AN INTRODUCTION TO COMPUTER NETWORKING

Kenneth C. Mansfield Jr.
James L. Antonakos

Prentice Hall

Upper Saddle River, New Jersey
Columbus, Ohio

Library of Congress Cataloging-in-Publication Data

Mansfield, Kenneth C.
   An introduction to computer networking / Kenneth C. Mansfield, Jr., James L. Antonakos.
     p. cm.
  ISBN 0-13-079693-X
   1. Computer networks.   I. Antonakos, James L.   II. Title.

TK5105.5 .M3578 2002   2001034592
004.6--dc21

Editor in Chief: Stephen Helba
Assistant Vice President and Publisher: Charles E. Stewart, Jr.
Production Editor: Alexandrina Benedicto Wolf
Production Coordination: Custom Editorial Productions, Inc.
Design Coordinator: Robin Chukes
Cover Designer: Thomas Mack
Cover Art: Marjory Dressler
Production Manager: Matthew Ottenweller
Product Manager: Scott Sambucci

This book was set in Palatino by Custom Editorial Productions, Inc. It was printed and bound by R. R. Donnelley & Sons Company. The cover was printed by The Lehigh Press, Inc.

All character names (e.g., Joe Tekk and Ken Koder) are registered trademarks of Prentice Hall.

Linux screen shots ©1999 courtesy of Red Hat, Inc. All rights reserved by Red Hat, Inc. Reprinted with permission. Microsoft screen captures courtesy of Microsoft, all rights reserved.

Pearson Education Ltd.
Pearson Education Australia Pty, Limited
Pearson Education Singapore, Pte. Ltd
Pearson Education North Asia Ltd
Pearson Education Canada, Ltd
Pearson Educación de Mexico, S.A. de C.V.
Pearson Education — Japan
Pearson Education Malaysia, Pte. Ltd
Pearson Education, Upper Saddle River, New Jersey

Prentice Hall

10 9 8 7 6 5 4 3 2
ISBN: 0-13-079693-X

Computer networks are everywhere. They span the globe, interconnecting with each other, weaving a web of communication that extends outward to the domain of satellites orbiting above the earth. They fail, they heal themselves, they move staggering amounts of information between distant locations. They are in our schools, our businesses, even our homes.

The purpose of this textbook is to explain the mystery behind the computer network, its hardware and software components, how it connects with other networks, the services it provides, network design and implementation, and how network problems can be solved. This book is suitable for students in computer engineering technology, electrical engineering technology, networking technology, and telecommunications technology programs.

Concepts and techniques are presented through actual real-world examples (such as examining all the packets captured while loading a web page or sending e-mail). A protocol sniffer/analyzer called LanExplorer is included on the companion CD-ROM that provides a detailed text and graphical interface into the world of networking. LanExplorer is capable of disassembling captured packets to examine every portion of the protocol embedded in the packet.

Where it is appropriate, the Internet is used to explain a new network service or mechanism. This includes heavy use of various sites located on the World Wide Web. In Part III, many of the networking concepts covered in Part II are put to use in several network client-server applications, including a virtual reality network maze game (NetMaze), Java applets, and CGI programming examples.

The social aspects of using computer networks in our everyday lives, and their technical challenges, are illustrated through the exploits of Joe Tekk, a fictitious network technician working at a fictitious software company called RWA Software. Joe encounters the successes and failures commonly associated with computer networks and their operation and also interacts with many different individuals regarding their networking experiences. Students are encouraged to consider the social implications of computer networking whenever possible.

OUTLINE OF COVERAGE

The textbook is divided into four parts.

Part I: Network Hardware
The basics of computer networking are presented, with a quick overview of network protocols and history. Networking hardware, topology, and technology (particularly Ethernet) are covered in detail.

Part II: Network Protocols
Wide coverage is provided on many of the typical hardware and software protocols employed in computer networks. These include the popular TCP/IP suite of protocols, the mechanics of switching and routing, network management and security, and the IEEE 802 standards.

Part III: Network Applications
The principles of operation behind many everyday networking applications are presented in this part, including e-mail, FTP, streaming audio and video, and the Internet browser. A working client-server network game (NetMaze) is presented as an example of network programming with Windows sockets.

Part IV: Network Operating Systems
This part covers the networking components of the Windows network operating systems (particularly NT Server). The operation of a network domain is examined, as are the details of file and printer sharing, dial-up networking, and setting up a network server.

The chapters in each part all have the same format. Each chapter begins with a short example of why the material is applicable to computer networking. Joe Tekk, a fictitious employee, is typically used to convey the problem or situation, as shown below.

Joe Tekk has just been hired by RWA Software as its new network technician. His manager was impressed during Joe's job interview by the fact that Joe had read RWA's company literature before the interview. When asked why, Joe said, "I like to be prepared, to know in advance what to expect of a situation."

Every chapter starts with **performance objectives**, which indicate what new skills and knowledge will be learned in the course of completing the chapter. The instructor will usually administer the requirements of the performance objectives.

The main section of each chapter presents all the information needed to perform the exercises and pass the review quiz. This section, which is usually the longest section in the chapter, contains important and detailed information.

The next section of each chapter contains a **troubleshooting** area. Tips, techniques, and actual problems and their solutions are presented.

Next is the **self-test** section to help the student verify understanding of the material covered in the chapter. The self-test is divided into several types of test questions: True/False, Multiple Choice, Completion, and Open-Ended. This is done to make the test more interesting and more reflective of what needs to be reviewed, and to help present the different types of questions asked during job interviews. Answers to odd-numbered self-test questions are given at the end of the book.

The **questions/activities** section follows the self-test. This section contains questions about the chapter just completed and is designed to help reinforce important concepts picked up during the reading. There may be times when other activities are suggested, and the instructor may or may not assign them. These other activities usually include outside assignments to provide the opportunity to broaden understanding of the subject.

The last section, the **review quiz**, restates the performance objectives.

Following each chapter is the **laboratory activity.** This is the "hands-on" application of what was just learned. The activity is usually performed in the lab. However, the instructor may assign some activities as outside work. This is usually the case for chapters on software. For these chapters, the activity usually consists of a series of software interactions with a computer. These interactions can be performed as a homework assignment or in some other place, such as a computer room, that provides access to computers for all students.

A rich set of appendices provides details on numerous network-related topics, including telecommunications technology, modems, and on becoming network certified.

THE NETWORKING POSTER

The pull-out networking poster provides a summary of many different networking topics. Understanding what is featured on the networking poster is a good way to measure progress.

THE COMPANION CD-ROM

The companion CD-ROM included with the textbook contains useful example programs and files designed to aid the student in developing and understanding the concepts presented in each part.

A demonstration version of LanExplorer, also included on the companion CD-ROM, allows the student to begin capturing and examining packets right away. Visit www.sunrisetelecom.com for additional details or to download a newer version.

View the README document (text, Microsoft Word, and HTML formats) to get a detailed description of the companion CD-ROM.

An Instructor's Manual is also available to instructors, which includes solutions to selected text problems, teaching suggestions, sample course syllabi, and many other teaching aids.

ACKNOWLEDGMENTS

We would like to thank our editor, Charles Stewart, and his assistant, Mayda Bosco, for their encouragement and assistance during the development of this project. Thanks also go to our copyeditor, Julie Hotchkiss, and our production supervisor, Megan Smith-Creed, at Custom Editorial Productions, Inc.

We are very grateful to Angelito Sarmiento of Sunrise Telecom for providing the LanExplorer software included on the CD-ROM, as well as for permission to use the numerous screen shots of LanExplorer in action.

We also thank Andy Wolf at OSDN for allowing screenshots of the internet-trafficreport.com website; Terri-Lyn Ross from SoftQuad for allowing screenshots of HoTMetaL; Liz Compton at AOL.com for allowing screenshots of Netscape and Instant Messenger; Mike Aalto at Ipswitch.com for allowing screenshots of WS_FTP; Phil Zimmermann of MIT and Sandra Brooks of PGP Security for allowing screenshots of PGP; and K. Claffy for allowing screenshots of the CAIDA website (www.caida.org).

We deeply appreciate the advice and assistance of our good friend Jeff Hatala, especially his help with our initial CGI applications.

Last, we thank our reviewers, who provided many useful and constructive suggestions: Sami Al-Salman, DeVry Institute of Technology; Ron Buchalski, Cisco Systems, Inc.; Jeffrey Hatala, Broome Community College; James McGuffee, Austin Community College; Edward F. Mikulski, IBM Global Services, Network Outsourcing; Asad Yousuf, Savannah State University; and Jerome Zornesky, Technical Career Institutes.

Kenneth C. Mansfield Jr.
mansfield_k@sunybroome.edu
http://www.sunybroome.edu/~mansfield_k

James L. Antonakos

CONTENTS

To our editors, Frank Burrows and Charles Stewart,
whom we cannot thank enough.

We could not have done this book
without them.

1

What Is a Computer Network?

Joe Tekk was visiting his friend Julie Plume, an instructor at a local community college. Julie was interested in setting up a network in her classroom.

"Joe," she began, "I need to know a number of things. How much will it all cost? Where do I buy everything? Who can set it up for me?"

Joe laughed. "Hold on, Julie, one thing at a time. The cost depends on how many computers you want to network, the type of network used, and who you buy your equipment from. I have a number of networking catalogs you can look at, and you can also browse the Web for networking products."

Joe looked around the room. There were 14 computers, two laser printers, and a color scanner. "You could probably buy a 16-port Ethernet hub that would take care of this entire room. One network interface card for each PC, some UTP cable, and that's about it. Probably a few hundred dollars will do it. I could set it up with you some afternoon."

Julie had more questions. "Will I need to buy software?"

"Most of the stuff you'll want to do, such as network printing and sharing files, is already built into Windows. You may need to purchase special network versions of some of your software."

"Just one more question, Joe," Julie said. "How does it all work?"

INTRODUCTION

A computer network is a collection of computers and devices connected so that they can share information. Such networks are called local area networks or **LANs** (networks in office buildings or on college campuses) and wide area networks or **WANs** (networks for very large geographical areas). Computer networks are becoming increasingly popular. With the **Internet** spanning the globe, and the *information superhighway* (also called the National Information Infrastructure), the exchange of information among computer users is increasing every day. In this chapter we will examine the basic operation of a computer network, how it is connected, how it transmits information, and what is required to connect a computer to a network. This chapter lays the foundation for the remaining chapters in the book.

COMPUTER NETWORK TOPOLOGY

Topology has to do with the way things are connected. The topology of a computer network is the way the individual computers or devices (called **nodes**) are connected. Figure 1.1 shows some common topologies.

Figure 1–1(a) illustrates a **fully connected network**. This kind of network is the most expensive to build, because every node must be connected to every other node in the network. The five-node network pictured requires 10 connections. A 20-node network would require 190 connections. The advantage of the fully connected network is that data need only traverse a single link to get from any node to any other node. This network is also called a *mesh* or *full-mesh network*.

Figure 1–1
Topologies for a five-node network.

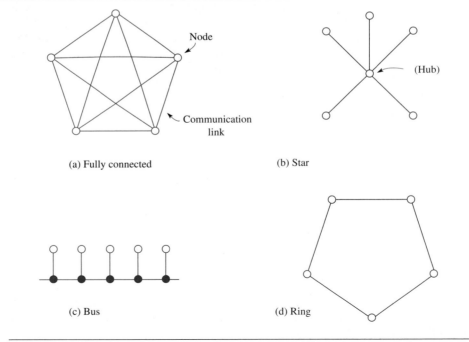

(a) Fully connected

(b) Star

(c) Bus

(d) Ring

Figure 1–1(b) shows the *star network*. Note that one node in the network is a centralized communications point. This makes the star connection inexpensive to build, since a minimum number of communication links are needed (always one less than the number of nodes). However, if the center node fails, the entire network shuts down. This does not happen in the fully connected network.

The *bus network* is shown in Figure 1–1(c). All nodes in the bus network are connected to the same communication link. One popular bus network is *Ethernet*, which we will be covering more completely in Chapter 4. The communication link in an Ethernet network is often a coaxial cable connected to each node through a T-connector. The bus network is inexpensive to build, and it is easy to add a new node to the network just by tapping into the communication link. One thing to consider in the bus network is the maximum distance between two nodes, because this affects the time required to send data between the nodes at each end of the link.

The last topology is the *ring network*, shown in Figure 1–1(d). This connection scheme puts the nodes into a circular communication path. Thus, as in the bus network, the maximum communication time depends on how many nodes there are in the network.

WIRED NETWORKS VERSUS WIRELESS NETWORKS

Pulling copper wire, or even fiber, throughout a building may be unsafe or prohibitively expensive. One solution involves the use of *wireless networking* equipment. In this topology, a base station connected to the network broadcasts data into the air in the form of a high-frequency RF signal (or through a line-of-sight infrared laser). Remote, or mobile, stations must stay within the range of the base station for reliable communication but are allowed to move about. We will examine wireless Ethernet in more detail in Chapter 4.

REPRESENTING DIGITAL DATA

The information exchanged between computers in a network is of necessity digital, the only form of data with which a computer can work. However, the actual way in which the digital data is represented varies. Figure 1–2 shows some of the more common methods used to represent digital data.

When an analog medium is used to transmit digital data (such as through the telephone system with a modem), the digital data may be represented by various forms of a *carrier-modulated* signal. Two forms of carrier modulation are amplitude modulation and frequency-shift keying. In amplitude modulation, the digital data controls the presence of a fixed-frequency carrier signal. In frequency-shift keying, the 0s and 1s are assigned two different frequencies, resulting in a shift in carrier frequency when the data changes from 0 to 1 or from 1 to 0. A third method is called *phase-shift keying,* in which the digital data controls the phase shift of the carrier signal.

Figure 1–2
Methods of
representing digital
data.

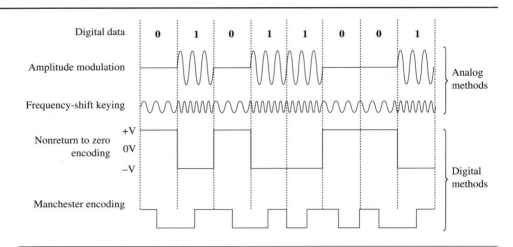

When a digital medium is used to transmit digital data (between COM1 of two PCs, for example), some form of digital waveform is used to represent the data. A digital waveform is a waveform that contains only two different voltages. Inside the computer, these two voltages are usually 0 volts and 5 volts. Outside the computer, plus and minus 12 volts are often used for digital waveforms. Refer again to Figure 1–2. The nonreturn to zero (NRZ) technique simply uses a positive voltage to represent a 0 and a negative voltage to represent a 1. The signal *never* returns to zero.

Another popular method is Manchester encoding. In this technique, phase transitions are used to represent the digital data. A one-to-zero transition is used for 0s and a zero-to-one transition is used for 1s. Thus, each bit being transmitted causes a transition in the Manchester waveform. This is not the case for the NRZ waveform, which may have long periods between transitions. The result is that Manchester encoding includes both data *and* a clock signal, which is helpful in extracting the original data in the receiver.

WORKING WITH DIGITAL DATA

What are some uses for digital data transmitted over a network? Let us examine a short list:

- Sharing files
- Printing to a network printer
- Loading a Web page
- Sending e-mail
- Listening to music (via streaming audio)

- Watching an MP3-encoded MPEG video
- Making a phone call
- Chatting
- Making a purchase
- Searching the Web
- Playing a network game

Many of these applications require large amounts of data to be exchanged. Some even require a secure connection. So, in addition to representing the digital data electronically (or physically), we also must represent it logically. Video files, for example, are compressed to reduce their storage requirements and downloading time. The information exchanged during a credit card purchase is typically encrypted to provide a measure of security. Compression and encryption are handled by software and are also supported by the use of communication protocols. Let us briefly examine the need for these protocols.

COMMUNICATION PROTOCOLS

Just throwing 1s and 0s onto a communication link is not enough to establish coherent communication between two nodes in a network. Both nodes must agree in advance on what the format of the information will look like. This format is called a *protocol* and is firmly defined. Figure 1–3 shows one of the accepted standards governing the use of protocols in computer networks. The Open Systems Interconnection (OSI) reference model defines seven layers required to establish reliable communication between two nodes. Different protocols are used between layers to handle such things as error recovery and information routing between nodes. A handy way to remember the names of each layer is contained in a simple statement: All Packets Should Take New Data Paths. The first letter of each word corresponds to the first letter of each OSI layer.

Not all of the seven layers are always used in a computer network. For example, Ethernet uses only the first two layers. The OSI reference model is really just a guide to establishing standards for network communications.

Layer   Function

7	Application
6	Presentation
5	Session
4	Transport
3	Network
2	Data Link
1	Physical

Figure 1–3
OSI reference model.

The Physical Layer

The Physical layer (layer 1) controls how the digital information is transmitted between nodes. In this layer, the encoding technique, the type of connector used, and the data rate, all of which are *physical* properties, are established. This layer is responsible for transmitting and receiving bits.

The Data-Link Layer

The Data-Link layer (layer 2) takes care of framing data, error detection, and maintains flow control over the physical connection. The Data-Link layer consists of two sublayers: LLC (Logical Link Control) and MAC (Media Access Control). We will examine these sublayers in more detail in Chapters 4 and 7.

The Network Layer

The Network layer (layer 3) is responsible for routing protocol-specific packets to their proper destination using logical IP addressing.

The Transport Layer

The Transport layer (layer 4) is the first layer that is not concerned with how the data actually gets from node to node. Instead, the Transport layer assumes that the physical data is error-free, and concentrates on providing correct communication between applications from a *logical* perspective. For example, the Transport layer guarantees that a large block of data transmitted in smaller chunks is reassembled in the proper order when received.

The Session Layer

The Session layer (layer 5) handles communication between processes running on two different nodes. For example, two mail programs running on different nodes establish a session to communicate with each other.

The Presentation Layer

The Presentation layer (layer 6) deals with matters such as text compression, conversion, and encryption.

The Application Layer

The Application layer (layer 7) is where the actual user program executes and makes use of the lower layers. We will examine the operation of each layer in more detail in the remaining chapters.

ETHERNET LANs

One of the most popular communication networks in use is Ethernet. Ethernet was developed jointly by Digital Equipment Corporation, Intel, and Xerox in 1980. Ethernet is referred to as a *baseband system*, which means that a single digital signal is transmitted. Contrast this with a *broadband system* (such as cable television), which uses multiple channels of data.

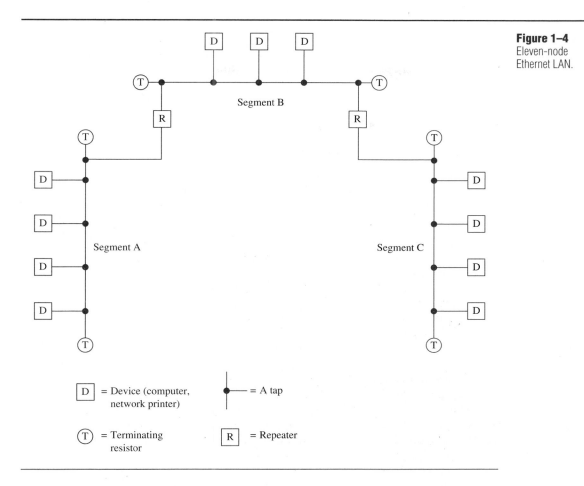

Figure 1–4
Eleven-node
Ethernet LAN.

Ethernet transmits data at the rate of 10 million bits per second (which translates to 1.25 million bytes per second). This corresponds to a bit time of 100 nanoseconds. Manchester encoding is used for the digital data. New 100-Mbps and 1000-Mbps Ethernet is already being used.

Each device connected to the Ethernet must contain a **transceiver** that provides the electronic connection between the device and the coaxial cable commonly used to connect nodes. Figure 1–4 shows a typical Ethernet installation. The 11 devices on the Ethernet are grouped into three **segments**. Each segment consists of a coaxial cable with a **tap** for each device. It is very important to correctly terminate both ends of the coaxial cable in each segment; otherwise, signal reflections will distort the information on the network and result in poor communications. Segments are connected to each other through the use of *repeaters,* which allow two-way communication between segments.

Each Ethernet device has its own unique binary address. The Ethernet card in each device waits to see its own address on the coaxial cable before

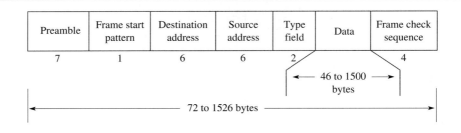

actually paying attention to the data being transmitted. Thus, when one device transmits data to another, every device listens. This is called *broadcasting*, much like the operation of a radio. However, Ethernet contains special hardware that detects when two or more devices attempt to transmit data at the same time (called a *collision*). When a collision occurs, all devices that are transmitting stop and wait a random period of time before transmitting the same data again. The random waiting period is designed to help reduce multiple collisions. This procedure represents a protocol called *Carrier Sense Multiple Access with Collision Detection* (*CSMA/CD*).

The format in which Ethernet transmits data is called a *frame*. Figure 1–5 details the individual components of the Ethernet frame. Recall that the physical and data-link layers are responsible for handling data at this level. Note that the length of the data section is limited to a range of 46 to 1500 bytes, which means that frame lengths are also limited in range. Because of the 10-Mbps data rate and the format of the Ethernet frame, the lengths of the various segments making up an Ethernet LAN are limited (either 185 meters for 10base2 or 500 meters for 10base5). This guarantees that a collision can be detected no matter which two nodes on a segment are active.

 TOKEN-RING LANS

Token-ring networks are not as popular as Ethernet but have their own advantages. The high collision rate of an Ethernet system with a lot of communication taking place is eliminated in a token-ring network.

The basic operation of a token-ring network involves the use of a special token (just another binary pattern) that circulates between nodes in the ring. When a node receives the token, it simply transmits it to the next node if there is nothing else to transmit. But if a node has its own frame of data to transmit, it holds onto the token and transmits the frame instead. Token-ring frames are similar to Ethernet frames in that both contain source and destination addresses. Each node that receives the frame checks the frame's destination address with its own address. If they match, the node captures the frame data and then retransmits the frame to the next node. If the addresses do not match, the frame is simply retransmitted.

When the node that originated the frame receives its own frame again (a complete trip through the ring), it transmits the original token again. Thus, even with no data being transmitted between nodes, the token is still being circulated.

Unfortunately, only one node's frame can circulate at any one time. Other nodes waiting to send their own frames must wait until they receive the token, which tends to reduce the amount of data that can be transmitted over a period of time. However, this is a small price to pay for the elimination of collisions.

NETWORK OPERATING SYSTEMS

In addition to the communication protocols that enable reliable communication across a LAN or WAN, a computer network also requires software to control the communication protocols and provide all of the networking functions. Windows 95/98/ME, Windows 2000, and Windows NT all contain built-in networking components, as do other network operating systems, such as Unix and Linux, Mac OS, and NetWare. Windows NT Server, in particular, is designed to manage large numbers of networked users through the services of a *domain*.

Windows provides a great deal of control over the operation of the network. Figure 1–6 shows a screen shot of the Network properties window. At a glance it is easy to see that the NetBEUI and TCP/IP protocols are installed and that the type of networking adapter is a plug-and-play ISA card. These details, and many others, are covered in Part IV.

IEEE 802 STANDARDS

The Institute of Electrical and Electronic Engineers (IEEE) has, over the years, established several committees dedicated to defining standards for computer networking. These standards are listed in Table 1–1. Any company entering the networking marketplace must manufacture networking hardware that complies with the published standards. For example, a new Ethernet network interface card must operate according to the standards presented in IEEE 802.2 and IEEE 802.3. We will encounter the IEEE standards many times in the remaining chapters.

TROUBLESHOOTING TECHNIQUES

Troubleshooting a network problem can take many forms. Before the network is even installed, decisions must be made about it that will affect the way it is troubleshot in the future. For example, Ethernet and token-ring networks use different data encoding schemes and connections, as well as different support software. Each has its own set of peculiar problems and solutions.

Figure 1–6
Network properties
window.

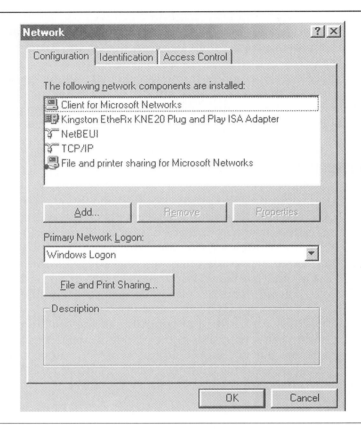

Table 1–1
IEEE 802 Standard.

Standard	Purpose
802.1	Internetworking
802.2	Logical Link Control
802.3	Ethernet LAN (CSMA/CD)
802.4	Token-Bus LAN
802.5	Token-Ring LAN
802.6	Metropolitan Area Network (MAN)
802.7	Broadband Technical Advisory Group
802.8	Fiber-Optic Technical Advisory Group
802.9	Integrated Voice/Data Network
802.10	Network Security
802.11	Wireless Networks
802.12	Demand Priority Access LAN (100 VG-AnyLAN)

Troubleshooting a network may take you down a hardware path (bad crimps on the cable connectors causing intermittent errors), a software path (the machine does not have its network addresses set up correctly), or both. There even may be nothing wrong with the network, the failure coming from the application using the network. So, a good deal of trial and error may be required to determine the exact nature of the problem. In the remaining chapters, many of these troubleshooting scenarios will be discussed.

SELF-TEST

This self-test is designed to help you check your understanding of the background information presented in this chapter.

True/False
Answer *true* or *false*.

1. The Internet is a computer network.

2. Both analog and digital media can be used to transmit digital data.

3. All seven layers of the OSI reference model are always used for communication in a network.

4. Ethernet uses collision detection to handle transmission errors.

Multiple Choice
Select the best answer.

5. The term LAN stands for
   a. Logical access node.
   b. Local area network.
   c. Large access network.

6. Phase transitions for each bit are used in
   a. Amplitude modulation.
   b. Carrier modulation.
   c. Manchester encoding.
   d. NRZ encoding.

7. Ethernet transmits data in
   a. Continuous streams of 0s and 1s.
   b. Frames.
   c. Blocks of 256 bytes.

8. Whic OSI network layer guarantees reliable data transmission?
   a. Physical.
   b. Data-Link.
   c. Network.

9. Ethernet segments are connected using
   a. Taps.
   b. Terminators.
   c. Repeaters.

Matching
Match a description of the topology property on the right with each item on the left.

10. Fully connected   a. The whole network shuts down when the central node fails.

11. Star   b. All nodes connect to the same communication link.

12. Bus   c. Uses a token to allow access to the network.

13. Ring   d. Most expensive to build.

Completion
Fill in the blank or blanks with the best answers.

14. The _____ of a network concerns how the nodes are connected.

15. A(n) _____ _____ network provides the fastest communication between any two nodes.

16. Using two different frequencies to represent digital data is called _____ _____.

17. The layer responsible for error detection and recovery is the _____ layer.

18. Collisions are eliminated in the _____ network.

19. _____ networking uses RF signals or infrared lasers.

20. The IEEE _____ Standards define the various network operations/technologies.

QUESTIONS/ACTIVITIES

1. Visit the computer center of your school. Find out who the network administrator is and discuss the overall structure of the school's network with him or her.

2. Visit a local computer store and find out how much it would cost to set up a 16-user LAN.

3. Visit the Internet2 Web site (www.internet2.edu). What is the Internet2? What is QBone?

REVIEW QUIZ

Under the supervision of your instructor

1. Sketch and discuss the different types of network topologies and their advantages and disadvantages.

2. Sketch and explain examples of digital data encoding.

3. Discuss the OSI reference model.

4. Explain the basic operation of Ethernet and token-ring networks.

Networking Concepts Laboratory

Experiment #1
Introduction to Computer Networks

Objective

To tour an actual networking laboratory.

Required Equipment

The following equipment is required for this experiment:

- Two or more networked computers running Windows, connected to the Internet

Procedure

Perform each of the following steps. Record your observations, results, and any difficulties you encounter. You will use this information when you develop your conclusions about the experiment.

1. Take a tour of a networking laboratory. Determine the following:
   a. The number of computers that are networked.
   b. The type of computers available (operating system, processor speed, RAM, etc.).
   c. The number of printers.
   d. The networking components used to connect the computers, including cable types, number of hubs or switches, and so on.
   e. The types of network applications available on each computer.
2. If the computers require each user to log in, the login window will contain fields for *Username* and *Password*. A third field may be used to specify the *Domain*. Obtain this information from your instructor and log in to a computer.
3. Open a browser (Internet Explorer, Netscape Navigator).
4. Enter **www.yahoo.com** in the address field of the browser.
5. Enter **computer network** in the search field and click the **Search** button.
6. Record the number of category hits for the **computer network** topic.
7. Click on **Web Pages** to determine the number of Web page hits and record it.
8. Close the browser.
9. Log off the computer.

Discussion and Conclusion

Using a word processor, write your own detailed explanations of the results and observations made during the experiment. To begin, try to say something about each procedure step.

In addition, provide answers to the following questions:

1. What most surprised you about the networking lab? What seemed familiar? What was new to you?
2. Consider the number of Web page hits returned during the Yahoo search. Is it more than 100,000? If so, did it seem like it took a long time to find all the hits, or a short time? If it only took a few seconds to find over 100,000 hits, do you think the entire Internet was searched during that time? Do you have the time to examine over 100,000 pages to find what you are looking for?

2

Network Topology

PERFORMANCE
OBJECTIVES
Upon completion of this
chapter, you will be able
to

• Describe the difference
between physical
topology and logical
topology.

• Sketch the physical
topologies of bus, star,
ring, and fully con-
nected networks.

• Explain what is meant
by network hierarchy.

Joe Tekk met Don, his manager, at 6 A.M., outside the doors of a local high school.

"Are you ready, Joe?" Don asked. Joe had never accompanied Don on a site upgrade before.

"Sure, Don," Joe replied. "I'm looking forward to it."

For the next four hours, Joe crawled around on the floor, poked his head up into drop ceilings and underneath benches, and traced cables down long corridors, between floors, and down into the boiler room. When he finished, he was tired, bruised, and dirty.

"Well, Joe," Don said, "We've mapped the whole network out. Now we can begin the upgrade."

"Now?" Joe asked wearily.

"No," Don laughed, "later. We have to order the network components first. Go get some rest. You did a good job today."

INTRODUCTION

Topology concerns the structure of the connections between computers in a network. Figure 2–1 shows three computers (A, B, and C) and a network *cloud*, a graphic symbol used to describe a network without specifying the nature of the connections. The network cloud may comprise only the network found in a small laboratory, or it may represent a wide area network (WAN) such as the Internet.

The three computers in Figure 2–1 are connected in two different ways: physically and logically. Let us examine these two types of connections.

Figure 2–1
Network cloud
connecting three
machines.

Figure 2–1
Network cloud
connecting three
machines.

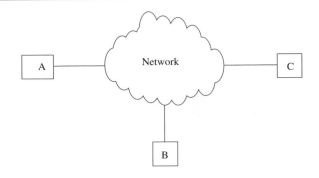

PHYSICAL TOPOLOGY VERSUS LOGICAL TOPOLOGY

Figure 2–2 shows the details of the connections inside the network cloud. Four intermediate network nodes (W, X, Y, and Z) are responsible for relaying data between each of the three machines A, B, and C. Five connections exist between the four intermediate nodes. This is the ***physical topology*** of the network. We will cover the details of each type of physical topology in the next few sections as well as in Chapters 3, 4, and 5.

The ***logical topology*** has to do with the path a packet of data takes through the network. For example, from machine A to machine C there are three different paths. These paths are as follows:

1. Link 3
2. Link 1 to link 2
3. Link 1 to link 4 to link 5

Figure 2–2
Physical network
topology.

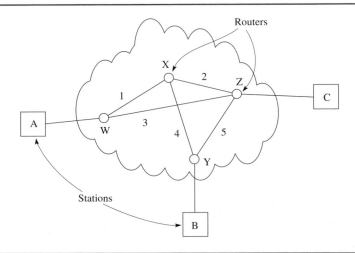

Clearly, data sent on link 3 will get from machine A to machine C in the shortest time (assuming all links are identical in speed), while the third path (links 1, 4, and 5) takes the longest. Due to the nature of the network, we cannot guarantee that link 3 is the one that is always used. It may become too busy; its noise level may unexpectedly increase, making it unusable; or a tree might have fallen on the fiber carrying link 3's data. Thus, packets of data may take different routes through the network, arriving *out of order* at their destination. It is the job of the network software protocol to properly reassemble the packets into the correct sequence. Chapters 7 through 10 provide the details of the many network protocols in use.

When a large amount of data must be sent between machines on a network, it is possible to set up a ***virtual circuit*** between the machines. A virtual circuit is a prearranged path through the network that *all* packets will travel for a particular session between machines. For example, for reasons based on the current state of the network, a virtual circuit is established between machines B and C through links 4 and 2. All packets exchanged between B and C will take links 4 and 2.

Another type of virtual connection is called a ***virtual private network (VPN)***. A VPN uses public network connections (such as the Internet or the telephone system) to establish private communication by encrypting the data. The data travels in ***tunnels***, logical connections between the nodes of the VPN.

FULLY-CONNECTED NETWORKS

Figure 2–3 shows four basic types of network connections. The fully connected network in Figure 2–3(a) is the most expensive to build, for each node has a link (communication channel) to every other node. Just adding one more node (for a total of six nodes) brings the number of links to 15. Seven fully connected nodes require 21 links. In general, the number of links *(L)* required in a fully connected network of N nodes is

$$L = \frac{N(N-1)}{2}$$

Table 2–1 shows the number of links for several values of N. It is easy to see that the number of links required in a fully connected network quickly becomes unmanageable. Even so, fully connected networks provide quick communication between nodes, for there is a one-link path between every two nodes in the network. Even if a link goes down, the worst-case path only becomes two links long. So, fully connected networks are very reliable and somewhat secure, since many links have to fail for two nodes to lose contact.

Figure 2–3
Network topologies.

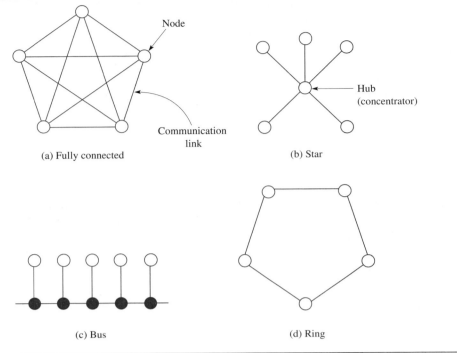

(a) Fully connected

(b) Star

(c) Bus

(d) Ring

Table 2–1
Number of links
in a fully connected
network.

N	L
2	1
3	3
4	6
5	10
6	15
10	45
100	4950

STAR NETWORKS

Figure 2–3(b) shows a star network. All nodes connect to a central **hub** (also called a *concentrator*). For small networks, only a single hub is required. Four, eight, and even sixteen or more connections are available on a single hub. Large star networks require multiple hubs, which increase the hardware and cabling costs. On the other hand, if a node on the network fails, the hub will isolate it so that the other nodes are not affected. Entire groups of nodes (machines) can be isolated at a time by disconnecting their hub. This helps narrow down the source of a network problem during troubleshooting.

BUS NETWORKS

A bus network uses a single common communication link that all nodes tap into. Figure 2–3(c) shows the bus connection; 10base2 and 10base5 Ethernet uses coaxial cable as the common connection. All nodes on the common bus compete with each other for possession, broadcasting their data when they detect the bus is idle. If two or more nodes transmit data at the same time, a *collision* occurs, requiring each node to stop and wait before retransmitting. This technique of sharing a common bus is known as Carrier Sense Multiple Access with Collision Detection (CSMA/CD), and is the basis of the Ethernet communication system.

Wiring a bus network is not too difficult. Suitable lengths of coaxial cable, properly terminated with BNC connectors on each end, are daisy-chained via T-connectors into one long *segment* of nodes. Each T-connector plugs into a network interface card. The problem with the daisy-chain bus connection is that bad crimps on the BNC connectors, poor connections in the T-connectors, or just an improperly terminated cable (no 50 ohm terminating resistor) can cause intermittent or excessive collisions; these problems can be difficult to find as well. A special piece of equipment called a *time domain reflectometer* (TDR) is used to send a pulse down the coaxial cable and determine where the fault is (by displaying a response curve for the cable).

In terms of convenience, the bus network is relatively easy to set up, with no significant hardware costs (no hubs are required). With 185 meters of cable possible in a segment (for 10base2 Ethernet), a large number of nodes can be wired together. Individual segments can be connected together with *repeaters* (more on this in Chapter 3).

RING NETWORKS

The last major network topology is the ring. As Figure 2–3(d) shows, each node in a ring is connected to exactly two other nodes. Data circulates in the ring, traveling through many intermediate nodes if necessary to get to its destination. Like the star connection, the number of links is the same as the number of nodes. The difference is that there is no central hub concentrating the nodes. Data sent between nodes will typically require paths of at least two links. If a link fails, the worst-case scenario requires a message to travel completely around the ring, through every link (except the one that failed). The increase in time required to relay messages around the bad link may be intolerable for some applications. The star network does not have this problem. If a link fails, only the node on that link is out of service.

Token-ring networks, although logically viewed as rings, are connected using central multistation access units (*MAU*s). The MAU provides a physical star connection.

HYBRID NETWORKS

A hybrid network combines the components of two or more network topologies. As Figure 2–4 indicates, two star networks are connected (with three additional nodes) via a bus. This is a common way to implement Ethernet, with coax running between classrooms or laboratories and hubs in each room to form small subnetworks. Putting together a hybrid network takes careful planning, for there are various rules that dictate how the individual components may be connected and used. For example, when connecting Ethernet segments, a maximum of four repeaters may be used with five segments. Furthermore, if a 4-Mbps token-ring network is interfaced with a 10-Mbps Ethernet, there are performance issues that must be taken into consideration also (since any Ethernet traffic is slowed down to 4 Mbps on the token ring side). In addition, the overall organization of the hybrid network, from a logical viewpoint, must be planned out as well. This will become clearer in the next section.

NETWORK HIERARCHY

The machines networked together in Figure 2–4 are not organized into a **hierarchy** (a layered organization). Data transmitted by any machine is broadcast through both hubs. Everyone connected to the network sees the same data and competes with everyone else for bandwidth.

The same network is illustrated in Figure 2–5, except for a few hardware modifications. Both hubs have been replaced by 10-Mbps switches, which act like hubs except they only forward data selectively. For example, any machine

Figure 2–4
Hybrid network.

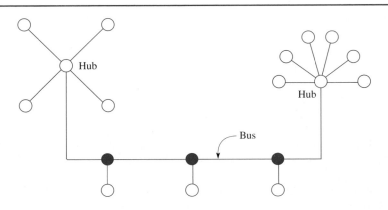

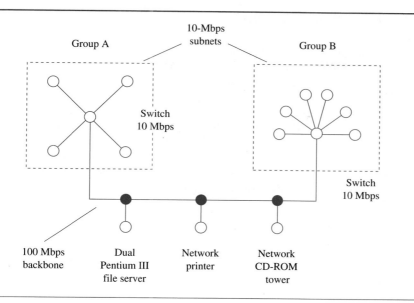

Figure 2–5
Hybrid network with hierarchy.

in group A can send data to any other machine in group A through the switch, without the data being broadcast on the 100-Mbps backbone. The same is true for machines in group B. Their traffic is isolated from the important, high-speed 100-Mbps backbone.

Now, when a machine from group A requests service from the file server, which in turn accesses the CD-ROM tower, the hierarchy of the network allows the file server to communicate with the CD-ROM tower at a high speed, while sending data back to the machine in group A only when it needs to. Machines from both groups can communicate with each other over the backbone as well, without significantly interfering with the other backbone traffic (since all machines in each group operate at 10 Mbps). The switches enforce hierarchy by learning where data packets should be forwarded (based on their destination addresses). Since the backbone is the main communication link in the hybrid network, its 100-Mbps speed allows each network component to communicate at its best speed. Switches are covered in more detail in Chapter 8.

SUBNETS

In Chapters 8 and 10 you will cover the structure and use of **IP addresses**, 32-bit numbers used to locate and identify nodes on the Internet. For example, the IP address of one computer in a classroom might be 192.203.131.137. Other computers on the same subnet may begin with 192.203.131 but have different numbers at the end, as in 192.203.131.130. This type of subnet is called a *class C subnet*. We will examine subnets in more detail in Chapter 8.

NETWORK ACCESS POINTS

In the beginning, an experimental network was created by connections between four major data processing facilities, located in Chicago, New York, San Francisco, and Washington, D.C. Today, facilities all across the country called *Network Access Points* (*NAPs*), provide access to national and global network traffic. Many companies have installed their own independent communication networks that connect to one or more NAPs or even act as NAPs themselves. Figure 2–6 shows the RWA Software national backbone, a fully connected network. Companies that connect to a NAP enter into *peering agreements* with each other that allow them to exchange traffic. When the traffic is Internet-based, the connection is called a *POP*, or *point-of-presence*.

Figure 2–6
RWA Software national backbone.

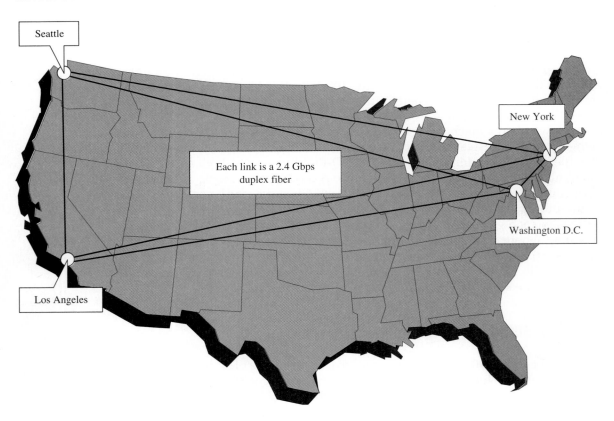

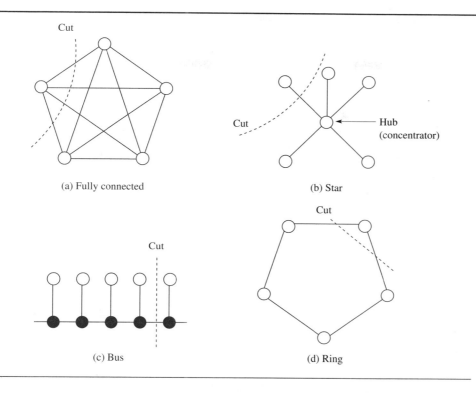

Figure 2–7
Partitioning a network.

 ## TROUBLESHOOTING TECHNIQUES

It is a fact of life that we must worry about intentional harm being done to our network. In terms of security and reliability, we must concern ourselves with what is required to *partition* our network, breaking it up into at least two pieces that cannot communicate with each other. Figure 2–7 shows how bus, star, ring, and fully connected networks are partitioned. Note that the star network is completely partitioned (all nodes isolated) if the central hub fails.

When troubleshooting a network, knowledge of its topology, both physical and logical, is essential to proper partitioning, so that testing and repairing can proceed smoothly.

SELF-TEST

This self-test is designed to help you check your understanding of the background information presented in this chapter.

True/False

Answer *true* or *false*.

1. Packets never exit once they enter a network cloud.

2. Fully connected networks require more links than star networks.

3. 10base2 Ethernet allows for 2000-meter segments.

4. A collision is required to exchange data over an Ethernet cable.

5. A hub is used to enforce network hierarchy.

Multiple Choice
Select the best answer.

6. A fully connected network of 10 nodes requires
   a. 10 links.
   b. 45 links.
   c. 90 links.

7. Star networks
   a. Require hubs.
   b. Are limited to 16 nodes.
   c. Both a and b.

8. A portion of an Ethernet bus is called a(n)
   a. CSMA module.
   b. Etherpath.
   c. Segment.

9. Assuming any single link fails, the worst-case path through the ring network of Figure 2–3(d) is
   a. Three links.
   b. Four links.
   c. Five links.

10. What is required to partition a fully connected network of six nodes?
   a. Cut one link.
   b. Cut one link at each node.
   c. Cut all links at a single node.

Matching
Match a description of the topology property on the right with each item on the left.

11. Bus
12. Star
13. Ring
14. Fully connected

a. All paths are one link long.
b. Each node has exactly two links.
c. All nodes share the same link.
d. All nodes share a central node.

Completion
Fill in the blank or blanks with the best answers

15. A prearranged connection between computers is called a(n) _____ circuit.

16. Hubs are also called _____.

17. CSMA/CD stands for _____ _____ _____ _____ with _____ _____.

18. Breaking a link in a network may _____ it.

19. A network that uses encryption to send secure data over public communication links is called a _____ _____network.

20. Companies connected to a NAP utilize _____ agreements.

QUESTIONS/ACTIVITIES

1. What are all the paths from machine B to machine C in the network of Figure 2–2?

2. Draw a fully connected eight-node network. How many links are there?

3. Repeat step 2 for a star network. Assume each hub has four connections available.

4. Find a laboratory or classroom that is networked. Make a diagram of the network, showing the various nodes and what they actually represent (computers, printers, etc.).

REVIEW QUIZ
Under the supervision of your instructor

1. Describe the difference between physical topology and logical topology.

2. Sketch the physical topologies of bus, star, ring, and fully connected networks.

3. Explain what is meant by network hierarchy.

Networking Concepts Laboratory

Experiment #2

Network Topology

Objectives

1. To further explore the characteristics of different network topologies.
2. To discover the details of Network Access Points like MAE East.

Required Equipment

The following equipment is required for this experiment:

- Two or more networked computers running Windows, connected to the Internet

Procedure

Perform each of the following steps. Record your observations, results, and any difficulties you encounter. You will use this information when you develop your conclusions about the experiment.

1. Sketch all the different network configurations possible using six communication links.
2. Search the Web for **fiber-distributed data interconnect (FDDI)**. Answer the following:
   a. What type of topology does FDDI use?
   b. What is FDDI used for?
   c. What is the maximum size of an FDDI network?
3. Search the Web for information on MAE East. Answer the following:
   a. What doe MAE stand for?
   b. What does MAE East do?
   c. Where is MAE East located?
   d. How many customers does MAE East have?
   e. What connection speeds and types are available?
4. Find out if there is a MAE West.
5. Search the Web for three companies using virtual private networking.

Discussion and Conclusion

Using a word processor, write your own detailed explanations of the results and observations made during the experiment. To begin, try to say something about each procedure step.

In addition, provide answers to the following questions:

1. Why would one topology be better than another when networking 225 computers together?
2. How do the terms *tier-1 provider* and *tier-2 provider* relate to NAP and POP?

3

Networking Hardware

PERFORMANCE OBJECTIVES
Upon completion of this chapter, you will be able to

- List and describe the basic networking hardware components.
- Explain the differences in 10base2 Ethernet and 10/100baseT Ethernet.
- Compare the advantages of fiber over copper wire.

Don, the senior technician, had his hands full of UTP cable. He had carefully stripped off 1 inch of outer insulation and was gingerly holding all eight twisted-pair conductors in a neat row by pinching them between his thumb and forefinger. In his other hand he held a clear plastic RJ-45 crimp-on connector and was slowly pushing all eight wires into their thin grooves in the connector.

Joe walked up and slapped Don on the back in a friendly way. "What are you doing, Don?" he asked.

Don let out a long-suffering sigh as all eight wires popped out of the connector. "Starting over again, Joe," he replied.

INTRODUCTION

In this chapter we will examine many of the different hardware components involved in networking. You are encouraged to look inside your machine to view your network interface card, around your lab to locate hubs and trace cables, and around your campus (especially the computer center) to see what other exotic hardware you can find.

ETHERNET CABLING

We begin our hardware presentation with Ethernet cabling. Ethernet cables come in three main varieties. These are

1. RG-58 coaxial cable, used for 10base2 operation (also called *thinwire*)

27

2. RG-11 coaxial cable, used for 10base5 operation (also called *thickwire*)
3. Unshielded twisted pair (*UTP*), used for 10baseT and 100baseT operation

There are other, specialized cables, including fiber (10baseFL), that are used as well.

RG-58 cable is typically used for wiring laboratories and offices, or other small groups of computers. Figure 3–1 shows the construction of a coaxial cable.

The maximum length of a thinwire Ethernet segment is 185 meters (606 feet), which is due to the nature of the CSMA/CD method of operation, the cable attenuation, and the speed at which signals propagate inside the coax. The length is limited to guarantee that collisions are detected when machines that are far apart transmit at the same time. BNC connectors are used to terminate each end of the cable. Figure 3–2 shows several different cables and connectors, including BNC T-connectors (one containing a terminating resistor).

When many machines are connected to the same Ethernet segment, a daisy-chain approach is used, as shown in Figure 3–3(a). The BNC T-connector allows the network interface card (*NIC*) to tap into the coaxial cable, and the coax to pass through the machine to the next machine. The last machines on each end of the cable (or simply the cable ends themselves) must use a terminating resistor (50 ohms) to eliminate collision-causing reflections in the cable. This connection is illustrated in Figure 3–3(b).

RG-11 coaxial cable is used as a *backbone cable*, distributing Ethernet signals throughout a building, an office complex, or other large installation. RG-11 is thicker and more sturdy than RG-58 coax. Thickwire Ethernet segments may be up to 500 meters (1640 feet) long with a maximum of five segments connected by repeaters. This gives a total distance of five times 500 meters, or 2500 meters. This is called the network *diameter*. The network diameter is different for other cable types and signal speeds. Chapter 4 provides additional details on network diameter. RG-11 cable is typically orange, with black rings around the cable every 2.5 meters to allow taps into the cable. The taps, called *vampire taps*, are used by transceivers that transfer Ethernet data to and from the cable.

UTP cable, used with hubs and other 10/100baseT equipment, uses twisted pairs of wires to reduce noise and crosstalk and allow higher-speed data rates (100 Mbit/second category 5 UTP for Fast Ethernet). The twists tend to cause

Figure 3–1
Coaxial cable
construction.

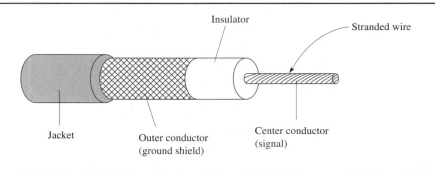

Insulator

Stranded wire

Jacket

Outer conductor
(ground shield)

Center conductor
(signal)

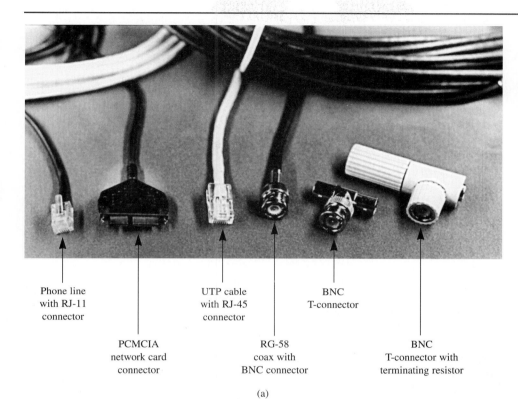

Figure 3–2
(a) Assorted connectors and cables *(photograph by John T. Butchko)*.
(b) Fiber optic cable with ST connectors.

Phone line
with RJ-11
connector

UTP cable
with RJ-45
connector

BNC
T-connector

PCMCIA
network card
connector

RG-58
coax with
BNC connector

BNC
T-connector with
terminating resistor

(a)

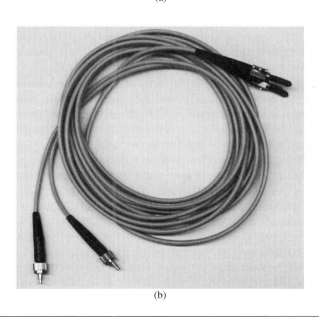

(b)

Figure 3–3
10base2 Ethernet
wiring.

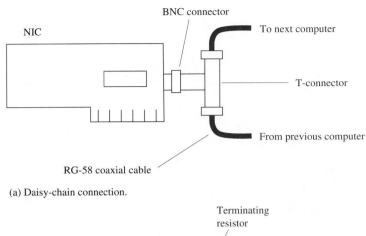

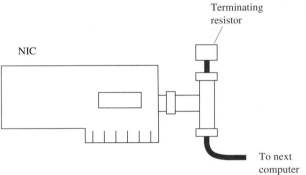

(a) Daisy-chain connection.

(b) Terminating connection (required at each end of the cable).

the small magnetic fields generated by currents in the wires to cancel, reducing noise on the signals. UTP cable length is limited to 100 meters (328 feet) and RJ-45 connectors are used for termination. The network diameter for UTP-based 10baseT networks is 500 meters. For 100baseT networks, the diameter drops to 200 meters for reasons discussed in Chapter 4.

The structure of the 8-pin RJ-45 connector is shown in Figure 3–4. Its modular format is similar to the telephone companies' 6-pin RJ-11 connector.

Table 3–1 shows the wire color combinations used in UTP cabling. Note that only two pairs are required for 10baseT operation, one pair for transmit and the other for receive.

UTP cables are wired as straight-through or crossover cables. Figure 3–5 shows the wiring diagrams for each type of cable. Straight-through cables typically connect the computer's network interface card to a port on the hub. Crossover cables are used for NIC-to-NIC communication, and for hub-to-hub connections when no crossover port is available. Sample wiring configurations are shown in Figure 3–6.

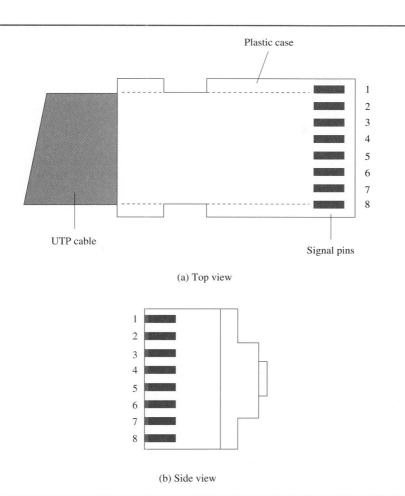

Figure 3–4
RJ-45 (10baseT)
connector.

Plastic case

UTP cable

Signal pins

(a) Top view

(b) Side view

Table 3–1
RJ-45 pin
assignments (568B
standard).

Pin	Color	Function	Used for 10baseT
1	White/Orange	T2	✔
2	Orange	R2	✔
3	White/Green	T3	✔
4	Blue	R1	
5	White/Blue	T1	
6	Green	R3	✔
7	White/Brown	T4	
8	Brown	R4	

Figure 3–5
RJ-45 cabling.

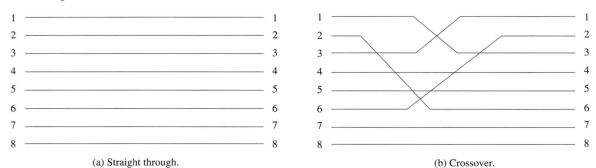

(a) Straight through.   (b) Crossover.

Figure 3–6
10baseT Ethernet
wiring.

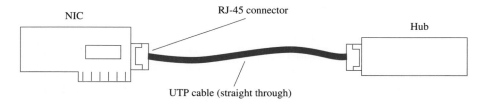

(a) Individual machine connection.

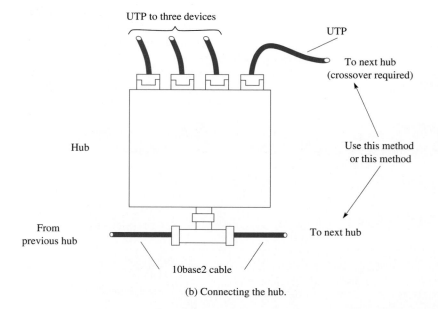

(b) Connecting the hub.

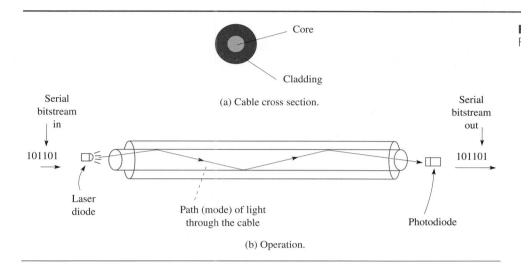

Figure 3–7
Fiber optic cable.

(a) Cable cross section.

(b) Operation.

Fiber optic cable relies on pulses of light to carry information. Figure 3–7(a) shows the basic construction of an optical fiber. Two types of plastic or glass with different physical properties are used (the inner *core* and the outer *cladding*) to allow a beam of light to reflect off the boundary between the core and the cladding. This is illustrated in Figure 3–7(b). Some fiber optic cables allow many different paths (or *modes*); others allow one single mode. These are called multimode and single-mode fibers. A popular multimode fiber has core/cladding dimensions of 62.5/125 nanometers.

High-speed laser diodes generate short bursts of light of a particular wavelength (typically 850 nanometers). These bursts travel down the fiber and affect a photodiode on the receiving end of the fiber. Since this light-based communication is one way, two fibers are used to make a two-way connection.

Fiber does not suffer from the problems found in copper wires, which are sensitive to electromagnetic interference, exhibit high signal loss, and are limited in bandwidth. The original 10baseFL fiber standard specifies a cable length of 2000 meters, significantly longer than the 10base5 segment length of 500 meters. In addition, fiber supports data rates in the gigabit range, providing the fastest communication method available for networking.

Table 3–2 compares each cabling system.

	10base5	**10base2**	**10baseT**	**10baseFL**
Cable Type	RG-11	RG-58	UTP	Fiber
Maximum Segment Length	500 meters (1640 feet)	185 meters (606 feet)	100 meters (328 feet)	2000 meters (6560 feet)
Max Nodes	100	30	2	2

Table 3–2
Comparing cabling systems.

🖥️🖥️ THE NIC

The network interface card (NIC) is the interface between the PC (or other networked device) and the physical network connection. In Ethernet systems, the NIC connects to a segment of coaxial or UTP cable (fiber NICs are available but not very common yet). As with any other type of adapter card, NICs come in ISA, PCMCIA, and PCI bus varieties. Figure 3–8 shows a typical Ethernet NIC. Since the NIC contains both BNC and RJ-45 connectors, it is called a *combo card*. The NE2000 Compatible stamp indicates that the NIC supports a widely accepted group of protocols.

The NIC in Figure 3–8 is an ISA adapter card. PCI networking cards are available in both non-bus-mastering and bus-mastering varieties. *Bus-mastering* means that the NIC can take over the system bus and access memory directly. Figure 3–9 shows a PCMCIA Ethernet NIC and cable.

The NIC is responsible for operations that take place in the physical layer of the OSI network model. It is only concerned with sending and receiving 0s and 1s, using the IEEE 802.3 Ethernet standard (or IEEE 802.5 token ring).

Windows identifies the installed NIC in Network Properties. Figure 3–10 shows the 3Com NIC entry. Note that the NetBEUI and TCP/IP protocols are

Figure 3–8
Network interface
card (Ethernet)
*(photograph by John
T. Butchko).*

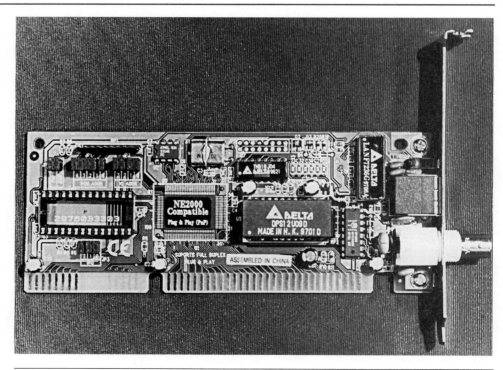

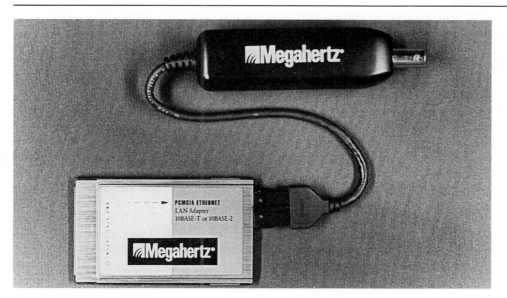

Figure 3–9
PCMCIA Ethernet
card with cable
*(photograph by
John T. Butchko).*

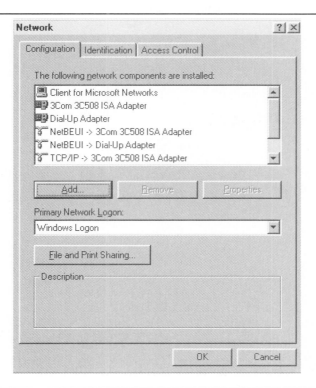

Figure 3–10
3Com 3C508 NIC
entry.

bound to the 3Com adapter. To use a protocol with a NIC you must bind the protocol to the adapter card. This is typically done automatically when the protocol is added.

Double-clicking the 3Com 3C508 entry brings up its Properties window, which is shown in Figure 3–11. The indicated driver type is NDIS, Microsoft's network driver interface specification, which allows multiple protocols to use a single NIC. An ODI (open data-link interface, developed by Novell) driver performs the same function for multiple protocol stacks used with the NetWare network operating system. Figure 3–12 shows the NDIS/ODI interface. Both are designed to *decouple* the protocols from the NIC. The protocols do not require any specific information about the NIC. They use the NDIS/ODI drivers to perform network operations with the drivers responsible for their specific hardware.

It is important to mention that all NICs are manufactured with a unique 48-bit MAC address (for example, 00-60-97-2B-E6-0F). You can view your NIC's MAC address using the WINIPCFG utility (from the Run menu). Figure 3–13 shows the initial WINIPCFG screen.

Figure 3–11
NIC Properties
window.

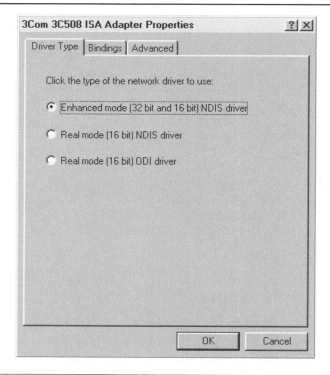

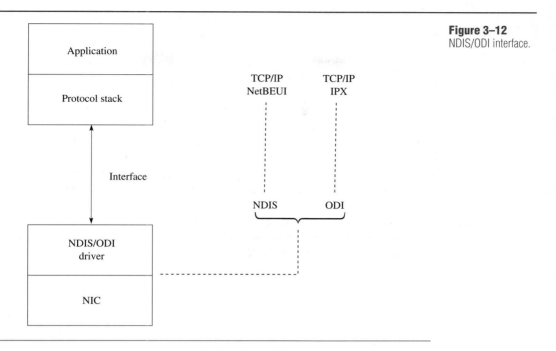

Figure 3–12
NDIS/ODI interface.

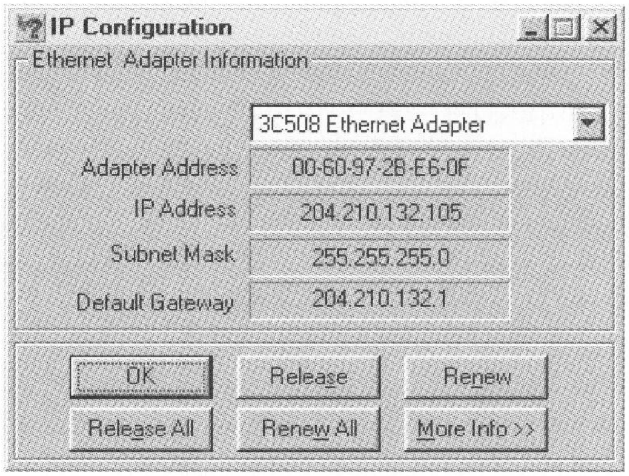

Figure 3–13
Viewing the NIC's
MAC address.

TOKEN RING

The IEEE 802.5 standard describes the token-ring networking system. IBM developed the initial 4 Mbit/second standard in the mid-1980s, with 16 Mbit/second token ring also available.

Figure 3–14
Token-ring network.

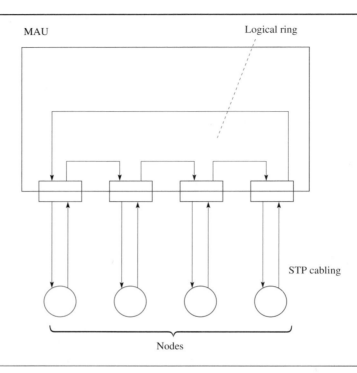

Token-ring networks use a multistation access unit (MAU), which establishes a logical ring connection even though the physical connections to the MAU resemble a star. Figure 3–14 shows the basic operation of the MAU. Computers in the ring circulate a software *token*. The machine holding the token is allowed to transmit data to the next machine on the ring (even if the data is not meant for that machine). One machine (typically the first to boot and connect) is identified as the *active monitor* and keeps track of all token-ring operations. If the active monitor detects that a machine has gone down (or been shut off), the connection to that machine is bypassed. If the active monitor itself goes down, the other machines vote to elect a new active monitor. Thus, we see that token-ring networks are *self healing,* unlike Ethernet, which is only capable of resolving collisions.

 Token-ring connections are made using STP (shielded twisted pair) cables. STP cable contains a metal shield around the twisted pairs that provides isolation from external crosstalk and noise. In general, do not substitute STP for UTP.

REPEATERS

A *repeater* connects two network segments and broadcasts packets between them. Since signal loss is a factor in the maximum length of a segment, a repeater is used to amplify the signal and extend the usable length. A common Ethernet rule is that no more than four repeaters may be used to join segments together. This is a physical limitation designed to keep collision detection working properly. Repeaters operate at layer 1 (Physical layer) of the OSI model.

TRANSCEIVERS

A transceiver converts from one media type to another. For example, a 10base2-to-fiber transceiver acts like a repeater, except it also interfaces 10base2 coaxial cable with a fiber optic cable. It is common to use more than one media type in an installation, so many different kinds of transceivers are available. Figure 3–15 shows two examples of Ethernet transceivers.

HUBS

Hubs, also called *concentrators,* expand one Ethernet connection into many. For example, a four-port hub connects up to four machines (or other network devices) via UTP cables. The hub provides a star connection for the four ports. Many hubs contain a single BNC connector as well to connect the hub to existing 10base2 network wiring. The hub can also be connected via one of its ports. One port is designed to operate in either straight-through or crossover mode, selected by a switch on the hub. Hubs that can connect in this fashion are called *stackable* hubs. Figure 3–16 shows an eight-port stackable Ethernet hub. Port 8 is switch selectable for straight through or crossover (cascade).

A hub is similar to a repeater, except it broadcasts data received by any port to all other ports on the hub. Most hubs contain a small amount of intelligence as well, examining received packets and checking them for integrity. If a bad packet arrives, or the hub determines that a port is unreliable, it will shut down the line until the error condition disappears.

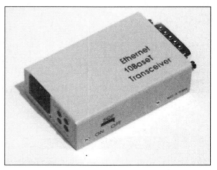

Figure 3–15
Transceivers.

(a) Thinwire coax to fiber

(b) UTP to AUI.

Figure 3–16
Ethernet hub
(photographs by John T. Butchko).

(a) Front view.

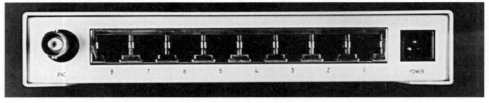

(b) Rear view.

Figure 3–17
Connecting five segments with hubs.

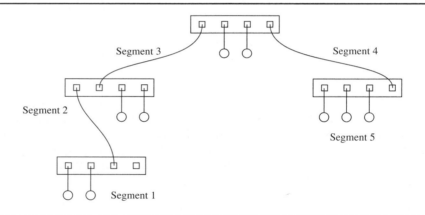

Note that a hub also acts like a repeater. Because of its slight delay when processing a packet, the number of hubs that may be connected in series is also limited. Figure 3–17 shows how several hubs are used to connect five Ethernet segments, within the accepted limits. Since each UTP cable may be as long as 100 meters, the maximum distance between nodes is 500 meters (the network diameter).

BRIDGES/SWITCHES

When a network grows in size, it is often necessary to partition it into smaller groups of nodes to help isolate traffic and improve performance. One way to

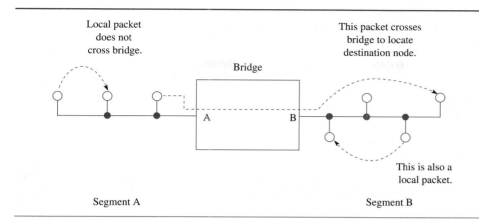

Figure 3–18
Operation of a
bridge.

do this is to use a *bridge*, the operation of which is indicated in Figure 3–18. The bridge keeps segment A traffic on the A side and segment B traffic on the B side. Packets from segment A that are meant for a node in segment B will cross the bridge (the bridge will permit the packet to cross). The same is true for packets going from B to A. The bridge learns which packets should cross as it is used.

A *switch* is similar to a bridge, with some important enhancements. First, a switch may have multiple ports, thus directing packets to several different segments, further partitioning and isolating network traffic in a way similar to a router. Figure 3–19 shows an eight-port N-way switch, which can route packets from any input to any output. Some or all of an incoming packet is examined to make the routing decision, depending on the switching method that is used. One common method is called *store and forward,* which stores the received packet before examining it to check for errors before retransmitting. Bad packets are not forwarded.

In addition, a switch typically has auto-sensing 10/100-Mbps ports and will adjust the speed of each port accordingly. Furthermore, a *managed* switch supports SNMP for further control over network traffic. Switches operate at layer 2 (Data-Link) of the OSI model.

ROUTERS

A *router* is the basic building block of the Internet. Each router connects two or more networks together by providing an interface for each network to which it is connected. Figure 3–20(a) shows a router with an interface for an Ethernet network and a token-ring network. The router examines each packet of information to determine whether the packet must be translated from one network to another, performing a function similar to a bridge. Unlike a bridge, a router can connect networks that use different technologies, addressing methods,

Figure 3–19
One configuration
in an eight-port
N-way switch.

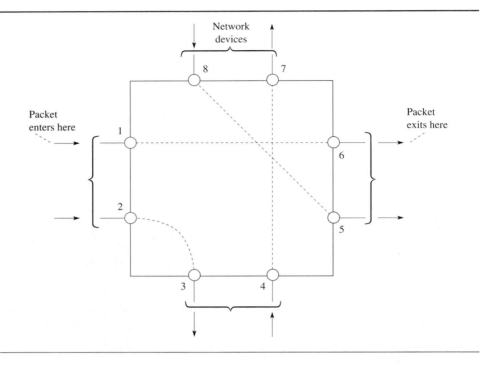

media types, frame formats, and speeds. Figures 3–20(b) and 3–20(c) show the top and rear views of the Cisco 1600 router. This router connects two Ethernet networks and has an expansion slot for a wide area network (WAN) connection.

Figure 3–20
(a) Router with two
interfaces.

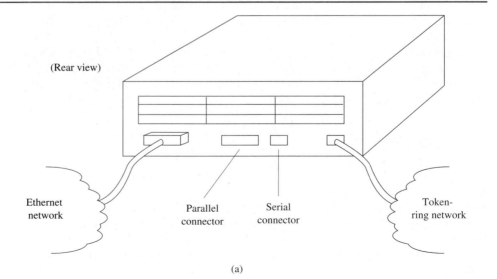

(b)

Figure 3–20
(continued) (b) Top view of Cisco 1600 router. (c) Rear view of Cisco 1600 router.

(c)

A router is a special-purpose device designed to interconnect networks. For example, three different networks can be connected using two routers, as illustrated in Figure 3–21. If a computer in network A needs to send a packet of information to network C, both routers pass the packets from the source network to the destination network.

Figure 3–21
Two routers connecting three networks.

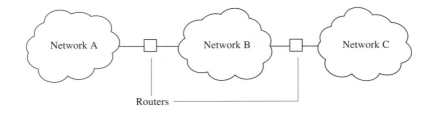

Figure 3–22
Packet routing.

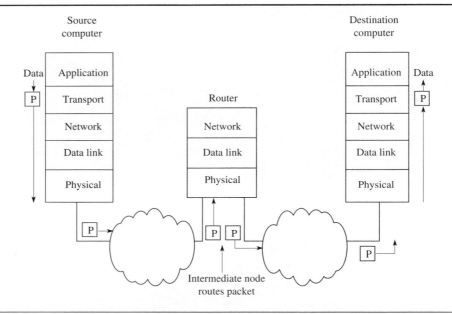

Routers maintain *routing tables* in their memories to store information about the physical connections on the network. The router examines each packet of data, checks the routing table, and then forwards the packet if necessary. Every other router in the path (between a source and a destination network) performs a similar procedure, as illustrated in Figure 3–22. Note that a router does not maintain any state information about the packets; it simply moves them along the network. Routers operate at layer 3 (Network) of the OSI model.

CABLE MODEMS

A *cable modem* is a high-speed network device connected to a local cable television provider. The cable television company allocates a pair of channels (one for transmit, one for receive) on the cable system to transmit data. At the

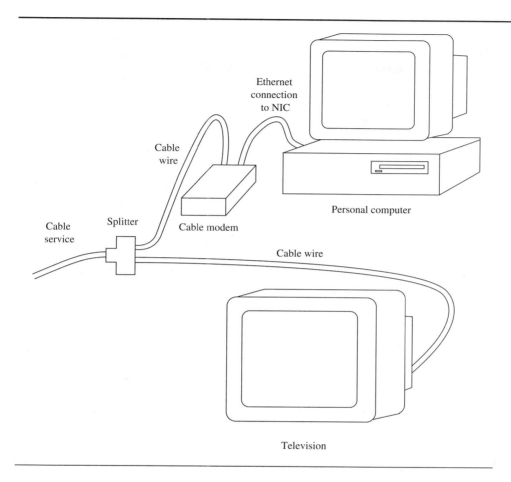

Figure 3–23
Cable service
connections.

Ethernet
connection
to NIC

Cable
wire

Cable
service

Splitter

Cable modem

Personal computer

Cable wire

Television

head-end of the network, located at the cable supplier offices, a traditional Internet service provider (*ISP*) service is established to service the network clients. The connection from the cable system ISP to the Internet uses traditional telecommunications devices, such as T1 or T3 lines.

The subscribers to the cable modem service use a splitter to create two cable wires. One wire is reconnected to the television and the second is connected to the new cable modem. This is illustrated in Figure 3–23. The cable modem itself requires just a few connections, as shown in Figure 3–24. After all the connections have been made, the power light on the front of the cable modem will be on. The other lights show the cable modem status. Both the cable and PC lights are on when the cable system ISP and the PC network card are set up properly. The test light is normally off, but comes on after a reset or when power is reapplied. Figure 3–25(a) shows the front panel display of a typical cable modem. Figure 3–25(b) shows the Motorola Wave modem.

Figure 3–24
Cable modem
connections.

Figure 3–24
Cable modem
connections.

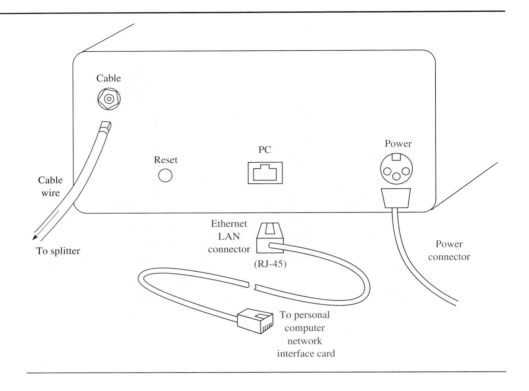

Figure 3–25
(a) Cable modem
indicator lights.

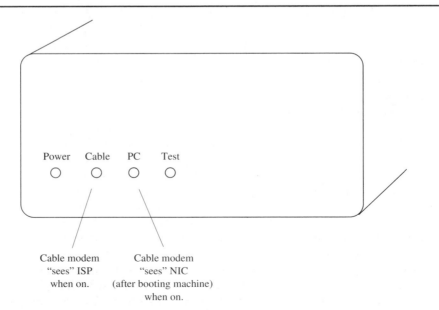

(a)

Figure 3–25
(continued)
(b) Motorola Wave
modem.

(b)

There is no maintenance for the cable modem subscriber other than providing adequate ventilation and keeping the power applied to the cable modem at all times. The cable system ISP may update the internal software or run tests on them during off-peak hours.

SATELLITE NETWORK SYSTEM

The Hughes Corporation offers a unique solution to low-speed Internet connections. For a few hundred dollars, you can buy their DirecPC Internet satellite networking system. Figure 3–26 shows the basic operation. Internet data comes to your PC via satellite at 400 Kbps. Through your modem and ISP, data goes back to Hughes's network operations center (NOC) where it is uploaded to the Internet. This is an ideal situation for browsing, when you need to receive information fast (if a Web page contains many images) but only send information out (clicking on a new URL to load a new page) occasionally. A low-speed line for transmitted packets is acceptable, unless you are uploading large files to an FTP site or sending e-mail with large attachments. If there is no cable where you live or work (for a cable modem connection), DirecPC may be the answer for you.

Figure 3–26
Satellite Internet.

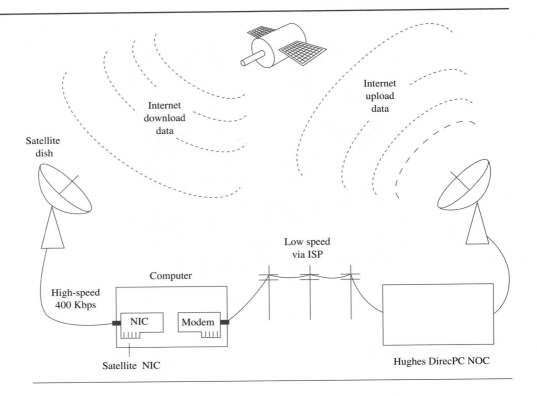

EXOTIC HARDWARE AND SOFTWARE

We have only examined the basic types of networking hardware in this chapter. Many more exotic (and expensive) networking components are available. For example, instead of using multiple 16-port switches, a single industrial switch with 64 ports or more, including port management, may be used. IP addresses can be assigned to specific ports, ports can be activated/deactivated with software, and the port speed can be controlled.

For networks that must be distributed over a large geographic area (such as a college or industrial campus), line-of-sight infrared lasers can be used to link separate networks together. If fiber is used instead, fiber repeaters may be necessary to obtain the required distance for a link.

Computer users can now walk around with their laptops, relying on wireless Ethernet technology to maintain the connection with the mobile machine. Other special-purpose devices called *cable modem routers* act like switches but allow multiple machines to share a single Internet connection.

Network software has also evolved. Network management software will display a graphic diagram of your network, with pertinent information (IP/MAC addresses, link speed, activity, and status). One system allows the network technician to be paged when a problem occurs.

A tour through a local industry will introduce you to a wide variety of sophisticated networking components. Bring a notebook to write down the names and model numbers on the equipment so you can search the Web for more information about them later.

TROUBLESHOOTING TECHNIQUES

One of the most important phases of a network installation is making the cables required for all the nodes. It is much less expensive to buy BNC connectors and spools of coax and make custom-length cables than it is to buy finished cables. This may not be the case for UTP cable, which is harder to terminate (four or eight wires) due to the rigid requirements of the UTP specifications.

A valuable tool to have at your disposal when preparing or checking cables is a *cable tester*. Figure 3–27 shows an electronic cable tester, capable of performing these (and many other) tests on UTP cable:

- Passive and active profiles
- Continuity

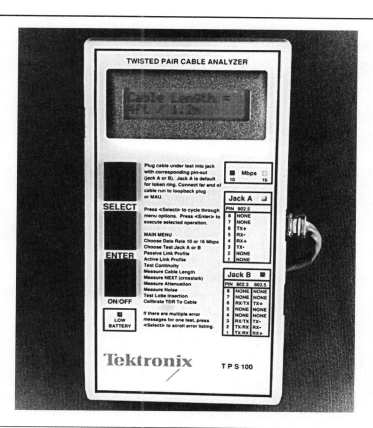

Figure 3–27
Electronic cable analyzer *(photograph by John T. Butchko).*

- Cable length
- NEXT (near-end crosstalk)
- Attenuation
- Noise

Other, more sophisticated network test equipment, such as the Fluke LANmeter, capture and diagnose network packets of many different protocols, gather statistics (collisions, packets sent), perform standard network operations such as PING and TRACERT, and can transmit packets for troubleshooting purposes. The power of this type of network analyzer is well worth the cost.

SELF-TEST

This self-test is designed to help you check your understanding of the background information presented in this chapter.

True/False
Answer *true* or *false*.

1. Only RG-58 coax is used in Ethernet systems.

2. Vampire taps are used with RG-11 cable.

3. All NICs have the same MAC address (for broadcasting).

4. Token-ring networks use an MAU.

5. Transceivers are only used with fiber and UTP.

6. The only type of fiber is single-mode fiber.

7. The network diameter is the same for all types of networks.

Multiple Choice
Select the best answer.

8. Hubs are also called
   a. Repeaters.
   b. Transceivers.
   c. Concentrators.

9. Hubs act like
   a. Repeaters.
   b. Transceivers.
   c. Routers.

10. A bridge between networks C and D
    a. Broadcasts all packets between C and D.
    b. Broadcasts selected packets between C and D.
    c. Broadcasts all packets from C to D, selected packets from D to C.

11. A router
    a. Connects two different networks.
    b. Ties all hubs together.
    c. Is not used for Internet connections.

12. Cable testers check
    a. Continuity.
    b. Crosstalk.
    c. Frequency response.
    d. a and b only.

13. Fiber optic cable consists of two parts: the core and the
    a. Cladding.
    b. Cloaking.
    c. Jacket.

14. To create a link between two network sites located 800 meters apart, use
    a. Seven hubs and eight 100-meter UTP cables.
    b. Two 500-meter thickwire segments and a repeater.
    c. A pair of infrared lasers.

Matching
Match each cable type on the right with each network system on the left.

15. 10base2	a.	Fiber
16. 10base5	b.	RG-11
17. 10/100baseT	c.	RG-58
18. 10baseFL	d.	UTP
19. IEEE 802.5	e.	STP

Completion

Fill in the blank or blanks with the best answers.

20. Connecting to RG-11 coaxial cable requires a(n) _____ tap.

21. A NIC that contains both types of connectors is called a(n) _____ card.

22. Protocols must be _____ to a NIC before they can be used.

23. The number of Ethernet segments that may be connected via repeaters is _____.

24. One technique used by switches is store and _____.

25. The path a pulse of light takes through a fiber is called a _____.

26. The maximum distance between two nodes on a network is the network _____.

QUESTIONS/ACTIVITIES

1. Why do you think fiber has not totally replaced coax and UTP cable?

2. What is the difference between the following:
   a. A repeater and a hub.
   b. A hub and a switch.
   c. A switch and a router.

3. What makes a hub stackable?

REVIEW QUIZ

Under the supervision of your instructor

1. List and describe the basic networking hardware components.

2. Explain the differences in 10base2 Ethernet and 10/100baseT Ethernet.

3. Compare the advantages of fiber over copper wire.

Networking Concepts Laboratory

Experiment #3
Ethernet LAN Components

Objectives

1. To become familiar with Ethernet LAN components such as cabling, network interface cards, and hubs.
2. To examine an operational Ethernet network.

Required Equipment

The following equipment is required for this experiment:

- Network Interface Card
- Ethernet hub
- Straight-through and crossover UTP cable
- Access to the Internet

Procedure

Perform each of the following steps. Record your observations, results, and any difficulties you encounter. You will use this information when you develop your conclusions about the experiment.

1. Carefully examine the components on a network interface card.
   a. What are the part numbers of the integrated circuits?
   b. Do you recognize any other components? If so, what are they?
   c. How many different types of components are there?
2. Repeat step 1 for an Ethernet hub. Use care when removing the cover.
3. Try to locate information on the Web about the integrated circuits you found in steps 1 and 2.
4. Place the ends of a single UTP cable side by side.
   a. How many wires are used?
   b. Are the wire colors in the same order in both connectors? (If so, the cable is a straight-through cable.)
   c. Record the colors of each wire.
5. Repeat step 4 for the opposite type of UTP cable.
6. Examine the Ethernet network in your building.
   a. What new components (transceivers, switches, routers, etc.) did you find?
   b. What are the lengths of the cables used?
   c. How fast are the segments?

d. What types of cables are used?

e. How does the network get from floor to floor and/or building to building?

f. Who is responsible for maintaining the network?

Discussion and Conclusion

Using a word processor, write your own detailed explanations of the results and observations made during the experiment. To begin, try to say something about each procedure step.

In addition, provide answers to the following questions:

1. How many different types of network interface cards are there (for example, ISA, PCI, PCMCIA, wireless, etc.)?

2. What are your thoughts about the internal circuitry of the hub? Were any components duplicated (one or two of each type for each port of the hub)?

3. How many computers are connected to the Ethernet network you examined?

4

Ethernet Technology

PERFORMANCE OBJECTIVES

Upon completion of this chapter, you will be able to

- Describe the format of an Ethernet frame.
- Explain the basic operation of collision detection.
- Compare the features of the different 10-Mbps Ethernet, Fast Ethernet, and Gigabit Ethernet technologies.
- Discuss the principles of wireless Ethernet.

Joe Tekk sat at a reference desk in the library of a local university. In front of him, folded open on the desk, was a thick manual titled IEEE Standard *for Carrier* Sense Multiple Access with Collision Detection (CSMA/CD) Access Method and Physical Layer Specifications. *Joe had been there for two hours, patiently scanning the manual page by page, reading some sections and glancing over others.*

Joe was fascinated by the amount of information contained in the specification. There were figures showing connector styles, state diagrams, cable impedances, and bit rates. Joe examined flowcharts, sample code that looked like Pascal, and data encoding methods.

The clock in the library gave a short tone. Joe looked at the time. It was 2:45 P.M. The IEEE Standard was open to page 720. Joe was glad there were only 500 pages to go.

INTRODUCTION

In this chapter we will examine the details and operation of the popular LAN technology called Ethernet. Since its development by Xerox, Intel, and Digital Equipment Corporation in 1980, Ethernet has evolved from its initial 10-Mbps data rate, to Fast Ethernet (100 Mbps), and now Gigabit Ethernet (1000 Mbps).

All of the properties, procedures, and definitions associated with Ethernet are contained in the IEEE Standard 802.3. This document contains over 1200 pages and includes such information as

- Flowcharts for transmitting and receiving a bit

55

Table 4–1
Selected IEE 802.3
standards.

Standard	Technology
802.3	10Base5
802.3a	10Base2
802.3i	10BaseT
802.3j	10BaseFL
802.3u	100BaseT
802.3z	1000BaseX

- Signal speed, noise, and other parameters for various media
- Data encoding methods (Manchester, 4B5B, etc.) used by each technology
- The method for computing the frame check sequence
- Detailed discussion of collision detection
- Autonegotiation using fast link pulses
- Repeater operation

The IEEE 802.3 document would be a valuable addition to your local library. Table 4–1 shows some of the many different Ethernet technologies covered by the IEEE 802.3 Standard. We will examine each technology, beginning with the 10-Mbps systems. Since each new technology must accomplish the same goal, reliable transmission of an Ethernet frame, our discussion begins there.

THE ETHERNET FRAME FORMAT

Figure 4–1 shows the format of an Ethernet 802.3 frame. A separate and practically identical frame format called Ethernet II has an 8-byte preamble of

Figure 4–1
IEEE 802.3 Ethernet
frame.

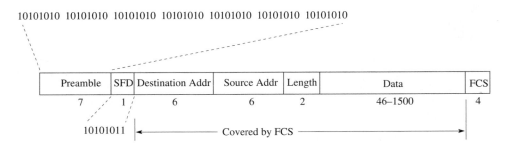

identical 10101010 patterns (no 10101011 SFD) and a 2-byte Type field in place of the Length field. Since the Data field of an 802.3 Ethernet frame is limited to 1500 bytes, a value larger than 1500 in the Type/Length field indicates an Ethernet II frame. Many companies, such as Xerox, DEC, and Novell, use Ethernet II frames in their networks.

All data is packaged into one or more frames for transmission over an Ethernet LAN. Let us look at each portion of the Ethernet frame.

Preamble (7 bytes)

The Preamble contains 7 bytes with the identical pattern 10101010. This alternating sequence of 1s and 0s are the first bytes transmitted. They are provided to help listening stations synchronize quickly on the new data stream.

SFD (1 byte)

The SFD (Start Frame Delimiter) is the 1-byte pattern 10101011. Note that the LSB is high, whereas all the bytes of the Preamble had their LSB low.

Destination Address (6 bytes)

This is the destination MAC address of the station that is to receive the frame. Every Ethernet device manufactured (NIC, router) contains a unique 48-bit MAC address assigned by the manufacturer. An example of a *MAC address* is 00-C0-F0-27-64-E2. The first 24 bits are the manufacturer code (00-C0-F0 is Kingston). The last 24 bits are chosen by the manufacturer. The WINIPCFG utility can be used to determine the MAC address (called the adapter address).

A MAC address of FF-FF-FF-FF-FF-FF (all 1s) is reserved for use as a broadcast address.

Source Address (6 bytes)

This is the MAC address of the source station transmitting the frame.

Length (2 bytes)

This field indicates the number of bytes in the Data field.

Data (46 to 1500 bytes)

The Data area is where all data from the upper networking layers is carried. In Chapters 7 through 10 we will see how upper layer protocols are encapsulated and stored in the Data area.

FCS (4 bytes)

The *FCS* (frame check sequence) is a 32-bit *CRC* (cyclic redundancy check) value used to determine the validity of the received Ethernet frame. The FCS is found using a generator polynomial defined mathematically as

$$G(x) = x^{32} + x^{26} + x^{23} + x^{22} + x^{16} + x^{12} + x^{11} + x^{10} + x^8 + x^7 + x^5 + x^4 + x^2 + x + 1$$

which is equivalent to the binary value 10000010011000001000111011011011011. The 1s in the pattern indicate where exclusive OR gates are used in a recirculating shift register circuit that is able to generate/check a valid stream of data of variable length. If even a single bit in the frame is received in error, the shift register will not generate the proper output and the error will be discovered.

All bits in the frame except those in the FCS are transmitted from LSB to MSB.

From the numbers provided in Figure 4–1, the minimum and maximum sizes of an Ethernet frame are 72 bytes and 1526 bytes, respectively. Many individuals refer to the smallest Ethernet frame as 64 bytes, by not including the 8 bytes of Preamble and SFD. The largest frame would then be 1518 bytes. For the purposes of the discussion in this exercise, the Preamble and SFD will be included in the length of the frame.

 ## THE INTERFRAME GAP

The *interframe gap* is a self-imposed quiet time appended to the end of every frame. This idle time gives the network media a chance to stabilize, and other network components time to process the frame. Figure 4–2 shows a sequence of frames separated by the fixed-size interframe gap. For 10-Mbps Ethernet, the interframe gap is 9.6 microseconds. This corresponds to 96 bit times (divide 9.6 microseconds by 100 nanoseconds/bit). Thus, the 576 bits of a minimum-length Ethernet frame are followed by 96 bit times of silence. Dividing 10 Mbps by 672 bits for each frame plus interframe gap gives a frame rate of 14,880 frames/second (minimum-sized frames). Since each frame is followed by 96 bits of silence, there are a total of 14,880 times 96, or 1,428,480 bits of the 10-Mbps bandwidth (14.28%) lost due to the interframe gap. These calculations are shown in Figure 4–3.

When the frame size is larger, more of the available bandwidth is utilized. This is illustrated in Table 4–2. Note that as the frame size increases, the 96 bits of interframe gap becomes less significant. The actual frame lengths in a real network will be constantly fluctuating, as shown in Figure 4–2, so the bandwidth utilization will be constantly changing. Note that the companion CD contains the Excel file FSVSBW.XLS, which generates the information shown in Table 4–2.

Figure 4–2
Interframe gap separates each Ethernet frame.

Frame ⟶ 0 1 2 3 4 5 6 7 8 9 ⟶ Time

Inter frame gap

9.6 µS @ 10 Mbps = 96 bit times
0.96 µS @ 100 Mbps = 96 bit times
0.096 µS @ 1000 Mbps = 96 bit times

Figure 4–3
Calculating effect of
frame size on lost
bandwidth.

$$
\begin{array}{r}
72 \text{ bytes/minimum Ethernet frame} \\
\times \quad 8 \text{ bits/byte} \\
\hline
576 \text{ bits/frame} \\
+ \quad 96 \text{ bits/interframe gap (IFG)} \\
\hline
672 \text{ bits/frame and IFG}
\end{array}
$$

$$
\begin{array}{r}
10,000,000 \text{ bits/second} \\
\div \quad 672 \text{ bits/frame and IFG} \\
\hline
14,880 \text{ frames/second}
\end{array}
$$

$$
\begin{array}{r}
14,880 \text{ frames/second} \\
\times \quad 96 \text{ bits/IFG} \\
\hline
1,428,480 \text{ bits lost/second}
\end{array}
$$

$$
\frac{1,428,480}{10,000,000} \times 100\% = 14.28\% \text{ lost bandwith}
$$

Table 4–2
Effect of frame size
on bandwidth
utilization.

Data Size (bytes)	Frame Size* (bits)	Frames per Second	Total Bits Lost	% Bandwidth Lost
46	672	14880	1428480	14.2848
64	816	12254	1176384	11.76384
100	1104	9057	869472	8.69472
128	1328	7530	722880	7.2288
150	1504	6648	638208	6.38208
200	1904	5252	504192	5.04192
256	2352	4251	408096	4.08096
512	4400	2272	218112	2.18112
1024	8496	1177	112992	1.12992
1500	12304	812	77952	0.77952

* Includes 96 bits for interframe gap.

 ## CSMA/CD

CSMA/CD stands for *Carrier Sense Multiple Access with Collision Detection.*
This is the technique used to share access to the available bandwidth. To
describe the basic operation of CSMA/CD, let us use the 10base5 network

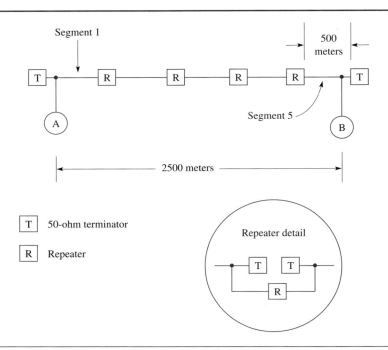

Figure 4–4
10base5 Ethernet
network.

shown in Figure 4–4. This network consists of five 500-meter coaxial segments connected by four repeaters. This is the largest network possible using 10base5 technology. Two stations, A and B, are located at the farthest ends of the network. There may be many more stations connected to each segment, all competing for bandwidth using the same CSMA/CD method. Collectively, these stations operate in a ***collision domain***. A collision domain is a portion of a LAN (or the entire LAN) where two or more stations transmitting at the same time will interfere with each other. For example, in Figure 4–4, the entire 2500-meter network is a single collision domain, due to the use of repeaters between each segment. In general, all ports on repeaters or hubs are in the same collision domain. Ports on switches and routers operate in their own individual collision domains.

Let us examine what occurs during good and bad frame transmissions in a collision domain.

No Collision During Frame

A station wishing to transmit a frame first listens to the coax, waiting for an idle period indicating no transmissions. Once the coax is quiet for a time equal to (or longer than) the interframe gap, the station begins transmitting the frame, one bit at a time. The electronic signal representing each bit travels at a limited speed within the thickwire coax, requiring 10.8 microseconds worst case to travel the 2500 meters from station A to station B or vice versa. This time is based on the speed coefficient of the cable (0.77 for thickwire coax), the length of the cable, and the speed of light (300,000,000 meters/second).

The signal is absorbed at the end of each coaxial segment by the terminating resistor. There are no reflections to cause a collision, and no other stations begin transmitting during the frame. One or more stations receive and process the frame.

A Collision Occurs During the Frame

At some point during the transmission of one station's frame, a new station begins transmitting its own frame. Their electronic signals eventually meet up with each other (a collision), causing signal and energy distortions that are sensed by the Ethernet transceivers. All affected stations then output a jam sequence and begin a random waiting period before transmitting again. The random period is used to help prevent the same stations from recolliding with each other and increases exponentially with successive collisions of the same frame.

It is important to note that the only way a station can detect a collision with its own frame is for the station to detect the collision *while it is still transmitting*. If the station finishes transmission and then a collision occurs, the station has no way of knowing if its frame was involved in the collision, or if two other stations had frames colliding. Since the diameter of the 10base5 network from Figure 4–4 is limited to 2500 meters, the worst-case round trip time of a signal is 21.6 microseconds (not including the delays associated with the four repeaters). Now, let us consider why the round-trip time is important to collision detection. Figure 4–5 shows an example timeline of how station A detects a collision with a frame from station B. In Figure 4–5(a), station A has listened to the coax and found it idle and has begun transmitting its frame. Station B is also listening and finding the coax idle.

The signal representing station A's frame travels towards station B, taking at least 10.8 microseconds for the 2500-meter trip, ignoring the delays of the four repeaters. Now, just as the signal is about to reach station B, station B begins transmitting its own frame (recall that station B also found the coax free of transmission). An instant later the collision occurs, indicated by the time t_1 in Figure 4–5(b). A distorted signal begins traveling back to station A, requiring an additional 10.8 microseconds (ignoring repeater delays again) to travel another 2500 meters. At time t_2 in Figure 4–5(c), station A detects the collision. The total time is 21.6 microseconds for the round trip. With each bit requiring 100 nanoseconds, this corresponds to 216 bits (27 bytes) transmitted during the round trip. So an Ethernet frame must be at least 27 bytes long to detect a collision. But remember that we have ignored the delays associated with the four repeaters. The IEEE 802.3 standard limits repeater delays to 8 bit times. This adds up to a total of 64 bits for the round trip, or another 8 bytes of length we must add to the Ethernet frame for collision detection. This gets us to 35 bytes for the minimum frame. Since an actual Ethernet frame is at least 72 bytes long, there is plenty of time for a round-trip collision signal to be detected.

Figure 4–5
Collision example.

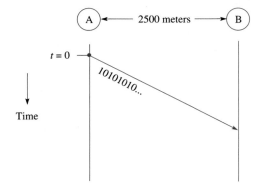

(a) Station A begins transmitting a frame.

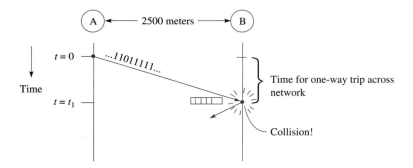

(b) Station B begins transmitting a frame
an instant before station A's frame arrives.

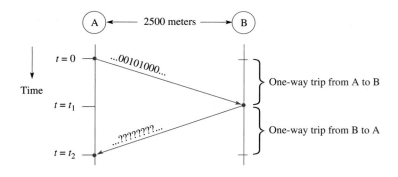

(c) Station A receives collision.

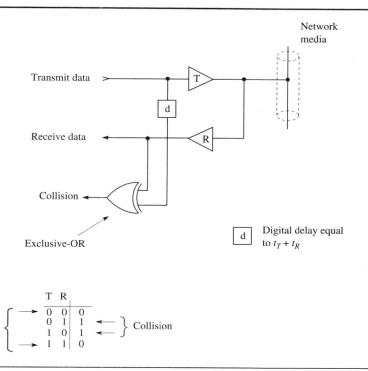

Figure 4–6
Hardware detection of collision.

Detecting Errors

Figure 4–6 shows a simplified circuit for detecting a collision by comparing the transmitted and received bitstreams with each other. In other words, the Ethernet transceiver listens to itself as it is transmitting. If a zero signal was transmitted, the receiver should see a zero. The same is true for a one signal. If the signals do not match, it is most likely due to a collision or some other network malfunction. As indicated in Figure 4–6, an exclusive-OR gate is used to identify when the transmitted and received bit streams are different. The delay is required on the transmitter input of the exclusive-OR gate to compensate for the time required by the transmitter and receiver circuits.

Figure 4–6 is based on information contained in the original Ethernet patent, which is titled MULTIPOINT DATA COMMUNICATION SYSTEM WITH COLLISION DETECTION. This patent, which was filed on March 31, 1975, can be viewed online at http://www.patents.ibm.com.

Jam Sequence

The *jam sequence* generated by stations detecting a collision is a 32-bit pattern designed to propagate the collision throughout the network. The contents of the jam pattern may not represent a valid FCS for the current frame.

Random Waiting Period

Retransmission of a frame is attempted after a random waiting period that is a multiple of an Ethernet *slot time*, the time required to transmit 512 bits (a total of 51.2 microseconds for 10-Mbps Ethernet). The actual name of the algorithm is "truncated binary exponential backoff," due to the method used to increase the waiting period. A collision counter keeps track of successive collisions (collisions involving the same frame). The higher the number of collisions, the longer the waiting period. Mathematically, we have

$$0 \le R \le 2^K$$

where K equals minimum $(N,10)$ and N is the number of successive collisions. R is a random integer chosen from the range 0 to 2^K. As K increases, the upper limit on the range increases exponentially (1, 2, 4, 8, 16, 32, 64, 128, 256, 512, 1024). The random integer R is thus chosen from an ever-increasing set of integers. As an example, after three collisions, R is chosen from the set of numbers 0 to 8. Suppose R is chosen to be 5. A total of 5 times 512 bit times is used as the delay period.

After 10 successive collisions, the waiting period becomes a maximum of 1024 slot times. When 16 successive collisions have occurred, transmission of the frame is aborted and an error is reported to the upper networking layer.

10-MBPS ETHERNET

The first three widely used Ethernet technologies were 10base5, 10base2, and 10baseT. Figure 4–7 shows the general 10-Mbps architecture of the Data-Link and Physical layers.

Beginning with the media (coax, UTP) we first encounter the MDI (medium dependent interface). The MDI is essentially the connection method used with the media, such as a vampire tap or RJ-45 connector.

The PMA (physical medium attachment) provides the functions necessary for transmission, reception, and collision detection. Together, the MDI and PMA make up the MAU (medium attachment unit).

The AUI (attachment unit interface) may be a transceiver cable up to 50 meters in length, connected via a 15-pin AUI connector. The AUI cable may be used, for example, to connect a thickwire vampire-tap transceiver to the upstream AUI port of a hub or switch. The PLS (physical signaling) is where Manchester encoding is applied to the bit stream.

Let us examine the properties of each 10 Mbps technology.

10base5
- Media: Thickwire coax
- Propagation velocity: 0.77 c
- Impedance: 50 ohms
- Connector: Vampire tap

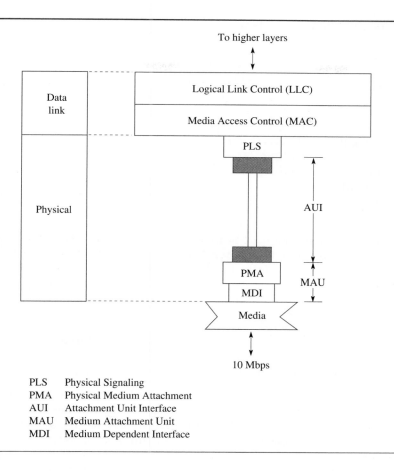

Figure 4–7
10-Mbps
architecture.

PLS   Physical Signaling
PMA   Physical Medium Attachment
AUI   Attachment Unit Interface
MAU   Medium Attachment Unit
MDI   Medium Dependent Interface

- Segment length: 500 meters
- Maximum nodes/segment: 100
- Node spacing: 2.5 meters
- Topology: Bus

The 2.5-meter spacing requirement is designed to prevent signal distortions from each station from adding together in phase. The number of nodes allowed on a segment is limited by the electrical properties of the cable.

10base2

- Media: Thinwire coax
- Propagation velocity: 0.65 c
- Impedance: 50 ohms
- Connector: BNC T
- Segment length: 185 meters
- Maximum nodes/segment: 30

- Node spacing: 0.5 meters
- Topology: Bus

Here we can see that different coaxial cable affects the allowable cable length as well as the number of nodes/segment.

10baseT

- Media: Category 3, 4, or 5 UTP
- Propagation velocity: 0.585 c
- Impedance: 100 ohms
- Connector: RJ-45
- Segment length: 100 meters
- Maximum nodes/segment: 2
- Topology: Star

The number of nodes/segment is misleading, since the UTP cable requires a point-to-point connection, typically a NIC to a port on a hub, or a hub-to-hub connection.

All three technologies have some common properties. These include

- 10 Mbps data rate
- Manchester encoding
- Maximum of 1024 stations in a single collision domain (Repeaters do not count towards this maximum limit.)
- Maximum of four repeaters in longest path through the network

Figure 4–8 shows a example of how a digital signal is Manchester encoded. A logic zero is encoded as a falling edge in the middle of a bit time. A logic one is encoded as a rising edge. This guarantees an edge during every bit time, making the signal easier to synchronize with and decode.

Figure 4–8
Manchester Encoding.

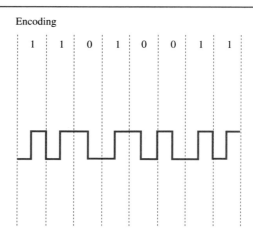

The four repeater limit, chosen to maintain CSMA/CD operation, is part of a larger set of restrictions, commonly referred to as the **5-4-3 Rule**, which has the following properties:

- 5 segments in the longest path
- 4 repeaters in the longest path
- 3 segments with nodes

Again, these rules apply to a single collision domain.

Figure 4–9 shows two ways of applying the 5-4-3 rule. In Figure 4–9(a) a 10base5/10base2 system is illustrated. Three of the five segments contain nodes. The longest path between stations (A and Z) is five segments, with four repeaters in between.

Figure 4–9(b) shows a 10baseT network. The A and Z stations are separated by five UTP segments with four hubs in between. Each UTP cable from a station to a hub, or from a hub to another hub, is considered a segment and may be up to 100 meters in length.

Collisions are detected in the 10baseT network whenever the transmit and receive pair in a single UTP cable are active at the same time. For example, a frame being transmitted from port 3 on a hub collides with a frame coming into port 3. Even though the transmit and receive wire pairs are different, and there is no electrical collision (as we see on coaxial cable), there is an attempt by two stations to use the network simultaneously, which results in a collision. This indicates half-duplex operation, since any station may send or receive,

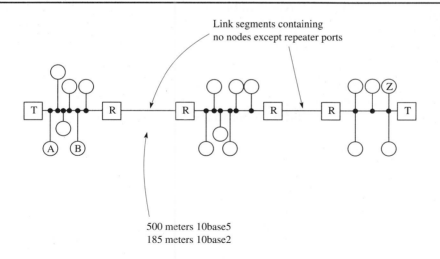

Figure 4–9
Utilizing the 5-4-3 rule.

(a) 10base5/10base2 network.

(continued on next page)

Figure 4–9
(continued)

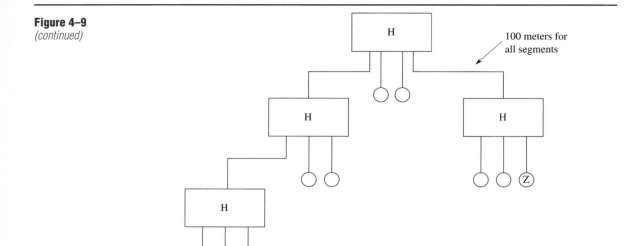

(b) 10baseT network.

but not at the same time. New, autonegotiating Ethernet transceivers are capable of operating in full-duplex, sending and receiving frames simultaneously.

10baseF

Originally, the FOIRL (fiber optic inter-repeater link) specification was used to standardize Ethernet communication over fiber. It allowed for a 1000-meter fiber between repeaters.

Eventually, the demand for fiber to the PC exceeded the FOIRL specifications, and a new set of fiber specifications was designed. Called 10baseF, it contains three categories: 10baseFL, 10baseFB, and 10baseFP.

10baseFL

- Fiber link specification
- Station-to-station, station-to-hub, and hub-to-hub connection
- 2000-meter segment length
- Manchester encoding
- Replaces FOIRL, works with existing FOIRL hardware
- Connector: ST

This specification is the most widely used. Figure 4–10 shows a portion of a 10baseFL network. Before fiber NICs became available, a 10baseFL to 10baseT (or 10base2) transceiver was used to interface fiber with the PC.

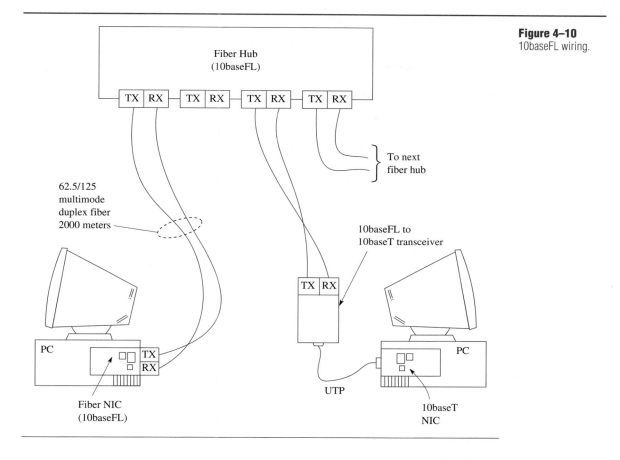

Figure 4–10
10baseFL wiring.

10baseFB

- Fiber backbone specification
- Hub-to-hub connection
- Synchronous operation
- 2000-meter segment length

The synchronous operation on the 10baseFB link is used to reduce the delays normally associated with Ethernet repeaters that cause the interframe gap to shrink as it propagates through multiple repeaters. This allows the segment distance to be extended without compromising the collision detection mechanism.

10baseFP

- Fiber passive specification
- Station-to-hub, hub-to-hub connection
- Hubs link up to 33 stations
- 500-meter segment length

This specification allows groups of 10baseFP computers to be passively connected via a hub that optically shares signals transmitted from any station. This technology is well suited for low-power environments.

 ## 100-MBPS ETHERNET (FAST ETHERNET)

Demand for bandwidth quickly exceeded the capacity of 10-Mbps Ethernet. Even moving from hub-based 10baseT networks to switch-based networks only provided temporary relief. Increasing the data rate by a factor of 10 over 10-Mbps Ethernet, 100-Mbps Ethernet, or *Fast Ethernet* as it is commonly called, is implemented in several different ways, all collectively referred to as 100baseT technology. One disadvantage of Fast Ethernet is its smaller network diameter, typically one tenth that of 10-Mbps Ethernet, or around 200 meters. This reduction in network diameter is necessary to maintain the parameters of CSMA/CD at the faster data rate, since the signals still move at the same speed in the cable, but the frame times are shorter by a factor of 10.

Figure 4–11 shows the 100-Mbps Ethernet interface definition. Several new sublayers have been added, due to the requirements of 100-Mbps transmission. For example, the Manchester encoding used in 10-Mbps Ethernet is not well suited to high-frequency operation. Other data encoding and signaling techniques are used instead, using special bit patterns and multilevel signaling to transfer data in 4-bit chunks instead of one bit at a time (as in 10-Mbps Ethernet).

Let us take a look at each 100-Mbps technology.

100baseT4
- Data is exchanged over 3 pairs of Category 3 (or higher) UTP.
- Data rate is 33.3 Mbps (25 M baud, 12.5 MHz) on each pair (total of 100 Mbps).
- 8B6T encoding is used.
- Fourth pair is used for collision detection.
- Half duplex only
- Maximum segment length: 100 meters
- Maximum network diameter: 205 meters
- Maximum number of repeaters: 2
- Connector: RJ-45

8B6T coding replaces 8-bit data values with 6 ternary codes that may have the values –, +, or 0. Table 4–3 shows a small sample of the 256 code patterns used in 8B6T encoding. The patterns are chosen to provide good DC characteristics, error detection, and reduced high-frequency effects. Special patterns can also be used as markers or control codes.

A multilevel signaling scheme is used, which allows more than one bit of data to be encoded into a signal transition. This is why a 12.5-MHz frequency

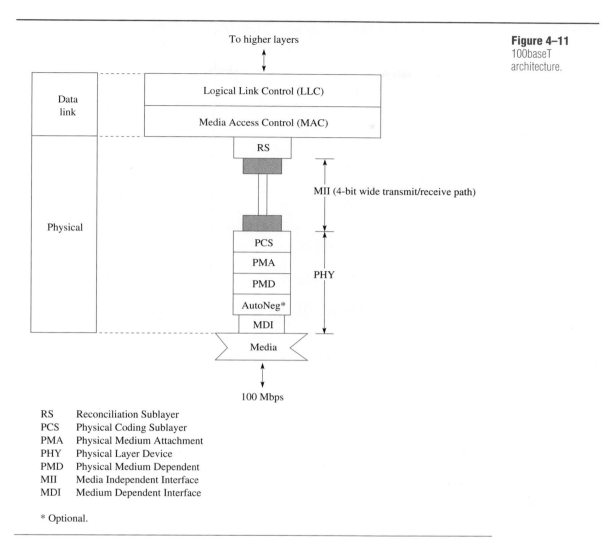

Figure 4–11
100baseT
architecture.

RS   Reconciliation Sublayer
PCS   Physical Coding Sublayer
PMA   Physical Medium Attachment
PHY   Physical Layer Device
PMD   Physical Medium Dependent
MII   Media Independent Interface
MDI   Medium Dependent Interface

* Optional.

carries a 33.3-Mbps stream. Think about it this way: Each cycle of the 12.5 MHz carrier contains two levels. This gives 25 million level changes per second on a single UTP pair. The signals on each of the three UTP pairs change a total of 75 million times each second. Dividing 75 million levels per second by 6 levels per 8B6T symbol gives 12.5 million symbols/second. Each symbol is equivalent to a unique 8-bit pattern, so multiplying 12.5 million symbols/second by 8 bits per symbol gives 100 million bits/second, the required data rate. Figure 4–12 shows a sample 8B6T encoded waveform. Note that the 12.5-MHz signaling frequency is within the 16 MHz limit of Category 3 cable.

Table 4–3
Selected 8B6T codes.

Hex Value	6T Code Group					
00	+	−	0	0	+	−
01	0	+	−	+	−	0
02	+	−	0	+	−	0
03	−	0	+	+	−	0
04	−	0	+	0	+	−
05	0	+	−	−	0	+
06	+	−	0	−	0	+
07	−	0	+	−	0	+
08	−	+	0	0	+	−
10	+	0	+	−	−	0
3F	+	0	−	+	0	−
5E	−	−	+	+	+	0
7F	0	0	+	−	−	+
80	+	−	+	0	0	−
C0	+	−	+	0	+	−
FF	+	0	−	+	0	0

Figure 4–12
8B6T encoding.

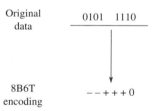

Original
data   0101   1110

8B6T   − − + + + 0
encoding

100baseTX

- Data is exchanged over 2 pairs of Category 5 UTP.
- Data rate is 125 Mbps on each pair (at 31.25 MHz).
- 4B5B encoding is used.
- Half and full duplex operation
- Maximum segment length: 100 meters
- Maximum network diameter: 205 meters
- Maximum number of repeaters: 2
- Connector: RJ-45

Table 4–4 shows the 4B5B coding for all 16 4-bit data patterns. Notice that there is always a mixture of 0s and 1s in each 5-bit pattern. This is done to

4-bit Data	5-bit Code
0000	11110
0001	01001
0010	10100
0011	10101
0100	01010
0101	01011
0110	01110
0111	01111
1000	10010
1001	10011
1010	10110
1011	10111
1100	11010
1101	11011
1110	11100
1111	11101

Table 4–4
4B5B coding.

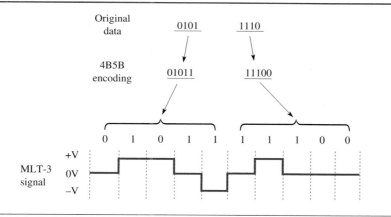

Figure 4–13
MLT-3 signaling for
4B5B encoded data.

prevent long strings of 0s or 1s from being encoded, which contributes to loss of synchronization on the signal.

Figure 4–13 shows how a three-level signal called MLT-3 (multiple level transition) is used to represent the 4B5B bitstream. Each 4-bit data value is replaced by its 5-bit 4B5B counterpart. Thus, the 100-Mbps data stream becomes a 125-Mbps 4B5B encoded data stream. Using MLT-3 allows the 125-Mbps

4B5B data stream to be carried using a signal rate of 31.25 MHz (31.25 MHz times 4 bits/cycle equals 125 Mbps).

Since the signaling frequency of 31.25 MHz is greater than the 16 MHz limit of Category 3 cable, a better cable, Category 5, is required. Category 5 cable has a frequency limit of 100 MHz.

100baseFX
- Single mode fiber limit: 10,000 meters
- Multimode fiber limit: 2000 meters (412 meters half duplex).
- 4B5B encoding is used.
- Connector: duplex SC, ST and FDDI MIC allowed

In this technology, the 4B5B encoded data is transmitted using NRZI (nonreturn to zero, invert on one). A 4B5B data rate of 125 Mbps is obtained using a 62.5-MHz carrier. Figure 4–14 illustrates a sample encoding and waveform. NRZI is well suited for fiber, due to its bi-level nature.

100baseT2
- Data is exchanged over 2 pairs of Category 3 (or higher) UTP.
- PAM5x5 encoding is used.
- Connector: RJ-45

Sending 100 Mbps over only two pairs of UTP requires yet another encoding and signaling scheme. Here, two 5-level PAM (pulse amplitude modulation) signals are sent over the UTP pairs, with a signaling rate of 12.5 MHz. Each cycle of the signal provides two PAM5x5 level changes, so there are 25 million level changes per UTP pair. Each pair of PAM signals (called A and B) encode a different 4-bit pattern (along with other, special patterns for idle mode) using combinations of these levels: {+2, +1, 0, −1, −2}. So 25 million PAM5x5 pairs times 4 bits/pair gives 100 Mbps.

Figure 4–14
NRZI signaling for
4B5B endoced data.

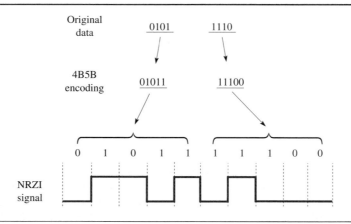

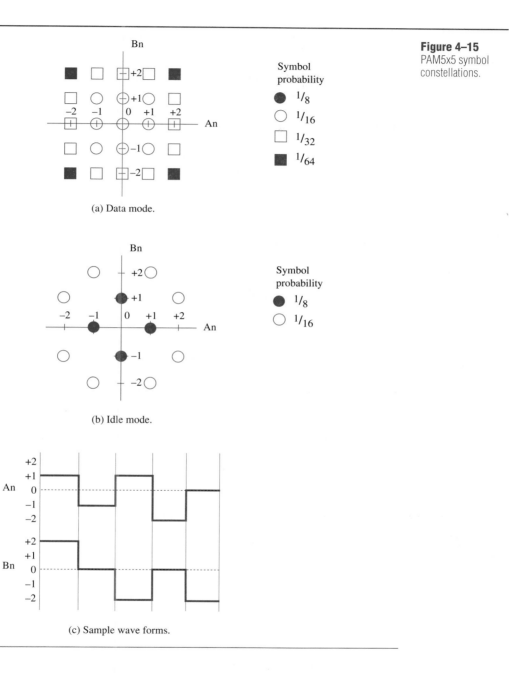

Figure 4–15
PAM5x5 symbol
constellations.

(a) Data mode.

(b) Idle mode.

(c) Sample wave forms.

Figure 4–15 shows the symbol constellations found in PAM5x5 encoding, as well as a sample pair of waveforms. Note that, when not transmitting data, the 100baseT2 link transmits an idle signal to maintain synchronization. During idle mode, the signals on A and B alternate between {+1, −1} and {+2, 0, −2}.

Fast Link Pulses

Beginning with 100baseT technology came the ability to perform autonegotiation between each end of a 100baseT connection. When the connection is established (plugging both ends of the UTP cable into their respective ports), a series of *fast link pulses* (FLP) will be exchanged between the ports. The 33 pulses contain 17 clock pulses and 16 data pulses. The 16 data pulses form a 16-bit code indicating the capabilities of the port, such as communication mode (half duplex, full duplex) and speed (10, 100, 10/100). Originally, 10baseT NICs used a single normal link pulse (NLP) to perform a link integrity test. An indicator LED on the NIC showed the status of the link. NLP pulses are typically generated every 16 milliseconds when the transmitter is idle, as indicated in Figure 4–16(a). NICs that support fast link pulses send an FLP burst containing 2 milliseconds of pulses, as illustrated in Figure 4–16(b). Note that the even pulses are the data pulses (one when a pulse is present 62.5 microseconds after a clock pulse, zero if there is no data pulse). The 125 microsecond spacing between the clock pulses allows the entire burst to complete in 2 milliseconds.

After the FLP bursts have been exchanged, the ports will decide on the best capabilities for the link according to the priority shown in Table 4–5. It is interesting to know that all this goes on as soon as you plug a live UTP cable into a port.

Figure 4–16
Fast link pulse details.

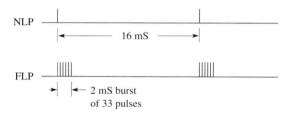

(a) General timing.

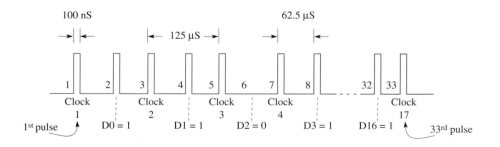

(b) FLP burst organization.

Priority	Link Choice
1 (Highest)	100baseT2 (full duplex)
2	100baseTX (full duplex)
3	100baseT2 (half duplex)
4	100baseT4
5	100baseTX (half duplex)
6	10baseT (full duplex)
7 (Lowest)	10baseT (half duplex)

Table 4–5
Autonegotiation priorities.

Two Repeater Types

The original 10-Mbps Ethernet specified a single repeater type to propagate frames between segments. Fast Ethernet contains specifications for two types of repeaters, Class I and Class II. Class I repeaters are slower (140 bit times for its round-trip delay) than Class II repeaters (92 bits times or less), but provide functions such as translation between the many different 100baseT technologies. Class II repeaters, although faster, only support a single technology.

Standard topologies for 100baseT networks are

- One Class I repeater. This provides a network diameter of 200 meters using copper cable. Stations may be 100 meters from the repeater.
- Two Class II repeaters connected via a 5-meter cable. This provides a diameter of 205 meters. Stations may be 100 meters from each repeater.

100VG-AnyLAN

Developed by Hewlett-Packard, the IEEE 802.12 standard 100VG-AnyLAN technology is a 100-Mbps LAN technology capable of handling both Ethernet and token-ring frames. 100VG-AnyLAN uses *domain-based priority access*, an access method whereby stations are polled in a round-robin fashion. Each polled station may make a normal-priority or high-priority request, which is processed by a higher-level 100VG-AnyLAN hub (not the same as an Ethernet hub). This access method eliminates collisions, allowing 100VG-AnyLAN networks to have a larger diameter than a 100baseT network. The high-priority requests are intended to support real-time multimedia applications such as voice and video.

Figure 4–17 shows a sample 100VG-AnyLAN network. The IEEE 802.12 specification provides for three levels of 100VG-AnyLAN hubs connected in a hierarchical manner. The entire network must support either Ethernet frames or token-ring frames.

For more information on 100VG-AnyLAN, visit http://www.100vg.com. This site contains detailed documentation and product information.

Figure 4–17
100VG-AnyLan network.

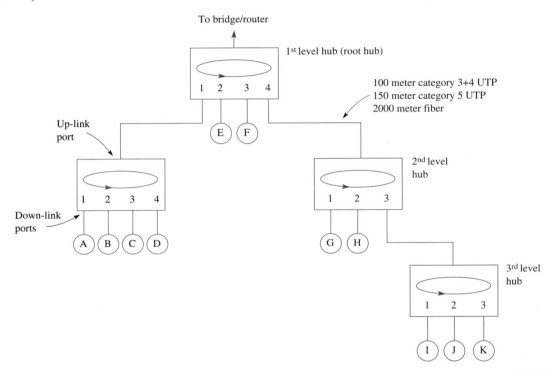

1000-MBPS ETHERNET (GIGABIT ETHERNET)

When the demand for bandwidth exceeded 100-Mbps Ethernet, it was natural to think about extending Ethernet to 1000 Mbps, rather than use some other, noncompatible technology like ATM (asynchronous transfer mode) or FDDI (fiber distributed data interface).

Extending the data rate, however, leads to a decrease in the network diameter (so that CSMA/CD is maintained). You might agree that a network diameter of 25 meters or less is not very practical. Two techniques used to increase the data rate from 100 Mbps to 1000 Mbps but still maintain a reasonable network diameter are carrier extension and frame bursting.

Carrier Extension
Figure 4–18 shows an Ethernet frame with a 0- to 448-byte carrier extension field. The carrier extension is used to maintain a minimum 512-byte Ethernet frame (not including the Preamble and SFD). So a 10/100-Mbps Ethernet frame containing

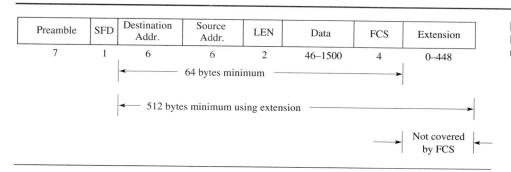

Preamble	SFD	Destination Addr.	Source Addr.	LEN	Data	FCS	Extension
7	1	6	6	2	46–1500	4	0–448

64 bytes minimum

512 bytes minimum using extension

Not covered by FCS

Figure 4–18
Ethernet frame with carrier extension.

only 100 bytes would require a carrier extension field of 412 bytes to be used over Gigabit Ethernet.

Frame Bursting

Frame bursting involves sending multiple frames in a burst of transmission. The first frame in the burst must be carrier extended if its length is less than 512 bytes. Additional frames in the burst do not require carrier extensions, but an interframe gap of 0.096 microseconds (still 96 bit times) is needed between frames. The transmitter continues transmitting during the interframe gap to maintain its hold on the network media. A burst timer started when the first frame is transmitted limits the length of the burst to a maximum of 65,536 bits.

Single Repeater Type

Unlike Fast Ethernet, Gigabit Ethernet goes back to a single repeater type. A Gigabit Ethernet repeater must support all 1000-Mbps technologies and operate at a fixed speed of 1000 Mbps (no 10/100/1000 or 100/1000 capabilities are defined, although there are multispeed Gigabit switches available on the market).

Gigabit Ethernet Architecture

Figure 4–19 shows the multilayer architectural model for Gigabit Ethernet. You may notice the similarties to 10-Mbps and 100-Mbps Ethernet. One notable difference is the new 8-bit wide transmit and receive paths.

In addition, you will notice that full duplex operation is available in every Gigabit technology, which was not the case for 10-Mbps Ethernet and Fast Ethernet. The MAC layer, described in IEE 802.3z, deals with issues such as half/full duplex operation, carrier extension, and frame bursting.

Let us examine the different Gigabit Ethernet technologies.

1000baseT

- IEEE standard 802.3ab
- Cable type: 4 pairs of Category 5 (or higher) UTP
- Maximum cable length: 100 meters

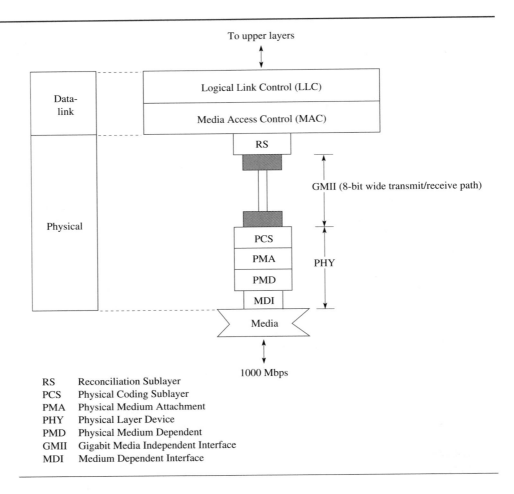

Figure 4–19
Gigabit Ethernet
architecture.

- Data rate: 1000 Mbps (2000 Mbps full duplex)
- PAM5x5 encoding
- Connector: RJ-45

The two-dimensional PAM5x5 encoding we were introduced to in 100baseT2 is extended here to a four-dimensional PAM5x5 system.

1000baseCX
- Short haul copper
- Cable: shielded, balanced copper (twinax)
- Maximum cable length: 25 meters
- Data rate: 1000 Mbps (2000 Mbps full duplex)
- 8B10B encoding
- Connector: 9-pin D or 8-pin Fibre Channel Type 2 (HSSC)

Transferring 8-bits of data reliably at Gigabit speeds requires another change in the method used to encode the data. The 8B10B coding method (originally developed for Fibre Channel) replaces 8-bit data values with 10-bit code words. The code words are chosen from groups such that the number of 0s and 1s transmitted is kept in balance. A signaling rate of 1.25 Gbps is required to encode the 1-Gbps data stream.

1000baseSX

- Short wavelength laser
- Wavelength: 770–860 nanometers
- Data rate: 1000 Mbps (2000 Mbps full duplex)
- 8B10B encoding
- 62.5/125 miltimode fiber length limit: 275 meters (half and full duplex)
- 50/125 multimode fiber length limit: 550 meters (full duplex), 316 meters (half duplex)
- Connector: SC

1000baseLX

- Long wavelength laser
- Wavelength: 1270–1355 nanometers
- Data rate: 1000 Mbps (2000 Mbps full duplex)
- 8B10B encoding
- Single-mode fiber length limit: 5000 meters (full duplex), 316 meters (half duplex)
- Multimode fiber length limit: 550 meters (full duplex), 316 meters (half duplex)
- Connector: SC

Table 4–6 summarizes the 10-, 100-, and 1000-Mbps Ethernet copper and fiber technologies. Even with this large number of technologies, there is still one more to examine: wireless Ethernet.

WIRELESS ETHERNET

Wireless Ethernet, the use of Ethernet over radio frequency (RF) or Infrared (IR), is covered by the IEEE 802.11 Wireless LAN Standard. A wireless Ethernet network consists of one or more fixed stations (base stations) that service multiple mobile stations. Some implementation details are as follows:

- Frame formats for IEEE 802.3 (Ethernet) and IEEE 802.5 (token ring) remain the same.
- CSMA/CA utilized.
- 1-Mbps and 2-Mbps operation. Faster speeds are becoming available.

CSMA/CA stands for *Carrier Sense Multiple Access with Collision Avoidance*. This method differs from CSMA/CD in that the wireless transceiver cannot listen to

Table 4–6
Comparison of Ethernet technologies.

Technology	Max Segment Length	Encoding Method	Topology	Media	Bit Rate (bits/sec)
10base5	500 meters	Manchester	Bus	50-ohm coax	10 M
10base2	185 meters	Manchester	Bus	50-ohm coax	10 M
10baseT	100 meters	Manchester	Star	2 pairs UTP Cat. 3, 4, 5	10 M
10baseFL	2000 meters	Manchester	Star	multimode fiber*	10 M
100baseT2	100 meters	PAM 5X5	Star	2 pairs UTP Cat. 3, 4, 5	100 M
100baseT4	100 meters	8B/6T	Star	4 pairs UTP Cat. 3,4,5	100 M
100baseTX	100 meters	4B/5B with MLT-3	Star	2 pairs UTP Cat. 5	100 M
100baseFX	412 meters/ 2000 meters	4B/5B with NRZI	Star	multimode* fiber	100 M
1000baseT	100 meters	PAM 5X5	Star	4 pairs UTP Cat. 5	1000 M
1000baseSX	275 meters	8B/10B	Star	multimode fiber +	1000 M
1000baseLX	316 meters/ 550 meters	8B/10B	Star	multimode fiber†	1000 M
1000baseCX	25 meters	8B/10B	Star	twinax	1000 M

* Fiber is duplex 62.5/125 μm mulitmode fiber.

+ Maximum segment length is 316 meters/550 meters with 50/125 μm multimode fiber.

† Maximum segment length is 316 meters/550 meters with 50/125 μm multimode fiber or 316 meters/5000 meters with 10/125 μm single-mode fiber.

the network for other transmissions while it is transmitting. Its transmitter simply drowns out any other signal that may be present. Instead, stations attempt to avoid collisions by using random backoff delays to delay transmission when the network is busy (when some other station is transmitting). A handshaking sequence is used between communicating stations (ready and acknowledge packets) to help maintain reliable delivery of messages over the air.

Types of Wireless LANs
There are two primary types of Wireless Ethernet LANs. They are RF-based and IR-based.

RF-based   Signals can propagate through objects, such as walls, reducing security. The ISM band (industrial, scientific, medical) is used for transmission at the following frequencies:

Industrial: 902 to 928 MHz
Scientific: 2.40 GHz to 2.4835 GHz
Medical: 5.725 GHz to 5.850 GHz

Data is transmitted using the spread spectrum technologies *frequency hopping* and *direct sequence*. In frequency hopping, the transmitter hops from frequency to frequency, seemingly at random, transmitting a portion of each frame at each frequency. The receiver hops to the same frequencies, using the same pseudo-random sequence as the transmitter. A measure of security is added to the data, since it is difficult to eavesdrop on all the associated frequencies and reassemble the frame fragments.

The Direct Sequence method involves exclusive-ORing a pseudo-random bitstream with the data before transmission. The same pseudo-random bit sequence is used in the receiver to get the original data back.

IR-based   Two types of IR wireless Ethernet are used: diffused IR and point-to-point IR. Diffused IR bounces signal off walls, ceilings, and floors. The data rate is limited by the *multipath effect*, whereby multiple signals radiate from a single transmission, each taking a different path to the receiving stations. This is illustrated in Figure 4–20.

Point-to-point IR uses line of sight IR lasers and provides a faster data rate than diffused IR. It also works over larger distances (up to 1 mile).

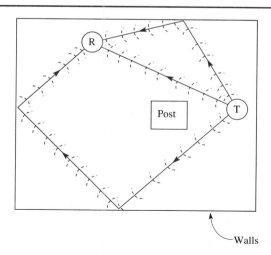

Figure 4–20
The multipath effect in diffused IR wireless Ethernet.

TROUBLESHOOTING TECHNIQUES

When working with Ethernet systems, it may be useful to be familiar with some common problems encountered in actual networks.

MTU Affects Available Bandwidth

The *MTU* (maximum transmission unit) is the maximum frame size allowed on the network. For Ethernet, the MTU may range from 68 to 1500, with many Internet service providers setting their lines to an MTU of 576. If the MTU is too small, large frames will be fragmented into two or more smaller frames, contributing to excess utilization of the bandwidth and increased collisions. Windows users may adjust their MTU by modifying the Registry.

Jabber

An out-of-control Ethernet transmitter may generate a frame that is longer than 1526 bytes. Other conditions on the network, such as bad terminations or a failing power supply in a hub or switch, may cause distortions that resemble a jabbering device. Repeaters are designed to prohibit retransmission of any frames for a short period of time when jabbering is detected, to prevent the network from being saturated with meaningless signals.

Runts

A *runt* is any transmitted frame whose length is less than the minimum frame size, even a short frame with a valid FCS.

Alignment Error

When all the bits of a frame have been received, it is possible that the last bit received is not the last bit of the final byte in the frame. In other words, the number of bits in the frame is not a multiple of eight. This is called an *alignment error*. This will most likely cause the FCS to be invalid and the frame will be discarded. Intermittent connections will contribute to this type of error, as will collisions (which terminate with an unknown number of bits transmitted followed by the jam sequence).

LanExplorer keeps track of many different Ethernet errors. Figure 4–21 shows a sample error display. The errors were created by pulling the RJ-45 connector out of its port on a hub while a large file download was in progress.

Cabling

Cabling errors are typically one of the following:

Coax

- Bad BNC connector crimp
- Improperly installed vampire tap
- Dirty (oxidized) connector
- Loose or missing terminator

Figure 4–21
LanExplorer Ethernet error display.

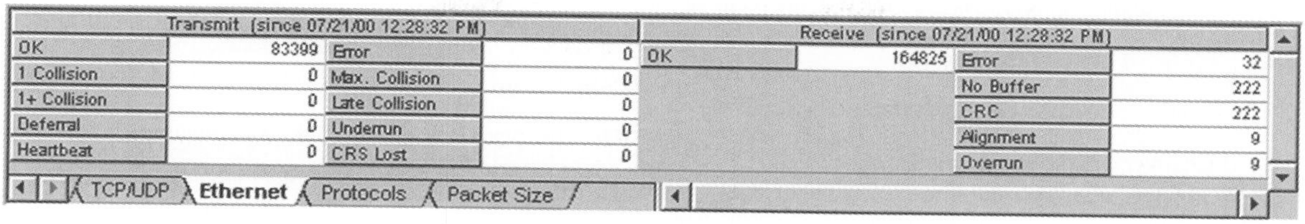

Transmit (since 07/21/00 12:28:32 PM)				Receive (since 07/21/00 12:28:32 PM)			
OK	83399	Error	0	OK	164825	Error	32
1 Collision	0	Max. Collision	0			No Buffer	222
1+ Collision	0	Late Collision	0			CRC	222
Deferral	0	Underrun	0			Alignment	9
Heartbeat	0	CRS Lost	0			Overrun	9

◄ ► TCP/UDP ⟍ **Ethernet** ⟋ Protocols ⟍ Packet Size ⟋   ◄   ►

UTP

- Wrong category cable
- Bad cable (open pair)
- Wrong cable type (crossover instead of straight-through)

Lost Termination

Removing the 50-ohm terminating resistor from the end of a 10base2 or 10base5 cable will cause distorted signals to reflect off the end instead of being absorbed by the terminating resistor (due to high-frequency properties of transmission lines). The signal reflections cause repeated collisions, effectively shutting down the entire cable segment.

Excess Utilization

Ethernet exhibits poor performance when its utilization is 60% or more. Excess utilization (including plenty of lost bandwidth due to collisions) is typically the result of too many stations operating in the same collision domain. Replacing hubs with switches or routers will partition the network into multiple collision domains, each containing a smaller number of stations. The improvement in performance will be very noticeable.

SELF-TEST

This self-test is designed to help you check your understanding of the background information presented in this chapter.

True/False

Answer *true* or *false*.

1. The minimum frame size is 32 bytes.

2. The maximum size of the data field in an Ethernet frame is 1500 bytes.

3. Ethernet uses CSMA/CA.

4. Fast Ethernet uses Manchester encoding.

5. Autonegotiation is accomplished using fast link pulses.

6. Point-to-point IR wireless Ethernet is faster than diffused IR.

Multiple Choice

Select the best answer.

7. The interframe gap is equivalent to how many bit times?
   a. 9.6.
   b. 96.
   c. 960.

8. The frame check sequence contains
   a. 8 bits.
   b. 16 bits.
   c. 32 bits.

9. In the 5-4-3 rule, the three stands for
   a. three segments with nodes.
   b. three repeaters.
   c. three terminators per segment.

10. 8B6T is a encoding method that converts
    a. 8 bits to 6 ternary voltage levels.
    b. 8 levels to 6 bits.
    c. Binary to decimal.

11. Which is not an encoding method?
    a. 4B5B.
    b. 6B9B.
    c. Manchester.

12. To eliminate collisions, 100VG-AnyLAN uses
    a. Domain based priority access.
    b. Ring/Hub contention management.
    c. Frame polling.

Completion

Fill in the blank or blanks with the best answers.

13. The preamble contains _____ bytes.

14. Due to the Interframe gap, a total of _____ minimum sized frames are possible in one second.

15. Typically, an error is reported after _____ successive collisions.

16. FOIRL stands for _____ _____ inter-repeater link.

17. Fast Ethernet has transmit and receive paths that are _____ bits wide.

18. Frame bursting is used by _____ Ethernet.

QUESTIONS/ACTIVITIES

1. There are many good Web sites containing information about Ethernet. Find five sites and compare their coverage.

2. Calculate the total amount of time required (including interframe gaps times) to transmit 10,000 bytes of data using 10-Mbit/second Ethernet. *Hint:* A total of seven frames will be required. Assume no collisions occur during transmission of the frames.

3. Make a chart showing the data encoding and signaling used in each Ethernet technology.

4. How is Gigabit Ethernet related to the Internet2? Visit http://www.gigabit-ethernet.org and http://www.internet2.edu.

5. What is the 10 Gigabit Ethernet Alliance? Visit http://www.10gea.org to find out.

REVIEW QUIZ

Under the supervision of your instructor

1. Describe the format of an Ethernet frame.

2. Explain the basic operation of collision detection.

3. Compare the features of the different 10-Mbps, 100-Mbps, and 1000-Mbps Ethernet technologies.

4. Discuss the principles of wireless Ethernet.

Networking Concepts Laboratory

Experiment #4
Ethernet LAN Fundamentals

Objectives

1. To set up an operational 10base2 Ethernet LAN.
2. To set up an operational 10baseT Ethernet LAN.

Required Equipment

The following equipment is required for this experiment:

- Two or more computers with network interface cards
- Straight-through and crossover UTP cable
- Thinwire coax cable with BNC connectors
- Two BNC terminators
- Two 10base2/10baseT hubs

Procedure

Perform each of the following steps. Record your observations, results, and any difficulties you encounter. You will use this information when you develop your conclusions about the experiment.

1. Use a crossover UTP cable to directly connect two computers through their network interface cards. For computers without a network interface card, install a NIC using the following instructions as a guide:
   - Remove computer cover.
   - Locate open expansion slot and install the network interface card.
   - Boot the computer and install software according to the manufacturer instructions. Depending on the NIC manufacturer, you may be asked to supply the Windows installation CD-ROM, a manufacturer's CD-ROM, or a floppy disk. *Note that several reboots may be necessary in order to complete the hardware installation.*
   - If the network interface card is not recognized by the operating system, it may be necessary to choose the correct software adapter driver from the list of supported manufacturers or from the CD-ROM or floppy disk that accompanies most network interface cards. *Note that the Windows operating system provides additional help via the Network Troubleshooter.*
   - After the card has been installed properly, replace the computer cover.
   - Verify that the NetBEUI and TCP/IP protocols are installed by reviewing the Network settings in the Control Panel. If one or both of these protocols are not listed, select the

Add option and then select protocols and pick them from the list of Microsoft protocols. Obtain proper settings information from your instructor or the network administrator.

2. Enable file sharing on each machine. This is done as follows:
   - Right-click on **Network Neighborhood**.
   - Select **Properties**.
   - Left-click on **File** and **Print Sharing**.
   - Check the box that allows file sharing.
   - Left-click on **OK**.
3. Now share the C: drive on each machine. This is done as follows:
   - Left double-click on **My Computer**.
   - Right-click on the drive **C:** icon.
   - Select **Sharing** from the pop-up menu.
   - Select the **Shared As** option.
   - Left click on **OK**.
4. Left double-click on **Network Neighborhood**. Does each machine see the other one?
   Note: It may take several seconds for any changes to be reflected in the Network Neighborhood. You should click the Refresh option in the View pull-down menu frequently to guarantee you have an accurate view of the network. Note how long it takes for the changes to occur.
5. If each Network Interface Card has a BNC connector, disconnect the UTP cable and attach a T-connector to the NIC. On one side of the T-connector, attach an end of a coaxial cable. On the other side, attach a 50-ohm terminator. If the NIC does not have a BNC connector, go to step 10.
6. Are the machines still visible in Network Neighborhood? Again, allow some time for the changes to be reflected in the Network Neighborhood.
7. Remove one of the 50-ohm terminators.
8. Are the machines still visible in Network Neighborhood?
9. Disconnect each T-connector.
10. Connect the computers to a hub using straight-through UTP cable.
11. Are the machines still visible in Network Neighborhood?

Discussion and Conclusion

Using a word processor, write your own detailed explanations of the results and observations made during the experiment. To begin, try to say something about each procedure step.

In addition, provide answers to the following questions:

1. What kind of problems are caused by the removal of a 50-ohm terminator in a 10base2 network?
2. Suppose two computers contain 10/100baseT network interface cards.
   a. What is the connection speed when the network interface cards are directly connected using a crossover UTP cable?
   b. What is the connection speed when each computer is connected to a 10baseT hub?
3. Repeat question 2, except now only one of the network interface cards is a 10/100baseT card. The other card is just 10baseT.

Token Ring, FDDI, and Other LAN Technologies

PERFORMANCE OBJECTIVES
Upon completion of this chapter, you will be able to

- Discuss the features of a token-ring LAN.
- Describe the topology of FDDI and its main characteristics.
- Explain the architecture of ARCnet.
- List some key features of token–bus and broadband LANs.

Joe Tekk was visiting his friend Michael Cippoli. They were both in the back room of Michael's pizza parlor, watching a video. Michael was also a fiber consultant, and the video was of him and two technicians pulling fiber in an underground mine. Michael explained that many of the tunnels and shafts in the mine were hundreds of meters long, and it was perpetually damp due to moisture seeping in from the walls. Michael had convinced the owner of the mine that using fiber instead of copper would help reduce the harmful effects of moisture and its associated corrosion, and also reduce the cost of the entire network, since repeaters would not be required for long runs of fiber. For reliability, FDDI was chosen as the network.

"That looks like fun, Mike," Joe said, when the video was over. "But why does the owner want a network in the mine?"

"I asked him the same question, Joe," Michael replied, as he pulled a fresh pizza out of the oven. "He just wants to be able to communicate with employees down in the mine. Walkie-talkies don't work down there due to interference from iron deposits in the ground, and the phone company wanted too much money."

The pizza was gone by the time they finished talking about the fiber installation.

INTRODUCTION

In this chapter we take a survey of several additional networking technologies. Even though Ethernet is by far the most popular, each of the

LAN technologies examined in this chapter have their own particular advantages and uses. In order, we will look at the following types of networks:

- Token ring
- Token bus
- FDDI
- Broadband LAN
- ARCnet

When you add Ethernet and wireless Ethernet LANs to the list, you have an impressive number of LAN technologies to choose from.

 TOKEN RING

Currently, token ring is the second most popular networking technology after Ethernet. A token-ring network, specified by the IEEE 802.5 standard, uses a token passing mechanism to regulate data flow in a ring-based topology. A *token* is a special group of symbols contained in a packet. The station possessing the token is able to transmit data onto the ring. The token circulates from one station to the next, helping to guarantee fair access to the available bandwidth. When a data frame makes a complete trip around the ring, the originating station releases the token.

Unlike Ethernet, token ring contains support for prioritized transmissions. In addition, there are no collisions in a token-ring network due to multiple stations transmitting at the same time. Thus, token ring performs better under heavy traffic loads than Ethernet does.

IEEE 802.5 specifies 4-Mbps and 16-Mbps speeds. Data is transmitted using differential Manchester encoding. Figure 5–1 illustrates the difference between Manchester encoding and differential Manchester encoding.

Figure 5–1
Comparing Manchester and differential Manchester encoding.

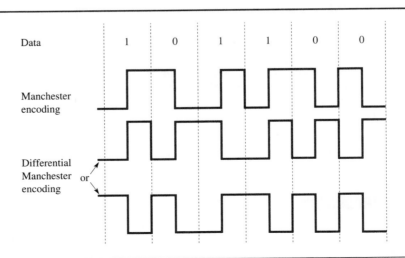

In *Manchester encoding,* a '0' is encoded as a falling edge in the middle of the bit time. A '1' is encoded as a rising edge in the middle of the bit time. In differential Manchester encoding, there is always a transition in the middle of the bit time. A transition at the beginning of a bit interval indicates a '0.' No transition indicates a '1.' An advantage of differential Manchester encoding is that the polarity of the signal is independent of the bitstream. In other words, inverting a differential Manchester signal will result in the same received data, whereas inverting an ordinary Manchester encoded signal will invert all the data bits.

 ## TOKEN-RING TOPOLOGY

Though the logical topology of a token-ring network is a ring, the physical topology is a combination of star and ring. As shown in Figure 5–2, stations (or *lobes*) in a token-ring network connect to an MAU (multistation access unit). Multiple MAUs are connected serially to form a ring. Shielded twisted pair (STP) is typically used for wiring, although UTP and fiber are also supported. The number of MAUs in the ring affects the maximum distance between MAUs. IEEE 802.5 limits the number of stations on any ring to 250 and the number of MAUs to 33. Stations can be added or removed without major disruption to the ring.

Figure 5–2
Token-ring topology.

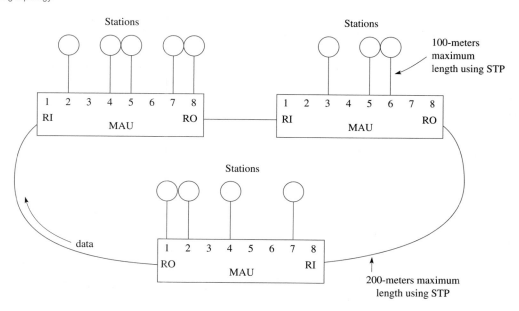

TOKEN-RING FRAME FORMATS

Figures 5–3 and 5–4 illustrate the formats of the token and information frame utilized by token ring. The token format in Figure 5–3 is a 24-bit frame generated by the active monitor (described in the following section). Notice that the Access Control field contains Priority and Reservation bits. The Priority bits indicate the current priority of the token and any associated information frames. The Reservation bits are used to reserve the next token at a specific priority. The Token bit is used to differentiate between Token frames and Information frames.

The Monitor bit helps identify a frame that is stuck circulating on the ring.

The J and K symbols are illegal differential Manchester codes (no transition in the middle of the bit time) used to identify the Starting and Ending delimiters.

Figure 5–3
Token-ring token format.

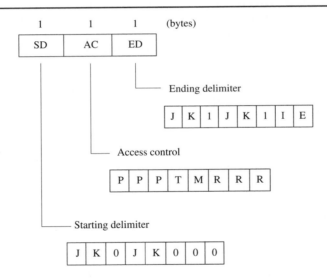

Key:

J—Nondata J symbol
K—Nondata K symbol
P—Priority bits (111 highest)
T—Token bit (0 = token, 1 = frame)
M—Monitor bit
R—Reservation bits
I—Intermediate frame bit
E—Error-detected bit

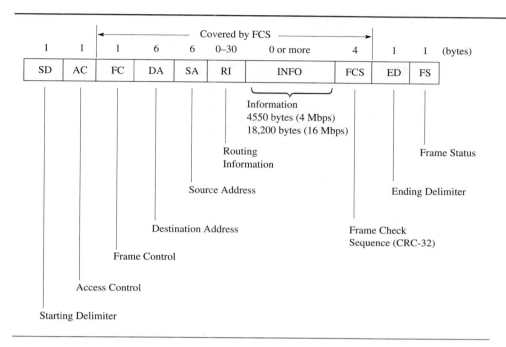

Figure 5–4
Token-ring frame format.

The Information frame diagramed in Figure 5–4 contains many of the same fields as the Ethernet frame covered in Chapter 4. One significant difference is the length of the INFO field, which may be 4550 bytes in length in 4-Mbps token ring, or 18,200 bytes for 16-Mbps token ring. Compare this with Ethernet's 1500-byte limit (for all Ethernet speeds).

RING MANAGEMENT

One station on the ring acts as the *active monitor* and is responsible for ensuring that valid tokens circulate on the ring. In addition, the active monitor controls the timing of the tokens on the ring, and initiates a *ring purge* operation to recover from errors such as lost or corrupted tokens, or timeouts during transmission of a frame. During a ring purge the logical ring is rebuilt from scratch.

All other stations on the ring act as standby monitors. If the active monitor fails, a standby monitor will initiate a "Claim Token" process to choose the new active monitor.

Catastrophic errors on the ring, such as a broken ring or an error during the "Claim Token" process, initiate the *beaconing procedure*. Beacon frames are then circulated to determine the nature of the fault (the *fault domain*) and possibly isolate the cause of the failure.

Item	Token Ring	Ethernet
Standard	IEEE 802.5	IEEE 802.3
Speed	4, 16 Mbps*	10, 100, 1000 Mbps
Max Nodes	250	1023
Self-healing	Yes	No
Max. Frame Size**	4550 bytes (4 Mbps) 18,200 bytes (16 Mbps)	1500 bytes
Encoding	Differential Manchester	Manchester, 4B/5B, 8B/6T, 8B/10B, PAM 5x5
Prioritized Access	Yes	No
Routing Information in Frame	Yes	No
Access Method	Token Passing	CSMA/CD
Physical Topology	Ring, Star	Bus, Star

* 100-Mbps and 1000-Mbps specifications exist but are not widely used.

** Amount of data in one packet

COMPARING TOKEN RING AND ETHERNET

Table 5–1 shows a comparison between token ring and Ethernet. Note that IBM developed the token-ring specification, which is very similar to the IEEE 802.5 standard.

TOKEN BUS

The IEEE 802.4 token-bus standard describes the mechanism by which multiple stations share access to a common bus. Figure 5–5 shows a sample token-bus network. Each station knows the address of the previous and next stations in the sequence of stations. Tokens are circulated in a logical ring, from station 10, to stations 8, 7, 5, and finally 3. Station 3 transmits back to station 10 to complete the logical ring. Note that the physical location of the station on the bus does not affect the sequence.

If a station fails, a special "who follows" frame is transmitted to determine the next station in sequence following the failed station.

Some additional details are as follows:

- Token bus is available in speeds of 1, 5, 10, and 20 Mbps
- Data frames may contain over 8000 bytes of information
- Four levels of priority are available
- Operates over coax and fiber

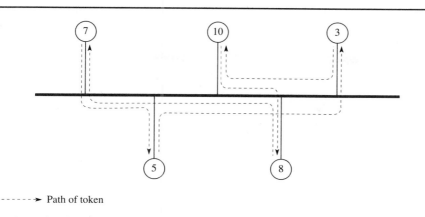

Figure 5–5
Token-bus operation.

- - - - - → Path of token

For more information on token bus operation, visit

http://www.relcominc.com/carrier-band/handbook/chapter04.htm

FDDI

FDDI (fiber-distributed data interface) is a self-healing baseband network technology similar to token ring. As indicated in Figure 5–6, an FDDI network consists of nodes connected together with dual fiber rings. Both rings, called primary and secondary (or backup), operate at 100 Mbps using 4B/5B encoding. An error detected with the primary ring will cause an instant changeover to the secondary ring to prevent loss of communication.

Using 4B/5B encoding, 4 bits of data are encoded as a 5-bit symbol. Bits are transmitted over the fiber as transitions of light (off-to-on or on-to-off). LEDs operating at 1300 nanometers provide the light source for the fiber. 62.5/125 micrometer multimode fiber is typically used.

The large circumference of an FDDI ring (100 kilometers for dual ring, 200 kilometers for single ring) makes it ideal for use over a large geographical area.

FDDI nodes come in two types:

- Single Attached Station (SAS). Attaches to the primary ring only.
- Dual Attached Station (DAS). Attaches to both rings.

Note that an SAS may not be directly connected to the primary ring, since the entire ring would fail if the SAS failed. Instead, the SAS is connected via a modified DAS called a *wiring concentrator*. These concentrators are also used to connect individual rings together.

Figures 5–7 and 5–8 provide the details of the token and information frames used over the FDDI ring. 4B/5B symbols are used. Note the large size of the FDDI information frame (up to 4500 bytes). This helps reduce overhead

Figure 5–6
FDDI topology.

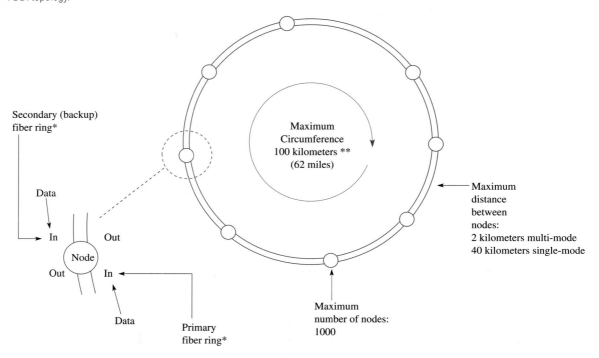

Secondary (backup)
fiber ring*

Data

In   Out

Node

Out   In

Data

Primary
fiber ring*

Maximum
Circumference
100 kilometers **
(62 miles)

Maximum
distance
between
nodes:
2 kilometers multi-mode
40 kilometers single-mode

Maximum
number of nodes:
1000

* Each ring operates at 100 Mbps.
** Maximum circumference is 200 kilometers (124 miles) if only primary ring is used.

Figure 5–7
FDDI token format.

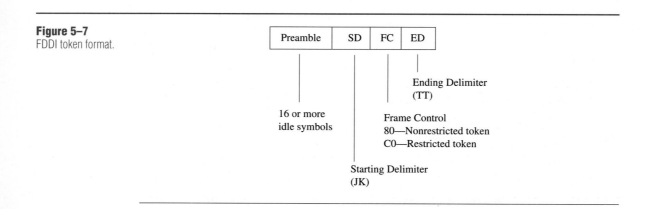

Preamble	SD	FC	ED

16 or more
idle symbols

Starting Delimiter
(JK)

Frame Control
80—Nonrestricted token
C0—Restricted token

Ending Delimiter
(TT)

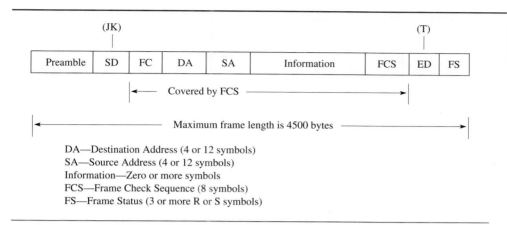

Figure 5–8
FDDI information frame format.

DA—Destination Address (4 or 12 symbols)
SA—Source Address (4 or 12 symbols)
Information—Zero or more symbols
FCS—Frame Check Sequence (8 symbols)
FS—Frame Status (3 or more R or S symbols)

when transmitting a large block of data that must be broken into multiple frames. The 4500-byte limit is a function of the maximum circumference of the ring, the data rate, and the allowable variation in clock speeds between nodes.

A newer variation of FDDI called FDDI-II (or *hybrid ring control*) contains support for voice, video, and other multimedia applications. This is accomplished through the addition of circuit-switching capability to the original packet-switching technique.

You can view an excellent tutorial on FDDI at

http://www.iol.unh.edu/training/fddi/htmls/index.html

BROADBAND LANS

Broadband LANs, in contrast to baseband LANs, use multiple carriers to exchange information. Just like your cable television allows you to select one of many different channels, broadband LAN technology divides the available bandwidth of the cable system into multiple channels (frequency division multiplexing). A *head-end* is used to maintain communication with each node on the broadband network. The broadband information signal is varied in both amplitude and phase to encode the digital data. One 6-MHz channel is capable of providing 27 Mbps using an encoding technique called *64 QAM* (quadrature amplitude modulation).

The IEEE 802.7 Standard describes broadband LAN operation. Broadband LAN cable technology is becoming increasingly popular in the home computing market due to its high speed compared to ordinary telephone modems. A detailed description of broadband technology can be found at

http://www.tristone.com/Broadband/broadband_whitepaper.htm

Table 5–2
ARCnet frame types.

Frame Type	Meaning	Function
ACK	Acknowledge	Acknowledge correct reception.
FBE	Free Buffer Enquiry	Determines if destination node is available to receive data.
ITT	Invitation to Transmit	Determines which node may transmit.
NAK	Negative Acknowledge	Indicates retransmission is required.
PAC	Packet	Carries data.

ARCNET

ARCnet (Attached Resource Computer Network) is a low-cost baseband network developed by the Datapoint Corporation in the late 1970s. Like token ring and FDDI, ARCnet uses tokens to exchange information. However, ARCnet physical topology is not ring based. Instead, ARCnet uses a bus architecture (*high-impedance* ARCnet) or a star topology (*low-impedance* ARCnet).

Nodes in an ARCnet network are addressed from 1 to 255 and organize themselves into a logical ring (not a physical ring). Address 0 is reserved for broadcasts. Nodes can be added or removed at will, their presence or absence automatically detected and accounted for. Communication speed is 2.5 Mbps (with a newer ARCnet Plus standard providing 20 Mbps). Coax, UTP, and fiber can all be used to connect ARCnet components. Both passive and active hubs are used to extend the size of the network.

Table 5–2 lists the different frame types used in ARCnet. The PAC frame may contain up to 508 bytes of data. Each byte of data is preceded by the bit pattern 110 during transmission. Thus, 11 bits are used to represent any 8-bit value. A 16-bit CRC is used as the FCS.

For more information on ARCnet, visit the ARCnet Trade Association Web site at http://www.arcnet.com.

TROUBLESHOOTING TECHNIQUES

Diagnosing problems with any of the LAN technologies covered in this chapter requires the following:

- Detailed knowledge of the LAN technology and its operation
- Diagnostic software
- Diagnostic hardware

Broadband LANs pose their own special troubleshooting scenarios, since multiple channels are operating simultaneously. Time domain reflectometers (TDR) and spectrum analyzers are two pieces of exotic (and expensive) equipment that might be required to diagnose errors. TDRs can be used to determine the distance to a fault in a cable. Spectrum analyzers can be used to examine the range of frequency bands that exist on the media. In a fiber-based LAN, an optical TDR (also expensive), fiber optic power meter, and even a fusion splicer may be needed.

In addition, a little common sense is also helpful. For example, never assume anything about the network before analyzing it. If you are working on a 16-Mbps token-ring LAN, make sure all the components are operating at 16 Mbps. It only takes one NIC running at 4 Mbps to keep the network from working properly. Also, token-ring MAC addresses may be locally administered (assigned by the network administrator), overriding the MAC address programmed into the NIC at the factory. Care must be taken to guarantee that no duplicate MAC addresses exist. This problem may also occur in an ARCnet network, except that the addresses need to be unique 8-bit IDs.

If the network is coax based, make sure the impedance of the cable is correct (and matches the impedance of the NICs). Also, make sure the terminators are attached.

SELF-TEST

This self-test is designed to help you check your understanding of the background information presented in this chapter.

True/False
Answer *true* or *false*.

1. Token-ring physical topology is purely ring based.

2. Only one token-ring station can be a standby monitor at one time.

3. Token-bus networks cannot recover from a failed station.

4. FDDI operates at 100 Mbps.

5. An FDDI SAS connects to the secondary ring only.

6. The maximum number of nodes on an ARCnet network is 1024.

Multiple Choice
Select the best answer.

7. IEEE 802.5 limits the number of stations on a token-ring network to
   a. 33.
   b. 127.
   c. 250.

8. Which token-ring station controls the timing of tokens?
   a. Active monitor.
   b. Standby monitor.
   c. Token monitor.

9. FDDI utilizes dual rings, the
   a. Major and minor.
   b. Forward and backward.
   c. Primary and secondary.

10. The maximum FDDI frame size is
    a. 1024 bytes.
    b. 4500 bytes.
    c. 45K bytes.

11. _____ LANs use multiple carriers to exchange information.
    a. Baseband.
    b. Broadband.
    c. Both a and b.

12. ARCnet's physical topology is
    a. Bus.
    b. Ring.
    c. Mesh.

Completion
Fill in the blank or blanks with the best answers.

13. Token ring uses a/an _____ monitor to help manage the ring.

14. Recovering from a catastrophic token ring failure is initiated through a process called _____.

15. Token _____ sends a "who follows" frame to recover from a failed station.

16. The maximum circumference of a dual-ring FDDI network is _____ kilometers.

17. FDDI SAS nodes are connected via wiring _____.

18. In ARCnet, an 8-bit number requires _____ bits during transmission.

QUESTIONS/ACTIVITIES

1. Search the Web for information comparing IBMs token-ring specification with IEEE 802.5.

2. Add FDDI and ARCnet to Table 5–1 and fill in any missing information with your own research.

3. Are any companies manufacturing wireless token-ring/bus network components?

REVIEW QUIZ

Under the supervision of your instructor

1. Discuss the features of a token-ring LAN.

2. Describe the topology of FDDI and its main characteristics.

3. Explain the architecture of ARCnet.

4. List some key features of token-bus and broadband LANs.

Networking Concepts Laboratory

Experiment #5
Token Ring, FDDI, and Other LAN Technologies

Objectives

1. To obtain additional information about token-ring and FDDI LAN technologies.
2. To develop a custom LAN technology based on your understanding of existing technologies.

Required Equipment

The following equipment is required for this experiment:

- One or more computers connected to the Internet

Procedure

Perform each of the following steps. Record your observations, results, and any difficulties you encounter. You will use this information when you develop your conclusions about the experiment.

1. If any of the network technologies discussed in this chapter are in use at your school or institution, contact the network administrator to arrange a tour of the network. Discuss the operating characteristics and any unique problems that have been discovered. Otherwise, locate a local business using one of the technologies and arrange a tour.
2. Visit the following Web sites and spend some time gathering details about the featured technology:
   - http://www.hstra.com/
   - http://www.nwfusion.com/research/fddi.html
3. Open the Network icon in Control Panel and click on the **Add** button. In the Select Network Component Type window, double-click the **Adapter** entry and examine the list of manufacturers. What percentage offer token-ring adapters? What percentage offer FDDI adapters?
4. Search the Web for additional LAN technologies. How many do you find? What are their basic characteristics, such as speed, topology, and media?
5. Develop a brand new networking technology according to these guidelines:
   - Fixed length frames of 64, 256, and 1024 bytes
   - Support for up to 512 nodes
   - Unicast and broadcast capability
   - Data rate: 100 Mbps
   - Switched star topology only
   - Cat 5 UTP cabling

Invent your own frame types (with all associated fields, such as preamble or start delim-iter, data field, FCS, etc.). Explain how to add and remove nodes from the network and how the network handles errors discovered in a frame.

Discussion and Conclusion

Using a word processor, write your own detailed explanations of the results and observations made during the experiment. To begin, try to say something about each procedure step.

In addition, provide answers to the following questions:

1. What kinds of test equipment are available for the LAN technologies examined in this experiment?
2. Do any of the LAN technologies dealt with in this experiment operate over modems?
3. Which LAN technologies offer redundancy?

6

Network Design and Troubleshooting Scenarios

PERFORMANCE OBJECTIVES
Upon completion of this chapter, you will be able to

- Discuss several considerations that must be made when networking computers together.
- Estimate the hardware components needed for a specific network.
- Discuss some initial steps to take when troubleshooting a network.

Joe Tekk and Don, the senior technician, were meeting with their boss, Bill Bestman, the president of RWA Software, Inc.

"Bill," Don was saying, "you need to upgrade the office network."

"Why, Don?" President Bestman asked.

Don looked at Joe, who had begged him weeks ago to do the president's presentation. "I'm going to let Joe explain the reasons, Bill."

Joe took over the meeting, expertly explaining why RWA Software needed to upgrade its existing network right away. Joe had researched the network hardware, looked up prices, and even estimated the number of man-hours required to complete the upgrade. Using his upgrade plan, no users would experience network downtime, since he planned on performing the upgrades in the evening, one department at a time.

When Joe finished the president said, "It sure sounds expensive, Joe. Do we really need to do this?"

"Yes, Bill, we do," Joe replied confidently. "There are local high schools that have better networks than we do."

President Bestman glanced at Don and then back to Joe. "Make it a showcase, you two, the best network in the area. I'm tripling your estimate, Joe. Buy whatever you need."

INTRODUCTION

In this chapter we will take a look at several different network scenarios, each more complex than the last. The goal is to provide you with ideas to begin designing your own network. Several network troubleshooting examples will also be examined.

NETWORKING TWO COMPUTERS

Connecting just two computers (in a dorm room or basement office) can be done several ways using

- Direct cable connection
- Network interface cards
- Modems

These methods are illustrated in Figure 6–1. The least expensive route is the direct cable connection. The connection may be through a serial cable or a parallel cable. Go to Start, Programs, Accessories, and finally Communications to initiate a connection. Figure 6–2 shows the initial Direct Cable Connection window. Note that the computer is set up as a Guest. Left-clicking the Change tab allows you to switch between Guest mode and Host mode. The Host computer provides the resources the Guest computer wants to access over the connection. Use a parallel cable to get the fastest data transfer speed.

Figure 6–1
Connecting two computers.

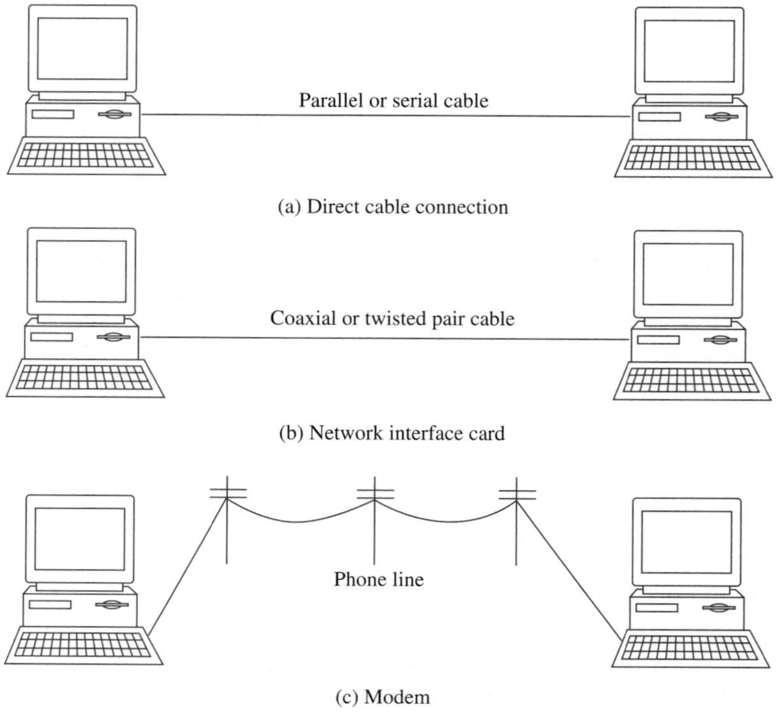

(a) Direct cable connection

Parallel or serial cable

(b) Network interface card

Coaxial or twisted pair cable

(c) Modem

Phone line

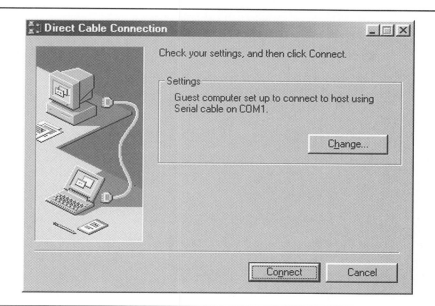

Figure 6–2
Direct Cable
Connection window.

Network interface cards do not cost as much as modems, and no hub is required to connect only two computers together, just a crossover cable (for 10/100baseT) or a length of coax (10base2).

Modems, by far the slowest connection, are useful when the two computers are separated by a large distance.

NETWORKING A SMALL LAB

The last few years have seen a tremendous increase in the number of schools connected to the Internet. On college campuses, many departments use networking laboratories to share resources, save money on equipment, and provide Internet access to their students and faculty.

What is required to network a small laboratory? Figure 6–3 shows an overhead diagram of the laboratory indicating the positions of computers, printers, and other devices.

Altogether a total of 11 machines are to be networked. With Ethernet as the desired technology, two possibilities exist:

1. Use one or more hubs or switches (10/100baseT)
2. Use coax (10base2)

Using hubs is more expensive, but may have advantages over using coax. For example, buying a 16-port hub will leave five ports free for future expansion. Using a 4-port hub and an 8-port hub will leave one port available (each

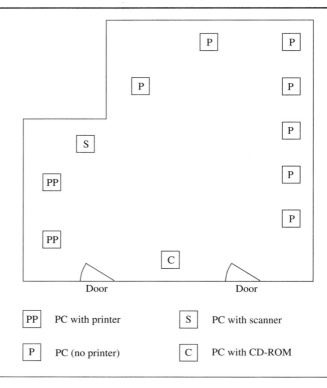

Figure 6–3
A small laboratory.

PP	PC with printer	S	PC with scanner
P	PC (no printer)	C	PC with CD-ROM

hub connected via its 10base2 port) and will allow the network to be partitioned if necessary. Switches may also be used if it is necessary to establish a network hierarchy or guarantee bandwidth.

Using coaxial cable saves on the hardware cost, since we need only buy a spool of cable, a box of BNC connectors, and some T-connectors. More time is required to install this type of network, unless preterminated lengths of coax are purchased.

In addition to the hardware, network software must also be configured. Windows machines with built-in networking support will automatically communicate over the network via *NetBEUI* (file sharing, Network Neighborhood). It may be necessary to also assign each machine an IP address (static or dynamic). Use any class C address in the range 192.168.xxx.xxx if the school does not have its own assigned address.

NETWORKING A SMALL BUSINESS

For the sake of this discussion, let us consider a small business with 80 employees. These employees are spread out over several floors of a small office

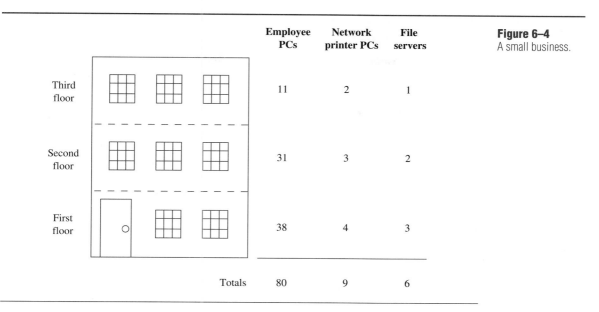

	Employee PCs	Network printer PCs	File servers
Third floor	11	2	1
Second floor	31	3	2
First floor	38	4	3
Totals	80	9	6

Figure 6–4
A small business.

building. In addition to one PC per employee, there are 15 additional PCs in various locations, mostly performing special duties as file servers or network print servers. Figure 6–4 shows the distribution of machines throughout the office building.

A network of this size (both the number of machines and the physical size of the office building) almost requires a hybrid network, with hubs or switches used to group bunches of PCs together, and coax, UTP, or fiber optic cable used to connect the hubs or switches. If hubs are used, whenever anyone sends a job to one of the network printers or requests a file from a file server, everyone (all 95 machines) must contend with the traffic. If switches are used, a network hierarchy can be established that isolates switched groups of users to their own local network printer so only members within the group contend with the printer traffic, not the entire network. File servers should be isolated in the same way. Using switches instead of hubs also allows the network to be repartitioned at a later time, to tweak performance or add new machines. A combination of switches and hubs may also be used, with switches isolating each floor of the building and hubs connecting all the users on a single floor.

It would be a mistake to wire the entire office building using only coax. First, the size of the building may prevent the use of a single length of coax, requiring different network segments connected by repeaters. Second, 95 *pairs* of crimps will be necessary to link all the machines together in a daisy chain. This situation is a disaster waiting to happen when just one of the 190 crimps goes bad. In addition, a coax-only network would provide less than 106,000 bits/second for each machine, a significantly smaller bandwidth than what a switch would provide.

Figure 6–5(a) and Figure 6–5(b) show two switch-based topologies that could be used to guarantee 10/100 Mbps to each machine. Using the star topology allows entire groups of machines to be disconnected for trouble-shooting purposes.

If the nature of the business is heavily data dependent (multimedia presentations, streaming audio/video), it may be necessary to connect each floor via fiber and utilize Fast or Gigabit Ethernet technology. This can be done using a fiber switch or a fiber ring topology. The high-speed fiber backbone between floors guarantees that floor-to-floor bandwidth is available for all applications. Figure 6–5(c) shows how duplex fiber is used to daisy-chain the fiber-10/100baseT switches. A star topology with a central fiber-only switch would also be acceptable, though at the cost of an extra switch.

Figure 6–5
Sample network topologies for office building.

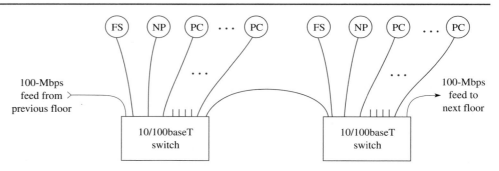

(a) Daisy-chained UTP.

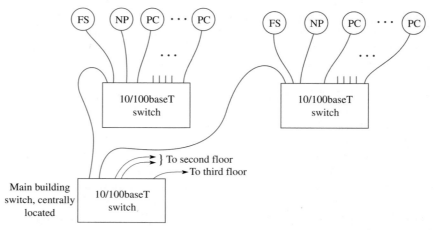

(b) Star of switches.

Figure 6–5
(continued)

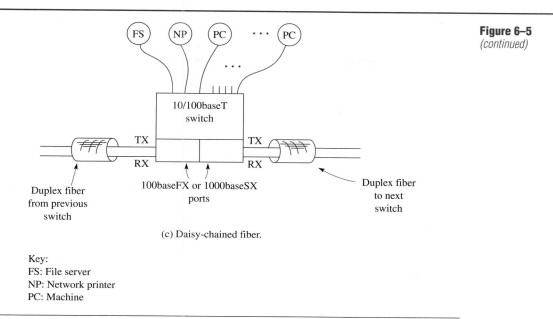

(c) Daisy-chained fiber.

Key:
FS: File server
NP: Network printer
PC: Machine

NETWORKING A COLLEGE CAMPUS

A typical community college may employ several hundred faculty and staff and host several thousand students. Computers for student use are grouped into laboratories, with several laboratories in each building on campus. Our sample college in Figure 6–6 has a total of 14 laboratories, each one containing 16 machines and a network printer (stand-alone, no PC required). The number of labs in each building is circled in the figure.

In addition to the lab computers, there are 350 faculty and staff wired to the network. Their numbers are indicated by the FAC and STA terms.

Each building connects to a central communications rack in the Computer Center. A pair of fibers (duplex cable) runs from each building to the Computer Center, where they all plug into a 100-Mbps fiber switch. Fiber was used instead of coax or UTP because of environmental concerns, as the college's geographical area is prone to thunderstorms. Fiber transceivers in each building convert between fiber and the 10base5 coaxial backbone cable used to distribute the network. Each floor has its own switch to isolate traffic. Figure 6–7 shows the layout of a typical campus building.

In the Computer Center, two mainframes connect to the central communications rack switch. One mainframe is for administrative use, the other for faculty/student use. The switch provides the necessary hierarchy separating the mainframes and their associated users. In addition, a router connected to the switch performs gateway duties, connecting the college to the Internet through a leased T1 (1.54 Mbps) line.

Figure 6–6
A college campus.

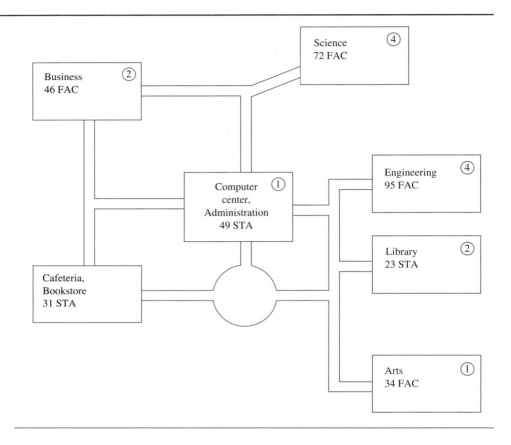

Because of the large number of machines (close to 240 in labs plus 350 faculty/staff), the college uses three class C subnets. With a number of IP addresses from each subnet reserved by the Computer Center, there are still over 700 IP addresses available for campus use. Taking away the lab and employee computers leaves 110 IP addresses, all available for future expansion.

Unfortunately, the use of 10base5 coaxial cable for the backbone in each building limits the network speed to 10 Mbps. Though the 10base5 technology was originally chosen for its 500-meter segment length (in order to connect all floors of a building), the bandwidth is inadequate for the campus traffic. Faculty and staff complaints about the "slow network" has prompted the administration to spend some money on a network upgrade. The proposed upgrade plan is as follows:

1. Replace the fiber-to-10base5 transceiver with a fiber-to-100baseT switch. Feed each floor with its own 100baseT cable.
2. Replace all hubs with 10/100baseT switches.
3. Install new 10/100baseT NICs in selected machines.

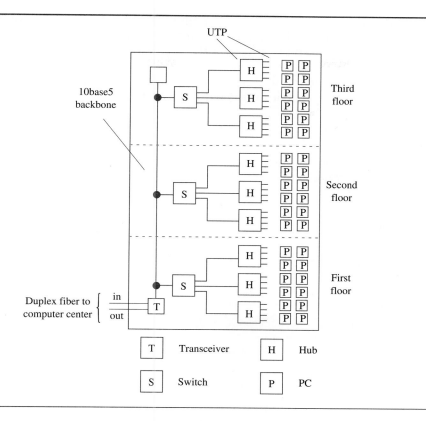

Figure 6–7
Network structure of
a typical campus
building.

The administration did not want to spend the money to run fiber to each floor. Even so, their upgrade plan gets many users up to 100 Mbps.

A counterproposal made by a committee of faculty, staff, and students came in with a cost 23% higher than the administration proposal but provided for fiber to each floor, a gigabit backbone, and an additional T1 line.

The administration accepted the committee's proposal.

TROUBLESHOOTING TECHNIQUES

This section will present a number of troubleshooting tips and also a few case studies involving actual networking problems and their solutions. Bear in mind that troubleshooting network problems requires time, patience, and logical thinking. The tips presented here offer a place to begin troubleshooting a network problem.

Checking the Hardware

Right-clicking on the My Computer icon and selecting Properties will bring up the System Properties window. Left-click the Device Manager tab to examine the list of installed hardware. If a small exclamation mark is present on the Network adapters device, there is a problem with the NIC or its driver. It is not uncommon for an interrupt conflict to arise when a sound card wants to use the same interrupt as the network adapter. Sometimes you can successfully change the interrupt of one of the devices. You may also be able to find and install a newer driver for the network card on the Web.

Using Test Equipment

For really nasty hardware problems, such as intermittent connections, it may be necessary to use sophisticated test equipment, such as a cable tester (UTP), time domain reflectometer (TDR) for coax, optical TDR (for fiber), or a network analyzer.

What's My IP?

It is a good idea to run WINIPCFG and view the network information (addresses, mask, lease details, etc.). Figure 6–8(a) shows a WINIPCFG display

Figure 6–8
(a) WINIPCFG display indicating invalid network information.

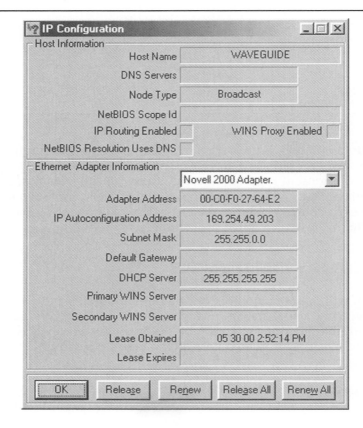

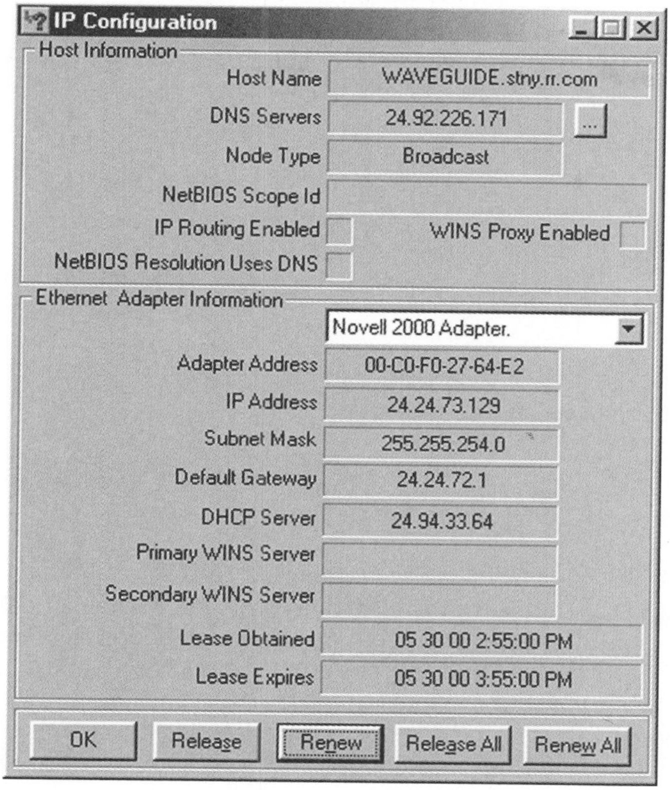

Figure 6–8
(continued)
(b) WINIPCFG display of valid network information.

for a machine that was not able to communicate with its network. Notice that the DNS Server and Default Gateway fields are blank and that the DHCP Server address is 255.255.255.255. Compare this display with the one shown in Figure 6–8(b). In addition to different addresses in each field, the Lease Expires field is now filled in, and the Host Name has changed (indicating that the machine WAVEGUIDE is now part of the stny.rr.com domain).

Check the Network Neighborhood

If your machine is properly networked you should be able to open up Network Neighborhood and see hosts sharing resources on the network. If all you get is a flashlight waving back and forth there is a problem with the NetBEUI protocol or some other low-level network component.

Can You PING?

Just being able to PING another network host (or not being able to) is valuable information. By successfully PINGing them we have proof that the network hardware and software is operating correctly. A sample PING report looks like this:

```
C> ping www.sunybroome.edu

Pinging sbccab.cc.sunybroome.edu [192.203.130.2] with 32 bytes of data:

Reply from 192.203.130.2: bytes=32 time=66ms TTL=245
Reply from 192.203.130.2: bytes=32 time=82ms TTL=245
Reply from 192.203.130.2: bytes=32 time=92ms TTL=245
Reply from 192.203.130.2: bytes=32 time=122ms TTL=245

Ping statistics for 192.203.130.2:
    Packets: Sent = 4, Received = 4, Lost = 0 (0% loss),
Approximate round trip times in milli-seconds:
    Minimum = 66ms, Maximum =  122ms, Average =  90ms
```

If you can PING a host using its IP address but not its domain name, there could be a problem with your DNS server.

Case Study #1: Cannot Browse the Network Neighborhood

One student in a networking lab was distressed because his machine was the only one that could not view the Network Neighborhood. The instructor spent a good deal of time checking properties before finally rebooting the machine and asking the student to try again. The instructor watched in surprise as the student cancelled the logon process to get to the desktop quicker. He then explained to the student that network privileges are only given to users who log on to Windows.

Case Study #2: RJ-45 Connector Partially Inserted

One user was confused when her machine would not connect to the network, even though the light on her hub was lit and the machine had been working on the network the previous evening. After spending a good deal of time on the phone with a technician and checking all hardware and software properties, she was about to give up. She began recalling her steps, thinking about everything she had done or seen since the computer last worked. She remembered that she pulled the mini-tower case to the front of her computer desk to adjust the volume control on her sound card. She carefully pulled the computer across the desk again, and saw that the RJ-45 connector was partially pulled out of its socket on the NIC. When she pushed on it she heard a snap as it clicked into place. After rebooting, her machine worked fine again.

Case Study #3: Missing Terminator

After rearranging the old networking hardware in a closet, a technician discovered that the entire 10base2 network was not functioning. Not a single machine worked on the network. Careful inspection of the rearranged equipment revealed that the technician forgot to reconnect the terminating resistor on the end of the coax.

Case Study #4: Wrong UTP Cable Type

Of the eight machines connected to a hub in a new networking lab, only seven can connect to the network. When the UTP cables are swapped between the bad machine and a good one, the problem moves to the good machine and the bad machine is able to connect to the network. When the two cables are swapped into different ports on the hub the problem also moves. Examining the ends of the original cable it was discovered that the cable was a crossover cable, not a straight-through cable, which normally connects a NIC to a hub or switch port.

Case Study #5: Cannot Map a Network Drive

One user tried everything to try to map a network drive (no password required) on the mainframe at his business. He changed NICs, reinstalled all the networking protocols, and finally reinstalled the operating system. Finally, with nothing else to try, he changed from using a static IP address to obtaining one via DHCP. After rebooting, he was able to map the network drive. Discussing the problem and its accidental solution with everyone he knew always brought up the same response: "What does a static IP address have to do with the problem?" The answer is, it should not make a difference. No satisfactory explanation for the solution exists. We just feel lucky to have solved it. It is now something else to try if a similar problem shows up in the future.

Case Study #6: Broadcast Storm

One business suffered frequent *broadcast storms*, a flooding of its network with so many packets that its switches were forced to drop packets to try to maintain their buffers. Eventually, by capturing network traffic with a protocol analyzer and examining it, the network technicians found a network packet used as a trigger for the broadcast storm, a message sent to a broadcast address on the business's subnet. Someone was PINGing their broadcast address!

After more digging, the technicians learned that a software engineer at the company was experimenting with a network application he downloaded from a hacker Web site. The application, whether intentional or not, was responsible for the broadcast storms.

Case Study #7: DHCP Not Working

On a particular college campus, a DHCP server is used to dynamically assign IP addresses to machines when they boot. One day the entire system stopped working, and no one could obtain an IP address. After isolating the building causing the DHCP server (in the computer center) to fail, the campus network technician went from lab to lab in the affected building. He finally found the problem: a Linux machine set up by a student as DHCP server for a project and accidentally connected to the college network. Once the machine was disconnected, the normal DHCP service resumed.

Baseband Versus Broadband

All of the networks discussed in this exercise were *baseband* communication networks. A baseband network has a single information carrier that is modulated with the digital network data. ***Broadband*** communication networks, like the television cable system, use many different carriers and thus support multiple channels of data. Broadband communication systems require more expensive hardware than baseband systems and are typically used for high-bandwidth applications, such as broadcast video and FM audio.

SELF-TEST

This self-test is designed to help you check your understanding of the background information presented in this chapter.

True/False

Answer *true* or *false*.

1. Only the direct cable connection can be used to connect two computers.

2. Coax should always be used when networking small laboratories.

3. Coax should always be used when networking small businesses.

4. Regarding Figure 6–7, machine-to-machine traffic on the second floor is also broadcast to the fiber.

5. Regarding Figure 6–7, machine-to-machine traffic from the second floor to the third floor is also broadcast to the fiber.

6. Interrupt conflicts do not prevent a NIC from operating correctly.

7. You must log on to Windows to have access to network services.

Multiple Choice

Select the best answer.

8. Modems are useful for
   a. PCs that are in the same room.
   b. PCs that have old 386 processors.
   c. PCs that are separated by large distances.

9. How many 4-port 10baseT hubs are needed to network the machines in the laboratory of Figure 6–3? Each hub also contains a 10base2 port.
   a. 2 hubs.
   b. 3 hubs.
   c. 4 hubs.

10. Assuming only 16-port hubs (with 10base2 ports) are used, how many are required for the small business shown in Figure 6–4?
    a. 4 hubs.
    b. 5 hubs.
    c. 6 hubs.

11. How many network connections are required for all the labs in Figure 6–6?
    a. 224.
    b. 238.
    c. 240.

12. To connect to the Internet you must use a
    a. Hub.
    b. Switch.
    c. Router.

13. Direct cable connection has two modes of operation, Guest and
    a. Client.
    b. Host.
    c. Server.

14. A network burdened by excessive packets is experiencing a
    a. Broadcast flood.
    b. Broadcast storm.
    c. Packet flood.

Completion

Fill in the blank or blanks with the best answers.

15. The direct cable connection is the _____ expensive way to connect two computers.

16. Modems provide the _____ speed connection between two computers.

17. Switches are used to establish a network _____.

18. Bad _____ are a problem in large coaxial (10base2) networks.

19. Fiber is used in the college campus scenario because of _____ conditions.

20. The IP address of a machine is displayed by the _____ utility.

21. Normally, a NIC connects to a port on a hub using a _____ UTP cable.

QUESTIONS/ACTIVITIES

1. Analyze the laboratory diagram in Figure 6–9. Determine how to network the computers. Assume that 4-port and 8-port hubs (with 10base2 ports) are available for use, if necessary. Explain why you would use 10base2 over 10/100baseT, or vice versa, how you considered the costs, future expansion of the lab, the amount of network traffic, and any other parameter that was significant.

2. This problem will require a good deal of time and effort. It involves the design of a network for a company called TriGen Laboratories.

The Site
The overhead view of the TriGen Research Laboratory is shown in Figure 6–10. Note in particular the dimensions of the office complex.

Detail Views
Figure 6–11 contains the detail views of Halls A, B, and C. Laboratories contain eight PCs each. Staff offices (O) contain two PCs each. Administrative offices (A) contain four PCs each. The I room is where the main Internet feed is present (T3 line to 100baseT).

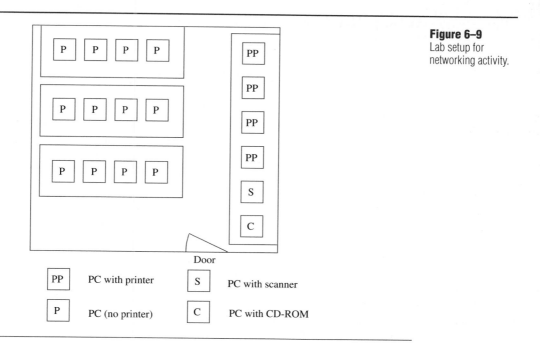

Figure 6–9
Lab setup for networking activity.

PP	PC with printer	S	PC with scanner
P	PC (no printer)	C	PC with CD-ROM

Door

Figure 6–10
Overhead view of
TriGen office complex.

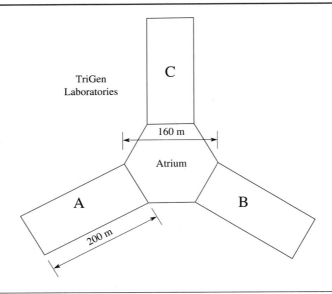

Figure 6–11
Details for each hall.

Lab	O	O	O	O		
Halls A and B						
Lab	O	O	O	O		

A	A	A		I
Hall C				
A	A	A		

Note: Halls A and B have two floors with identical layouts. The distance between floors is 4 meters. Hall C has only one floor.

The Plan

- Determine the total number of machines to be networked.
- Choose a physical network (10base2, 10/100baseT, fiber, or hybrid).
- Design the network.
- Cost out your design.

When designing the network, the following considerations should be part of your decision process:

- Traffic in each hall should be isolated from each other (i.e., switched).
- Every machine should be capable of sharing files.
- One class C subnet is available (208.210.112.xxx).

- The I room where the Internet feed originates contains the company router. The 100baseT router port address is 208.210.112.254.
- Every office (A and O) and each lab has a networked printer. Printers may be connected to printer ports or may have their own network connections.
- Labs are fed separately from all other offices.
- Future expansion (adding more machines) should be built in.
- The use of multimedia should be addressed.
- Assume that all machines and printers are already purchased and that conduit exists for any wiring scenario. The machines do not contain a network interface card.
- Do not include the cost of the installation in your pricing.

Document your decision process from the beginning. Find prices for your equipment on the Web. To really be impressive, suggest how IP addresses will be administered.

REVIEW QUIZ

Under the supervision of your instructor

1. Discuss several considerations that must be made when networking computers together.

2. Estimate the hardware components needed for a specific network.

3. Discuss some initial steps to take when troubleshooting a network.

Networking Concepts Laboratory

Experiment #6
Ethernet LAN Design and Troubleshooting

Objectives

1. To set up and analyze several different Ethernet LAN topologies.
2. To gain experience troubleshooting Ethernet problems.

Required Equipment

The following equipment is required for this experiment:

- Four or more computers containing network interface cards
- At least four straight-through UTP cables
- At least one crossover UTP cable
- At least three BNC-terminated coaxial cable segments
- At least two 50-ohm BNC terminators
- At least two Ethernet 10baseT/10base2 hubs

Procedure

Perform each of the following steps. Record your observations, results, and any difficulties you en-counter. You will use this information when you develop your conclusions about the experiment.

1. If your network interface cards do not contain BNC connectors (10base2 Ethernet), skip to step 8.
2. Daisy-chain four computers together using three lengths of coaxial cable, four T-connec-tors, and two 50-ohm terminators.
3. Copy BIGFILE.DAT from the companion CD-ROM to the C: drive on two of the machines.
4. Share the C: drive on each machine.
5. Make sure all machines are visible in Network Neighborhood.
6. Record the amount of time it takes to transfer BIGFILE.DAT from one machine to another. To transfer the file, do the following:
   - On the destination domputer, map the C: drive on the source computer using Windows Explorer.
   - Locate BIGFILE.DAT on the mapped drive and right-click on it.
   - Select **Copy** from the pop-up menu.
   - Right-click on the destination computer's C: drive.
   - Select **Paste** on the pop-up menu and begin timing the transfer.

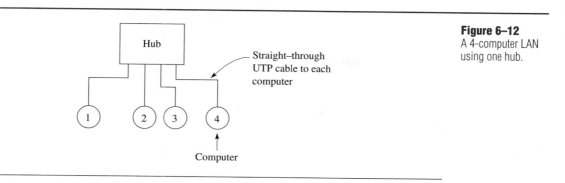

Figure 6–12
A 4-computer LAN using one hub.

7. Record the amount of time it takes to transfer BIGFILE.DAT from two machines to the other two *at the same time*.
8. Disconnect the coax daisy chain and connect the four computers using a single hub (10baseT Ethernet) and four straight-through UTP cables, as indicated in Figure 6–12.
9. Perform the single and dual BIGFILE.DAT file transfers and record the times. How does the transfer time of the 10baseT network compare to the 10base2 network?
10. Add a second hub to the LAN. Connect it to the first hub using coax. Do not forget to use T-connectors and terminators on each end of the coax. Figure 6–13(a) shows the desired network cofiguration.
11. Repeat the single and dual file transfers and record the transfer times. Note that there are many ways to do the transfers. For example, a single transfer may be done from machine 1 to 2, or from machine 1 to machine 3 or machine 4. The dual transfer has more combinations.
12. Disconnect the coax and add a crosover UTP cable between each hub, as indicated in Figure 6–13(b).
13. Repeat the file transfers.
14. Reconnect the coax while the crossover UTP is still attached. Does this cause any problems?

Figure 6–13
A 4-computer LAN using two hubs.

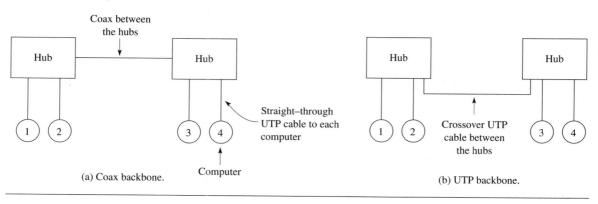

15. Disconnect the coax and add a faulty UTP cable between the machines or between the machines and the hub. *Note that a faulty UTP cable is one that is miswired or has one or more open connections.*
16. Record what problems, if any, are experienced. *Note:* Depending on the specific cable fault, many different errors may be experienced.

Discussion and Conclusion

Using a word processor, write your own detailed explanations of the results and observations made during the experiment. To begin, try to say something about each procedure step.

In addition, provide answers to the following questions:

1. What are the basic factors to consider when designing an Ethernet LAN?
2. What other combination of UTP and coax connections can be used to connect four computers?
3. Is it possible to network all the computers in your lab with the equipment you have?
4. What are the basic steps to take when troubleshooting an Ethernet LAN?

7

Low-Level Protocols

PERFORMANCE OBJECTIVES

Upon completion of this chapter, you will be able to:

- Describe the format of a serial data transmission.
- List the differences between SLIP and PPP.
- Explain the operation of the Logical Link Control sublayer.
- Discuss the role of NetBEUI and NetBIOS in a Windows network.

Joe Tekk was sitting in on a lecture at a local community college. His friend, Dan Russ, was lecturing about protocols, high level and low level. It was almost time to quit.

"I just want to finish with something for you to think about," Dan said. "All protocols have something in common: They are all agreements. These agreements exist between clients and servers, or between transmitters and receivers. From high-level protocols that specify how a Web page should be coded, to low-level protocols that require Manchester encoding to represent 1s and 0s, there are agreements between the parties involved."

Dan looked at his watch. "We agreed to finish 5 minutes early today. This is the end of my transmission."

INTRODUCTION

This chapter is the first of four chapters designed to provide coverage of the wide number of hardware and software protocols used in modern network communications. In this chapter we examine the low-level protocols used to establish serial communication, exchange data over different hardware technologies, and provide peer-to-peer communication.

SERIAL DATA COMMUNICATION

Serial data communication takes place one bit at a time over a single communication line. For example, an 8-bit binary number is transmitted

Figure 7–1
11-bit transmission
code.

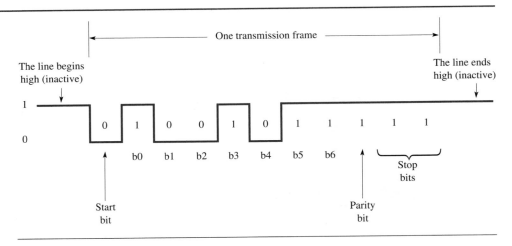

one bit at a time, beginning with the least significant bit. Examples of devices that use serial data communication are the keyboard, mouse, and COM1 port on a PC, MODEMs, and Ethernet NICs.

One popular standard for transmitting ASCII characters uses the 11-bit transmission waveform shown in Figure 7–1. Here the ASCII character being transmitted is a lowercase i. Its ASCII code is 69 hexadecimal, or 1101001 binary. The first bit in the waveform is the start bit, which is always low. This identifies the beginning of a new transmission, since the normal inactive state of the line is high. The next 7 bits are the ASCII code, beginning with the least significant bit. Do you see the 1001011 levels in the waveform?

Following the last data bit is a parity bit. Parity bits are used to help determine if there is an error in the received character. Count the number of 1s in the data. There are four. Including the 1 in the parity bit we have five 1s. This is an odd number, thus, the waveform has odd *parity*.

Suppose that the waveform in Figure 7–1 is transmitted correctly, but during transmission the 1 in b_5 is changed to a 0 by noise. The received waveform will then have even parity. If we expect received waveforms to have odd parity, an even parity waveform must contain an error.

The last two bits in the transmission frame are the stop bits, which are always high. This gets the transmission line back to its normal inactive state, and also provides some time for processing the received waveform. Note that there may be one, one and one-half, or two stop bits used.

Each bit of the waveform takes the same amount of time. This time is related to the *baud rate* of the serial transmission (it is the inverse). Baud rate is generally regarded to be the number of bits per second in a transmission, but is actually the number of transitions per second. For instance, a 9600 bits/second modem may only require 2400 baud (when each signal transition represents 4 bits). We will use bits/second here. As an example, if the time of one bit is 833.3 microseconds, the baud rate is 1 divided by 833.3 microseconds, or 1200 bits/second.

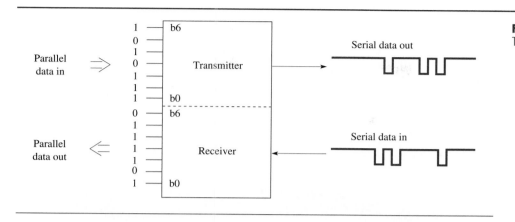

Figure 7–2
The UART.

An advantage of serial data transmission is its simple connection requirements: a single transmit wire and a single receive wire (plus a ground wire). With only one transmit wire, it is not possible to send a clock signal with the waveform. This is referred to as *asynchronous communication*. To compensate, the start and stop bits are used to synchronize the transmitter and receiver.

Serial data transmission is handled by digital devices called UARTs (universal asynchronous receiver transmitter). Figure 7–2 shows the basic operation of a UART. Parallel input data is converted to serial output data and serial input data is converted into parallel output data. In a modem, the UART interfaces with analog circuitry that converts bits to varying frequencies within the bandwidth of the telephone connection.

SLIP

The Serial Line Interface Protocol, or **SLIP**, was the first protocol used to transmit the Transmission Control Protocol/Internet Protocol, or **TCP/IP**, over dial-up phone lines. Note that TCP/IP is covered in detail in Chapter 8. SLIP provides a basic method to encapsulate the TCP/IP data but does not provide support for error detection, Internet Protocol (**IP**) address assignments, link testing, synchronous communication (clock included with data), or protocols other than TCP/IP to be transmitted. Compressed SLIP (CSLIP) is also available to increase the amount of data that can be transmitted. However, due to the many limitations, SLIP has been replaced by use of PPP, the Point-to-Point Protocol.

PPP

The Point-to-Point Protocol, or **PPP**, provides the ability to encapsulate many different protocols over a serial connection. In fact, PPP supports TCP/IP, IPX, NetBEUI, AppleTalk, and other protocols. The format of a PPP frame is shown

Figure 7–3
PPP frame format.

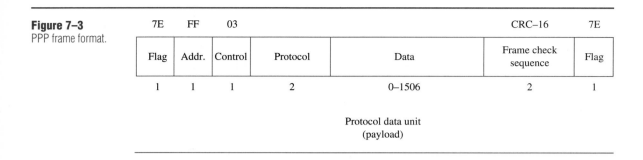

7E	FF	03			CRC–16	7E
Flag	Addr.	Control	Protocol	Data	Frame check sequence	Flag
1	1	1	2	0–1506	2	1

Protocol data unit
(payload)

Table 7–1
Comparing SLIP
and PPP.

SLIP	PPP
Static IP addresses	Dynamic IP addresses
Supports TCP/IP only	Supports TCP/IP, IPX, NetBEUI, AppleTalk, and others
Asynchronous	Asynchronous and synchronous
No compression	Compression supported
No security	Security supported (password logon)
56 Kbps maximum	No speed limit
No link testing	Link testing supported

in Figure 7–3. In addition, unlike SLIP, PPP provides for error detection, the ability to assign IP addresses, link testing, both synchronous and asynchronous communication modes, security (user name and password authentication), and compression.

Error detection over PPP uses a checksum value to test for data validity. The ability for address assignment in PPP allows for an address to be assigned as needed during the duration of the session. Link testing provides a mechanism to periodically test the status of the PPP link operation. Security is available in PPP using either the Password Authentication Protocol (PAP) or the Challenge Handshake Authentication Protocol (CHAP). Due to these additional features, PPP is widely used. Table 7–1 summarizes the differences between SLIP and PPP. Additional coverage of communication via PPP is provided in Chapters 17 and 18.

IEEE 802.2 LOGICAL LINK CONTROL

The Data-Link layer of the OSI networking model contains two parts, as indicated in Figure 7.4. These are the Logical Link Control (*LLC*) sublayer and the Media Access Control (MAC) sublayer.

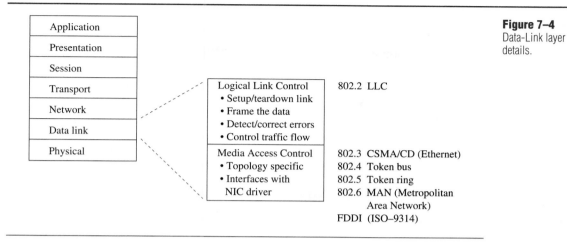

Figure 7–4
Data-Link layer details.

The IEEE 802.2 standard describes the operating characteristics of Logical Link Control, which provides three types of service:

- Type 1: Connectionless communication
- Type 2: Connection-oriented communication
- Type 3: Acknowledged connectionless communication

Connectionless communication is unreliable. The sending station makes a *best effort* to deliver its information. Connection-oriented communication is reliable, with the sending and receiving stations exchanging acknowledgement messages to guarantee error-free delivery. Connectionless communication relies on upper layer protocols to provide reliability.

How is reliable communication established? The sender and the receiver must send messages back and forth, according to an established protocol. For example, the sender sends four messages of information, and the receiver acknowledges getting four. If an error occurs, and the receiver only acknowledges getting two messages, the sender knows to resend the missing messages.

The LLC protocol is based on a popular protocol called HDLC (High-Level Data-Link Control), which provides a mechanism for sending commands and responses over a communication link.

The format of an LLC protocol data unit is shown in Figure 7–5. The values of the DSAP and SSAP fields indicate how the payload will be interpreted. One type of payload, called SNAP (sub network access protocol), is used when a high-level protocol is being handled by the LLC sublayer.

The MAC sublayer is designed to interface the LLC sublayer with different network technologies, without the LLC sublayer having to know any of the details. This allows the same LLC sublayer to work with different network technologies (and therefore different MAC sublayers). Additional responsibilities include controlling access to the network media, recovering from errors, and addressing (i.e., working with MAC addresses).

Figure 7–5
Logical Link
Control PDU.

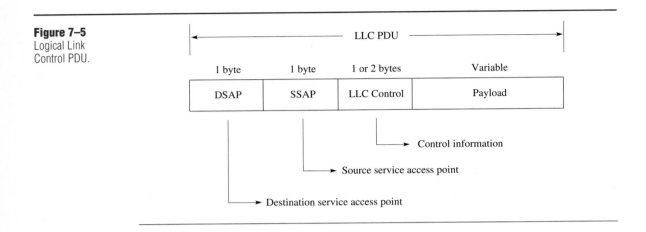

NETBIOS

NetBIOS (Network Basic Input/Output System) provides all the functionality needed to share resources between networked computers, such as files and printers. Originally developed by IBM and Sytek, NetBIOS defines an interface to the network service protocols, acting as an API (application programming interface) for clients accessing LAN resources. NetBIOS is a layer 2 (Data-Link) protocol.

NetBIOS utilizes three types of services: name, session, and datagram. The features of each service are as follows:

- Name: Finding and naming machines
- Session: Connection-oriented reliable transfer of messages
- Datagram: Connectionless non-reliable datagram transfer

The main component of a NetBIOS message is the *SMB* (server message block) it carries. SMBs provide all of the functionality possible under NetBIOS. Table 7–2 shows a sample of the operations possible under NetBIOS.

A sample SMB message, decoded by LanExplorer, looks like this:

```
Destination    Source        Protocol          Summary Size Time Tick
-----------------------------------------------------------------------------
030000000001   00C0F02764E2   NetBIOS SMB C Transaction  LLC UI  193  12/06/99 14:15:48

Addr.  Hex. Data                                          ASCII
0000:  03 00 00 00 00 01 00 C0 F0 27 64 E2 00 B3 F0 F0   .........'d.....
0010:  03 2C 00 FF EF 08 00 00 00 00 00 00 00 52 41 59   .,...........RAY
0020:  43 41 53 54 20 20 20 20 20 20 20 20 1E 57 41 56   CAST        .WAV
0030:  45 47 55 49 44 45 20 20 20 20 20 20 00 FF 53 4D   EGUIDE      ..SM
0040:  42 25 00 00 00 00 00 00 00 00 00 00 00 00 00 00   B%..............
```

Table 7–2
Sample NetBIOS
commands.

Command	Description
Bad command	Invalid SMB command
Change/check dir	Change to directory or check path
Change password	Change password of user
Copy file	Copy file to specified path
Delete file	Delete the specified file
Find unique	Search directory for specified file
Get resources	Get availability of server resources
Mailslot message	Mail slot transaction message
Named pipe call	Open, write, read, or close named pipe
Rename file	Rename the specified file to a new name
Reserve resources	Reserve resources on the server
Session setup	Log-in with consumer-based authentication

```
0050:   00 00 00 00 00 00 00 00 00 00 00 00 00 11 00 00   ................
0060:   2E 00 00 00 00 00 00 00 00 00 00 00 00 00 00 00   ................
0070:   00 00 00 00 2E 00 56 00 03 00 01 00 01 00 02 00   ......V.........
0080:   3F 00 5C 4D 41 49 4C 53 4C 4F 54 5C 42 52 4F 57   ?.\MAILSLOT\BROW
0090:   53 45 00 0F 08 C0 27 09 00 57 41 56 45 47 55 49   SE....'..WAVEGUI
00A0:   44 45 00 00 00 00 00 00 00 04 00 03 22 45 00 15   DE.........."E..
00B0:   04 55 AA 6A 6C 61 27 73 20 6D 61 63 68 69 6E 65   .U.jla's machine
00C0:   00                                                .
```

```
802.3 [0000:000D]
   0000:0005   Destination Address: 030000000001 (NetBEUI Multicast)
   0006:000B   Source Address: 00C0F02764E2 (Kingston2764E2)
   000C:000D   Ethernet Length: 179
LLC [000E:0010]
   000E:000E   Destination SAP: NETBIOS
   000F:000F   Source SAP: NETBIOS (Command)
   0010:0010   LLC Control: UI (Unnumbered Information) frame
NETBIOS [0011:003C]
   0011:0012   Header Length: 44
   0013:0014   Delimiter: 0xEFFF
   0015:0015   Command: Datagram
   0016:0016   Data1: Reserved
   0017:0018   Data2: Reserved
   0019:001A   Transmit Correlator: Reserved
   001B:001C   Response Correlator: Reserved
   001D:002C   Destination Name: RAYCAST      (name of receiver)
```

```
  002D:003C  Source Name: WAVEGUIDE        (name of sender)
SMB [003D:005C]
  003D:0040  ID: 0xFF, 'SMB'
  0041:0041  Command Code: Transaction (Client Command)
  0042:0042  Error Class: Success
  0043:0043  Reserved: 0
  0044:0045  Error Code: Success
  0046:0046  Flag: 0x00
  0047:0048  Flag2: 0x0000
  0049:0054  Reserved: Not Used
  0055:0056  Tree ID: 0x0000
  0057:0058  Process ID: 0x0000
  0059:005A  User ID: 0x0000
  005B:005C  Multiplex ID: 0x0000
```

Notice that the source and destination addresses are 6-byte MAC addresses, and not 4-byte IP addresses. The SMB is being transmitted from the machine named WAVEGUIDE.

Machine names are the NetBIOS names that identify each machine on a Windows network. To view or alter your machine name, right-click on the Network Neighborhood icon and select Properties to bring up the Network properties display. Left-click the Identification tab to see the machine name. Figure 7–6 shows the Identification display for the WAVEGUIDE machine.

NetBIOS names may be up to 15 characters including letters, numbers, and a limited set of symbols. Figure 7–7 shows the error display resulting from entering an invalid machine name.

Windows uses the machine name to identify a computer so that it can share resources and engage in other network activities, such as locating other machines in the network neighborhood.

NETBEUI

NetBEUI (NetBIOS Extended User Interface) provides a transport mechanism to deliver NetBIOS messages over a LAN. NetBEUI does not comform to the OSI model (it uses Transport, Network, and the LLC part of Data-Link). NetBEUI is not a routable protocol since it uses MAC addresses to specify source and destination computers and is thus only used on small networks (up to 254 machines). A special dynamic database called WINS (Windows Internet Name Service) maps NetBIOS names to IP addresses when larger networks are needed. Clearly, it is easier for a human to remember the name of a machine than its IP address, so the WINS database provides an important function.

NetBIOS over TCP/IP allows NetBIOS messages to be transported using *TCP*, which is a routable protocol used to connect computers in different networks

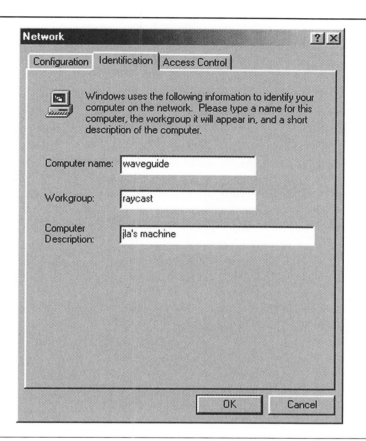

Figure 7–6
Network Identification display.

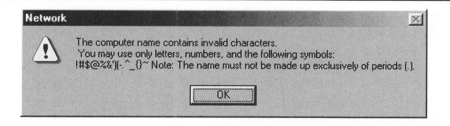

Figure 7–7
Invalid NetBIOS computer name error message.

(i.e., computers on the Internet). NetBIOS over TCP/IP can therefore be used to share resources over a WAN, instead of just a LAN environment. This is supported by a look at the Network properties window shown in Figure 7–8 (right-click on Network Neighborhood and choose Properties, or left-double-click the Network icon in Control Panel).

Figure 7–8
Network properties
showing protocol
bindings.

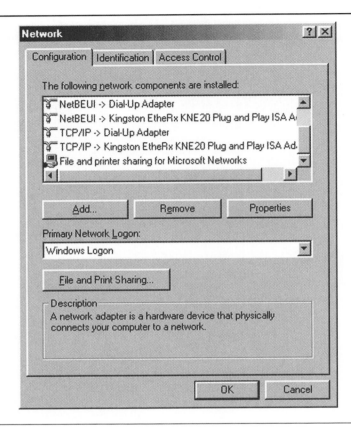

Although NetBEUI was originally used by IBM for its LAN Manager network, it has been adapted by Microsoft for use in Windows for Workgroups 3.11 and Windows 95/98/ME/NT. Figures 7–9(a) and 7–9(b) show the NetBEUI Properties windows. These are displayed by selecting one of the bound protocols from the Network properties window and examining its properties. It is normally not necessary to adjust any of the NetBEUI parameters.

 ## TROUBLESHOOTING TECHNIQUES

It is often necessary to dig deeper into the specifics of a protocol. An excellent source of protocol information can be found on the Web at www.protocols.com. Just click the Search icon and enter the name of the protocol you are looking for.

Another good site is www.whatis.com, which provides short descriptions of the items being searched for, with links to additional information provided. Use both sites to supplement your study of the protocols covered in this chapter, and those you will be exposed to in Chapters 8 through 10.

Figure 7–9
(a) NetBEUI Properties, Bindings.(b) NetBEUI Properties, Advanced.

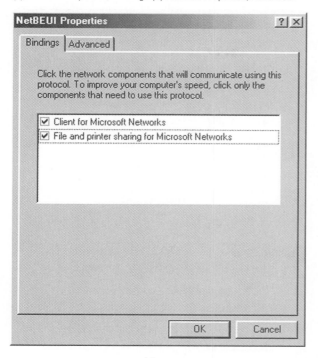

(a)

(b)

SELF-TEST

This self-test is designed to help you check your understanding of the background information presented in this chapter.

True/False
Answer *true* or *false*.

1. In a serial transmission, the start bit is always low.

2. SLIP is more advanced than PPP.

3. Logical Link Control interfaces directly with the NIC drivers.

4. WINS maps NetBIOS names to MAC addresses.

5. NetBEUI is a routable protocol.

Multiple Choice
Select the best answer.

6. Errors may be detected in a serial transmission by examining the
   a. Start bit.
   b. Frame-check bit.
   c. Parity bit.

7. Which protocol supports dynamic IP address allocation?
   a. SLIP.
   b. PPP.
   c. DYNIP.

8. A SNAP payload encapsulates a
   a. Low-level protocol.
   b. High-level protocol.
   c. Both a and b.

9. Which is not a valid NetBIOS name?
   a. FASTCPU
   b. FAST CPU
   c. FASTCPU!!!

10. What type of address does NetBEUI use?
    a. IP.
    b. MAC.
    c. Both a and b.

Completion
Fill in the blank or blanks with the best answers.

11. The last bit transmitted over a serial connection is the _____ bit.

12. LLC provides connectionless and connection-_____ communication.

13. MAC stands for Media _____ Control.

14. NetBIOS names may be up to _____ characters in length.

15. NetBIOS uses _____ message blocks to exchange information.

QUESTIONS/ACTIVITIES

1. Look up information on the RS-232 standard.

2. Try to explain why a computer connected to the Internet that is using NetBIOS over TCP/IP may be vulnerable.

For a demonstration of vulnerability, go to www.grc.com and look for "Shields UP."

REVIEW QUIZ

Under the supervision of your instructor

1. Describe the format of a serial data transmission.

2. List the differences between SLIP and PPP.

3. Explain the operation of the Logical Link Control sublayer.

4. Discuss the role of NetBEUI and NetBIOS in a Windows network.

Networking Concepts Laboratory

Experiment #7
NetBIOS and NetBEUI

Objectives

1. To examine the use of NetBIOS and NetBEUI on a Windows network.
2. To see how file and printer sharing are supported through NetBEUI.

Required Equipment

The following equipment is required for this experiment:

- Four computers connected by a network
- LanExplorer software

Procedure

Perform each of the following steps. Record your observations, results, and any difficulties you encounter. You will use this information when you develop your conclusions about the experiment.

1. Use a browser to open the README.HTML document in the LANEXP folder of the companion CD-ROM. Carefully follow the instructions and install LanExplorer on *one computer only*. Keep track of this computer and any others you may install LanExplorer on. (*Note:* The LanExplorer program on the companion CD-ROM only allows installation on ONE computer ONE time, and then it can only be run for a limited number of times over a limited number of days. Keep good track of the installations that you perform so that you are not in the position of not being able to run LanExplorer at all.)
2. Review Appendix F.
3. Build a network of two or more computers.
4. Use LanExplorer to capture network activity for 10 minutes. What kind of packets are present?
5. Examine the captured packets for those containing NetBIOS messages. Are there any SMB transactions? If so, decode one of them.
6. Capture packets while changing the name of one of the computers. Since you will have to reboot the computer after changing its name, you will be able to capture the packets exchanged by Windows while it is booting.

Discussion and Conclusion

Using a word processor, write your own detailed explanations of the results and observations made during the experiment. To begin, try to say something about each procedure step.

In addition, provide answers to the following questions:

1. What is the nature of the traffic on a Windows network when the machines are simply on and no one is using them?
2. Explain how a protocol is really an agreement between sender and receiver.

8

The TCP/IP Protocols

PERFORMANCE OBJECTIVES

Upon completion of this chapter, you will be able to

- Describe how the TCP/IP protocol stack is organized compared to the ISO/OSI protocol stack.
- Discuss the different protocols that make up the TCP/IP suite.
- Show how TCP/IP data is encapsulated inside a hardware frame for transmission.
- Describe the relationship between IP addresses and MAC addresses.
- Discuss the role of the PING and TRACERT applications.

Joe Tekk walked by Don, the senior technician, muttering under his breath. "Arp, rarp. Arp, rarp."

Don looked at Joe with a quizzical expression. "What are you saying, Joe?" he asked.

Joe laughed. "Arp, rarp. They're abbreviations for two networking procotols. ARP stands for address resolution protocol. RARP stands for reverse address resolution protocol. You know, arp, rarp. I like the sound of it."

Don just shook his head, bewildered. "You sound like my three-year-old grandson."

Joe was shocked. "Really? Does he know anything about networking?"

INTRODUCTION

In this chapter we will examine the features of the TCP/IP (Transmission Control Protocol/Internet Protocol) suite. The TCP/IP protocol suite is unquestionably one of the most popular networking protocols ever developed. TCP/IP has been used since the 1960s as a method to connect large mainframe computers together to share information among the research community and the Department of Defense. Now TCP/IP is used to support the largest computer network, the Internet. Most manufacturers incorporate TCP/IP into their operating systems, allowing all types of computers to communicate with each other.

To help understand TCP/IP, let us begin our discussion by reviewing the characteristics of the ISO/OSI model that is shown in Table

ISO/OSI Layer	Operation (purpose)
7 = Application	Use network services via an established protocol (TCP/IP, NetBEUI)
6 = Presentation	Format data for proper display and interpretation
5 = Sesson	Establish, maintain, and teardown session between both networked computers
4 = Transport	Break application data into network-sized packets
3 = Network	Handle network addressing
2 = Data Link	Flow control, reliable transfer of data
1 = Physical	All hardware required to make the connection (NIC, cabling, etc.) and transmit/receive 0s and 1s

8–1. The ISO/OSI model breaks network communication down into seven layers. In contrast, the TCP/IP network model contains only five layers. Figure 8–1 shows the relationship between the ISO/OSI network model and the TCP/IP network model. These particular network models are also called the *protocol stacks*.

The Physical layer is responsible only for sending and receiving digital data, nothing else. Any errors that show up in the data at the Physical layer are handled by the next higher layer up in the protocol stack. In the TCP/IP network model, the next higher level up is referred to as the Network Interface layer. The Network Interface layer performs the same functions as the Data-Link layer in the ISO/OSI model. The functions of the Physical layer and the Data-Link layer are determined by the type of LAN hardware in use, such as Ethernet, token ring, and so forth.

The next layer up, called the Internet layer, performs the same function as the Network layer in the ISO/OSI model. The Internet layer uses the Internet Protocol (IP) and provides what is called *machine-to-machine* communication.

The Transport layer is the same in both the ISO/OSI and TCP/IP network stacks. There are two transport layer protocols in TCP/IP, the Transmission Control Protocol (TCP) and the User Datagram Protocol (UDP). The transport protocols provide *application-to-application* communication. TCP provides for connection-oriented reliable transport and UDP provides for connectionless unreliable transport.

The TCP/IP Application layer provides the same functionality as the Session, Presentation, and Application layers in the ISO/OSI network model. The Application layer is where the communicating application programs running on the source computer and the destination computer reside. The packet of data that is transmitted from the source computer contains an informational header for each layer in the protocol stack (except layer 1). This concept is shown in Figure 8–2.

When a hardware frame is sent out onto the network, it contains all of the information necessary to be forwarded to and received properly by the

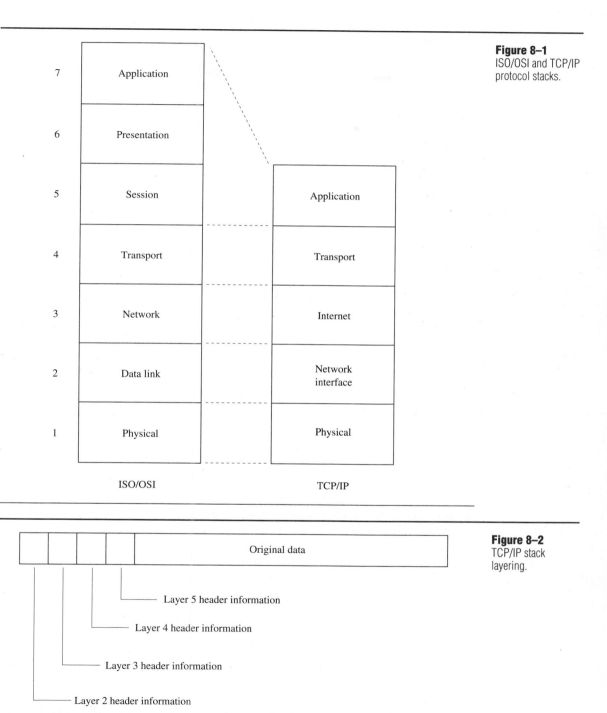

Figure 8–1
ISO/OSI and TCP/IP protocol stacks.

Figure 8–2
TCP/IP stack layering.

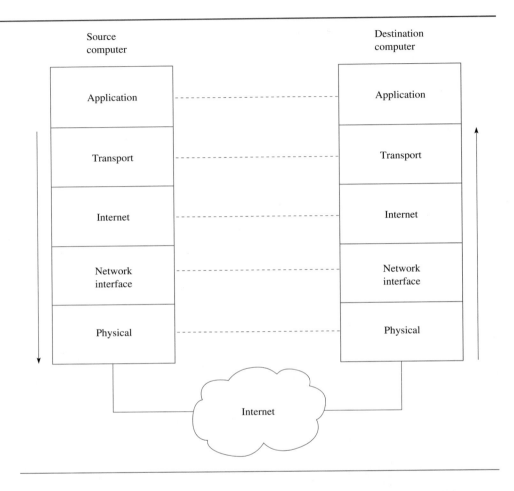

Figure 8–3
TCP/IP message
layering.

Source computer — Destination computer

Application — Application

Transport — Transport

Internet — Internet

Network interface — Network interface

Physical — Physical

Internet

destination computer without errors. At the destination computer, as the received message moves up the stack toward the application, identical copies of the packaged information are available at each layer, just as it was on the source computer. This is illustrated in Figure 8–3. TCP/IP uses this layering technique to transmit all data between the applications running on the communicating computers.

Figure 8–4 shows which protocols are used at each specific layer in the TCP/IP protocol stack. Each of the protocols in the TCP/IP protocol stack is described in detail by an RFC.

 RFCs

Official standards for the Internet are published as electronic documents called Request for Comments, or *RFCs*. The RFC series of documents on networking

ISO/OSI Layer	TCP/IP Protocols	
7 = Application	Telnet	DHCP
6 = Presentation	FTP	SNMP
5 = Session	SMTP	DNS
4 = Transport	TCP	UDP
3 = Network	IP ARP RARP	
2 = Data link	LLC 802.2 MAC	
1 = Physical	802.3 Ethernet 802.5 Token Ring	

Figure 8–4
TCP/IP protocol suite.

began in 1969 as part of the original Advanced Research Projects Agency wide-area networking project called ARPAnet. RFCs cover a wide range of topics in addition to Internet standards, from early discussion of new research concepts to status memos about the current state of the Internet.

Refer to Table 8–2 for a list of RFCs associated with some of the most popular protocols in TCP/IP. The Internet Engineering Task Force (IETF) Web site

Protocol	RFC	Name
Telnet	854	Remote Terminal Protocol
FTP	959	File Transfer Protocol
SMTP	821	Simple Mail Transfer Protocol
SNMP	1098	Simple Network Management Protocol
DNS	1034	Domain Name System
TCP	793	Transport Control Protocol
UDP	768	User Datagram Protocol
ARP	826	Address Resolution Protocol
RARP	903	Reverse Address Resolution Protocol
ICMP	792	Internet Control Message Protocol
BOOTP	951	Bootstrap Protocol
IP	791	Internet Protocol

Table 8–2
Several important TCP/IP RFCs.

located at www.ietf.org/rfc.html provides quick access to all of the RFC documents. Appendix D contains a list of RFC numbers and their titles. The RFC number is used (entered into an HTML form) on the IETF Web site to examine the individual RFCs. You are encouraged to review the RFC documents, as they provide much insight into how TCP/IP and the Internet work.

Now, let us take a look at the most fundamental protocol in TCP/IP, the Internet Protocol.

IP

The Internet Protocol (IP) is the base layer of the TCP/IP protocol suite. IP is used at the Internet layer in the TCP/IP stack. All TCP/IP data is packaged in units called IP datagrams. All other TCP/IP protocols, except for the address resolution protocols, are encapsulated inside of an IP datagram for delivery on the network. IP datagrams are eventually encapsulated inside of a hardware frame, such as Ethernet for transmission on a LAN. This is illustrated in Figure 8–5.

The IP datagram is transmitted on a local network to a special purpose device called a *router* whose job is to forward the packet onto another router or possibly deliver the packet to the LAN where the destination computer is located. The whole routing process is covered in detail in Chapter 10.

There is no direct link between the source and destination computers on the Internet. The source computer system sends packets out onto the local LAN network where they are then forwarded onto their destination. When an IP datagram is sent, it is treated as an independent entity on the network, with no relationship to any other datagrams. Datagrams sent to the same location may take different routes as network conditions change. This may cause the destination computer to receive the packets out of order if packets are delayed.

The Internet Protocol is considered to be unreliable due to the fact there is no guarantee the datagram will reach its destination. IP provides what is called *best effort* delivery. For example, a common reason for packet loss is network congestion. Figure 8–6 shows a reason why congestion might occur.

Figure 8–5
An IP datagram encapsulated into an Ethernet frame.

Frame header	Frame data	

	IP Datagram header	Datagram data

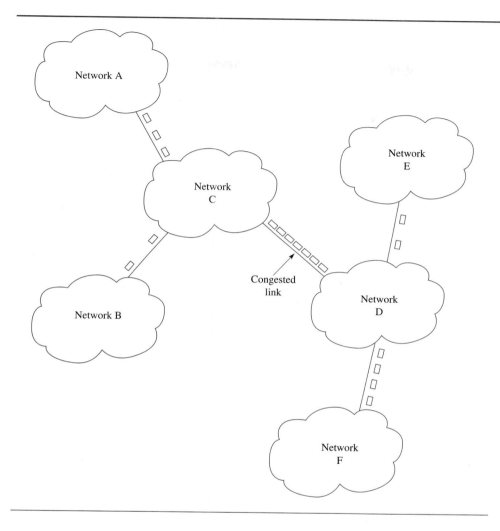

Figure 8–6
A source of network
congestion.

Consider the situation in which computers connected to network C are trying to communicate with computers in the E and F networks that are connected to network D. The link between networks C and D may not be able to handle all of the traffic, creating network *congestion*. On a congested network, some network traffic may simply be discarded to eliminate the congestion. Usually, when an IP datagram runs into trouble on the network, it is simply discarded. An error contained in an *ICMP* (Internet Control Message Protocol) message may or may not be returned to the sender. Figure 8–7 illustrates an example of how an ICMP message is encapsulated in an IP datagram. Additional information about ICMP will be provided later in this chapter. Because of IP's best effort delivery, the higher layers of the Internet Protocol provide for transmission reliability (using TCP) if it is required.

Figure 8–7
ICMP encapsulated in
an IP datagram.

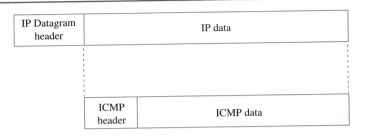

The IP datagram header and data field containing the ICMP message is shown in Figure 8–8. An IP datagram has a maximum size of 64K, or 65536 bytes. This total includes the header and the data area. Table 8–3 shows the size and purpose of each of the fields in the IP datagram header. Basically, the IP datagram header contains data fields to identify the version of IP, the length of the IP header (usually 20 bytes), the type of service, the total length of the datagram, and other fields that are used to identify the source and destination addresses and various error detection, reassembly, and delivery options.

When an IP datagram is encapsulated in a hardware frame, it is done so according to the local network maximum transmission unit, or MTU. A typical value for an MTU is 1500 bytes. This MTU value specifies the maximum size of an IP packet that may be transmitted on that particular network. Some

Figure 8–8
IP encapsulated message.

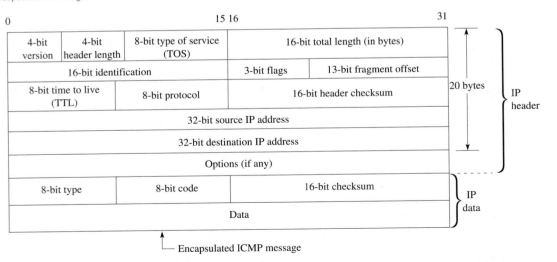

Header Field	Size	Meaning
Version	4 bits	Indicates the IP version number.
Hlen	4 bits	Length of the header in 32-bit words. The minimum value is 5 (20 bytes).
Service Type	8 bits	Specifies various parameters for throughput, reliability, precedence, and delay.
Total Length	16 bits	Specifies the total datagram length in bytes.
Identification	16 bits	Used to uniquely identify a datagram.
Flags	3 bits	Parameters used to specify information about fragmentation. Only two of these bits are defined.
Fragment Offset	13 bits	Indicates where in the original datagram the fragment belongs.
Time to Live (TTL)	8 bits	Used to specify how many hops a datagram can travel on the network.
Protocol	8 bits	Specifies the next higher level protocol to receive the data.
Header Checksum	16 bits	Used to detect errors in the header field only. This value is recomputed at each router since some of the header fields such as TTL are changed.
Source Address	32 bits	Sender IP address.
Destination Address	32 bits	Destination IP address.
Options and Padding	32 bits	User requested options.
Data	Variable	The data field is an integer multiple of 8 bits. The maximum size of the IP datagram is 64K bytes.

Table 8–3
IP header field information.

networks may set the MTU to a larger or smaller value. During transit, a packet generated with an MTU value of 1500 might encounter a network where the MTU is smaller. This is illustrated in Figure 8–9. When this situation occurs, it is necessary to fragment the IP datagram to comply with the network's lower MTU value, as shown in Figure 8–10.

When a datagram is fragmented, additional information is coded in the fragment offset field in the IP header to allow the receiving computer to correctly reassemble the data segments data back into the original state.

To understand how an IP datagram is forwarded to the destination, it is necessary to understand how the IP datagrams are addressed.

IP ADDRESSES

IP datagrams are routed on the network using an IP address. The IP address consists of a 32-bit number, divided into four sections, each containing 8 bits. These four sections are called *octets* and may contain a decimal value in the

Figure 8–9
Networks with
different MTUs.

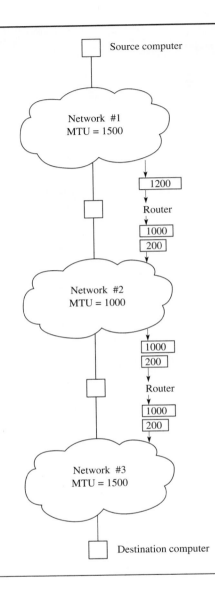

Source computer

Network #1
MTU = 1500

1200

Router

1000
200

Network #2
MTU = 1000

1000
200

Router

1000
200

Network #3
MTU = 1500

Destination computer

range 0 to 255. The four values from each section are separated by periods in the IP address. This is called *dotted decimal notation*. An example of dotted decimal notation is shown in Figure 8–11 illustrating a class C Internet address.

The IP address is assigned by software (statically or dynamically) and must be a unique address on the network. IP addresses thus differ from MAC addresses, which are fixed 48-bit addresses encoded into the hardware of every Ethernet controller, assigned by the manufacturer.

Figure 8–10
IP datagram fragmentation.

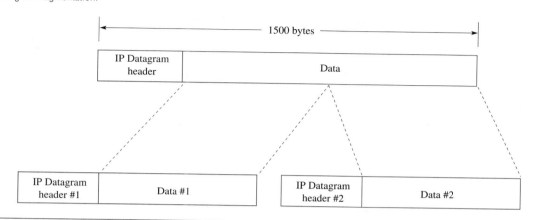

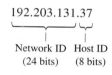

192.203.131.37

Network ID   Host ID
(24 bits)   (8 bits)

Figure 8–11
Class C network
IP address.

Address Classes

The Internet addresses are classified into five address classes. These addresses are shown in Figure 8–12. Each address class consists of a network ID and a host ID.

The network ID in a class A address contains a maximum number of 128 possible networks and over 16 million hosts. A class B address allocates more bits in the IP address to the network ID and less bits to the host ID, creating a possible 16,384 networks and 65,536 hosts. The class C address provides over two million networks, each with a possible 256 hosts. Class D addresses are reserved for *multicast* data and class E addresses are reserved.

Some of the IP addresses are reserved for special functions. For example, the class A address 127 is reserved for loopback testing, allowing a local method to test functionality of the TCP/IP software and applications. Other addresses are used as masks to identify each network type, such as 255.255.255.0 to identify a class C address.

There are also several other types of IP addresses that have a special use and meaning as well. These special addresses are listed in Table 8–4. The first

Figure 8–12
IP address classes.

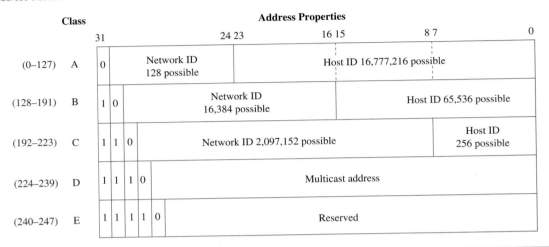

Table 8–4
Special IP addresses.

IP Address		Description
Network ID	Host ID	
All zeros	All zeros	This host (used during boot)
All zeros	Host number	A host on this network
All ones	All ones	Limited broadcast to local network
Network Number	All ones	Directed broadcast to a remote network
127	Any number	Loopback address (used for testing)

special IP address contains all zeros for both the network and the host portion of the address. This special address is used on a computer during booting. It is not a valid address for communicating on the network. The second address type consisting of zeros in the host portion and a valid host address identifies a host on the current (default) network. This address can be used to communicate with a computer in the same network. The third address type, consisting of all ones in the network and host portion of the address, is called a *limited broadcast*. A limited broadcast message will be received by all computers on a local network. The fourth special address type contains a network ID in the network portion of the address and all ones in the host portion. This is called a *directed broadcast*. A directed broadcast is used to send a broadcast message to all computers on a remote network. The directed broadcast is usually done to obtain the physical address of a computer if only the IP address is known. This is known as *address resolution*.

One of the shortcomings in the design of IP version 4 is in the addressing scheme. Class A networks, while being able to support 16 million hosts, rarely contain that many hosts. The same is true for class B addresses (though there are not as many wasted addresses, since class B networks have a limit of 65,536 hosts). The popular class C networks have had such a high demand that there is now a shortage of these addresses. A solution to this problem was established by introducing a classless IP address that can take advantage of the unused addresses. This addressing is accomplished using the *CIDR* (Classless Inter-Domain Routing) protocol. We will examine CIDR in detail in Chapter 10.

With an understanding of addressing and how messages are transmitted using IP, let us examine the transport protocols that are used to get the data from an application running on a source computer to the application running on a destination computer.

TCP

The Transmission Control Protocol defines a standard way that two computers can reliably communicate together over interconnected networks. Applications using TCP establish *connections* with each other, through the use of predefined *ports* or *sockets*. A TCP connection is reliable, with error checking, acknowledgment for received packets, and packet sequencing provided to guarantee the data arrives properly at its destination. Telnet and FTP are examples of TCP/IP applications that use TCP.

The TCP provides the communication link between the application program and IP. A set of function calls provides an application process a number of different options. For example, there are calls to open and close connections and to send and receive data on previously established connections. These functions will be discussed in detail in Chapter 16.

The TCP datagram format is illustrated in Figure 8–13. A brief description of the purpose of each field in the header is provided in Table 8–5. The TCP header and associated data are encapsulated into a hardware frame, such as Ethernet.

The primary purpose of the TCP is to provide reliable communication between applications running on a source computer and a destination computer. To provide guaranteed delivery on top of IP requires attention to the following areas:

- Data transfer
- Reliability
- Flow control
- Multiplexing
- Connections
- Message precedence and security

Let us take a look at each of these areas.

Figure 8–13
TCP datagram format.

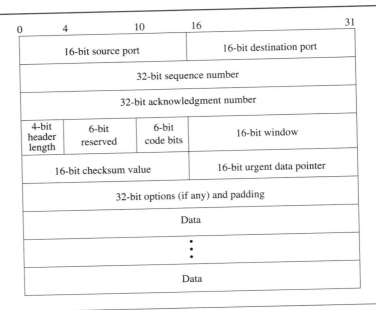

Table 8–5
TCP header field information.

Header Field	Size	Meaning
Source Port	16 bits	Source port service access point
Destination Port	16 bits	Destination port service access point
Sequence Number	32 bits	Sequence number of the current data segment
Acknowledgment Number	32 bits	The acknowledgment number contains the sequence number of the next data byte that TCP expects to receive
Header Length	4 bits	Number of 32 bits words in the TCP header
Reserved	6 bits	Flags reserved for future use
Code Bits	6 bits	Flags used to control the Urgent pointer, Acknowledgment field, Push function, Reset function, Sequence number synchronization, and final data indication
Window	16 bits	Contains the number of data bytes starting with the one in the acknowledgment field
Checksum	16 bits	The checksum value of the entire data segment to be transmitted
Urgent Pointer	16 bits	Indicates the amount of urgent data in the segment
Options and Padding	32 bits	One option currently defined that specifies the maximum data segment size that will be accepted

TCP is used to transfer a stream of data in each direction between the applications by packaging some data into segments for transmission through the network. When a user needs to be sure that all the data has been sent to the destination computer, a special function called **PUSH** is defined. This function indicates that the data that has been sent should be pushed through to the receiving application. A PUSH causes the TCP to initiate delivery of all the data currently in the pipeline.

To provide reliability, the TCP must be able to recover from data that is lost, damaged, delivered out of order, or duplicated by the network. This reliability is accomplished by assigning sequence numbers to the data as it is transmitted and requiring a positive acknowledgment (ACK) from the destination computer after the data has been received without error. If the ACK is not received within a certain timeout interval, the data is automatically retransmitted by the source computer. The timeout interval is based on an estimate of the time it takes for a packet to be sent to the destination computer and then acknowledged. This value is also called the *round trip estimation* time. A good estimated value for the round trip time allows for the highest level of network utilization.

At the destination computer, the sequence numbers are used to correctly reassemble the data segments. Duplicate packets that may be received are discarded. To ensure that a complete data segment has not been damaged, a checksum value is assigned to each segment that is transmitted. The destination computer checks the checksum value and discards any damaged segments. The TCP checksum field is based on a pseudo TCP header that contains only the source address, the destination address, the protocol, and the TCP segment length. In addition to error checking, the checksum field gives protection against misrouted datagrams.

TCP flow control provides a means for the receiver to govern the amount of data sent by the sender. This is achieved by returning a "window" with every ACK indicating a range of acceptable sequence numbers beyond the last segment successfully received. The window indicates an allowed number of octets that the sender may transmit before receiving further permission to send more. As the data is acknowledged, the window can be slid over the data that must still be transmitted. This is known as *sliding window flow control*. Figure 8–14 shows a simplistic example of two flow control methods. In Figure 8–14(a), the stop-and-go flow control requires that an acknowledgment be received before the next packet can be sent. The stop-and-go flow control method turns out to be extremely inefficient when compared to the sliding window flow control, as shown in Figure 8–14(b). Using a sample window size of five, the source computer sends the first five packets and then waits for an acknowledgment from the receiver. Additional packets are sent as the receiver indicates it is ready to receive them. Figure 8–15 shows a sliding window in the process of sending 15 data packets. In practice, window sizes are much larger and can accommodate large transfers of data very efficiently. One of the problems associated with the sliding window is called the *silly window syndrome*. The silly window syndrome occurs when the receiver repeatedly advertises a small window size due to what began as a temporary situation. The sender then transmits small segments to fit the small window size. Whereas less information is transmitted, some of the network bandwidth

Figure 8–14
Stop-and-go versus sliding window flow control.

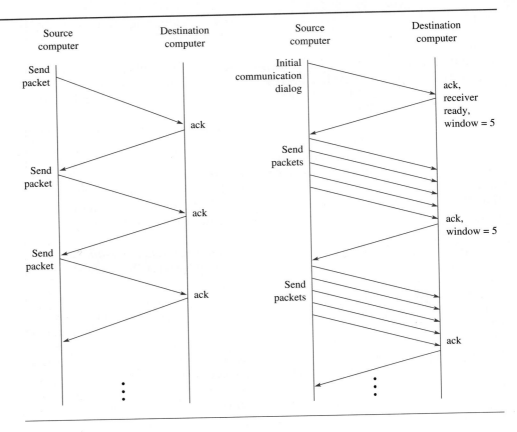

Figure 8–15
Sliding window flow control in operation.

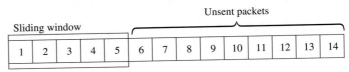

(a) Beginning of transmission.

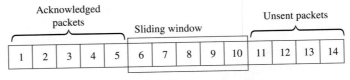

(b) After one acknowledgment.

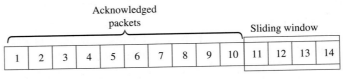

(c) After two acknowledgments.

is unused and therefore wasted. When examining TCP packets using LanExplorer, pay attention to the window size field. Try to determine how often the window size changes, if at all.

Port Numbers

All data communicated between two TCP applications take place through specific *ports*. A port is associated with the network *socket* created and used by the application. A pair of sockets uniquely identifies a *connection*.

So, a single computer may receive several TCP packets, with the port number associated with the TCP application stored in each packet. The port number is used to demultiplex the packet stream and forward the correct TCP packet to each application's input buffer. The binding of port numbers to application programs is handled independently by each operating system. However, commonly used network applications are assigned to fixed socket numbers (or port numbers) that are publicly known. The services then can be accessed through the well-known port numbers. In general, port numbers less than 1024 are reserved for well-known services. Port numbers greater than or equal to 1024 but less than 65536 are available for general use by applications. The official list of well-known port numbers are published in RFC 762.

When two applications want to communicate, the TCP is used to establish a connection (initialize the status information on both sides). After the connection has been established, data can be exchanged as necessary. After the communication is complete, the connection can be closed. Since these connections are established between hosts using the unreliable Internet Protocol, a *three-way handshake* is used to avoid the error condition when a connection is closed before all of the data has been transmitted. Essentially, this handshaking consists of three messages sent back and forth between the hosts, with each successive message containing information based on the previously received message.

Lastly, the precedence and security of TCP communication may be specified. The TCP may have a requirement to indicate the security and precedence of the data or it may use default values when these special features are not needed.

See how much of this information you can extract from a LanExplorer captured packet that shows a portion of a file transfer that uses the TCP:

```
Capture 1:Packet 61
```

Destination	Source	Protocol	Summary	Size	Time Tick
24.24.78.84	192.203.130.2		File Transfer Protocol (ACK,PSH)	60	[Default Data] TCP 07/15/00 12:37:57.477

```
Addr.  Hex. Data                                              ASCII
0000:  00 60 97 9E EA D5 08 00 3E 02 07 8D 08 00 45 00    .'......>.....E.
0010:  00 2E 90 A6 00 00 75 06 0B EA C0 CB 82 02 18 18    ......u.........
0020:  4E 54 00 14 04 19 54 1C 3A 01 00 15 32 6A 50 18    NT....T.:...2jP.
0030:  24 00 28 DF 00 00 74 65 73 74 0D 0A                $.(...test..
```

```
802.3 [0000:000D]
  0000:0005   Destination Address: 0060979EEAD5 (3Com9EEAD5)
  0006:000B   Source Address: 08003E02078D (Motorola02078D)
  000C:000D   Ethernet Type: DOD Internet Protocol (IP)
IP [000E:0021]
  000E:000E   Version: 4; Header Length: 20
  000F:000F   TOS, Precedence: Routine; Delay: Normal; Throughput: Normal;
Reliability: Normal
  0010:0011   Packet Length: 46
  0012:0013   Identification: 0x90A6
  0014:0014   DF: May Fragment; MF: Last Fragment
  0014:0015   Fragment Offset: 0
  0016:0016   Time to Live: 117
  0017:0017   Transport: Transmission Control
  0018:0019   Header Checksum: 0x0BEA (correct)
  001A:001D   Source Address: 192.203.130.2
  001E:0021   Destination Address: 24.24.78.84
TCP [0022:0035]
  0022:0023   Source Port: File Transfer Protocol [Default Data]
  0024:0025   Destination Port: 1049
  0026:0029   Sequence Number: 1411136001
  002A:002D   Acknowledgment Number: 1389162
  002E:002E   Header Length (bit 7..4): 20
  002F:002F   Control Bit - ACK; PSH;
  0030:0031   Window Size: 9216
  0032:0033   Checksum: 0x28DF (correct)
  0034:0035   Urgent Pointer: 0x0000
```

Compare each of the protocols (IP and TCP) shown in the Ethernet frame to their respective headers to determine what value each header field contains.

Next, let us examine the other transport protocol that we use when guaranteed reliable data transfer is deemed unnecessary, the User Datagram Protocol.

UDP

The User Datagram Protocol is similar to TCP except it is *connectionless*. Data is transmitted with no acknowledgment of whether it is received or not. **UDP** is thus not as reliable as TCP. There are many applications that do not require the additional overhead and complexity of TCP handshaking, such as the Domain Name Service (**DNS**), the Dynamic Host Configuration Protocol (**DHCP**), and network games. For example, a DNS or DHCP request will use the UDP and will retransmit the request if a response is not obtained in a timely fashion. A multiplayer network game might use UDP because it is simple to implement, requires less overhead to manage than TCP, and also because the game may not be severely affected if a few packets are lost now and then.

The format of a UDP header is shown in Figure 8–16, and a description of the data fields inside of the header are provided in Table 8–6. The UDP header

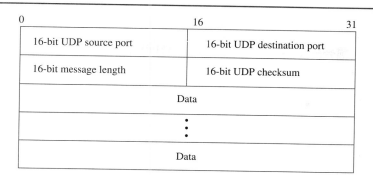

Figure 8–16
UDP datagram format.

Header Field	Size	Meaning
Source Port	16 bits	Source port service access point
Destination Port	16 bits	Destination port service access point
Length	16 bits	Contains the length of the segment including the header field and the data
Checksum	16 bits	The checksum value of the complete data segment

Table 8–6
UDP header field information.

format is quite a bit simpler than TCP, with fields used to identify the port number of the source computer, the port number on the destination computer, the length of the message in bytes, and a checksum value used to insure that the data was received properly. The port numbers used in UDP are used to identify the specific application running on the source computer and the destination computer. Similar to TCP, port numbers less than 1024 are reserved for well-known services. Port numbers greater than or equal to 1024 but less than 65536 are available for general use by applications. The complete list of well-known port numbers is found in RFC 762.

The UDP checksum field is based on a pseudo header that will work under any conditions. The pseudo header contains the source address, the destination address, the protocol, and the UDP segment length. The use of the UDP checksum field is optional. It must contain zeros to indicate that no checksum is supplied. A good reason to use the checksum field is that it gives protection against misrouted datagrams.

A packet captured using LanExplorer provides a good look at UDP in action while it is performing a DNS request:

```
Capture 1:Packet 6


Destination  Source       Protocol    Summary       Size   Time   Tick
----------------------------------------------------------------------
24.92.226.171   24.24.78.84  Domain Name Server   Query    78    07/15/00
```

                                                    12:37:28.351

```
Addr.   Hex. Data                                    ASCII
0000:   08 00 3E 02 07 8D 00 60 97 9E EA D5 08 00 45 00    ..>....'......E.
0010:   00 40 11 01 00 00 80 11 C8 38 18 18 4E 54 18 5C    .@.......8..NT.\
0020:   E2 AB 04 16 00 35 00 2C 06 74 00 01 01 00 00 01    .....5.,.t......
0030:   00 00 00 00 00 00 03 66 74 70 0A 73 75 6E 79 62    .......ftp.sunyb
0040:   72 6F 6F 6D 65 03 65 64 75 00 00 01 00 01          roome.edu.....
```

802.3 [0000:000D]
  0000:0005   Destination Address: 08003E02078D (Motorola02078D)
  0006:000B   Source Address: 0060979EEAD5 (3Com9EEAD5)
  000C:000D   Ethernet Type: DOD Internet Protocol (IP)
IP [000E:0021]
  000E:000E   Version: 4; Header Length: 20
  000F:000F   TOS, Precedence: Routine; Delay: Normal; Throughput: Normal;
Reliability: Normal
  0010:0011   Packet Length: 64
  0012:0013   Identification: 0x1101
  0014:0014   DF: May Fragment; MF: Last Fragment
  0014:0015   Fragment Offset: 0
  0016:0016   Time to Live: 128
  0017:0017   Transport: User Datagram
  0018:0019   Header Checksum: 0xC838 (correct)
  001A:001D   Source Address: 24.24.78.84
  001E:0021   Destination Address: 24.92.226.171
UDP [0022:0029]
  0022:0023   Source Port: 1046
  0024:0025   Destination Port: Domain Name Server
  0026:0027   Packet Length: 44
  0028:0029   Checksum: 0x0674 (correct)
DNS [002A:004D]
  002A:002B   ID: 0x0001
  002C:002C   QR: Query, Opcode: Standard Query, AA: No, TC: No, RD: Yes
  002D:002D   RA: No, Reserved: 0, Response Code: No Error
  002E:002F   Question Count: 1
  0030:0031   Answer Count: 0
  0032:0033   Authority Count: 0
  0034:0035   Additional Count: 0
  0036:0049   Question Name: ftp.sunybroome.edu
  004A:004B   Question Type: host address
  004C:004D   Question Class: Internet

ARP AND RARP

Before any packet can be transmitted, the hardware address of its destination computer must be known. This address is called a *MAC address*. MAC stands for media access control, and it takes the form of a 48-bit binary number that uniquely identifies one machine from every other. Every network interface card manufactured has a preassigned MAC address that it responds to.

The Address Resolution Protocol (*ARP*) uses a directed broadcast message to obtain the MAC address for a given IP address. For example, an ARP request may say, "What is the MAC address for 204.210.133.51?" The ARP reply may be "The MAC address is 00-60-97-2B-E6-0F."

Once the ARP reply has been received, it is possible for the source computer and destination computer to communicate directly. Figure 8–17 shows the format of the ARP message. Notice that there is a place to hold the hardware address (MAC) and software address (IP) for both the source and destination computer systems. The purpose of each of these data fields is shown in Table 8–7.

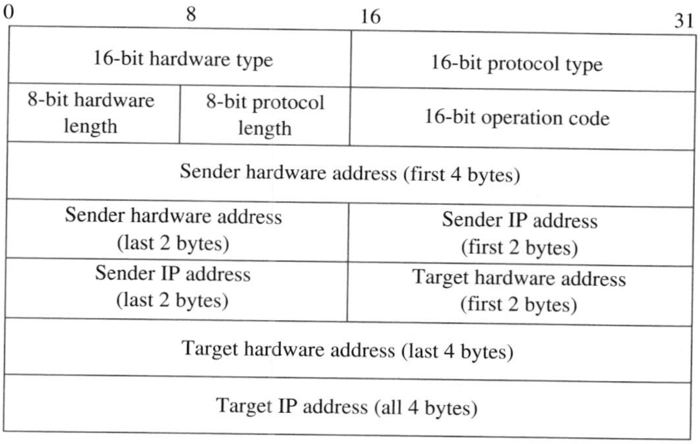

Figure 8–17
ARP/RARP message format.

Header Field	Size	Meaning
Hardware Type	16 bits	Specifies the type of hardware interface
Protocol Type	16 bits	Specifies the type of high level protocol to get
Hardware Length	16 bits	Indicates the length of the hardware address
Protocol Length	16 bits	Indicates the length of the protocol address
Operation Code	16 bits	Specifies the ARP/RARP operation (request or reply) to perform
Sender Hardware Address	48 bits	Identifies the senders hardware address
Sender Protocol Address	32 bits	Identifies the senders IP address
Target Hardware Address	48 bits	Place for the target hardware address to be stored (contains zeros in ARP request)
Target Protocol Address	32 bits	Identifies the target computer IP address

Table 8–7
ARP/RARP header field information.

Let us examine a LanExplorer packet capture of an ARP request and the subsequent reply message. First, the ARP request:

```
Capture 3:Packet 18

Destination  Source       Protocol     Summary         Size Time Tick
-----------------------------------------------------------------
24.24.78.1   24.24.78.84  ARP     Request    60         07/17/00 17:37:55.279

Addr.  Hex. Data                                       ASCII
0000:  FF FF FF FF FF FF 00 60 97 9E EA D5 08 06 00 01  .......'........
0010:  08 00 06 04 00 01 00 60 97 9E EA D5 18 18 4E 54  .......'......NT
0020:  00 00 00 00 00 00 18 18 4E 01                    ........N.

802.3 [0000:000D]
  0000:0005   Destination Address: FFFFFFFFFFFF (Broadcast)
  0006:000B   Source Address: 0060979EEAD5 (3Com9EEAD5)
  000C:000D   Ethernet Type: Address Resolution Protocol (ARP)
ARP [000E:0029]
  000E:000F   Hardware Type: Ethernet (10Mbps)
  0010:0011   Protocol Type: DOD Internet Protocol (IP)
  0012:0012   Hardware Address Length: 6
  0013:0013   Protocol Address Length: 4
  0014:0015   Opcode: Request
  0016:001B   Source HW Address: 0060979EEAD5
  001C:001F   Source IP Address: 24.24.78.84
  0020:0025   Destination HW Address: 000000000000
  0026:0029   Destination IP Address: 24.24.78.1
```

Notice that the destination hardware address contains all zeros. The ARP request is transmitted to the destination network in the form of a directed broadcast, asking which machine in that network has the IP address 24.24.78.1. The machine with that particular address responds with the ARP reply message as shown below:

```
Capture 3:Packet 19

Destination  Source       Protocol     Summary       Size  Time Tick
-----------------------------------------------------------------
24.24.78.84  24.24.78.1   ARP   Reply    60          07/17/00 17:37:55.324

Addr.  Hex. Data                                       ASCII
0000:  00 60 97 9E EA D5 08 00 3E 02 07 8D 08 06 00 01  .'......>.......
0010:  08 00 06 04 00 02 08 00 3E 02 07 8D 18 18 4E 01  ........>.....N.
0020:  00 60 97 9E EA D5 18 18 4E 54 8F 1E 76 01 00 00  .'......NT..v...
0030:  00 00 00 00 00 00 18 5E 3E 8A 60 51              .......^>.'Q

802.3 [0000:000D]
```

```
0000:0005   Destination Address: 0060979EEAD5 (3Com9EEAD5)
0006:000B   Source Address: 08003E02078D (Motorola02078D)
000C:000D   Ethernet Type: Address Resolution Protocol (ARP)
ARP [000E:0029]
000E:000F   Hardware Type: Ethernet (10Mbps)
0010:0011   Protocol Type: DOD Internet Protocol (IP)
0012:0012   Hardware Address Length: 6
0013:0013   Protocol Address Length: 4
0014:0015   Opcode: Reply
0016:001B   Source HW Address: 08003E02078D
001C:001F   Source IP Address: 24.24.78.1
0020:0025   Destination HW Address: 0060979EEAD5
0026:0029   Destination IP Address: 24.24.78.84
```

There is one more point worth noting with ARP messages. They are not encapsulated within an IP datagram and instead are encapsulated directly into an Ethernet frame as illustrated in Figure 8–18.

The Reverse Address Resolution Protocol (**RARP**) performs the opposite of ARP, providing the IP address for a specific MAC address. The message format for RARP is the same as the ARP message shown in Figure 8–17. RARP is usually performed on diskless computer workstations that do not have any other way of obtaining an IP address. A RARP server is used to perform the required translations. Figure 8–19 gives an example of both protocols at work.

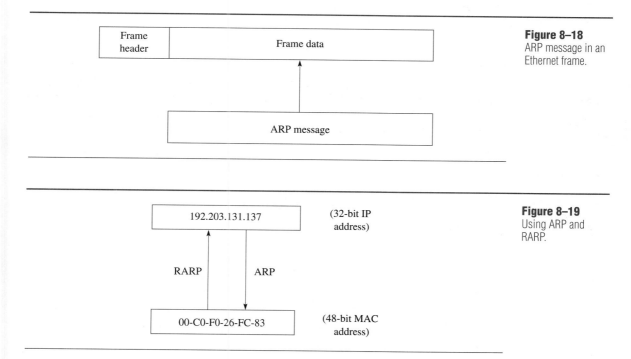

Figure 8–18
ARP message in an Ethernet frame.

Figure 8–19
Using ARP and RARP.

ARP is also the name of an application program that can be run from the DOS prompt. Online help for ARP appears as follows:

```
C:\>arp

Displays and modifies the IP-to-Physical address translation tables used by
address resolution protocol (ARP).

ARP -s inet_addr eth_addr [if_addr]
ARP -d inet_addr [if_addr]
ARP -a [inet_addr] [-N if_addr]

  -a              Displays current ARP entries by interrogating the current
                  protocol data.  If inet_addr is specified, the IP and Physical
                  addresses for only the specified computer are displayed.  If
                  more than one network interface uses ARP, entries for each ARP
                  table are displayed.
  -g              Same as -a.
  inet_addr       Specifies an Internet address.
  -N if_addr      Displays the ARP entries for the network interface specified
                  by if_addr.
  -d              Deletes the host specified by inet_addr.
  -s              Adds the host and associates the Internet address inet_addr
                  with the Physical address eth_addr.  The Physical address is
                  given as 6 hexadecimal bytes separated by hyphens. The entry
                  is permanent.
  eth_addr        Specifies a physical address.
  if_addr         If present, this specifies the Internet address of the
                  interface whose address translation table should be modified.
                  If not present, the first applicable interface will be used.
Example:
  > arp -s 157.55.85.212   00-aa-00-62-c6-09  .... Adds a static entry.
  > arp -a                                    .... Displays the arp table.
```

A display of the ARP table on a typical computer would reveal the physical address of the default router or gateway on the network. For example

```
C:\WINDOWS>arp -a

Interface: 24.24.78.84 on Interface 0x1000002
  Internet Address      Physical Address      Type
  24.24.78.1            08-00-3e-02-07-8d      dynamic
```

This is the only address that is required to send data back and forth across the Internet using the connection to a LAN. Try running ARP on your computer to see what the ARP table contains.

TCP/IP SUPPORT PROTOCOLS

DNS

Every machine on a network must be uniquely identified. On the Internet, this identification takes the form of what is called an *IP address*. The IP address consists of a 4-byte number, commonly represented in dotted decimal notation. For example, 204.210.133.51 specifies the IP address of some machine on some network somewhere in the world. To make it easier to remember an address, a *host* name can be associated with an IP address. The Domain Name Service provides the means to convert from a host name to an IP address and vice versa. Instead of using the IP address 204.210.133.51, we may instead enter "raycast.rwa.com" as the host name. Typically a DNS server application running on the local network has the responsibility of converting names to IP addresses.

DHCP

DHCP stands for Dynamic Host Configuration Protocol. DHCP is a protocol for dynamically assigning IP addresses to devices on a network during the bootstrap process. Using DHCP, a device may be assigned a different IP address every time it connects to the network. Sometimes a computer's IP address can even change while it is still connected to the network.

IP addresses are *leased* to a computer for a period of time set by the network administrator. Look ahead to Figure 8–26 for an example of a leased IP address. Before the lease expires, the network software will request a renewal of the lease.

DHCP addressing simplifies network administration because the software keeps track of IP addresses rather than requiring an administrator to manage the task. This means that a new computer can be added to a network without the hassle of manually assigning it a unique IP address. Many Internet service providers use dynamic IP addressing for dial-up users.

The basic operation of DHCP is outlined by the mnemonic ROSA, which stands for Request, Offer, Select, and Acknowledge. The DHCP client *requests* an IP address at boot time. The DHCP server *offers* an IP address. The client notifies the server of its *selection*. The server then *acknowledges* the selection.

Some additional properties of DHCP are as follows:

- Carried by UDP datagrams
- Based on earlier BOOTP protocol
- Found in RFCs 1533, 1534, 1541, and 1542
- DHCP client support is built into most operating systems including Windows, Unix/Linux, and many others.
- DHCP server support is provided by Windows NT Server, Unix/Linux, and other mainframe operating systems. Refer to Chapter 18 for additional information about running a DHCP server on Windows NT.

ICMP

Usually, when an IP datagram runs into trouble on the network, an error message is generated (which is sent back to the source computer) and then it is simply discarded. An error contained in an ICMP message may or may not be returned to the sender due to use of the UDP as the transport protocol. If an ICMP message must be discarded, no ICMP error message is generated. This is because of a specific rule in the implementation that prohibits error messages being generated about other error messages. Why do you think this rule exists? What are the consequences of not having such a rule?

The format of the ICMP header is shown in Figure 8–20. The entire message header contains only three fields. These fields and their descriptions are shown in Table 8–8. Depending on the value of the Type and Data fields, one or more additional descriptive data messages will follow. These messages will provide the necessary details to determine what happened when the message was generated.

Table 8–9 shows a list of the different ICMP messages. When Netscape gives you its "host unreachable" error message, it is an ICMP message that is responsible.

SMTP

The Simple Mail Transport Protocol (*SMTP*) is responsible for routing electronic mail on the Internet using TCP and IP. The process usually requires connecting to a remote computer and transferring the e-mail message, but due to problems with the network or a remote computer, messages can be temporarily undeliverable. The electronic mail server will try to deliver any messages by periodically trying to contact the remote destination. When the remote computer becomes available, the message is delivered using SMTP. Refer to Chapter 12 for more information on SMTP.

Figure 8–20
ICMP message format.

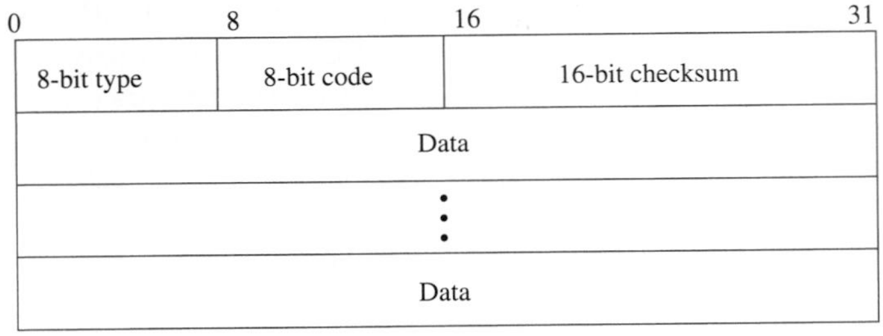

Table 8–8
ICMP header field information.

Header Field	Size	Meaning
Type	8 bits	Identifies the message type
Code	8 bits	Additional information based on the Type field
Checksum	16 bits	Checksum value computed using the ICMP message

Type	Code	Description	Query	Error
0	0	Echo reply	✔	
3		Destination unreachable		
	0	network unreachable		✔
	1	host unreachable		✔
	2	protocol unreachable		✔
	3	port unreachable		✔
	4	fragmentation needed but don't fragment bit set		✔
	5	source route failed		✔
	6	destination network unknown		✔
	7	destination host unknown		✔
	8	source host isolated (obsolete)		✔
	9	destination network administratively prohibited		✔
	10	destination host administratively prohibited		✔
	11	network unreachable for TOS		✔
	12	host unreachable for TOS		✔
	13	communication administratively prohibited by filtering		✔
	14	host precedence violation		✔
	15	precedence cutoff in effect		✔
4	0	Source quench (elementary flow control)		✔
5		Redirect		
	0	redirect for network		✔
	1	redirect for host		✔
	2	redirect for type-of-service and network		✔
	3	redirect for type-of-service and host		✔
8	0	Echo request	✔	
9	0	Router advertisement	✔	
10	0	Router solicitation	✔	
11		Time exceeded		
	0	time to live equals 0 during transit (trace route)		✔
	1	time to live equals 0 during assembly		✔
12		Parameter problem		
	0	IP header bad (catchall error)		✔
	1	required option missing		✔
13		Timestamp request	✔	
14		Timestamp reply	✔	
15		Information request (obsolete)	✔	
16		Information reply (obsolete)	✔	
17		Address mask request	✔	
18		Address mask reply	✔	

Table 8–9
ICMP messages.

SNMP

Network managers responsible for monitoring and controlling the network hardware and software use the Simple Network Management Protocol. *SNMP* defines the format and meaning of messages exchanged by the manager and agents. The network manager (*manager*) uses SNMP to interrogate network devices (*agents*) such as routers, switches, and bridges in order to determine their status and also retrieve statistical information. Chapter 11 contains additional details about SNMP.

HTTP

HTTP, the HyperText Transport Protocol, is used to transfer multimedia information over the Internet, such as Web pages, images, audio, and video. An HTTP client, such as a browser, sends a request to an HTTP server (also called an HTTP *daemon*), which services the request.

Figure 8–21 shows a portion of the sequence of HTTP messages exchanged between client and server while a Web page is being loaded. It is important to

Figure 8–21
A sequence of HTTP messages to display a Web page.

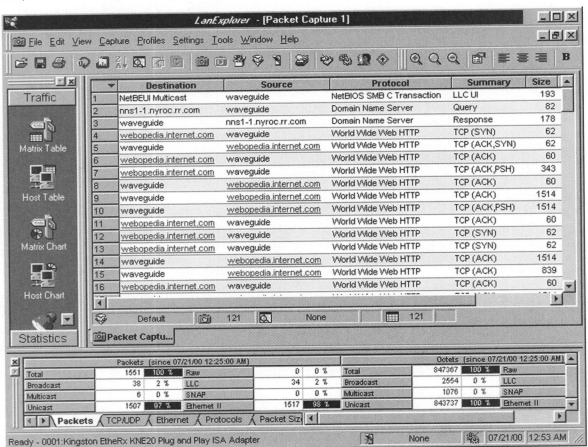

note that HTTP is carried via TCP and not UDP. There is a great deal of back and forth between the client and server, with many acknowledgment messages insuring reliable communication.

A packet containing the HTTP GET request is decoded for you to examine:

```
Capture 1:Packet 7

Destination Source       Protocol    Summary    Size    Time Tick
----------------------------------------------------------------------
63.236.73.230       192.168.1.105   World Wide Web HTTP   343   07/21/00
                                    TCP (ACK,PSH)        00:25:16.384

Addr.  Hex. Data                                         ASCII
0000:  00 20 78 C6 78 14 00 C0 F0 27 64 E2 08 00 45 00   . x.x....'d...E.
0010:  01 49 1F 07 40 00 40 06 CE C4 C0 A8 01 69 3F EC   .I..@.@......i?.
0020:  49 E6 05 0B 00 50 00 F6 E6 00 21 60 F5 5E 50 18   I....P....!'.^P.
0030:  FF FF 19 86 00 00 47 45 54 20 2F 54 45 52 4D 2F   ......GET /TERM/
0040:  73 2F 73 77 69 74 63 68 2E 68 74 6D 6C 20 48 54   s/switch.html HT
0050:  54 50 2F 31 2E 30 0D 0A 43 6F 6E 6E 65 63 74 69   TP/1.0..Connecti
0060:  6F 6E 3A 20 4B 65 65 70 2D 41 6C 69 76 65 0D 0A   on: Keep-Alive..
0070:  55 73 65 72 2D 41 67 65 6E 74 3A 20 4D 6F 7A 69   User-Agent: Mozi
0080:  6C 6C 61 2F 34 2E 35 31 20 5B 65 6E 5D 20 28 57   lla/4.51 [en] (W
0090:  69 6E 39 38 3B 20 49 29 0D 0A 48 6F 73 74 3A 20   in98; I)..Host:
00A0:  77 65 62 6F 70 65 64 69 61 2E 69 6E 74 65 72 6E   webopedia.intern
00B0:  65 74 2E 63 6F 6D 0D 0A 41 63 63 65 70 74 3A 20   et.com..Accept:
00C0:  69 6D 61 67 65 2F 67 69 66 2C 20 69 6D 61 67 65   image/gif, image
00D0:  2F 78 2D 78 62 69 74 6D 61 70 2C 20 69 6D 61 67   /x-xbitmap, imag
00E0:  65 2F 6A 70 65 67 2C 20 69 6D 61 67 65 2F 70 6A   e/jpeg, image/pj
00F0:  70 65 67 2C 20 69 6D 61 67 65 2F 70 6E 67 2C 20   peg, image/png,
0100:  2A 2F 2A 0D 0A 41 63 63 65 70 74 2D 45 6E 63 6F   */*..Accept-Enco
0110:  64 69 6E 67 3A 20 67 7A 69 70 0D 0A 41 63 63 65   ding: gzip..Acce
0120:  70 74 2D 4C 61 6E 67 75 61 67 65 3A 20 65 6E 0D   pt-Language: en.
0130:  0A 41 63 63 65 70 74 2D 43 68 61 72 73 65 74 3A   .Accept-Charset:
0140:  20 69 73 6F 2D 38 38 35 39 2D 31 2C 2A 2C 75 74    iso-8859-1,*,ut
0150:  66 2D 38 0D 0A 0D 0A                              f- ....

802.3 [0000:000D]
  0000:0005  Destination Address: 002078C67814 (RuntopC67814)
  0006:000B  Source Address: 00C0F02764E2 (Kingston2764E2)
  000C:000D  Ethernet Type: DOD Internet Protocol (IP)
IP [000E:0021]
  000E:000E  Version: 4, Header Length: 20
  000F:000F  TOS, Precedence: Routine, Delay: Normal, Throughput: Normal,
Reliability: Normal
  0010:0011  Packet Length: 329
  0012:0013  Identification: 0x1F07
  0014:0014  Fragment Flag (bit 6..5): Don't Fragment
```

```
0014:0015   Fragment Offset: 0x0000
0016:0016   Time to Live: 64
0017:0017   Transport: Transmission Control
0018:0019   Header Checksum: 0xCEC4
001A:001D   Source Address: 192.168.1.105
001E:0021   Destination Address: 63.236.73.230
TCP [0022:0035]
0022:0023   Source Port: 1291
0024:0025   Destination Port: World Wide Web HTTP
0026:0029   Sequence Number: 16180736
002A:002D   Acknowledgment Number: 560002398
002E:002E   Header Length (bit 7..4): 20
002F:002F   Control Bit - ACK; PSH;
0030:0031   Window Size: 65535
0032:0033   Checksum: 0x1986
0034:0035   Urgent Pointer: 0x0000
```

The GET request is contained within the data area of the TCP message. Some additional HTTP details are as follows:

- Version 1.1 is defined in RFC 2616.
- Well-known port number is 80.
- Methods are operations performed on HTTP objects. Some methods are GET, PUT, POST, DELETE, LINK, and TEXTSEARCH.
- Supports MIME.
- Supports compression on certain data types (HTML pages, for example).
- Utilizes a *persistent connection* to enable multiple requests and responses to use the same connection, eliminating the overhead of opening and closing a session for each item transferred.

TCP/IP APPLICATIONS

PING

PING is a TCP/IP application that sends datagrams once every second in the hope of an echo response from the machine being PINGed. If the machine is connected and running a TCP/IP protocol stack, it should respond to the PING datagram with a datagram of its own. If PING encounters an error condition, an ICMP message is returned. PING displays the time of the return response in milliseconds or one of several error messages (request timed out, destination host unreachable, etc.).

PING can be used to simply determine the IP address of a www site if you know its URL. For example, the IP address for www.yahoo.com is 204.71.200.75, which can be found with PING by opening a DOS window and entering

```
C> ping www.yahoo.com
```

You should see something similar to this:

```
Pinging www.yahoo.com [204.71.200.75] with 32 bytes of data:

Reply from 204.71.200.75: bytes=32 time=180ms TTL=245
Reply from 204.71.200.75: bytes=32 time=127ms TTL=245
Reply from 204.71.200.75: bytes=32 time=145ms TTL=245
Reply from 204.71.200.75: bytes=32 time=146ms TTL=245
```

So PING performed DNS on the URL to find out the IP address and then sent datagrams to Yahoo's host machine and displayed the responses. If you know the IP address you can enter it directly and PING will skip the DNS phase.

To get a list of PING's features, enter PING with no parameters. You should see something similar to this:

```
Usage: ping [-t] [-a] [-n count] [-l size] [-f] [-i TTL] [-v TOS]
            [-r count] [-s count] [[-j host-list] | [-k host-list]]
            [-w timeout] destination-list

Options:

    -t              Ping the specified host until interrupted.
    -a              Resolve addresses to hostnames.
    -n count        Number of echo requests to send.
    -l size         Send buffer size.
    -f              Set Don't Fragment flag in packet.
    -i TTL          Time To Live.
    -v TOS          Type Of Service.
    -r count        Record route for count hops.
    -s count        Timestamp for count hops.
    -j host-list    Loose source route along host-list.
    -k host-list    Strict source route along host-list.
    -w timeout      Timeout in milliseconds to wait for each reply.
```

PING can also be used to determine the MTU value between two networks. Normally, packet fragmentation automatically occurs without the knowledge of the source computer. PING can determine the MTU value between a source and destination computer by specifying that no fragmentation is allowed and choosing a custom message length to send. PING will display an ICMP error message if fragmentation is required to send the data but is not allowed to do so. For example, setting the do not fragment flag (-f) and sending a buffer size of 1472 bytes (-l 1472) of data is permitted when sending to www.yahoo.com as shown below:

```
C:\> ping -f -l 1472 www.yahoo.com

Pinging www.yahoo.akadns.net [204.71.200.75] with 1472 bytes of data:
```

```
Reply from 204.71.200.75: bytes=1472 time=140ms TTL=241
Reply from 204.71.200.75: bytes=1472 time=146ms TTL=241
Reply from 204.71.200.75: bytes=1472 time=145ms TTL=241
Reply from 204.71.200.75: bytes=1472 time=161ms TTL=241

Ping statistics for 204.71.200.75:
    Packets: Sent = 4, Received = 4, Lost = 0 (0% loss),
Approximate round trip times in milli-seconds:
    Minimum = 140ms, Maximum =  161ms, Average =  148ms
```

A packet capture using LanExplorer of a successful PING exchange looks like the following:

```
Capture 1:Packet 24


Destination  Source     Protocol   Summary      Size Time Tick
------------------------------------------------------------------------
204.71.200.67  24.24.78.84   ICMP   Echo   ID=0001  Seq=0020  1514  07/17/00
10:33:55.754


Addr.  Hex. Data                                              ASCII
0000:  08 00 3E 02 07 8D 00 60 97 9E EA D5 08 00 45 00    ..>....'......E.
0010:  05 DC 4C 02 40 00 20 01 0E 28 18 18 4E 54 CC 47    ..L.@. ..(..NT.G
0020:  C8 43 08 00 1F 48 01 00 20 00 61 62 63 64 65 66    .C...H.. .abcdef
0030:  67 68 69 6A 6B 6C 6D 6E 6F 70 71 72 73 74 75 76    ghijklmnopqrstuv
0040:  77 61 62 63 64 65 66 67 68 69 6A 6B 6C 6D 6E 6F    wabcdefghijklmno
.
.                  (1500 bytes of data)
.
0590:  63 64 65 66 67 68 69 6A 6B 6C 6D 6E 6F 70 71 72    cdefghijklmnopqr
05A0:  73 74 75 76 77 61 62 63 64 65 66 67 68 69 6A 6B    stuvwabcdefghijk
05B0:  6C 6D 6E 6F 70 71 72 73 74 75 76 77 61 62 63 64    lmnopqrstuvwabcd
05C0:  65 66 67 68 69 6A 6B 6C 6D 6E 6F 70 71 72 73 74    efghijklmnopqrst
05D0:  75 76 77 61 62 63 64 65 66 67 68 69 6A 6B 6C 6D    uvwabcdefghijklm
05E0:  6E 6F 70 71 72 73 74 75 76 77                      nopqrstuvw

802.3 [0000:000D]
  0000:0005  Destination Address: 08003E02078D (Motorola02078D)
  0006:000B  Source Address: 0060979EEAD5 (3Com9EEAD5)
  000C:000D  Ethernet Type: DOD Internet Protocol (IP)
IP [000E:0021]
  000E:000E  Version: 4; Header Length: 20
  000F:000F  TOS, Precedence: Routine; Delay: Normal; Throughput: Normal;
Reliability: Normal
  0010:0011  Packet Length: 1500
  0012:0013  Identification: 0x4C02
  0014:0014  DF: Don't Fragment; MF: Last Fragment
```

```
 0014:0015   Fragment Offset: 0
 0016:0016   Time to Live: 32
 0017:0017   Transport: Internet Control Message
 0018:0019   Header Checksum: 0x0E28 (correct)
 001A:001D   Source Address: 24.24.78.84
 001E:0021   Destination Address: 204.71.200.67
ICMP [0022:0029]
 0022:0022   Type: Echo
 0023:0023   Code: 0x00
 0024:0025   Checksum: 0x1F48
 0026:0027   Identifier: 0x0001
 0028:0029   Sequence Number: 32
```

Again, notice how the ICMP data is encapsulated inside of an IP datagram which is further encapsulated into an Ethernet frame.

During the experiment to determine the MTU value, what happens if one additional byte is added to the PING packet size? The PING operation fails and an ICMP error is returned as the following shows:

```
C:\>ping -f -l 1473 www.yahoo.com

Pinging www.yahoo.akadns.net [204.71.200.67] with 1473 bytes of data:

Packet needs to be fragmented but DF set.
Packet needs to be fragmented but DF set.
Packet needs to be fragmented but DF set.
Packet needs to be fragmented but DF set.

Ping statistics for 204.71.200.67:
    Packets: Sent = 4, Received = 0, Lost = 4 (100% loss),
Approximate round trip times in milli-seconds:
    Minimum = 0ms, Maximum =  0ms, Average =  0ms
```

It may seem strange to pick a PING buffer size value like 1472 when checking the MTU value, but the buffer size specifies only the data portion of the IP datagram. When the size of the IP header (20 bytes) is added to the size of the ICMP header (8 bytes) for a total header size of 28 bytes, the 1500 byte MTU is determined. So, as you can see, the 1473-byte message that was attempted is 1 byte too many.

You are encouraged to experiment further with all of the PING parameters.

TRACERT

TRACERT (trace route) is a TCP/IP application that determines the path through the network to a destination entered by the user. Creative use of ICMP messages is the basis for the trace route application.

For example, running

```
C> tracert www.yahoo.com
```

generates the following output:

```
Tracing route to www7.yahoo.com [204.71.200.72]
over a maximum of 30 hops:

  1     20 ms     19 ms     19 ms   bing100b.stny.lrun.com [204.210.132.1]
  2     10 ms     14 ms      9 ms   m2.stny.lrun.com [204.210.159.17]
  3     12 ms     24 ms     10 ms   ext_router.stny.lrun.com [204.210.155.18]
  4     46 ms     40 ms     44 ms   border3-serial4-0-6.Greensboro.mci.net [204.70.83.85]
  5     42 ms     53 ms     46 ms   core1-fddi-0.Greensboro.mci.net [204.70.80.17]
  6    109 ms    160 ms    122 ms   bordercore2.Bloomington.mci.net [166.48.176.1]
  7    123 ms    126 ms    113 ms   hssi1-0.br2.NUQ.globalcenter.net [166.48.177.254]
  8    125 ms    117 ms    115 ms   fe5-1.cr1.NUQ.globalcenter.net [206.251.1.33]
  9    114 ms    125 ms    113 ms   pos0-0.wr1.NUQ.globalcenter.net [206.251.0.122]
 10    125 ms    124 ms    121 ms   pos1-0-OC12.wr1.SNV.globalcenter.net [206.251.0.74]
 11    122 ms    139 ms    115 ms   pos5-0.cr1.SNV.globalcenter.net [206.251.0.105]
 12    128 ms    129 ms    138 ms   www7.yahoo.com [204.71.200.72]

Trace complete.
```

The trace indicates that it took 12 *hops* to get to Yahoo. Every hop is a connection between two routers on the network. Each router guides the test datagram from TRACERT one step closer to the destination. TRACERT specifically manipulates the TTL (time to live) parameter of the datagram, adding 1 to it each time it rebroadcasts the test datagram. Initially the TTL count is 1. This causes the very first router in the path to send back an ICMP time-exceeded message, which TRACERT uses to identify the router and display path information. When the TTL is increased to 2, the second router sends back the ICMP message, and so on, until the destination is reached (if it ever is).

It is fascinating to examine TRACERT's output. Notice that hop 5 contains a reference to *FDDI*, which means that the datagram spent some time traveling around a fiber-distributed data interface network.

Online help for the TRACERT program is availably by simply entering TRACERT at the DOS prompt as shown:

```
C:\tracert

Usage: tracert [-d] [-h maximum_hops] [-j host-list] [-w timeout] target_name

Options:
    -d                 Do not resolve addresses to hostnames.
    -h maximum_hops    Maximum number of hops to search for target.
    -j host-list       Loose source route along host-list.
    -w timeout         Wait timeout milliseconds for each reply.
```

You are encouraged to experiment with the TRACERT program.

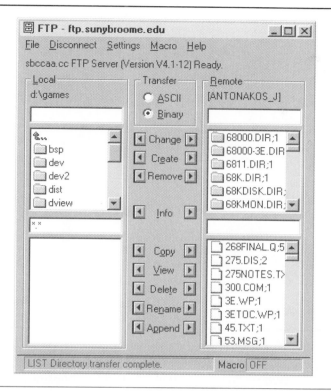

Figure 8–22
FTP application.

FTP

The File Transfer Protocol (*FTP*) allows a user to log in to a remote computer and transfer files back and forth through simple commands. Many FTP sites allow you to log in as an *anonymous* user, an open account with limited privileges, but still capable of file transfers. A typical FTP application might look like the one shown in Figure 8–22. Files may be transferred in either direction. Refer to Chapter 13 for more information about FTP.

Telnet

A Telnet session allows a user to establish a terminal emulation connection on a remote computer. For example, an instructor may Telnet into his or her college's mainframe to do some work. Figure 8–23 shows how the Telnet connection is set up.

Once the connection has been made, Telnet begins emulating the terminal selected in the Connection Dialog window. Figure 8–24 shows this mode of operation.

Refer to Chapter 13 for additional information about Telnet.

Figure 8–23
Establishing the
Telnet connection.

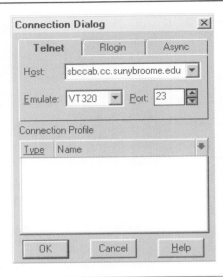

Figure 8–24
Sample Telnet
session.

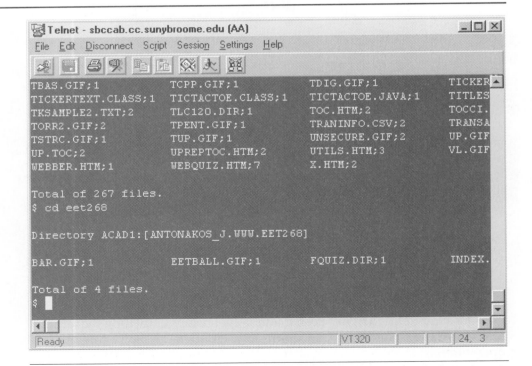

IP VERSION 6

One of the problems with the current version of the Internet is the lack of adequate addresses. Basically, there are no more conventional addresses available. Thanks to classless addressing techniques, however, some address space has been freed up and is still available. A new version of the Internet, sometimes called the "next generation Internet," has resolved many of the problems experienced by its predecessor.

For example, the address for the next generation Internet is 128 bits as opposed to 32 bits. This additional address space is large enough to accommodate network growth for the foreseeable future. Addresses are grouped into three different categories, *unicast* (single computer), *multicast* (a set of computers with the same address), and *cluster* (a set of computers that share a common address prefix), routed to one computer closest to the sender.

Other changes include different header formats, new extension headers, and support for audio and video. Unlike IP version 4, IP version 6 does not specify all of the possible protocol features. This allows for new features to be added without the need to update the protocol.

A review of all of the changes that IP version 6 introduces would actually require a complete reexamination of the same material that we have examined looking at version 4. Your best source about the next generation Internet is available to you right on the Web using a browser. You may also get to take a look at the competition to the next generation Internet version 6, the Internet 2.

PROTOCOL ANALYZERS

Protocol analyzers (or *sniffers*) are hardware or software devices that listen to the traffic on a network and capture various packets for examination. Hardware analyzers also double as cable testers.

Figure 8–25 shows a demo version of the LanExplorer protocol analyzer at work. LanExplorer displays an ongoing update of network traffic statistics, allows packets to be captured, disassembled, and saved, and can also transmit packets to facilitate testing and troubleshooting. You have already seen many of LanExplorer's abilities.

TROUBLESHOOTING TECHNIQUES

Windows provides a very useful utility called WINIPCFG, which you can run from the Run menu. Figure 8–26 shows the display window with all details included. Notice the various IP addresses indicated. Because the network software used by the system receives an IP address *on the fly*, via DHCP, the IP address of the DHCP server (24.94.33.64) is known to the system. DHCP is not used when your system has been allocated a fixed IP address by your network administrator.

Figure 8–25
LanExplorer protocol
analyzer window.

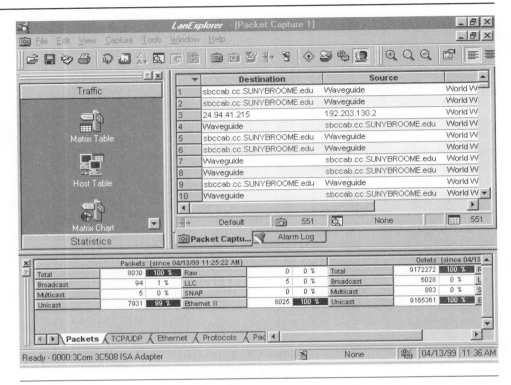

Figure 8–26
Windows IP
Configuration
window.

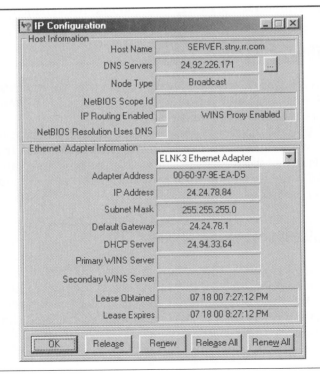

If you have difficulty with your network connection, the information displayed by WINIPCFG will be valuable to the individual troubleshooting the connection. Note that a similar application program is available on other operating systems as well.

SELF-TEST

This self-test is designed to help you check your understanding of the background information presented in this chapter.

True/False

Answer *true* or *false*.

1. IP addresses and MAC addresses are the same thing.

2. The ISO/OSI network model defines the nine network layers.

3. RFCs are documents that describe how each of the TCP/IP protocols are implemented.

4. IP datagrams are guaranteed to be delivered.

5. Loopback testing allows for a remote method to test TCP/IP and application functionality.

Multiple Choice

Select the best answer.

6. TCP connections are
   a. Unreliable and must rely on the IP protocol to provide the necessary reliability.
   b. Created using predefined ports or sockets.
   c. Considered connectionless without the need to acknowledge the received data.
   d. Limited to class A addresses.

7. Dotted decimal notation is used to describe
   a. Each of the five address classes.
   b. All of the networks and hosts on the Internet.
   c. Reserved addresses used for special purposes.
   d. All of the above.
   e. None of the above.

8. DNS servers provide
   a. The MAC address for every host address.
   b. The error checking protocol for ICMP messages.
   c. A mapping from a host name to an IP address.
   d. A mechanism to transfer IP packets over serial lines.

9. How many different class C networks are shown in the TRACERT output for Yahoo?
   a. 8.
   b. 9.
   c. 10.

10. To find out the adapter address (MAC address), use
   a. PING.
   b. TRACERT.
   c. WINIPCFG.

Matching

Match a description of the items on the right with each item on the left.

11. TCP
12. Flow Control
13. TCP/IP
14. UDP
15. FTP

a. Unreliable protocol
b. Connection-oriented File Transfer Protocol
c. Connection-oriented protocol
d. Sliding window
e. UDP, TCP, and ICMP protocols

Completion

Fill in the blank or blanks with the best answers.

16. Most FTP sites allow for _____ login.

17. DHCP is used to assign IP _____.

18. A _____ describes each of the TCP/IP protocols.

19. IP addresses are commonly shown in _____ _____ _____.

20. To determine the path to an IP address use _____.

QUESTIONS/ACTIVITIES

1. What is the purpose of a set of protocols?

2. Why do you think IP addresses are used for routing instead of MAC addresses?

3. How can the value of a remote computer's MAC address be determined?

4. What do you think is the problem with generating error messages about error messages?

5. How can you stop a packet from being fragmented while in transit on the network?

6. How does an IP message get delivered to the correct computer on a remote LAN?

REVIEW QUIZ

Under the supervision of your instructor

1. Describe how the TCP/IP protocol stack is organized compared to the ISO/OSI protocol stack.

2. Discuss the different protocols that make up the TCP/IP suite.

3. Show how TCP/IP data is encapsulated inside a hardware frame for transmission.

4. Describe the relationship between IP addresses and MAC addresses.

5. Discuss the role of the PING and TRACERT applications.

Networking Concepts Laboratory

Experiment #8

TCP/IP

Objectives

1. To examine the properties of various TCP/IP protocols using LanExplorer.
2. To capture the client-server message exchanges for several client-server applications.

Required Equipment

The following equipment is required for this experiment:

- Two or more computers connected by a network, with access to the Internet
- LanExplorer software

Procedure

Perform each of the following steps. Record your observations, results, and any difficulties you encounter. You will use this information when you develop your conclusions about the experiment.

1. Using LanExplorer, do the following:
   - Capture several packets and note the type of packets captured.
   - Watch the network statistics for several minutes.
   - Identify all the different protocols present on the network.
2. Visit the computer center at your school and ask the network technicians to share information about the IP classes in use, what network management protocols are used, and how many nodes are on the network.
3. Look up the term *broadcast storm* in a networking dictionary (or search the Web for it). What is a broadcast storm, what are its effects, and how can it be prevented?
4. PING all of the following addresses. Capture the results using LanExplorer.
   - www.yahoo.com
   - www.intel.com
   - www.whitehouse.gov
   - www.nasa.gov
   - 192.203.131.137

   PING an additional five addresses of your own choosing.
   Make a note of the response time for each. If possible, PING the same addresses at a different time of the day. State your findings.

5. Run TRACERT on the addresses in step 4. Comment on any interesting router names that show up.
6. Run WINIPCFG to determine the lease of the DHCP address for the computer you use in the lab. Make a note of the IP address currently assigned.
7. Capture a complete exchange of the packets exchanged while a Web page is loading. What do you find interesting about the packets?

Discussion and Conclusion

Using a word processor, write your own detailed explanations of the results and observations made during the experiment. To begin, try to say something about each procedure step.

In addition, provide answers to the following questions:

1. What are the port numbers used by the server and client connections for each of the packet captures?
2. What is the window size for TCP transfers for each of the packet captures? Does the window size change?
3. Which protocol, TCP or UDP, is used most often in each of your packet captures?

9

IPX/SPX, AppleTalk, and Other Network Protocols

PERFORMANCE OBJECTIVES

Upon completion of this chapter, you will be able to

• Discuss the features of the IPX/SPX, AppleTalk, DECnet, and SNA protocols.

• Describe how IPX/SPX is similar to TCP/IP.

Joe Tekk watched while his friend, Ken Koder, tried to get a software module to compile.

"What are you working on, Ken?" Joe asked, always curious about Ken's projects.

"I'm converting some IPX/SPX network code over to TCP/IP," Ken answered, "so I can use it in my remote security application."

Joe examined several pages of program listings. "Where did you get the code, from the Web?"

"Yes, "Ken said, "There's code all over the place."

That night, Joe spent several hours locating and archiving his own library of networking code.

INTRODUCTION

In this chapter we continue our examination of networking protocols. Each protocol family (except for IPX/SPX) was developed by a computer manufacturer in order to network their own computers together.

In order, we will look at

- IPX/SPX (from Novell)
- AppleTalk (from Apple Computer)
- DECnet (from Digital Equipment Corporation)
- SNA (from IBM)

As you read about each new suite of protocols, try to find similarities between them.

⬛⬛ IPX/SPX

The IPX/SPX protocol suite, developed by Novell for its NetWare network operating system, is based on the Xerox Network System (XNS), which was developed in the 1970s. It is similar to the TCP/IP protocol suit, offering connectionless and connection-oriented delivery. Figure 9–1 shows the IPX/SPX protocols and their relationship to the OSI networking model. Let us take a look at each protocol.

IPX

The Internet Packet Exchange (IPX) protocol is similar to UDP under TCP/IP, providing connectionless, unreliable network communication. IPX packets are used to carry higher-level protocols such as SPX, RIP, NCP, and SAP.

Figure 9–2 shows the 30-byte IPX header format. The Checksum field is normally set to FFFF hexadecimal and is typically not used for error detection. The Length field indicates the number of bytes in the IPX packet, including the 30-byte header. The maximum size of an IPX packet is 576 bytes, providing 546 bytes of data.

The Transport Control field is initially set to 0 by the transmitting station (the source node) and is incremented each time the IPX packet passes through a router. Thus, it indicates the number of hops the packet has encountered on the way to its destination. Using RIP, this field may not exceed 16 (the maximimum hop count), or the packet is discarded.

The Packet Type field indicates the higher-level protocol encapsulated in the IPX packet. Table 9–1 lists the values associated with each higher-level protocol.

Figure 9–1
NetWare protocol suite.

ISO/OSI Layer	IPX/SPX Protocols		
7 = Application	NCP	SAP	RIP
6 = Presentation			
5 = Session			
4 = Transport	SPX		
3 = Network	IPX		
2 = Data link	LSL 802.2 MAC		
1 = Physical	802.3 Ethernet 802.5 Token ring		

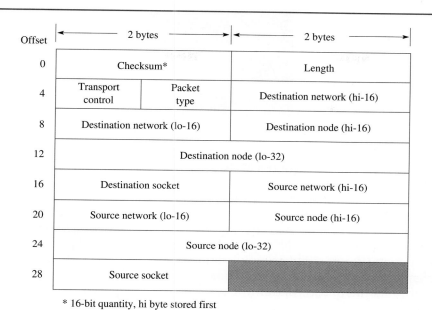

Figure 9–2
30-byte IPX header.

Offset				
	◄——— 2 bytes ———►		◄——— 2 bytes ———►	
0	Checksum*		Length	
4	Transport control	Packet type	Destination network (hi-16)	
8	Destination network (lo-16)		Destination node (hi-16)	
12	Destination node (lo-32)			
16	Destination socket		Source network (hi-16)	
20	Source network (lo-16)		Source node (hi-16)	
24	Source node (lo-32)			
28	Source socket			

* 16-bit quantity, hi byte stored first

Table 9–1
IPX packet types.

Packet Type Value	Protocol
0	Unknown
1	RIP
2	Echo packet
3	Error packet
4	PEP
5	SPX
17	NCP

The remainder of the IPX header is dedicated to storing the Destination and Source Network, Node, and Socket addresses. The 32-bit Network address is similar to, but not the same as, an IP address. The IPX network addressing space is flat, meaning there is no subnetting allowed. An address of 00000000H indicates the Source and Destination nodes are on the same network and no routing is required.

Node addresses are unique 48-bit MAC addresses. Broadcasting is accomplished by using FFFFFFFFFFFFH for the Destination node.

The Socket number is similar to the port number used in TCP/IP. Table 9–2 lists some well-known IPX Socket numbers.

Socket	Function
451H	NCP Server
452H	SAP
453H	RIP
455H	NetBIOS

NCP

The NetWare Core Protocol (NCP) is the workhorse of NetWare, responsible for the majority of traffic on a NetWare network. Spanning three layers of the OSI protocol stack (Session, Presentation, and Application), NCP carries all file system traffic in addition to numerous other functions, including printing, name management, and establishing connection-oriented sessions between servers and workstations. NCP provides connection-oriented packet transmission allowing for positive acknowledgment of each packet. A more efficient implementation called NCPB (NetWare Core Protocol Burst) was added to reduce the amount of control traffic necesary when using NCP.

SPX

The Sequenced Packet Exchange (SPX) protocol is similar to TCP under TCP/IP, providing connection-oriented communication that is reliable (lost packets are retransmitted). SPX packets contain a sequence number that allow packets received out of order to be reassembled correctly. Flow control is used to synchronize both ends of the connection to achieve maximum throughput.

Figure 9–3 compares an ordinary IPX packet and one encapsulating the SPX protocol. Since the overall IPX packet length is limited to 576 bytes, the size of the Data portion must shrink by 12 bytes to accommodate the SPX header. The 12 bytes are allocated as indicated in Figure 9–4.

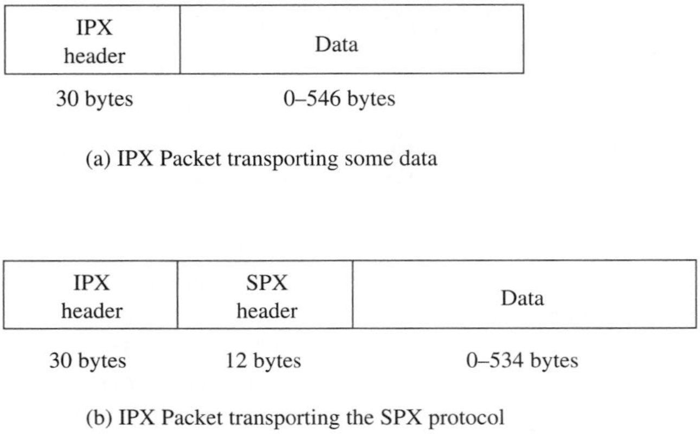

Figure 9–3
Different types of IPX packets.

IPX header	Data
30 bytes	0–546 bytes

(a) IPX Packet transporting some data

IPX header	SPX header	Data
30 bytes	12 bytes	0–534 bytes

(b) IPX Packet transporting the SPX protocol

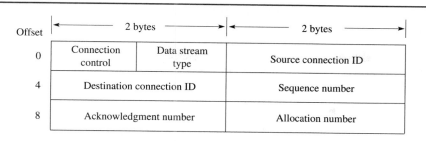

Figure 9–4
SPX header.

The meaning and purpose of each portion of the SPX header is as follows:

- Connection Control: A set of four flags that are used to help control the connection. Table 9–3 lists the flags values and their meanings. Note that only the upper 4 bits of the 8-bit Connection Control number are used.
- Data Stream Type: This number provides information on the type of data included in the SPX packet. As indicated in Table 9–4, values between 0 and 253 are ignored by SPX (and can be used by applications for identification). The values 254 and 255 are used when a connection terminates.
- Source Connection ID and Destination Connection ID: Used to identify the connection associated with the packet.

The reliability of SPX is a function of the Sequence and Acknowledgment numbers. Every SPX packet in a stream of packets making up a large message contains a unique Sequence number. The Acknowledgment number indicates which Sequence number the receiving application expects next and also serves to acknowledge reception of all previous (lower) Sequence numbers.

Connection Control Flag	Meaning
10H (bit 4)	Last packet in message
20H (bit 5)	Attention
40H (bit 6)	Acknowledgment
80H (bit 7)	System packet

Table 9–3
Connection Control flag values.

Data Stream Type	Meaning
0–253	Ignored by SPX
254	End of connection
255	End of connection Ack

Table 9–4
Data Stream Type values.

For example, an Acknowledgment number of 100 acknowledges that packets numbered up to 99 have already been received.

The number of receive buffers available to be managed by flow control are indicated by the Allocation number.

For more information on IPX and SPX, check out a good comparison of TCP/IP and IPX/SPX located at

http://www.odyssea.com/WHATS_NEW/tcpipnet/tcpipnet.html

SAP

The Service Advertising Protocol (SAP) is a broadcast protocol that is used to maintain a database of servers and routers connected to the NetWare network.

RIP

Like SAP, the Routing Information Protocol (**RIP**) is also a broadcast protocol. RIP is used by routers to exchange their routing tables. Multiple routers on the same network discover each other (during a RIP broadcast) and build entries for all networks that can be reached through each other. When conditions on the network change (a link goes down or is added), the change will be propagated from router to router (using RIP packets).

MLID

The Multiple Link Interface Driver (MLID) provides the interface between the network hardware and the network software. A specification called *ODI (Open Data-Link Interface)* is supported by MLID. ODI allows NetWare clients to use multiple protocols over the same network interface card. The LSL (Link Support Layer) provides the ODI facilities.

APPLETALK

The AppleTalk suite of protocols were developed in the 1980s for use in networks of Macintosh computers. The two versions of AppleTalk are called Phase 1 and Phase 2. AppleTalk Phase 1, the initial version, limited networks to 127 workstations and 127 servers. This limited network is called a *nonextended* network. AppleTalk Phase 2 breaks the restriction and allows workstation/server numbers to be anything between 1 and 253. Larger networks are made possible by assigning multiple network numbers to a network. AppleTalk Phase 2 networks are called *extended* networks.

As indicated in Figure 9–5, AppleTalk contains a rich set of protocols. Brief descriptions of each protocol are shown in Table 9–5.

There is wide support for AppleTalk in the Data-Link and Physical layers, with several different Link Access Protocol drivers available (such as EtherTalk for Ethernet and TokenTalk for token ring).

Once again, connectionless (DDP) and connection-oriented (ADSP) packet delivery is provided. Note that reliable ADSP messages are carried by unreliable DDP packets. In fact, every protocol above the Network layer is carried by a DDP packet.

ISO/OSI Layer	Apple Talk		Protocols		
7 Application				AFP	Postscript
6 Presentation					
5 Session	ZIP	ASP	PAP	ADSP	
4 Transport	AEP	ATP	NBP	RTMP	AURP
3 Network	AARP		DDP		
2 Data link	ELAP	TLAP	FLAP	LLAP	ARAP
1 Physical	Ethernet 802.3	Token ring 802.5	FDDI	Local talk	Serial (RS–422)

Figure 9–5
AppleTalk protocol suite.

Protocol	Name	Function
AFP	AppleTalk Filing Protocol	Allows applications to communicate with network
ZIP	Zone Information Protocol	Maintains zone information
ASP	AppleTalk Session Protocol	Start-up/tear-down session
PAP	Printer Access Protocol	Provides network printing service
ADSP	AppleTalk Data Stream Protocol	Reliable packet delivery
AEP	AppleTalk Echo Protocol	Echo's packet from receiver back to sender
ATP	AppleTalk Transaction Protocol	Reliable packet delivery
NBP	Name Binding Protocol	Associates device names with network addresses
RTMP	Routing Table Maintenance Protocol	Discovers routing information
AURP	AppleTalk Update Routing Protocol	Updates routing tables only during changes to network
AARP	AppleTalk Address Resolution Protocol	Maps AppleTalk address to physical addresses
DDP	Datagram Delivery Protocol	Unreliable packet delivery
ELAP	EtherTalk Link Access Protocol	IEEE 802.3 Ethernet
TLAP	TokenTalk Link Access Protocol	IEEE 802.5 Token Ring
FLAP	FDDITalk Link Access Protocol	100 Mbps FDDI
LLAP	LocalTalk Link Access Protocol	230 Kbps RS-422 Serial
ARAP	AppleTalk Remote Access Protocol	Network access using serial line

Table 9–5
AppleTalk protocols.

Table 9–6
Network Node
number
assignments.

Network Node Number	Assignment
0	Reserved
1–127	Workstation
128–254	Server
255	Reserved

File sharing is accomplished using AFP, which relies on a session controlled by ATP and ASP.

ZIP is used to help manage the *zones* used in an AppleTalk extended network. A zone is a logical group of computers that may belong to different networks. Every computer on an extended network belongs to a single zone, or to no zone at all.

NBP is used to associate AppleTalk names with network addresses. Network addresses are composed of three parts:

- 16-bit Network number
- 8-bit Node number
- 8-bit Socket number

For example, in the network address 50.66.100, the Network number is 50, the Node number is 66, and the Socket number is 100. Phase 1 Node numbers are assigned as indicated in Table 9–6.

Figure 9–6 illustrates the different fields of the DDP header. Most of the header is devoted to storing the Source and Destination network addresses. The Hop Count is used by RIP to control the lifetime of the packet during routing. There are many excellent Web sites containing detailed discussions of AppleTalk networking. Visit

http://www.ieng.com/univercd/cc/td/doc/cisintwk/ito_doc/applet.htm

for additional information.

 **DECNET**

The DECnet suite of protocols was created by Digital Equipment Corporation (DEC) in 1974 to connect DEC minicomputers together. The DECnet protocols are based on a network architecture that is referred to as the Digital Network Architecture (DNA). Figure 9–7 shows the relationship between DNA and the OSI model. The DNA link access protocols that span the bottom two layers of the OSI model may be Ethernet, DDCMP (Digital Data Communication Message Protocol), X.25, token ring, FDDI, CI (a proprietary DEC computer interconnect), and several others. Note that the CI was originally used to establish cluster communications on the DEC Open-VMS operating system. Today, cluster communications can simply be made through a NIC card running Ethernet.

Figure 9–6
DDP header fields.

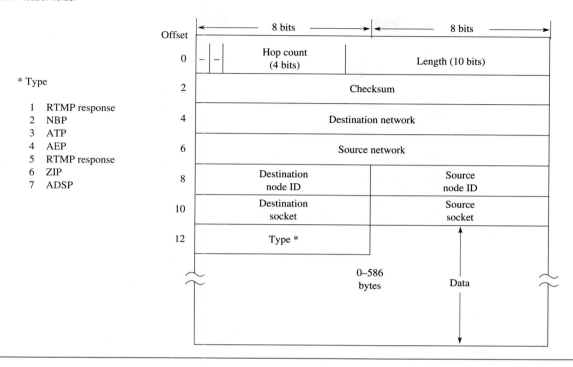

The DECnet protocol suite includes the following:

- CTERM—Command Terminal
- DAP—Data Access Protocol
- LAT—Local Area Transport
- LAVC—Local Area VAX Cluster
- MOP—Maintenance Operation Protocol
- NSP—Network Service Protocol
- RP—Routing Protocol
- SCP—Session Control Protocol
- STP—Spanning Tree Protocol

This list of names would only be familiar to someone with a DEC computer background.

The two most common versions of the DECnet protocol are Phase IV (released in 1982) and Phase V (released in 1987). DECnet Phase IV is fully compatible under DECnet Phase V. DECnet Phase V supports all of the OSI protocols, but in addition it also supports DEC proprietary protocols and maintains compatibility with DECnet Phase IV. DECnet Phase V is commonly referred to as DECnet OSI.

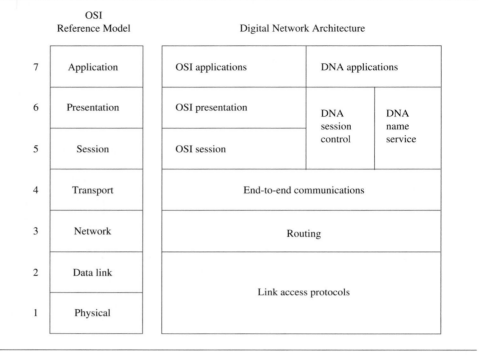

The address format of these two versions of DECnet is shown in Figure 9–8. In a DECnet Phase IV network, the address consists of two parts, each 1 byte in length. These two parts are called the Area number and the Node number. The Area number must be between 1 and 63, and the Node number must be between 1 and 1023. The combination of these two values allows for almost 65,000 computers per DECnet network.

In a DECnet Phase V network, the address also consists of two parts but may contain up to 20 bytes, as illustrated in Figure 9–8(b). The first part of the address is called the initial domain part (IDP). The IDP contains two fields:

- Authority and format identifier (AFI)
- Initial domain identifier (IDI)

The second part of the address, called the domain-specific part (DSP), has four fields called

- PreDSP
- Local area
- Node ID
- Selector (SEL)

The increased size of the address provides for a much larger network.

In an Ethernet network, the DEC network protocols are assigned several different Ethernet type fields. Refer to Table 9–7 for a list of the assigned Ethernet

(a) DECnet phase IV address (2 bytes).

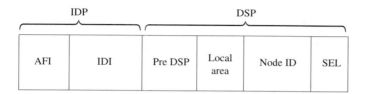

(b) DECnet phase V address (up to 20 bytes).

Figure 9–8
DECnet address
formats.

Table 9–7
Ethernet type fields
for DEC network
protocols.

Ethernet Type (hex)	DEC Protocol Description
6000	DEC unassigned, experimental
6001	DEC Maintenance Operation Protocol (MOP) Dump/Load Assistance
6002	DEC Maintenance Operation Protocol (MOP) Remote Console
6003	DECNET Phase IV, DNA Routing
6004	DEC Local Area Transport (LAT)
6005	DEC diagnostic protocol
6006	DEC customer protocol
6007	DEC Local Area VAX Cluster (LAVC), System Communication Architecture (SCA)
6008	DEC AMBER
6009	DEC MUMPS
8038	DEC LanBridge Management
8039	DEC DSM/DDP
803A	DEC Argonaut Console
803B	DEC VAXELN
803C	DEC DNS Naming Service
803D	DEC Ethernet CSMA/CD Encryption Protocol
803E	DEC Distributed Time Service
803F	DEC LAN Traffic Monitor Protocol
8040	DEC PATHWORKS DECnet NETBIOS Emulation
8041	DEC Local Area System Transport
8042	DEC unassigned

types. An enhanced version of DECnet provides the ability to use DECnet in an IBM token-ring environment. Note that Compaq Corporation purchased DEC in 1998.

 ## SNA

The SNA (Systems Network Architecture) protocol was designed by IBM to allow communication between IBM mainframe computers and any other types of computers that support SNA. In the early days of SNA, all traffic on the network required processing by a mainframe computer.

The architecture of the SNA protocols contains seven layers, the same as in the OSI model. The names of the layers are different, as shown in Figure 9–9. The SNA protocol stack is further divided into two segments called the Path Control network and the NAU network. The Path Control network portion is responsible for the delivery of network information. The Advanced Communications Function/Network Control Program (ACF/NCP) is used to manage the Path Control network.

The NAU layers of the network are responsible for controlling the process to move the data between the source and the destination. A NAU is any entity on the network that can be assigned a network address. These entities are

Figure 9–9
SNA protocol stack.

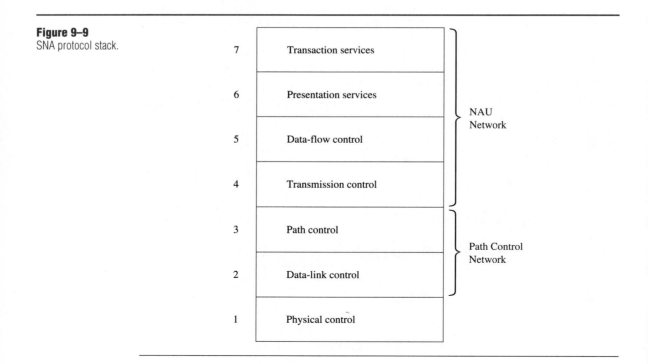

grouped into three categories called a host, a communications controller, and a peripheral. The communication between two NAUs is called a session.

SNA categorizes the network entities into physical units and logical units. A physical unit contains all of the necessary hardware and software to control a logical unit. A logical unit is used to access the programs run by the end user. A physical unit is designed to manage many logical units. To connect the logical units together, IBM developed several systems to offer different types of network application services. These application services are

- CICS (Customer Information Control System)
- CMS (Conversational Monitor System)
- IMS (Information Management System)
- TSO (Time Sharing Option)

In general, these services are provided by system applications that are bundled inside of the operating system that are able to take full advantage of all network resources. You are encouraged to learn more about each of these network services.

When the capabilities of the personal computer were added to SNA in the 1980s, a new feature called Advanced Program-to-Program Communication (APPC) was developed. This allowed for communication directly between two PCs. To accommodate the additional network communication requirements, a physical unit and a logical unit were added to the SNA protocol. APPC allows for two programs on the same computer to communicate, as well as client-server applications. Table 9–8 lists the physical unit types and Table 9–9 lists the logical unit types within an SNA network. The System Service Control Point (SSCP) services are used to manage all (or part) of the sessions on the physical and logical units within a network, which collectively make up a domain. An SNA network session can take on many different forms. For example, a session can be established between any of the following entities:

- Logical unit to logical unit
- Physical unit to physical unit
- SSCP to logical unit
- SSCP to physical unit

Physical Unit Types	Description
1	Low-end peripheral node (obsolete)
2.0	Peripheral node
2.1	APPC peripheral node
4	Sub-area node
5	Host processor

Table 9–8
SNA physical unit types.

Table 9–9
SNA logical unit types.

Logical Unit Types	Description
0	User-defined logical unit
1	Printer supporting SCS (SNA character strings)
2	Terminal device
3	Printer that does not support SCS
4	Peer-to-peer communication using SCS
6.0	Program-to-program communication using CICS
6.1	Program-to-program communication using CICS or IMS
6.2	General purpose program-to-program communication not requiring the service of a host computer (APPC)
7	Communication between a host and terminal supporting SCS or stream data

Two additional types of communication are also provided. SSCP to SSCP is used to enable communication between two host computers and control point to control point is used to provide communication between two APPN applications.

An even more advanced networking solution from IBM is called Advanced Peer-to-Peer Networking (APPN). APPN is part of the IBM Systems Applications Architecture and offers more flexibility than SNA with the added benefits of dynamic routing.

In summary, each of the protocols in this chapter provides a unique and elegant solution to solve the problem of computer communications.

 TROUBLESHOOTING TECHNIQUES

The large number of protocols in use on today's networks requires a good understanding of their basic principles of operation. There are many excellent online references that provide valuable protocol information. Some places to examine can be found at

- http://www.protocols.com
- http://www.techfest.com/networking/prot.htm

In addition, many companies will send you a free networking poster, such as one showing several protocols and their OSI model layers, or another detailing Voice over IP protocols. Try searching the Web for "networking poster" or something similar. You will have to navigate through the search results carefully. Some sites make it easy to find their free poster, others will require you to dig through them. It took one student only five minutes to order posters from three different companies, so spending a few minutes doing this research on the Web will be very rewarding.

SELF-TEST

This self-test is designed to help you check your understanding of the background information presented in this chapter.

True/False

Answer *true* or *false*.

1. IPX is a reliable packet delivery protocol.

2. DDP is a reliable packet delivery protocol.

3. Nonextended AppleTalk networks may be larger than extended networks.

4. DECnet Phase IV protocols are fully compatible with the OSI model.

5. Advanced Program-to-Program Communication (APPC) is part of SNA.

6. The SNA protocol stack is implemented in 8 layers.

7. DECnet is part of the Systems Applications Architecture.

Multiple Choice

Select the best answer.

8. The maximum length of an IPX packet is
   a. 534 bytes.
   b. 546 bytes.
   c. 576 bytes.

9. A TCP/IP port is similar to an SPX
   a. Socket.
   b. Port.
   c. I/O channel.

10. In the AppleTalk network address 10.20.30, the Node number is
    a. 10.
    b. 20.
    c. 30.

11. Digital Equipment Corporation created the _____ _____ architecture.
    a. Digital Network.
    b. Systems Applications.
    c. Network Application.

12. In an SNA network, a _____ can be assigned an address.
    a. DAU.
    b. MAU.
    c. NAU.

13. A DECnet Phase V network address may contain up to _____ bytes.
    a. 2.
    b. 10.
    c. 20.

Completion

Fill in the blank or blanks with the best answers.

14. MLID stands for _____ Link Interface Driver.

15. A logical group of AppleTalk computers is called a _____.

16. The Ethernet driver for AppleTalk is called _____.

17. A collection of logical unit and physical units in an SNA network is called a _____.

18. The communication between two _____ is called a session.

19. SSCP to SSCP communication is used to communicate between two _____ computers.

20. DECnet Phase V is commonly referred to as DECnet _____.

QUESTIONS/ACTIVITIES

1. Search the Web for information about the Banyan VINES protocol suite. Create any figures and tables that are needed to explain the basic operation of the protocol suite and where the protocols are used.

2. How is the reliable protocol SPX possible, when it is transported using the unreliable protocol IPX?

3. What is XNS? Generate a small table of features and a diagram, if necessary, to explain its architecture.

REVIEW QUIZ

Under the supervision of your instructor

1. Discuss the features of the IPX/SPX, AppleTalk, DECnet, and SNA protocols.

2. Describe how IPX/SPX is similar to TCP/IP.

Networking Concepts Laboratory

Experiment #9
IPX/SPX, AppleTalk, and Other Network Protocols

Objectives

1. To examine the properties of various non-TCP/IP protocols.
2. To capture one or more non-TCP/IP protocols using LanExplorer.

Required Equipment

The following equipment is required for this experiment:

- One or more computers connected by a network, with access to the Internet
- LanExplorer software

Procedure

Perform each of the following steps. Record your observations, results, and any difficulties you encounter. You will use this information when you develop your conclusions about the experiment.

1. Examine the following decoded IPX packet. What do you find that is similar to a TCP/IP packet? What do you find is different?

```
Protocol Summary: SAP Response, Raw IPX


Addr.   Hex. Data                                            ASCII
0000:   FF FF FF FF FF FF 00 60 B0 4B E9 96 00 60 FF FF      .......'.K...'..
0010:   00 60 00 00 00 00 00 01 FF FF FF FF FF FF 04 52      .'.............R
0020:   00 00 00 01 00 60 B0 4B E9 96 04 52 00 02 03 0C      .....'.K...R....
0030:   30 30 36 30 42 30 34 42 45 39 39 36 38 33 43 52      0060B04BE99683CR
0040:   4E 50 49 34 42 45 39 39 36 00 00 00 00 00 00 00      NPI4BE996.......
0050:   00 00 00 00 00 00 00 00 00 00 00 00 00 00 00 00      ................
0060:   00 00 00 01 00 60 B0 4B E9 96 40 0C 00 01            .....'.K..@...

802.3 [0000:000D]
  0000:0005   Destination Address: FFFFFFFFFFFF (Broadcast)
  0006:000B   Source Address: 0060B04BE996 (Hewlett-Packard4BE996)
  000C:000D   Ethernet Length: 96
IPX [000E:002B]
  000E:000F   Checksum: 0xFFFF
  0010:0011   Packet Length: 96
```

```
0012:0012   Transport Control: 0x00
0013:0013   Packet Type: Unknown Packet Type
0014:0017   Destination Network: 0x00000001
0018:001D   Destination Node: FFFFFFFFFFFF
001E:001F   Destination Socket: Service Advertising Protocol
0020:0023   Source Network: 0x00000001
0024:0029   Source Node: 0060B04BE996
002A:002B   Source Socket: Service Advertising Protocol
SAP [002C:006D]
002C:002D   Operation: Response
002E:002F   (1) Service Type: Intel Netport 2 or HP JetDirect or HP
Quicksilver
0030:005F   (1) Server Name: 0060B04BE99683CRNPI4BE996
0060:0063   (1) Network Address: 0x00000001
0064:0069   (1) Node Address: 0060B04BE996
006A:006B   (1) Socket: 0x400C
006C:006D   (1) Hops to Server: 1
```

2. **Repeat step 1 for this AppleTalk packet:**

```
Protocol Summary: Apple ARP, Request

Addr.  Hex. Data                                          ASCII
0000:   09 00 07 FF FF FF 00 50 E4 66 00 5B 00 24 AA AA   .......P.f.[.$..
0010:   03 00 00 00 80 F3 00 01 80 9B 06 04 00 01 00 50   ...............P
0020:   E4 66 00 5B 00 00 C8 65 00 00 00 00 00 00 00 00   .f.[...e........
0030:   C8 5A 55 55 55 55 55 55 55 55 55 55               .ZUUUUUUUUUU

802.3 [0000:000D]
0000:0005   Destination Address: 090007FFFFFF (AppleTalk Multicast)
0006:000B   Source Address: 0050E466005B
000C:000D   Ethernet Length: 36
LLC [000E:0015]
000E:000E   Destination SAP: SNAP
000F:000F   Source SAP: SNAP (Command)
0010:0010   LLC Control: UI (Unnumbered Information) frame
0011:0013   SNAP Organization Code: 0x000000
0014:0015   SNAP Protocol Type: AppleTalk ARP
Apple ARP [0016:0031]
0016:0017   Hardware Type: Ethernet (10Mbps)
0018:0019   Protocol Type: EtherTalk (AppleTalk over Ethernet)
001A:001A   Hardware Address Length: 6
001B:001B   Protocol Address Length: 4
001C:001D   Opcode: Request
001E:0023   Source HW Address: 0050E466005B
0024:0027   Source Protocol Address: 0.0.200.101
0028:002D   Destination HW Address: 000000000000
002E:0031   Destination Protocol Address: 0.0.200.90
```

3. Repeat step 1 for this DECnet packet:

```
Protocol Summary: DECnet Routing, Ethernet Router Hello

Addr.   Hex. Data                                                ASCII
0000:   AB 00 00 03 00 00 AA 00 04 00 02 9C 60 03 22 00   ............'.".
0010:   0B 02 00 00 AA 00 04 00 02 9C 02 DA 05 40 00 0F   .............@..
0020:   00 00 0F 00 00 00 00 00 00 00 07 AA 00 04 00 FF   ................
0030:   9C C0 00 00 00 00 00 00 00 00 00 00               ............

802.3 [0000:000F]
   0000:0005   Destination Address: AB0000030000 (DECNET Multicast)
   0006:000B   Source Address: AA000400029C (DEC00029C)
   000C:000D   Ethernet Type: DECNET Phase IV, DNA Routing
   000E:000F   Length: 34
DECnet Routing [0010:0021]
   0010:0010   PF: 0; Reserved: 0; Type: Ethernet Router Hello; Packet: Control
   0011:0011   Version: 2
   0012:0012   ECO: 0
   0013:0013   User ECO: 0
   0014:0019   TX Node ID: AA000400029C
   001A:001A   Info: 2
   001B:001C   Block Size: 1498
   001D:001D   Priority: 64
   001E:001E   Area: 0
   001F:0020   Timer: 15
   0021:0021   MPD: 0
```

4. Use LanExplorer to capture and decode your own IPX/SPX, AppleTalk, or DECnet packets. Save at least one decoded packet for each protocol and print it out.

Discussion and Conclusion

Using a word processor, write your own detailed explanations of the results and observations made during the experiment. To begin, try to say something about each procedure step.

In addition, provide answers to the following questions:

1. What are the various names used for sources and destinations in each packet?
2. Compare the IPX header details from Figure 9–2 with the decoded packet from step 1. Does each field match?
3. Describe the type of encapsulation found in each packet.
4. Which non-TCP/IP protocol is used most often in each of your packet captures?

10

Switching and Routing

PERFORMANCE OBJECTIVES

Upon completion of this chapter, you will be able to

- Explain the basic differences between hubs and switches.
- Discuss the difference between store-and-forward switching and cut-through switching.
- Describe the operation of a router.
- Explain the differences between distance-vector and link-state routing protocols and give examples of each.
- Illustrate the differences between interior and exterior routing protocols.

Joe Tekk and his friend Richard Majestic finished their examination of the network installed several years ago in a local hospital. The network was a mixture of 10base5 and 10baseT technology. There were no switches, just hubs providing the 10baseT connections. The hospital administration wanted the network upgraded so that some stations had access to 100-Mbps dedicated bandwidth (to support their medical imaging database). In addition, the administration wanted an Internet connection.

Joe and Richard devised an upgrade plan and discussed it with Don, the senior technician. The plan included pulling lots of Category 5 UTP cable, replacing most hubs with 10/100 Mbps managed switches, and adding two routers to partition the hospital network into manageable groups. Joe and Richard presented the plan to the hospital administration and it was approved.

Within three weeks the new network was in place and the hospital was online. The hospital was so pleased they hired Richard as their new network administrator.

INTRODUCTION

In Chapter 8 we examined the many different TCP/IP protocols and their use. Several higher-layer protocols provided the methods required for two stations to communicate, reliably or unreliably. In this chapter we take a look at the routing protocols used to transport the higher-layer protocols between LANs (across a WAN). We will also explore the details of switching and make comparisons between hubs, switches, and routers.

199

HUBS VERSUS SWITCHES

The essential difference between hubs and switches is that hubs broadcast frames received on one port to all other ports, whereas a switch will forward a received frame to a specific port. This is illustrated in Figure 10–1, in which a small network of six stations (A through F) are connected two different ways.

Figure 10–1
Comparing a hub and a switch.

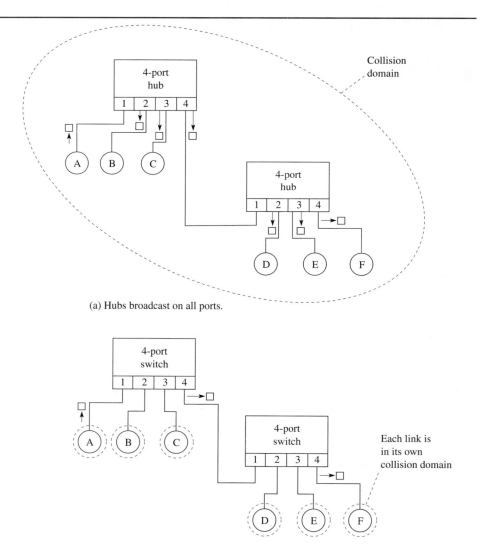

(a) Hubs broadcast on all ports.

(b) Switches forward frames to specific ports.

In Figure 10–1(a), station A transmits a frame whose destination is station F. This does not matter to the 4-port hubs, which simply broadcast copies of the frame from station A to the other five stations. This amounts to a good deal of wasted bandwidth. Furthermore, all six stations operate in the same collision domain, making them compete for bandwidth.

Figure 10–1(b) shows the same network with the 4-port hubs replaced by 4-port switches. Now, a frame transmitted from station A with a destination of station F is forwarded between the switches and sent directly to station F on port 4. Stations B, C, D, and E do not receive copies of the frame as they do in Figure 10–1(a). Thus, network traffic has been reduced.

The switches also partition the network into six separate collision domains. Now each station has unrestricted access to its own dedicated bandwidth (the speed of the switch port).

The switch is capable of specific forwarding because it learns what MAC addresses are associated with each port. Recall that every Ethernet frame contains a source MAC address and a destination MAC address. When a frame is received by a port on a switch, the switch will save a copy of the source MAC address and its associated port number in a special internal lookup table. Though we are storing the source MAC address, it is a destination MAC address to every other station in the network. Now, when a frame requires forwarding, the switch examines the destination MAC address stored in the frame, and looks for it in the lookup table. If the destination MAC address is found in the table, the frame is forwarded to the associated port. If the destination MAC address is not found, the frame is broadcast to all ports. Eventually the destination station will most likely respond with its own frame, and its port will be identified. Further broadcasts for that station will not be required.

Figure 10–2 shows the results obtained when a hub and switch are used together. Stations A, B, and C are in one collision domain (competing for bandwidth). Stations D, E, and F are in their own collision domains, each having full access to the available bandwidth. In Figure 10–2(a), station A transmits a frame destined for station F. The frame is broadcast by the hub and forwarded by the switch. Stations B and C must contend with the broadcast frame, waiting their turn for access. Neither station is allowed to transmit while the hub is broadcasting (or a collision will result). So, even though station A is sending a frame to station F, stations B and C are affected.

Figure 10–2(b) shows station A sending a frame to station C. The hub still broadcasts the frame, which affects station B but not stations D, E, or F.

In Figure 10–2(c), station F sends a frame to station A. The frame is forwarded by the switch and broadcast by the hub. Stations B and C are affected by F's frame; stations D and E are not.

Figure 10–2(d) shows station F sending a frame to station D. Station E is unaffected and may transmit a frame to stations A, B, or C without affecting the F-to-D transmission.

Figure 10–2
Mixing hubs and
switches.

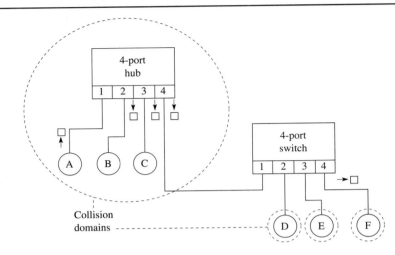

(a) A sending to F.

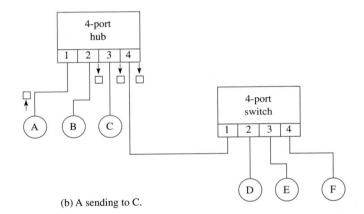

(b) A sending to C.

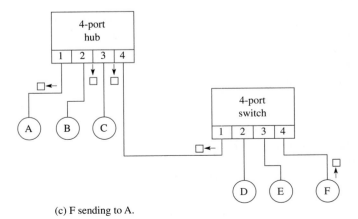

(c) F sending to A.

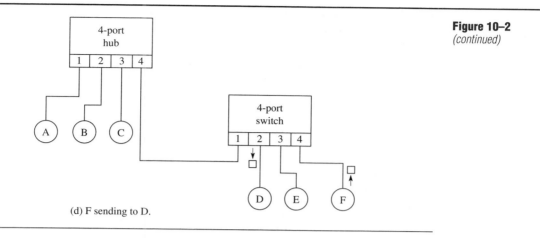

Figure 10–2
(continued)

(d) F sending to D.

INSIDE A SWITCH

If you wanted to start your own networking company and begin designing and manufacturing switches, where would you begin? Let us examine the block diagram of a simple switch, shown in Figure 10–3.

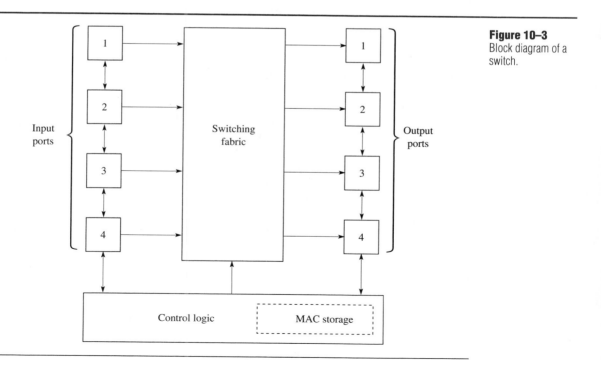

Figure 10–3
Block diagram of a switch.

As illustrated, the switch contains the following components:

- Input port logic
- Output port logic
- Switching fabric
- Control logic

What would be required of each component?

Input Port Logic

This section contains the Ethernet receiving logic and buffers for received frames. Buffering received frames lowers the rate of collisions and allows the switching fabric to be busy for short periods of time without losing data. If the frame buffer fills up, any new frame received by the port will trigger a collision. The random delay of CSMA/CD will then give the switch time to empty a portion of the input buffer before the station attempts retransmission.

Output Port Logic

Each output port contains an Ethernet transmitter and output frame buffer. Again, the buffer allows the switch fabric to service multiple output ports on a demand basis. For example, several frames may arrive simultaneously, with each frame directed to the same output port. The buffer is required to prevent the switching fabric from stalling. In addition, the input and output frame buffers allow different speeds between ports (port 1 operating at 10 Mbps and port 3 operating at 100 Mbps, for example). The buffers may be filled at one speed and emptied at another speed.

Switching Fabric

The switching fabric is responsible for directing the received frames from each input port to the appropriate output port. In addition, the switching fabric must also be able to handle a broadcast to all output ports. In general, there are two ways to build the switching fabric: crossbar switch and high-speed multiplexed bus. Both methods are shown in Figure 10–4.

The crossbar switch in Figure 10–4(a) is a two-dimensional set of data buses. Any combination of input-to-output connections is possible, even broadcasting. Each intersection of input wires and output wires in the crossbar switch contains an electronic switch that is either open or closed. A small amount of control information is required to configure the crossbar switch. Changing the control information changes the input-to-output connections.

The multiplexed bus in Figure 10–4(b) effectively makes one input-output connection at a time, with each input port getting its turn at using the bus. When many signals are multiplexed in this fashion, the data rate on the multiplexed bus must be much faster than the individual speeds of each port. For example, on a 4-port switch, with each port running at 100 Mbps, the multiplexed bus would need to operate at 400 Mbps. An 8-port switch would require an 800-Mbps bus. The speed requirement of this technique makes it unsuitable for switching at high speeds. This problem is overcome by the parallel nature of the crossbar switch.

Figure 10–4
Switching fabrics.

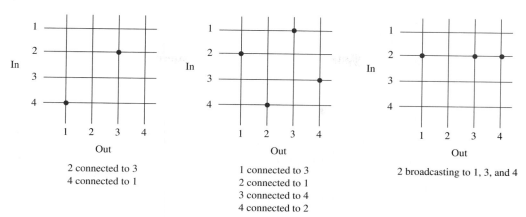

2 connected to 3
4 connected to 1

1 connected to 3
2 connected to 1
3 connected to 4
4 connected to 2

2 broadcasting to 1, 3, and 4

(a) Crossbar switch.

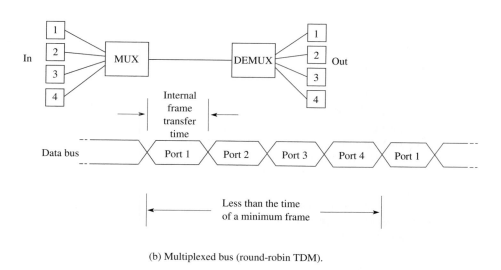

(b) Multiplexed bus (round-robin TDM).

Control Logic

The control logic must perform several chores, including

- Updating and searching the MAC address table
- Configuring the switching fabric
- Maintaining proper flow control through the switch fabric

Recall that the switch learns which ports are associated with specific stations by storing copies of the source MAC address from each received frame. The

Figure 10–5
CAM organization.

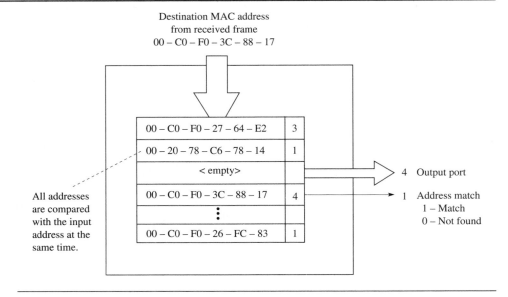

Destination MAC address
from received frame
00 – C0 – F0 – 3C – 88 – 17

00 – C0 – F0 – 27 – 64 – E2	3
00 – 20 – 78 – C6 – 78 – 14	1
< empty>	
00 – C0 – F0 – 3C – 88 – 17	4
⋮	
00 – C0 – F0 – 26 – FC – 83	1

All addresses
are compared
with the input
address at the
same time.

4   Output port

1   Address match
    1 – Match
    0 – Not found

MAC address and port number are stored in a special high-speed memory called CAM (content addressable memory). The hardware architecture of the CAM allows its internal memory to be searched for a desired data value, such as a 48-bit MAC address. Figure 10–5 shows a simple example of a CAM being searched for the MAC address 00-C0-F0-3C-88-17. It is important to note that all of the MAC addresses being stored in the CAM are compared with the input value, *at the same time*. For example, the MUSIC LANCAM MU9C1480 from MUSIC Semiconductor (http://www.music-ic.com) stores 1024 64-bit entries and performs comparisons in 70 nanoseconds.

The control logic uses the lookup results from the CAM to configure the switching fabric. In the event that an output port becomes unavailable due to congestion or some other problem, a flow control mechanism will prevent access to the port until it becomes available again.

STORE-AND-FORWARD SWITCHING

Initially, switches handled frames using a technique called *store-and-forward switching*. In this technique, the entire frame is stored as it is received. If the FCS is valid, the destination MAC address is used to select an output port, and the frame is forwarded to the appropriate output port via the switching fabric. Since the entire frame is stored before any decisions are made, there is a delay between the time the frame is received and the time it begins transmission on the appropriate output port. This delay is called *latency*, and it varies depending on the length of the frame. The minimum latency is obtained with a minimum size frame. For 10 Mbps Ethernet, the minimum latency is 57.6 microseconds (576 bit times at 100 nanoseconds/bit, including Preamble). Maximum length frames have a latency just over 1.2 milliseconds.

Some applications, such as streaming audio and video, are sensitive to latency.

CUT-THROUGH SWITCHING

Cut-through switching reduces the latency of a switch tremendously. In this technique, as soon as the destination MAC address of an incoming frame is received, the forwarding process can begin (assuming there is a free output port and the switching fabric is available). This reduces the latency to just 11.2 microseconds, plus any additional time for internal switch operations. In addition, the latency of the cut-through method is fixed, since forwarding can always begin as soon as the destination MAC address is received. Unfortunately, errors can be propagated using the cut-through method, since there is no way to know if a frame being forwarded is good until it has been completely received. Cut-through switches will revert to store-and-forward when multiple errors occur while using the cut-through method.

SWITCHES VERSUS ROUTERS

Switches are considered Layer 2 (Data-Link) devices, using MAC addresses to forward frames to their proper destination. Routers, Layer 3 (Network) devices, are much more complex, using microprocessor-based circuitry to route packets between networks based on their IP address. Routers provide the following services, among others:

- Route discovery
- Selection of the best route to a destination
- Adaptation to changes in the network
- Translation from one technology to another, such as Ethernet to token ring
- Packet filtering based on IP address, protocol, or UDP/TCP port number
- Connection to a WAN

Because of the additional processing required for each packet, a router has a higher latency than a switch. In addition, a router requires an initial setup sequence, in which the ports are programmed and certain protocols and characteristics enabled or disabled. A switch may be simply plugged into the network, automatically learning how to forward frames as the network is used. Note that some protocols, such as NetBEUI, are nonroutable. These protocols will pass through a switch but not a router.

Finally, switches are used within networks to forward local traffic intelligently. Routers are used between networks, to route packets between networks in the most efficient manner. In the following sections, we will examine the many different routing protocols used to enable communication between LANs.

ROUTING PROTOCOLS

When an organization chooses what type of routing protocols to use, it is a complex task based on the answers to at least the following questions:

- What is the size and complexity of the network?
- What types of physical networks must be connected?
- Which service provider will handle the network data?
- What is/are the network traffic levels?
- What are the security needs?
- What level of reliability is required?
- What are the organizational policies within the organization?
- How does the organization implement changes?
- What type of hardware and software support from the manufacturer is required?
- How long will it take to repair or replace the equipment if it fails?

Routing protocols perform a different type of switching than discussed previously. Routing protocols operate at the Network layer (Layer 3) in the TCP/IP and OSI protocol stacks. Using a device called a *router*, various types of networks are connected together to form one *logical* network. The Internet is an example of one logical network. A router is a special-purpose computer whose only responsibility is to move the data around on the network between source and destination computers. The individual networks can be made up of different types of LAN hardware and topologies, such as Ethernet, token-ring, or ATM networks, to name just a few. The router is able to move the data between the different network types and perform any necessary translations, such as between ASCII and EBCDIC and vice versa. On the Internet, the routing protocols are based on the Internet Protocol and use IP addresses.

In general, each router must follow a few ground rules to allow it to process Network layer data:

- Communicate on a LAN just like any other station. For example, on an Ethernet network, a router communicates using CSMA/CD and monitors the media for their MAC address and any broadcast messages.
- Maintain tables with routing information for all reachable networks.
- Forward or block traffic based on the destination network address.
- Drop all frames to unknown destinations.
- Forward directed broadcasts (such as ARP) between networks.
- Perform CRC checks on each transferred packet.

Using a router, messages are passed from one device (host computer or router) to another until the message eventually reaches the destination. Figure 10–6 shows a typical network connected to the Internet through a router. Any

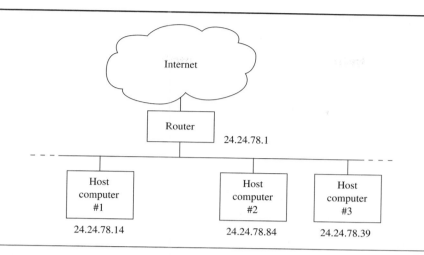

Figure 10–6
A router connecting a network to the Internet.

traffic exchanged between any of the nodes on the local network can be delivered directly without the need for a router. All traffic that is destined for the Internet must be passed on to the router.

A Windows application program called NETSTAT is used to show the routes that are currently active on a personal computer running the Windows operating system. Running the NETSTAT program with the -r option produces the following output:

```
C:\WINDOWS>netstat -r

Route Table

Active Routes:

  Network Address            Netmask   Gateway Address      Interface   Metric
          0.0.0.0            0.0.0.0         24.24.78.1    24.24.78.84        1
       24.24.78.0      255.255.255.0        24.24.78.84    24.24.78.84        1
      24.24.78.84    255.255.255.255         127.0.0.1      127.0.0.1        1
   24.255.255.255    255.255.255.255        24.24.78.84    24.24.78.84        1
        127.0.0.0          255.0.0.0         127.0.0.1      127.0.0.1        1
        224.0.0.0          224.0.0.0        24.24.78.84    24.24.78.84        1
  255.255.255.255    255.255.255.255        24.24.78.84    24.24.78.84        1

Active Connections

  Proto  Local Address          Foreign Address             State
  TCP    server:1025            sbccab.cc.sunybroome.edu:139   ESTABLISHED
  TCP    server:4424            ftp-eng.cisco.com:ftp  CLOSE_WAIT
  TCP    server:4970            mail3-1.nyroc.rr.com:pop-3   TIME_WAIT
  TCP    server:4981            sunc.scit.wlv.ac.uk:80  CLOSE_WAIT
```

As you can see, NETSTAT shows the routing table and active connections for the computer. To deliver a message to a remote network, it must be transmitted from the source host to a local router (sometimes called the *default gateway*). In the NET-STAT display, the default gateway has the address 24.24.78.1. Do any of the other addresses look familiar, such as the loopback address or the network masks?

After the data is send to the default gateway router, it is passed on to another router or to the host computer on the destination LAN. Each router implements the routing process by forwarding messages (one hop at a time) toward their final destination using information stored in a *routing table*. The routing table contains an entry that indicates the best path (or interface) to send the data on to the destination.

The routing table in a router can be created and maintained using two different methods: statically or dynamically. In a static router, a number of predefined routes are created and the router lacks the ability to discover new routes. In a router with statically configured routing tables, the network administrator needs a detailed knowledge of the network topology and must take the time to manually build and update the routing table as conditions change. Basically this involves programming all of the routes into the router memory. Static routers can work well for small networks but do not work well in large or dynamically changing networks due to the manual effort required by them. In addition, static routers are not fault tolerant. The lifetime of a manually configured static route is infinite. Therefore, statically configured routers do not recover from a bad link or a malfunctioning router.

In contrast, using dynamic routing, new routes can be discovered, and old routes can be updated as required. Dynamic routing consists of maintaining routing tables automatically using either periodic or on-demand messages through an ongoing communication between routers using the routing protocols. Except for their initial configuration, dynamic routers require little ongoing maintenance. Dynamic routing is fault tolerant. Dynamic routes learned from other routers have a finite lifetime. If a router or link goes down, the routers sense the change in the network topology through the expiration of the lifetime of the learned route in the routing table. This change can then be propagated to other routers so that all the routers on the network *realize* the new network topology. The router chooses the "best" path to send the data by implementing a *distance-vector* or *link-state* algorithm. In the distance-vector algorithm, each router in the network contains a partial view of the complete network topology. In the link-state algorithm, each router is aware of the entire network.

Before we can discuss how the routing algorithms and protocols operate, it is necessary to understand where a LAN fits into the logical network as a whole. Each connected network is part of a larger network called an ***autonomous system***.

AUTONOMOUS SYSTEMS

Routing is based on the individual networks that are called autonomous systems, commonly abbreviated to AS. An autonomous system is a network or

Number	Network
3300	ATT Unisource
9744	E-Z NET Internet Service Provider
7487	Idea Net Co., Ltd.
4618	Internet Thailand Service Center
786	JANET
6453	Teleglobe Montreal
8297	Teleglobe Virginia
1849	UUnet UK

Table 10–1
A list of autonomous system numbers.

group of networks and routers controlled by a single administrative authority. The authority can be an institution, corporation, or any other type of organization. An autonomous system number is associated with each autonomous system. Table 10–1 shows a brief list of autonomous system numbers. Each autonomous system has a single and clearly defined external routing policy. A new AS needs to be created if a network connects to more than one AS with a different routing policy.

Different routing protocols are used when routing inside autonomous system and between them. The Interior Gateway Protocol (IGP) is used inside of autonomous systems. Exterior Gateway Protocols (EGP) exchange information between different autonomous systems. Figure 10–7 illustrates the how the different routing protocols are used to connect autonomous systems together.

Many of the protocols we will examine in this exercise are shown in Table 10–2 along with the RFC numbers that describe their operation in detail. As you will see, some of these protocols may be used as IGPs, EGPs, or both. Let us begin with a discussion of the Interior Gateway Protocols.

INTERIOR GATEWAY PROTOCOLS

Interior Gateway Protocols (IGPs) are used from communication inside of autonomous systems. The following protocols are used as IGPs for IP networks:

- *Gateway-to-Gateway Protocol (GGP)*: An RFC-based distance-vector IGP
- *Routing Information Protocol (RIP)*: An RFC-based distance-vector IGP
- *Routing Information Protocol 2 (RIP-2)*: An enhanced version of RIP that includes support for Classless Inter-Domain Routing (CIDR)
- *Interior Gateway Routing Protocol (IGRP)*: A distance-vector IGP developed by Cisco Systems, Inc. in the 1980s. IGRP is capable of load balancing multiple network paths based on delay and bandwidth.

Figure 10–7
Interior versus
Exterior Gateway
Protocols.

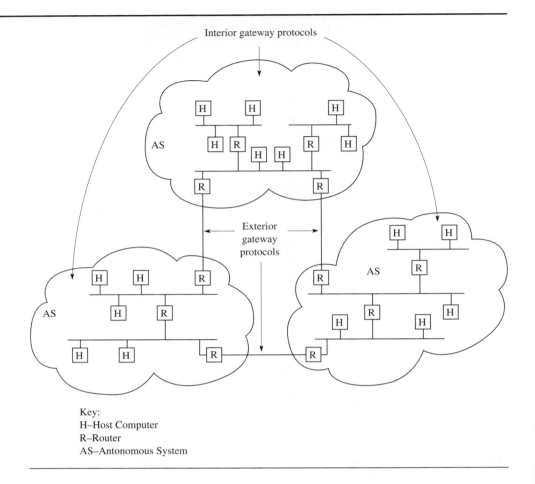

Key:
H–Host Computer
R–Router
AS–Antonomous System

- *Extended Interior Gateway Routing Protocol (EIGRP)*: An enhanced distance-vector IGP developed by Cisco Systems, Inc. EIGRP extends IGRP to support CIDR and provides several other enhancements.
- *Open Shortest Path First (OSPF)*: Link-state IP protocol that is primarily used within an autonomous system but can also be used as an EGP as well. OSPF includes authentication and has become the IP routing protocol of choice in large environments.
- *Intermediate System to Intermediate System (IS-IS)*: OSI-based connectionless link-state protocol

We will examine each of these protocols in more detail shortly.

The autonomous systems that use the IGPs are connected to other autonomous systems. The Exterior Gateway Protocols are used for the communication between the autonomous systems.

RFC Number	Description
791	IP
792	ICMP
823	DARPA Internet Gateway
827	EGP
995	Telecom and Information Exchange Between Systems
1058	RIP
1105	BGP
1131	OSFP
1142	OSI IS-IS Intra-Domain Routing Protocol
1163	BGP-2
1247	OSPF V2
1248	OSPF-MIB
1253	OSPF Version 2 Management Information Base
1267	BGP-3
1387	RIP Protocol Analysis
1388	RIP Version 2 Protocol Extensions
1389	RIP-MIB
1403	BGP OSPF Interaction
1466	IP Address Space Management
1517	Applicability Statement for the Implementation of Classless Inter-Domain Routing (CIDR)
1518	IP Address Allocation with CIDR
1519	A CIDR Address Assignment and Aggregation Strategy
1520	Exchanging Routing Information Across Provider Boundaries in the CIDR Environment
1631	IP Network Address Translator (NAT)
1654	BGP-4
1655	Application of the Border Gateway Protocol
1656	BGP-4 Document Roadmap and Implementation Experience
1771	BGP-4 (revised)
1774	BGP-4 Protocol Analysis
1930	Guidelines for Creation, Selection, and Registration of an Autonomous System (AS)
2080	RIPng for IPv6
2082	RIP-II MD5 Authentication
2385	BGP Protection Using TCP
2453	RIP Version 2

Table 10–2
RFCs associated with routing protocols.

EXTERIOR GATEWAY PROTOCOLS

Exterior Gateway Protocols (EGPs) are used between different autonomous systems. EGPs define the way that all of the networks within the AS are advertised outside of the AS. Each EGP advertises the "reachability" to the networks it can connect to. Figure 10–8 shows what messages an EGP might broadcast to other EGPs. Note that the EGPs are independent of the IGPs used within the autonomous system. EGPs can facilitate the exchange of routes between autonomous systems that may use different IGPs. Notice that each autonomous system contains two EGP routers for redundancy. If one EGP is down, the second must temporarily handle the additional load. In practice, the internal and external router may be located within the same box, performing both internal and external routing decisions simultaneously. For

Figure 10–8
EGP messages.

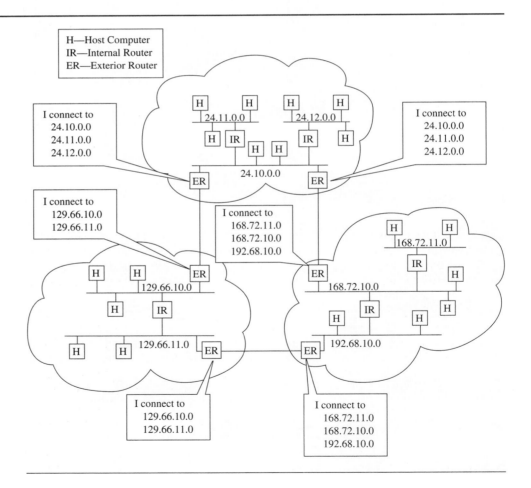

example, on a Cisco router, as many as 30 different routing protocols may be operating simultaneously. The combinations are made up as follows:

- Up to 30 EGP routing processes
- Up to 30 IGRP routing processes
- Up to 30 OSPF routing processes
- One RIP routing process
- One IS-IS process
- One BGP routing process

As you might agree, this is a rather impressive list of supported combinations. The following protocols are used for EGPs in IP networks:

- *Exterior Gateway Protocol (EGP)*: An RFC-based protocol that was developed for use between ASs on the Internet. EGP is no longer used on the Internet due to its lack of support for complex, multipath environments and Classless Inter-Domain Routing (CIDR).
- *Border Gateway Protocol (BGP)*: An RFC-based protocol that is currently used between ASs on the Internet. BGP overcomes the weaknesses of EGP. For example, BGP is better at detecting routing loops than EGP.
- *Open Shortest Path First (OSPF)*: Link-state IP protocol. OSPF includes authentication and has become the IP routing protocol of choice in large environments. OSPF is also used as an IGP.

We will examine many of the details of these protocols shortly as well. First, let us examine Classless Inter-Domain Routing, a new addressing scheme used by newer IGPs and EGPs.

CLASSLESS INTER-DOMAIN ROUTING

Classless Inter-Domain Routing (CIDR) was initially developed to recover many of the unused addresses in class A and class B networks. The CIDR technique is supported by interior and exterior gateway protocols and is based on route aggregation. CIDR is also known as *supernetting*. CIDR is a new way of looking at IP addresses that eliminates the concept of classes (class A, class B, and so on). With CIDR, IP addresses and their *subnet* masks are written as 4 octets, separated by periods, followed by a forward slash and a 2-digit number that represents the length of the subnet mask. For example, the class B network 178.217.0.0, which is an illegal class C network address, is a legal class C supernet address when it is represented in CIDR notation as 178.217.0.0/24. The /24 indicates that the subnet mask consists of 24 bits (counting from the left). Therefore, 178.217.0.0/24 represents the address 178.217.0.0 with a mask of 255.255.255.0.

CIDR makes it easy to aggregate or combine routes. *Route aggregation* is the process of using several different routes in such a way that a single route can be advertised, which minimizes the size of the routing tables maintained by a router. Table 10–3 shows various CIDR prefixes with the number of class C

Table 10–3
CIDR address prefix and number of class C addresses.

CIDR Prefix	Number of Equivalent Class C Addresses	Number of Host Addresses
/28	1/16 of one class C	16 hosts
/27	1/8 of one class C	32 hosts
/26	1/4 of one class C	64 hosts
/25	1/2 of one class C	128 hosts
/24	1 class C	256 hosts
/23	2 class Cs	512 hosts
/22	4 class Cs	1,024 hosts
/21	8 class Cs	2,048 hosts
/20	16 class Cs	4,096 hosts
/19	32 class Cs	8,192 hosts
/18	64 class Cs	16,384 hosts
/17	128 class Cs	32,768 hosts
/16	256 class Cs	65,536 hosts
/15	512 class Cs	131,072 hosts
/14	1,024 class Cs	262,144 hosts
/13	2,048 class Cs	524,288 hosts

equivalent addresses. Currently, big blocks of addresses are assigned to the large Internet service providers (ISPs), who then reallocate portions of their address blocks to their customers. The implementation of CIDR has been critical to the continued growth of the Internet, allowing more organizations and users to take advantage of this increasingly vital global networking and information resource.

Let us continue with a brief introduction to the routing algorithms. The routing algorithms are based on one of two different approaches to finding the "best" or shortest path to the destination. The first method, called *distance-vector routing*, is based on determining the fewest number of hops to the destination. The metric (or measure) of distance is based on the number of exchanges between routers that must be performed. The second routing method, called *link-state routing*, is more complex and more efficient than distance-vector algorithms. First, let us examine the distance-vector routing algorithm and a few of the protocols that use it.

DISTANCE-VECTOR ROUTING

The distance-vector routing algorithm (also called the Bellman-Ford algorithm) is a type of routing algorithm that is based on the number of hops in a

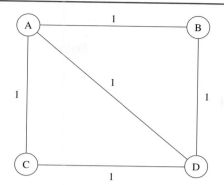

Figure 10–9
Routing based on
hop count.

route between a source and destination computer. The shortest path algorithm is attributed to Bellman and the distributed nature of the algorithm is attributed to Ford. Distance-vector routing algorithms call for each router to send its entire routing table (to its neighbor) in each update. An update is performed every 30 seconds. The distance-vector routing algorithm is distributed between the routers on the network.

The most common measure of distance (metric) is based on the number of hops the data needs to take to reach the destination. To keep the metric value simple, the number of hops from any router to itself is 0 and a connection to a neighbor is assigned a value of 1. Figure 10–9 shows a small network containing 4 LANs, labeled A, B, C, and D. Network A is connected directly to networks B, C, and D. Network B is connect to networks A and D. Network C is connected to networks A and D. Lastly, network D, like network A, is connected to all of the other networks. Notice that the best route between nodes A and B is the direct connection between them with the cost of 1. Similarly, connections between B and C have a cost of 2. As you will see, it is possible to use other metrics as well.

Although distance-vector protocols are usually easy to implement, they have many weaknesses. For example, the distance-vector algorithm is susceptible to routing loops, cannot differentiate between the speeds of different links, cannot determine the lifetime of a single packet, and the time it takes to propagate all messages to every router in a large network is painfully slow.

Each router that implements the distance-vector routing algorithm maintains a routing table that contains one entry for each router in the network. The routing table entry contains two fields: one is used to indicate the distance to the destination and the other one indicates the network interface adapter to use to get there. The distance-vector routing algorithm was chosen as the original ARPAnet routing algorithm, the predecessor to the modern Internet. A common distance-vector protocol is called the Routing Information Protocol, more commonly known as RIP.

RIP

The Routing Information Protocol (RIP) is a commonly used distance-vector routing protocol that uses the underlying UDP transport. RIP is based on a 1970s Xerox design that was ported to TCP/IP when LANs first appeared in the 1980s. RIP uses a 4-bit metric to count router hops to a destination. Due to the size of this field, a RIP network can be no larger than 15 hops between the furthest connected stations. The value 16 is used to represent infinity. If hop counts are elevated on slower or less reliable links, this can quickly becomes a problem.

Every 30 seconds a RIP router will broadcast its routing table of networks and subnets it can reach to its neighbor. The neighboring router in turn will pass the information on to its next neighbor and so on, until all routers within the network have the same knowledge of routing paths, a state known as network *convergence*, or network *realization*. RIP uses a hop count as a way to determine network distance.

Depending on the length of the routing table, which depends on the size of the network, bandwidth usage can be excessive as the size of the routing table increases. Unfortunately, RIP is also difficult to debug when a problem does occur, since the routing algorithm is distributed over many different routers. In addition, RIP has no security features.

RIP also has several benefits. It is in widespread use, the only Interior Gateway Protocol that can be counted on to run on every router platform. Configuring the RIP protocol requires little effort beyond setting up the cost associated with each path. Finally, RIP uses an algorithm (distance-vector) that does not impose serious computation or storage requirements on hosts or routers.

Each entry in a RIP routing table contains

- Address of the destination
- Address of the next router
- Metric value
- Recently Updated Flag
- Various timers

RIP has changed little in the past few decades and suffers from several limitations previously identified, some of which have been overcome with a newer version of the protocol called RIP-2. RIP-2 maintains compatibility with RIP-1. RIP-2 provides for these additional routing features:

- Authentication
- Classless Inter-Domain Routing (CIDR)
- Next Hop
- Multicasting

The message headers for both RIP and RIP-2 are shown in Figure 10–10. A brief description of each of the header fields is provided in Table 10–4. Note that as many as 25 routes may be broadcast inside of every single RIP message.

Let us continue with another distance vector routing algorithm called the Inter-Gateway Routing Protocol.

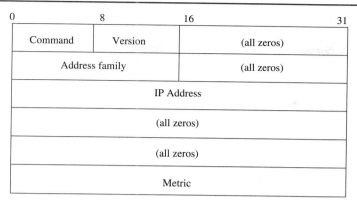

(a) RIP-1.

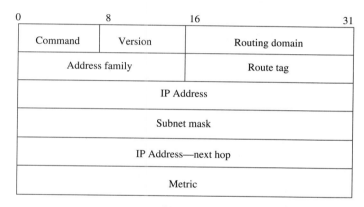

(b) RIP-2.

Figure 10–10
Routing Information
Protocol packets.

Field Name	Version	Size	Meaning
Command	1, 2	8 bits	RIP command value
Version	1, 2	8 bits	RIP version
Routing Domain	2	16 bits	Network routing domain
Address Family	1, 2	16 bits	Type of address
Route Tag	2	16 bits	Used to separate internal and external routes
IP Address	2	32 bits	IP address
Subnet Mask	2	32 bits	Subnetwork mask applied to the IP address
IP Address (next hop)	2	32-bits	Immediate IP address of the next hop
Metric	1, 2	32 bits	Hop count, etc.

Table 10–4
Routing Information
Protocol header field
information.

Inter-Gateway Routing Protocol

The Inter-Gateway Routing Protocol (IGRP) is a Cisco-proprietary solution to many of the problems associated with the RIP protocol. In general, IGRP is characterized by the following properties:

- IP transport
- Updates broadcast every 90 seconds instead of 30
- Hold down–protocol enhancement
- New metrics
  - Bandwidth
  - Delay
  - Load
  - Reliability
- Protection against loops
- Multipath routing
- Default route handling

IGRP is regarded as an Interior Gateway Protocol (IGP) but has also been used extensively as an Exterior Gateway Protocol for inter-domain routing. IGRP uses distance-vector routing technology. The methods used to implement IGRP are one of the reasons why Cisco routers are often used on the Internet. The proprietary nature of the IGRP protocol means that Cisco routers are the only routers that can use it.

A brief look the most important properties that set IGRP apart from RIP include less bandwidth consumed with broadcast updates, newer, more efficient methods to compensate for changing network conditions, additional metric parameters that can be used to allow a network administrator to provide additional measure of control as to how routes are chosen, increased prevention against routing loops, better handling of multiple paths, and the selection of a default route.

To prevent routing loops several new features are included. These features include

- Hold down
- Poison-reverse update
- Split horizon

A hold down feature is used to prevent the condition where a route that has become unstable is used prematurely. A poison reverse update is used to eliminate routing loops by removing the routes from routing tables. Lastly, a split horizon is used to prevent information from being sent back on a link from the direction in which it was originally received.

The IGRP enhancements also include the addition of several new timer variables. These timers are

- Flush
- Hold-time
- Invalid
- Update

The flush timer variable is used to control the lifetime of each entry in the routing table. The hold-time timer variable determines how long a route is kept in a hold down condition. The invalid timer variable determines how long a route remains valid in the absence of an update message. The update timer variable is used to determine how often update messages are distributed. The values specified for each of these timer variables allows for the most efficient use of the router processor and network bandwidth utilization.

You are encouraged to spend some additional time on your own exploring the features of IGRP and the advantages that Cisco routers provide.

Although IGRP has many advantages over RIP, a more advanced version called EIGRP provides many other capabilities.

Enhanced Inter-Gateway Routing Protocol

Cisco developed Enhanced IGRP in the early 1990s to improve the operating efficiency of IGRP. Improvements to IGRP include

- A distributed update algorithm
- MD5 authentication
- Protocol Independent Routing
- Metric changes (not entire routing tables) exchanged every 90 seconds
- CIDR support

Due to the proprietary nature of the EIGRP protocol, it is only supported by Cisco routers.

Another set of routing protocols that offer additional capabilities are based on the link-state routing algorithm. Generally speaking, it is simply a different method to select the "best" route to the destination. Let us begin with an examination of how link-state routing works and then at some of the most common link-state protocols.

LINK-STATE ROUTING

In contrast to the distance-vector algorithm, the link-state routing algorithm broadcasts information about the cost of reaching each of its neighbors to all other routers in the network. This allows the link-state algorithm to create a consistent view of the network at each router. The method used to compute the shortest distance is based on *Dijkstra's algorithm*, an open shortest path algorithm. The primary difference between distance-vector routing and link-state routing is that a path with the least hops may not be chosen as the least-cost route. For example, take a look at Figure 10–11. Notice that the best path from A to B is not the single hop that directly connects the two. This could be due to the fact that the direct connection between the two of them contains a 56K link whereas all of the other links operate at T1 speed. In a large network, route computations are more complex.

Figure 10–11
Routing based on
weighted connections.

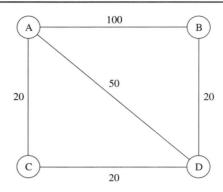

The implementation of the link-state routing algorithm is specified in the following steps:

1. Initialize a set called "S" to contain all of the routers in the network except for the source router.
2. Initialize a destination array to the metric value associated between each of the routers in set S and the source router if a connection exists. If no connections exist, the distance is set to infinity.
3. Initialize values in a routing table array such that the metric distance value is assigned, otherwise the value is set to zero.
4. While the set S is not empty
   a. Choose a router from set S such that the metric distance is minimum.
   b. If the minimum distance is infinity
      i. No path exists to the router.
   c. Else
      i. Remove the router from set S.
      ii. For each router in set S
         1. Compute a sum of the metric value.
         2. If the sum of the metric value is less than the current destination value
            a. Store the sum metric value in the distance array.
            b. Identify this router as the "best" path in the routing table array.

In a small network, it may be easy to work through the algorithm. In a large network, it is much more difficult.

The link-state routing algorithm is not prone to routing loops or any of the other problems that are common to distance-vector routing algorithms. The problem with link-state algorithms lies in its complexity.

A link-state router has the following characteristics:

- Automatically discover any neighboring routers
- Shared information via multicast transmissions
- Routing tables are built using first-hand information only

- Hello packets containing route information are forwarded to all routers
- Use metrics other than hop count
- Supports load balancing
- No assumption that routing information is accurate and has been received from a trusted source
- Compute the shortest path to every router in the network

In link-state protocols, the router keeps a list of all routers that it knows in a table. In the routing table the distance to each network is specified. Routers update their routing tables periodically according to other router's routing tables and advertise their own routing tables to other routers. Each of the routes is calculated during every link-state modification. A special *flooding protocol* is used to propagate the changes in a link's status quickly throughout the network. To reduce the amount of multicast router traffic on the network, a *spanning tree* is used to create nonlooping paths between the routers in the network. Figure 10–12 illustrates a spanning tree example on a small network. To build a spanning tree path between all of the nodes in the network, we begin at node A and examine each of the paths to the other nodes that are connected to A, choosing the smallest. Next, it is necessary to examine each of the remaining paths between each of the currently linked nodes, again choosing the link to a new node which is the smallest. This process continues until all nodes are in the tree. Figure 10–12(b) shows each of the individual steps required to build the spanning tree between each of the nodes in the small network. Figure 10–12(c) shows the complete spanning tree with the darkened lines

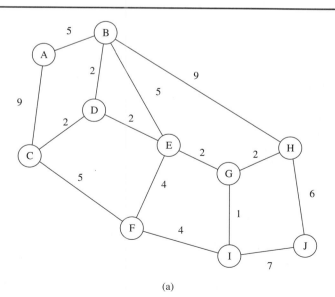

Figure 10–12
Choosing the best route between nodes using a spanning tree.

(a)

(continued on next page)

Figure 10–12
(continued)

#1

#2

#3

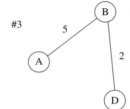

#4

#5

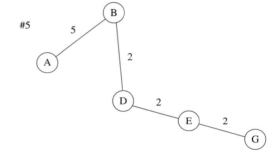

#6

#7

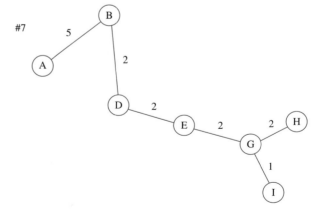

(b)

Figure 10–12
(continued)

Figure 10–12
(continued)

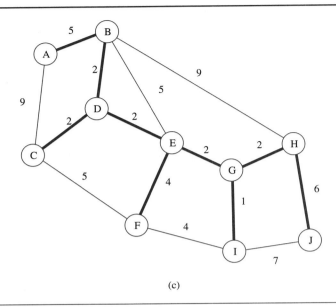

(c)

indicating the resulting path. Verify for yourself that all nodes have been added. There are six basic steps used to create the tree:

1. Let the distance $D(n)$ = the set of the weighted links for a given path.
2. Let the cost $C(i, j)$ = the cost between the two nodes i and j
3. Initialize the set $N = \{1\}$
4. For each node (n), not in N set $D(n) = C(n, j)$ for all nodes j in N
5. Find a new node (m) not in N for which the value of $D(m)$ is the minimum.
6. Add m to set N.
7. Repeat steps 4 through 6 until all nodes are in set N.

Note that spanning trees were originally implemented in 802.3 MAC bridges. Newer and more efficient methods called *reverse-path forwarding, Steiner trees,* and *center-based trees* are also used to deliver routing messages across a network. You are encouraged to examine the details of these different traffic reduction strategies on your own.

Although link-state routing requires much more computation power it is more efficient. The advantages of link-state routing include

- Fast, loopless convergence
- Support for multiple metrics
- Support for multiple paths

The link-state header is shown in Figure 10–13. Table 10–5 describes each of the fields in the header.

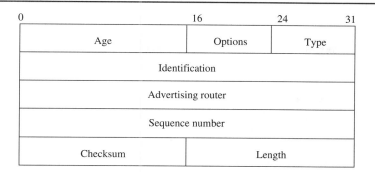

Figure 10–13
Link-state header fields.

Field Name	Size	Meaning
Age	16 bits	Time in seconds since first advertisement
Options	8 bits	Description of the capabilities of the advertising router
Type	8 bits	Type of link state connection: • External link • Network link • Router link • Summary Link (Border network) • Summary Link (IP network)
Identification	32 bits	Link Identification chosen by the advertising router
Advertising Router	32 bits	Address of the advertising router
Sequence Number	32 bits	Identifier associated with the advertisement
Checksum	16 bits	Computed checksum value
Length	16 bits	Length of the record including the 20-byte header

Table 10–5
Link-state header field information.

One of the first types of routing protocols based on a link-state algorithm was end system (hosts) to intermediate systems (routers) (ES-IS) and intermediate system to intermediate system (IS-IS), which are described in several of the early RFC documents. ES-IS and IS-IS routing were originally used on the NSFnet when it was spun off from the ARPAnet in the early 1980s.

End System to Intermediate System

End system to intermediate system (ES-IS) is an OSI protocol that defines how end systems (hosts) and intermediate systems (routers) learn about each other, a process known as *configuration*. Configuration happens before routing between end systems can occur. Once configured, data can be exchanged between the end systems and intermediate systems and vice versa. Note that ES-IS is more of a *discovery* protocol than a routing protocol but is a necessary step in the routing process. Being able to communicate between end systems and an intermediate system is the first of two steps. Next, the data must be transferred between the intermediate systems until the data reaches the intermediate system that can communicate with the end system, the destination. This is where the intermediate system–to–intermediate system protocol is used.

Intermediate System to Intermediate System

Intermediate system to intermediate system (IS-IS) is an OSI link-state hierarchical routing protocol that floods the network with link-state information to build a complete, consistent picture of network topology. To simplify router design and operation, IS-IS distinguishes between Level 1 and Level 2 ISs. Level 1 ISs communicate with other Level 1 ISs in the same area. Level 2 ISs route between Level 1 areas and form an intradomain routing backbone. Hierarchical routing simplifies backbone design because Level 1 ISs only need to know how to get to the nearest Level 2 IS. The backbone routing protocol also can change without impacting the intra-area routing protocol.

IS-IS uses a single required default metric with a maximum path value of 1,024. IS-IS uses three basic packet formats: *IS-IS hello packets*, *link-state packets (LSPs)*, and *sequence-number packets (SNPs)*. Each of the three IS-IS packets has a complex format with the following three different logical parts. The first part consists of an 8-byte fixed header shared by all three packet types. The second part is a packet-type–specific portion with a fixed format. The third part is also packet-type–specific but of variable length. Figure 10–14 illustrates the logical format of IS-IS packets. Table 10–6 shows the common header fields of the IS-IS packets.

Following the common header, each packet type has a different additional fixed portion, followed by a variable length portion. A more robust version of the protocol is called integrated IS-IS.

Integrated IS-IS

Integrated IS-IS is a routing protocol based on the OSI routing protocol, but it also supports IP and other protocols. Integrated IS-IS implementations send only one set of routing updates, making it more efficient than two separate implementations, formerly called the dual IS-IS routing method. Integrated IS-IS is a version of the OSI IS-IS routing protocol that uses a single routing algorithm to support connection-oriented communication also.

The Netware Link Services Protocol (also used to route IP packets in a Novell network) is based on IS-IS routing.

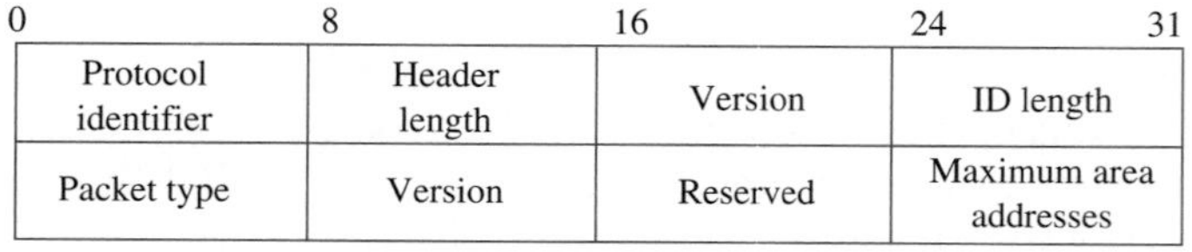

Figure 10–14
IS-IS packet header.

0	8	16	24	31
Protocol identifier	Header length	Version	ID length	
Packet type	Version	Reserved	Maximum area addresses	

Table 10–6
IS-IS header field
descriptions.

Field Name	Description
Protocol Identifier	Identifies the IS-IS protocol and contains the constant 131.
Header Length	Contains the fixed header length. The length is always equal to 8 bytes.
Version	Contains a value of 1 in the current IS-IS specification.
ID Length	Specifies the size of the ID portion of an NSAP address. If the field contains a value between 1 and 8 inclusive, the ID portion of an NSAP address is that number of bytes. If the field contains a value of 0, the ID portion of an NSAP address is 6 bytes. If the field contains a value of 255 (all ones), the ID portion of an NSAP address is 0 bytes.
Packet Type	Specifies the type of IS-IS packet (hello, LSP, or SNP).
Version	Repeats after the Packet Type field.
Reserved	Is ignored by the receiver and is equal to 0.
Maximum Area Addresses	Specifies the number of addresses permitted in this area.

NetWare Link Services Protocol

The NetWare Link Services Protocol (NLSP) is a link-state routing protocol based on IS-IS. NLSP is the successor to the IPX protocol. Routers employing NLSP use incremental updates (as opposed to periodic updates) when exchanging network topology changes with their immediate neighbors. NLSP was designed to overcome some of the limitations associated with the IPX Routing Information Protocol (based on RIP) and its companion protocol, the Service Advertisement Protocol (SAP). NLSP was designed to replace RIP and SAP, Novell's original routing protocols that were designed when networks were local and relatively small.

As compared to RIP and SAP, NLSP provides improved routing, better efficiency, and scalability. In addition, NLSP-based routers are backward-compatible with RIP-based routers. NLSP-based routers use a reliable delivery protocol, so delivery is guaranteed. Furthermore, NLSP facilitates improved routing decisions because NLSP-based routers store a complete map of the network, not just next-hop information such as RIP-based routers use. Routing information is transmitted only when the topology has changed, not every 30 seconds as RIP-based routers do, regardless of whether the topology has changed. Additionally, NLSP-based routers send service-information updates only when services change, not every 60 seconds as SAP does.

In terms of scalability, NLSP can support up to 127 hops. Recall that RIP supports only 15 hops. Compared to RIP, NetWare Link Services Protocol offers the following benefits:

- Improved routing
- Reduced network overhead
- Very low WAN overhead
- Faster data transfer
- Increased reliability

- Less CPU usage
- Better scalability
- Superior manageability
- Backwards compatibility
- Support for multiple networking media
- Optional manual link-cost assignment

Inter-Domain Routing Protocol

The Inter-Domain Routing Protocol (IDRP) is an OSI protocol that specifies how routers communicate with routers in different domains. IDRP is designed to operate seamlessly with ES-IS and IS-IS implementations. IDRP is based on the Border Gateway Protocol (*BGP*), an inter-domain routing protocol that originated in the IP community that will be discussed shortly. Using IDRP, a partial route recalculation occurs when one of three events occurs: An incremental routing update with new routes is received, a neighboring router goes down, or a neighboring router comes up. Unfortunately, IDRP was not able to keep up with the dramatic growth of the Internet.

Exterior Gateway Protocol

The Exterior Gateway Protocol (EGP) is a protocol for exchanging routing information between two neighbor gateway hosts in a network of autonomous systems. The format of the EGP header is shown in Figure 10–15. A brief description of the purpose of each of the fields is shown in Table 10–7. EGP is commonly used between hosts on the Internet to exchange routing table information. The routing table contains a list of known routers, the addresses they can reach, and a cost metric associated with the path to each router so that the best available route is chosen. Each router polls its neighbor at intervals between 120 to 480 seconds and the neighbor responds by sending its complete routing table. The latest version of EGP is called EGP-2.

Another Exterior Gateway Protocol called the Border Gateway Protocol (BGP) provides additional capabilities.

Border Gateway Protocol

The Border Gateway Protocol (*BGP*), defined in RFC 1771, provides loop-free inter-domain routing between autonomous systems. BGP is often run among the networks of Internet service providers (ISPs), although BGP can be used as a

Figure 10–15
EGP header format.

0	8	16	24	31
Version	Type	Code	Information	
Checksum		Autonomous system #		
Sequence #		Data...		

Field Name	Size	Meaning
Version Number	8 bits	Current version number (currently = 2)
Type	8 bits	Subprotocol message type
Code	8 bits	Identification of a message within subprotocol
Information	8 bits	Information message codes
Checksum	16 bits	Computed checksum value
Autonomous System number	16 bits	Number of AS of sending router
Sequence number	16 bits	Used to correlate queries and responses
Data	Varies	Information to be exchanged between routers such as errors, neighbors, etc.

Table 10–7
EGP header fields.

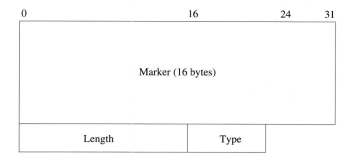

Figure 10–16
BGP header fields.

Field Name	Size	Meaning
Marker	16 bytes	Identification number used for security purposes
Length	2 bytes	Message length in bytes
Type	1 byte	Four types are defined: • Keep Alive • Notification • Open • Update

Table 10–8
BGP header fields.

protocol for both internal and external routing. The format of a BGP header is shown in Figure 10–16 and a description of the fields is provided in Table 10–8.

Before BGP exchanges information with an external autonomous system it ensures that networks within the AS are reachable. This is done by a combination of internal BGP peering among routers within the AS and by redistributing BGP routing information to Interior Gateway Protocols (IGPs) that run within the AS, such as Interior Gateway Routing Protocol (IGRP), Intermediate System to Intermediate System (IS-IS), Routing Information Protocol (RIP), and Open Shortest Path First (*OSPF*).

BGP uses the Transmission Control Protocol (TCP) as its transport protocol (specifically port 179). Any two routers that have opened a TCP connection to each other for the purpose of exchanging routing information are known as *peers* or *neighbors*. BGP peers initially exchange their full BGP routing tables. Thereafter, BGP peers send incremental updates only. BGP peers also exchange keep-alive messages (to ensure that the connection is up) and notification messages (in response to errors or special conditions).

When a BGP router receives updates that describe different paths to the same destination, it chooses the single best path for reaching that destination. Once chosen, BGP propagates the best path to its neighbors. The decision is based on the value of attributes (such as next hop, administrative weights, local preference, the origin of the route, and path length) that the update contains and other BGP-configurable factors.

The latest version of BGP, called BGP-4, has been used on the Internet since 1995. BGP-4 includes support for CIDR.

POLICY ROUTING

Policy-based routing refers to any type of routing that is based on factors other than the selection of the "shortest path." One of the primary uses of policy routing is used to accommodate acceptable use policies of the various interconnected networks. Other considerations are also incorporated, such as

- Contract obligations
- Quality of service (resource reservation)
- Service provider selection

The BGP is used to support policy-based routing. Policy-based routing is a newer type of protocol that is even more complex to set up and manage, although the rewards for doing so are great.

Other types of routing algorithms are also possible, such as those based on routing IP information over ATM, like Multi-Protocol Label Switching and the Private Network-Network Interface.

MULTI-PROTOCOL LABEL SWITCHING

Multi-Protocol Label Switching (MPLS) allows for faster, cheaper IP routers based on ATM technology. The label is used similarly to the ATM virtual circuit identifier.

Since the labels are shorter than IP addresses, the packets can be forwarded at a faster rate. The labels are independent of IP addresses allowing for policies. Multiprotocol Label Switching is an IETF initiative that integrates Layer 2 information about network links (bandwidth, delay, and bandwidth utilization) into Layer 3 (IP) within a particular autonomous system in order to simplify and improve the IP datagram exchange.

MPLS gives network operators a great deal of flexibility to divert and route traffic around link failures, congestion, and bottlenecks. From a quality-of-service standpoint, ISPs will better be able to manage different kinds of data streams based on priority and service plan. For instance, those who subscribe to a premium service plan or those who receive a lot of streaming media or high-bandwidth content can see minimal latency and packet loss.

When packets enter a MPLS-based network, label edge routers (LERs) give them a label (identifier). These labels not only contain information based on the routing table entry (i.e., destination, bandwidth, delay, and other metrics), but also refer to the IP header field (source IP address), Layer 4 Socket number information, and differentiated service. Once this classification is complete and mapped, different packets are assigned to corresponding labeled switch paths (LSPs), where label switch routers (LSRs) place outgoing labels on the packets. With these LSPs, network operators can divert and route traffic based on data-stream type and Internet-access customer.

Additional information about MPLS is available from http://www.mplsrc.com and http://www.ietf.org/ids.by.wg/mpls.html. You are encouraged to visit these Web sites for more information.

PRIVATE NETWORK-NETWORK INTERFACE

The Private Network-Network Interface (PNNI) is an ATM Forum specification for the protocols between switches in a private ATM network. The PNNI protocol has two main functions:

- PNNI includes a routing protocol for reliably distributing network topology information so that paths can be computed to any addressed destination.
- PNNI includes a signaling protocol for the establishment and take-down of point-to-point and point-to-multipoint connections.

The PNNI routing protocol is built upon concepts drawn from existing routing protocols (in particular OSPF) extended to support QoS routing and scalability. PNNI introduces full dynamic routing and enables the deployment of multivendor networks.

The PNNI protocol was developed to address the needs of applications with real-time requirements such as guaranteed bandwidth and bounded delay. These requirements place special demands on routing and signaling that are addressed by PNNI, and that are not found in protocols in use in existing data networks.

🖥️🖥️ LAYER 3 SWITCHING

A layer 3 switch is essentially a switch and a router combined into one package. *Layer 3 switching* has become popular due to the ever-increasing demand for bandwidth and services. Traditional routers have become bottlenecks in the campus and corporate LAN environments, due to their microprocessor-based operation and high latency. Layer 3 switches utilize ASIC (application specific integrated circuit) technology to implement the routing functions in hardware. This enables the layer 3 switch to perform router duties while forwarding frames significantly faster than an ordinary router. In fact, layer 3 switches are capable of forwarding millions of frames per second, compared to several hundred thousand frames per second for a router.

Replacing the campus or corporate routers with layer 3 switches, or adding layer 3 switching to a router-less network, has many benefits:

- Less expensive than routers
- Fewer network components to manage (via SNMP)
- Faster forwarding (close to *wire speed*, the speed of the frames on the wire)
- Helps provide QoS (quality of service) to the LAN environment
- Compatible with existing routing protocols (RIP, OSPF)
- Easier to configure than a router

There is a great deal of information about layer 3 switching available on the Web. Visit

http://www.3com.com/technology/tech_net/white_papers/500660.html

for an interesting white paper on layer 3 switching.

Figure 10–17 summarizes the layer-based networking components we have examined in this chapter, including the layer 3 switch. Let us see how these hardware components and protocols work together in an Internet service provider.

🖥️🖥️ INSIDE AN ISP

Figure 10–18 shows an overhead view of the networking and telecommunications room at a small ISP (Internet service provider). Along the east wall are

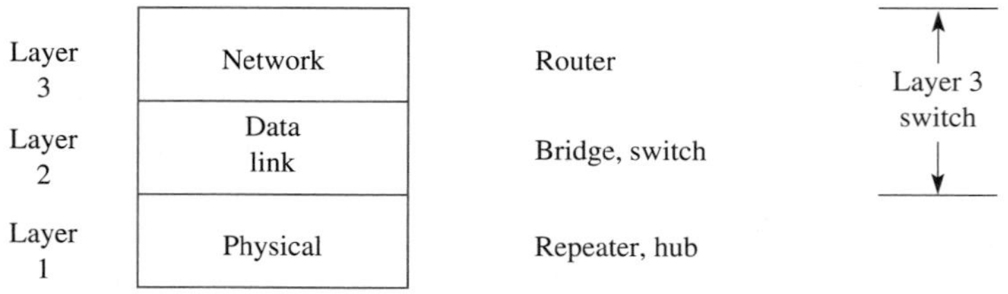

Figure 10–17
Network components and their associated layers.

Layer 3	Network	Router	↑ Layer 3 switch ↓
Layer 2	Data link	Bridge, switch	
Layer 1	Physical	Repeater, hub	

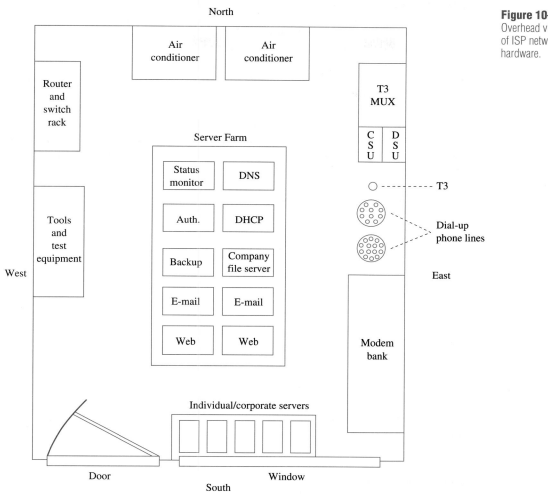

Figure 10–18
Overhead view
of ISP network
hardware.

the incoming phone lines (200 pairs), modem bank (groups of sixty-four 56K-baud modems in a rack-mountable case), and the 44.7-Mbps T3 connection (to a higher-level ISP).

The west wall contains the routers and switches that make up the ISP topology and logical networks.

The center of the room contains the server farm, where all of the servers required for operation of the ISP reside. These include servers for DNS, DHCP, electronic mail, Web pages, and authentication. One machine is dedicated to monitoring the network (via SNMP) and another for performing backups.

The south wall contains server space for individual and corporate servers, which, along with the dial-up users, help generate income for the ISP.

Numerous UPS (uninterruptible power source) units provide 30 minutes of power in the event of a main power loss.

Figure 10–19 illustrates the actual layout of the network. The T3 connection is the WAN connection to the higher-level ISP providing the actual Internet connection. Traffic in the T3 connection is filtered by the *firewall*. The I-router connects the individual subnetworks together and acts as the gateway to the Internet through the firewall. Employee computers (some of which have 100-Mbps switched service) communicate with their own file server or may tap into the server farm via the I-router. Individual and corporate servers share their own switch, as do the modems in the modem bank and the servers in the server farm. The F-router is used to lighten the load on the I-router for traffic moving between the server farm and the modem bank.

Figure 10–19
ISP network diagram.

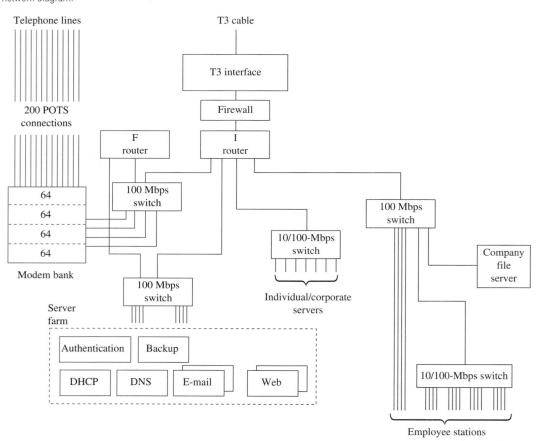

The network was designed in this fashion to allow the subnetworks to keep operating in the event that the main I-router goes down. Dial-up users can still check e-mail or work on their Web pages. Employees can continue to work as well, although without access to the Internet or the server farm.

TROUBLESHOOTING TECHNIQUES

It is good for network technicians and administrators to look at the big picture as well as concentrating on the little details. For example, a network administrator concerned with slow Internet access may first look for the cause in the local LAN. If no reason can be found, the slowdown may be due to slow traffic over the WAN connection. Perhaps a router central to the traffic flow has failed. One interesting way to check on the status of routers all across the Internet, as well as traffic characteristics, is to use the Internet Traffic Report located at http://www.internettrafficreport.com. Figure 10–20 shows the Internet Traffic Report home page.

The first item displayed shows each of the continents where major amounts of Internet traffic are concentrated. Left-clicking on a traffic icon brings up a page like the one shown in Figure 10–21. Here, additional details about the routers in Asia are displayed. Notice that the actual response time of three of the first four routers is less than the average response time of all the routers. The Beijing router, on the other hand, has a much higher response time. Left-clicking on the Beijing routers entry will provide additional details about the router, possibly suggesting a reason for the slow response time. Figure 10–22 shows one of several interesting graphs of the Beijing routers activity. Do you see any pattern for the day's activity index? Is there any relation between the index value and the time of day?

It would be time well spent looking through all of the information provided by the Internet Traffic Report.

To discover information about the topology of the underlying networks on the Internet, visit http://www.caida.org. This site is hosted by the Cooperative Association for Internet Data Analysis. The CAIDA home page is shown in Figure 10–23. There is a great deal of information about the structure of the Internet at the CAIDA site. An interactive tool called MAPNET allows you to choose a service provider, such as AT&T WorldNet, and examine its backbone. Figure 10–24 shows the USA view of AT&T's WorldNet backbone topology. Moving the mouse over any of the links causes a message to be displayed containing the speed of the link and the two cities connected by the link. Similar information is displayed when the mouse passes over a node.

Using the services provided by the CAIDA site may help you choose what service provider to use for your own Internet connection. You are encouraged again to spend time touring the site and seeing what other information is available.

Figure 10–20
Main Internet Traffic Report display.

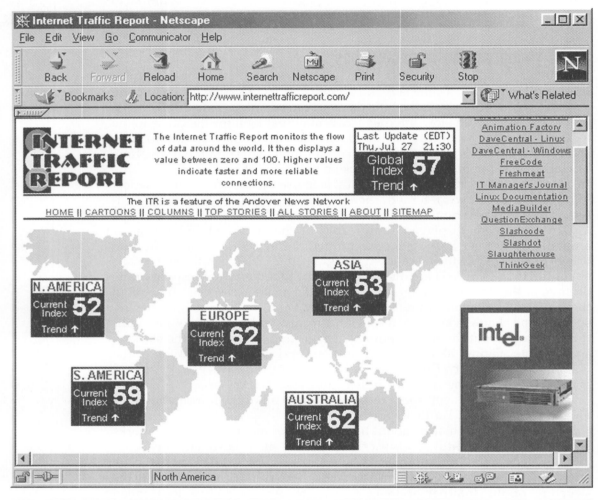

Figure 10–21
Router information for Asia.

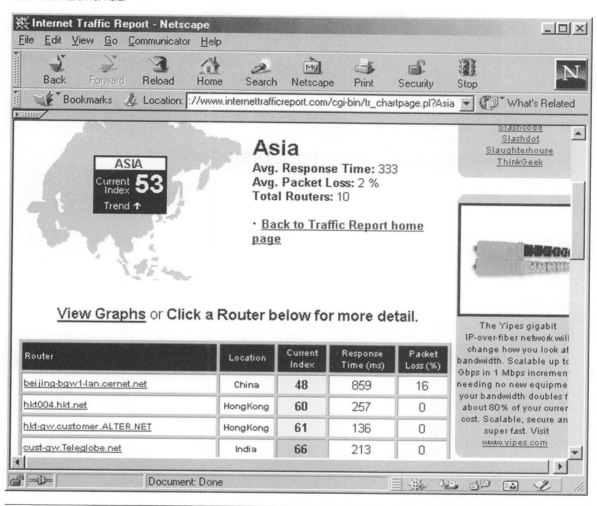

Figure 10–22
Detailed router history.

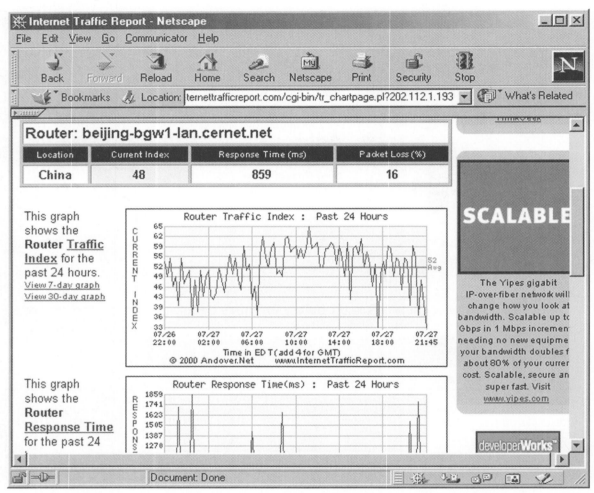

Figure 10–23
The CAIDA home page.

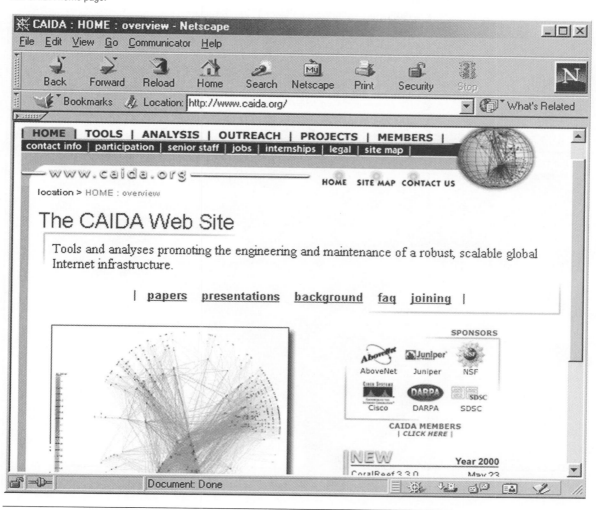

Figure 10–24
View of the AT&T WorldNet network topology.

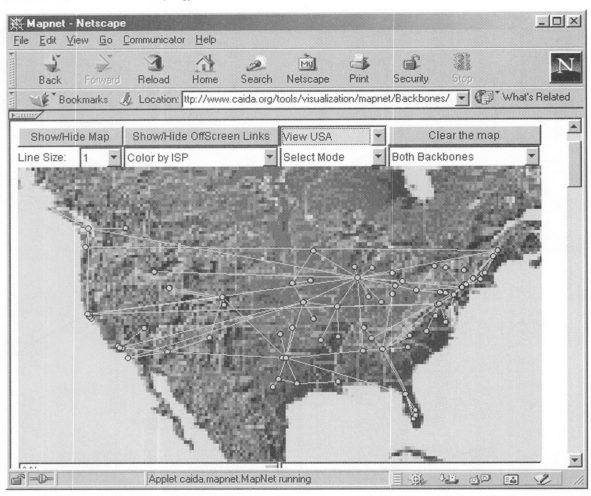

SELF-TEST

This self-test is designed to help you check your understanding of the background information presented in this chapter.

True/False

Answer *true* or *false*.

1. Hubs and switches both broadcast all received frames.

2. A switch uses the source MAC address to forward a frame.

3. Store-and-forward switching has a longer latency than cut-through switching.

4. Routers operate at Layer 3 (Network).

5. Routers require no configuration; they automatically learn their own addresses.

6. RIP is a link-state routing protocol.

7. Hop count is the only metric used in routing decisions.

Multiple Choice

Select the best answer.

8. A 4-port hub has how many collision domains?
   a. 1.
   b. 2.
   c. 4.

9. A 4-port switch has how many collision domains?
   a. 1.
   b. 2.
   c. 4.

10. Delay in a switch is called
    a. Latency.
    b. Stall time.
    c. Packet wait.

11. A local router is also called the
    a. Internal router.
    b. External router.
    c. Default gateway.

12. RIP has a hop count limitation of _____ hops.
    a. 15.
    b. 31.
    c. 127.

13. The _____ Gateway Protocol is used inside of autonomous systems.
    a. Interior.
    b. Exterior.
    c. Border.

14. CIDR uses _____ length subnet masks.
    a. Variable.
    b. Fixed.
    c. Static.

Completion

Fill in the blank or blanks with the best answers.

15. CAM, the memory used in a switch, stands for _____ Addressable Memory.

16. In a LAN, a _____ forwards traffic intelligently.

17. Networks are connected together using a

    _____.

18. Network realization time is the same as network _____ time.

19. RIP broadcasts up to _____ routes in a single message.

20. Hold downs are used in the _____ protocol.

21. A _____ tree contains nonlooping paths.

QUESTIONS/ACTIVITIES

1. Explain how four stations (A, B, C, and D) connected to a hub are able to communicate if stations A and B are talking to each other and stations C and D are talking to each other.

2. Repeat question 1 for a four-port switch.

3. The network shown in Figure 10–25 consists of five class C networks connected via six routers. Each network has a single machine on it. Study the diagram before continuing.

4. How many hops are there from one node to another? Make up a detailed table.

5. What are all the IP addresses? Assign IPs for each machine and all router ports. Some IP addresses are already suggested.

6. Estimate how long it takes (assuming all routers come on line at the same time with their port-0 and port-1 IP

addresses set) for the routing tables to stabilize. Use a 30-second RIP interval in your calculations.

7. What entries are in router Ra's routing table?

8. If router Rf goes down, how does machine 4 talk to machine 5?

9. What is the minimum number of routers required to connect all five networks?

10. What is the impact of eliminating one router from the network in Figure 10–25?

11. What is the impact of eliminating two routers?

Figure 10–25
Routers connecting
five class C networks.

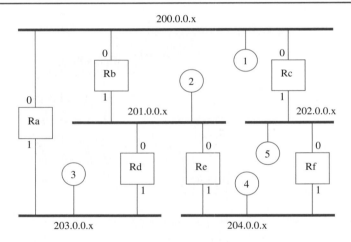

REVIEW QUIZ

Under the supervision of your instructor

1. Explain the basic differences between hubs and switches.

2. Discuss the difference between store-and-forward switching and cut-through switching.

3. Describe the operation of a router.

4. Explain the differences between distance-vector and link-state routing protocols and give examples of each.

5. Illustrate the differences between interior and exterior routing protocols.

Networking Concepts Laboratory

Experiment #10

Hubs, Switches, and Routers

Objectives

1. To explore the differences between hubs, switches, and routers.
2. To learn about the different types of routing protocols.

Required Equipment

The following equipment is required for this experiment:

- Two or more computers connected by a network
- Two hubs
- Two switches (optional)
- One router (optional)
- Crossover and straight-through cables

Procedure

Perform each of the following steps. Record your observations, results, and any difficulties you encounter. You will use this information when you develop your conclusions about the experiment.

1. Set up the small network of four machines shown in Figure 10–26. Assign the indicated IP addresses using the IP Address tab in the TCP/IP Properties window, as shown in Figure 10–27. In addition, share the C: drive on each computer.

   After rebooting each machine to enable the IP address, verify that the network is working by PINGing each machine.

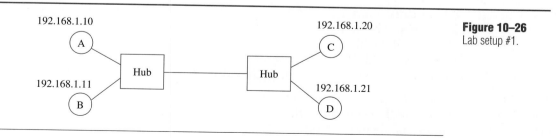

Figure 10–26
Lab setup #1.

Figure 10–27
Setting the IP address
of a machine.

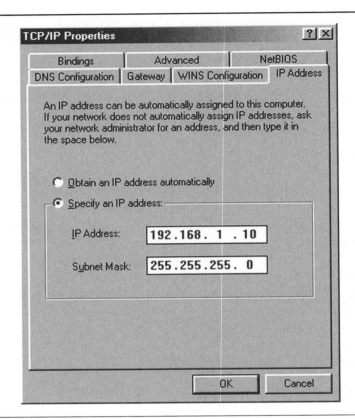

2. View the network using Network Neighborhood. If all four machines do not show up, check the File and Printer Sharing settings in the Network window.
3. Locate a large file or directory on the hard drive. Choose a file that is at least 10MB in size. The 25-MB file BIGFILE.DAT on the companion CD-ROM can be used for this purpose.
4. Using a stopwatch, record the amount of time required to cut and paste the large file or directory from one machine to another across the network. Specifically, transfer the file or directory from machine A to C and from machine B to D at the same time. Repeat the test three times and average the times together.
5. Change the IP address on machine A to 192.168.2.10. Change the IP address on machine C to 192.168.2.11. Reboot both machines.
6. Are all machines still visible in the Network Neighborhood?
7. Can all four machines still PING each other?
8. Switch the IP addresses back to their original values and reboot both machines.

Optional Procedure (if two switches are available)
9. Replace each hub with a switch, so that two switches are connecting the four computers.
10. Are all machines visible in the Network Neighborhood?
11. Can all four machines PING each other?

12. Run the same file transfer test performed in step 4. How do the hubs compare to the switches?

    Optional Procedure (if a router is available)
13. Setup the network shown in Figure 10–28. Switches may be used in place of hubs if desired.
14. Set the gateway address on each machine using the Gateway tab in the TCP/IP Properties window, as indicated in Figure 10–29. After entering the gateway address click the **Add** button. Machines A and B use router port 0 as their gateway. Machines C and D use router port 1.

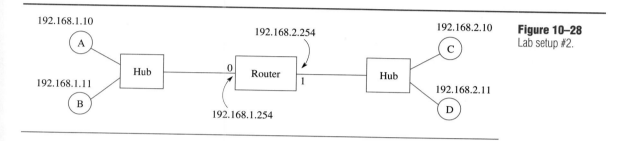

Figure 10–28
Lab setup #2.

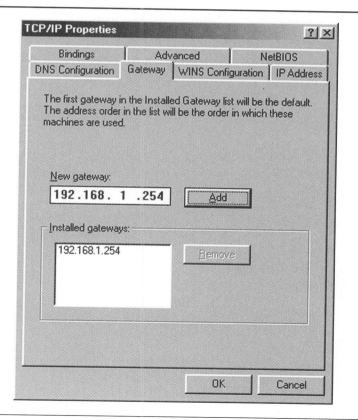

Figure 10–29
Setting the gateway address.

15. Configure the router according to its packaged directions. Use RIP to enable the two different networks to communicate.
16. Are all four machines visible in Network Neighborhood?
17. Can all machines PING each other?

Discussion and Conclusion

Using a word processor, write your own detailed explanations of the results and observations made during the experiment. To begin, try to say something about each procedure step.
    In addition, provide answers to the following questions:

1. How do routers and layer 3 switches differ? How are they the same?
2. What metrics are most important in the newer routing technologies? Why?
3. What is the advantage of a cut-through switch type over store-and-forward switching?

11

Network Management and Security

PERFORMANCE OBJECTIVES
Upon completion of this chapter, you will be able to

- Discuss the various elements of network management and security.
- Explain various encryption and authentication techniques.
- Describe the purpose of IP masquerading and tunneling.

Joe Tekk was always concerned about network security. One day he decided to sit down and install Pretty Good Privacy, a security program that is used to secure e-mail messages and files.

Joe downloaded the ZIP file from the Massachusetts Institute of Technology Web site and then proceeded to extract the files to a temporary directory for use during the installation. As the installation program executed, Joe was surprised by the amount of interaction that was necessary. He selected the PGP components to install, generated the key pair using the default key pair size of 2048 bits, and uploaded the key pair to the PGP server. After the installation was complete he had to reboot his machine.

Later that day, Joe was very excited to receive his first PGP encoded e-mail from his friend Ken Koder. He had no idea what it said but it looked cool.

INTRODUCTION

In this chapter, we examine two important areas of computer networking: network management and network security. Network management involves managing the network technologies to provide a business or organization a cost efficient, reliable computer network. Network security (a subset of network management) involves the methods used to secure data as it is transmitted on a network and the methods used to regulate what packets are transmitted. Let us begin by looking at network management.

NETWORK MANAGEMENT

Network management is one of the most important tasks that is performed in a networked computer environment. The network management function within a company or an organization is performed by a system administrator, network manager, or network engineer. Planning what network topology is used, what computers are part of the network, how they participate in the network, what type of information they can access and share, how they get backed up, and how they get restored in the event of a hard drive crash or corruption are each an essential element of network management. Other important elements include how physical access to the network hardware is granted, how network printers are configured, and other network resources can be shared. Each of the essential elements requires careful planning and record keeping to maintain a current view (or status) of the network. These items can be expanded into several different categories that must be reviewed. A partial list of these categories follows:

- System hardware and software configuration and management
- Network storage management
- Security management
- Traffic management
- Performance management
- Hardware and software maintenance
- Disaster planning and backup management
- Consulting and outside resource management

In addition to these items, a network manager is also interested in answering a host of questions and concerns that involve reviewing and selecting new network technology. Some of these concerns are as follows:

- What can a new technology do for a business?
- How is the current environment affected?
- What is the cost of new technology?
- What is the learning curve asociated with new technology?
- What are the risks?
- How does it compare with alternative technologies?
- How would the new technology affect business partners?
- How does the new technology impact clients and customers?
- What effect will the new technology have on employees?
- If the technology breaks, how does it affect the rest of the network?
- How easy can the technology be repaired?
- Can the technology be made fault tolerant?
- How difficult is the technology to administer and maintain?
- Can existing staff manage the new technology?
- Will retraining of staff be required? How much will it cost?

- What are the recurring costs associated with the technology?
- What is the useful life of the new technology?
- How does the technology compare with that of other companies or organizations of about the same size?
- What technologies are other companies and organizations using?

Obviously, some of these questions will require an investment of time and energy to perform the necessary research and to make an informed decision.

Let us continue with a look at some of the tools that a network manager or administrator would use to perform their jobs.

Protocol Analyzers

The protocol analyzer is used to report the traffic type and usage on a computer network. The purpose of a protocol analyzer is to quickly identify network problems. Using the information provided by a protocol analyzer, it is easier to proactively monitor and plan for future network growth. Many different companies such as Network General Corporation, Fluke, and Cisco provide equipment and software to monitor and analyze network traffic.

A protocol analyzer is a stand alone unit that connects to the network, collecting statistical information about the network performance. These statistics are usually converted into graphical real-time views that are useful to identify and isolate network problems.

LanExplorer provides a breakdown of the protocols in a small window located at the bottom of the screen under the Protocols tab, as shown in Figure 11–1. Notice that a small set of protocol categories are provided. These numbers are updated in real time as LanExplorer monitors the network traffic. Review Appendix F for additional information on LanExplorer.

The RMON and RMON2 standards provide for support of packet capturing and protocol decoding. Using these standards, it is almost as easy to access data from remote network locations as it is to access it from the local segment of a LAN. RMON allows for traffic monitoring at the MAC layer and the RMON2 standard provides access to information at higher layers in the

Figure 11–1
LanExplorer Protocols display window.

Packets (since 05/16/99 01:17:33 PM)						Octets (since 05/16/99 01:17:3 ▲		
NetBIOS	8887 ▮ 15 %	AppleTalk	0	0 %	NetBIOS	7834077 ▮ 16 %	AppleTalk
IP	51756 ▮ 85 %	SNA	6	0 %	IP	40110014 ▮ 84 %	SNA
IPX	237	0 %	Vines	0	0 %	IPX	34478	0 %	Vines
XNS	0	0 %	DEC	0	0 %	XNS	0	0 %	DEC ▼

◄ ► \ Packets ⟨ TCP/UDP ⟨ Ethernet ⟩ **Protocols** ⟨ Pad ◄ |

protocol stack. RMON2 can provide access to additional information such as the protocol breakdown by

- Segment
- Network address
- Traffic between different network addresses
- Application layer for a network address
- Application layer for exchanges between different network addresses

The Simple Network Management Protocol provides support for these standards.

SNMP

Unlike a protocol analyzer, the mechanism to gather the statistics on a device-by-device basis is performed using the Simple Network Management Protocol, or SNMP. Network devices that are categorized as *managed* support SNMP. These devices include hubs, switches, routers, and other network devices. SNMP has existed since 1990 and is described by RFCs. SNMP uses *agents* to gather network statistics and *management stations* to report on the data.

SNMP has become very popular because of its usefulness, and it is simple to use. Four operations involved in SNMP are shown in Table 11–1. Of these four operations, two of them, GET and GET-NEXT, are used to retrieve the information from the managed device; the SET operation is used to manage (create or modify) the network object; and the TRAP operation is used to capture network events of interest.

To fully understand how SNMP is used, we will examine three categories. Together, they define the full scope of how SNMP is used. The first category is the SNMP protocol itself, which specifies the format of SNMP messages and the rules on how the messages are exchanged. The second category to consider is the rules for specifying what type of management information is collected. These rules are called the *structure of management information*, or SMI. The SMI rules are used both to name and define the individual objects that we choose to manage. Third, we must examine how the information is organized and used. The *management information base*, or MIB, is a collection of the entire list of managed objects used by a device.

With this set of tools available to the network administrator, we can begin to focus our attention on the area of network security.

Table 11–1
Fundamental simple network management protocol operations.

Operation	Description
GET	Retrieve a specific object
GET-NEXT	Retrieve a collection of objects in a MIB tree
SET	Create or modify a specific object
TRAP	Send notification of an event to a management station

NETWORK SECURITY

Network security begins with the security measures in place on a host computer. Protection of files and limited access to resources are simple measures that can be instituted on every host. With adequate measures in place for the hosts, the network security issues can be addressed. Network security is grouped into two categories: the methods used to secure the data and the methods used to regulate what data can be transmitted.

The methods used to secure data can go from one extreme, in which a computer should not even be connected to a network, to the other, in which all of the information on a computer can be publicly accessed. A middle-of-the-road approach is usually adequate for most businesses and organizations that involve some type of encryption. Access to data is allowed on a "need to know" basis. A secret key or keys can be distributed as needed.

The methods used to regulate the transmission of data are accomplished by placing devices (router, firewall, etc.) between the data and the users. If the transmission of the data is authorized, the transmission can be allowed. Otherwise the transmission must be blocked and a notification sent to the security administrator. This becomes a difficult task to handle if many users require varying amounts of access to data.

To gain a better understanding, it is useful to be knowledgeable about the types of threats and the types of problems that a security administrator faces on a daily basis.

Threats

The threats to a networked computer environment are many. Essentially, the goal for networked computers is to transmit information from a source location to a destination, as shown in Figure 11–2. Figure 11–2(a) shows a rather simplistic view of the exchange of information between a source and a destination location. In practice, the communication may be encrypted for added security, or IP tunneling may be employed to further restrict access to sensitive information. Figure 11–2(b) through Figure 11–2(e) shows several different scenarios that are commonly associated with exchanging information between computers. Different security measures are employed to deal with each of the problems highlighted in Figure 11–2. Table 11–2 describes the common security measures that are employed to strengthen network security.

One of the most commonly encountered scenarios in a computer network involves computer viruses. A computer virus can infect a corporate network, small business, or personal computer and stop or reduce regular network activity.

Viruses

A computer *virus* is a piece of software that has been written to enter a computer system and corrupt the files on the hard drive. Some computer viruses are a nuisance, like the common cold, and others can be as deadly to your hard drive as cancer. With more than 50,000 known strains, the chances that your computer will contract one at some point are high.

Figure 11–2
Typical information
exchange scenarios
between A and B.

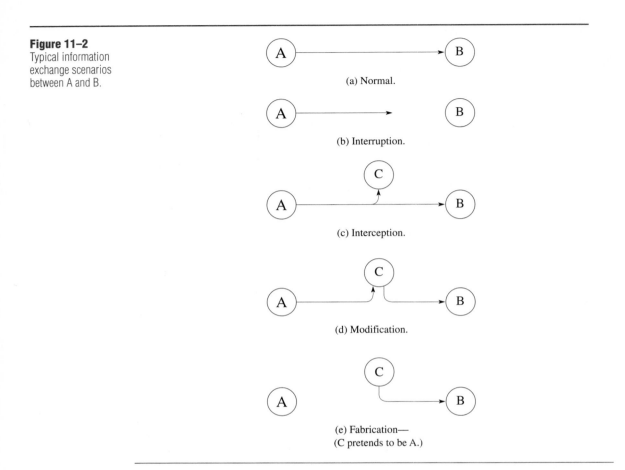

(a) Normal.

(b) Interruption.

(c) Interception.

(d) Modification.

(e) Fabrication—
(C pretends to be A.)

Table 11–2
Different types of
security measures.

Security Measure	Description
Accessibility	Allow access to information on a restricted basis
Authentication	Correctly identify the origin of an electronic message
Availability	Make sure that computer resources are available when needed
Confidentiality	Allow only authorized parties to access information
Integrity	Allow only authorized parties to update information
Nonrepudiation	Provide a mechanism to prevent the sender or receiver the ability to deny an electronic transmission

Computer viruses are categorized into four main types: boot sector, file or program, macro, and multipartite viruses. **Boot sector viruses** are usually transmitted when an infected floppy disk is left in the drive and the system is rebooted. The virus is read from the infected boot sector of the floppy disk and written to the master boot record of the system's hard drive. The master boot sector is the first place your system reads from when booting up from the hard drive. Then, whenever the computer is booted up, the virus will be loaded into the system's memory.

Program or **file viruses** are pieces of viral code that attach themselves to executable programs. Once the infected program is run, the virus is transferred to your system's memory and may replicate itself further.

Macro viruses are currently the most commonly found viruses. They infect files run by applications that use macro languages, like Microsoft Word or Excel. The virus looks like a macro in the file, and when the file is opened, the virus can execute commands understood by the application's macro language.

Multipartite viruses have characteristics of both boot sector viruses and file viruses. They may start out in the boot sector and spread to applications, or vice versa.

While they are not technically viruses, other malicious programs like worms and Trojan horses usually are included in the virus category, too. They typically have the same type of results as viruses and are written to wreak havoc on a system or networks, or both. The latest types of viruses are called *stealth*, *polymorphic*, and *armored*.

A *worm* is a program that replicates itself, but does not necessarily infect other programs. The Melissa and ILOVEYOU e-mail viruses, which caused widespread problems, are good examples of recent worms. These worms replicated themselves by using e-mail systems, making use of Microsoft Outlook address books.

Trojan horses (as in Greek mythology) contain a concealed surprise. A Trojan horse program resides hidden in another seemingly harmless piece of software until some condition triggers execution.

Viruses can be written to affect almost any type of file, so it is important to be aware of this when installing software on a system. Note that there are many instances of viruses being accidentally included in licensed, shrink-wrapped software, although you are generally safe when installing legally purchased software that has been obtained through normal channels.

The process of tracking and developing methods to render a computer virus harmless is a big business since it can affect governments, corporations, educational institutions, and individuals. As far as network and security administrators are concerned, they are interested in virus prevention, virus detection, and virus elimination, in that order. With proper virus prevention safeguards, it is likely that a catastrophic event can be avoided. Unfortunately, a virus is not the only threat to a computer network. Let us take a look at another common danger that can be used to compromise network security.

Network Sniffers

A *network sniffer* can be a device like a protocol analyzer, or LanExplorer. Using a network sniffer, it is possible for network traffic to be captured and decoded. This includes passwords, trade secrets, or other proprietary information that may be considered highly secret. A network sniffer operates in a passive mode. The device is attached to the network and then proceeds to silently collect information.

Table 11–3
Common terminology used in computer and network security.

Term	Description
Cipher	The method used to encrypt and decrypt data
Ciphertext	An encrypted message
Cleartext	Original data in unmodified form
Cryptography	Process to encode data to keep information secret
Cryptoanalysis	Process to break a ciphertext message without knowledge of the key
Cryptology	Branch of mathematics that studies cryptographic methods
Decryption	Retrieving a plain text message from Ciphertext
DES	Data Encryption Standard
DSS	Digital Signature Standard
Key	A secret key used to encrypt or decrypt data
NIST	National Institute of Standards and Technology
NSA	National Security Agency
Plain text	Original data in unmodified form
Private Key	A key used to decrypt a message
Public Key	A key used to encrypt a message
RSA	Rivest-Shamir-Adelman encryption algorithm

After a period of time, the contents of the data that have been collected can be reviewed and the sensitive information extracted. This is one of the worst types of security breaches due to the fact that no one knows that network security has been compromised. Can you think of any ways to determine if a sniffer is attached to a network or prevent a sniffer from capturing sensitive information? One popular technique is data encryption. There are many different forms of data encryption and we will examine just a few of them.

Plain-Text Encryption

A first line of defense in protecting network data is to prevent passwords from being exchanged on the network in plain text. It may be helpful to review the common terms associated with network security shown in Table 11–3 before continuing. One of the methods used to prevent disclosure of sensitive information like a password is to *encrypt* it. In a Windows environment, the password used to gain access to a domain must be transmitted to the server for authentication. While in transit, the packet can be intercepted and decoded. For example, examine the following decoded NetBIOS packet. Note in particular the information between addresses 0030 and 0070:

```
Destination   Source        Protocol     Summary       Size   Time Tick
----------------------------------------------------------------------------
200.200.200.255  200.200.200.200  SMB C Transaction  UDP NETBIOS Datagram Service
268     12/13/99 13:46:41.415
```

```
Addr.  Hex. Data                                                    ASCII
0000:  FF FF FF FF FF FF 00 C0 F0 25 0B 2A 08 00 45 00   .........%.*..E.
0010:  00 FE 39 00 00 00 80 11 DD 95 C8 C8 C8 C8 C8 C8   ..9.............
0020:  C8 FF 00 8A 00 8A 00 EA 9C CD 11 02 00 3E C8 C8   .............>..
0030:  C8 C8 00 8A 00 D4 00 00 20 45 45 46 43 45 50 45   ........ EEFCEPE
0040:  4F 45 46 44 43 43 41 43 41 43 41 43 41 43 41 43   OEFDCCACACACACAC
0050:  41 43 41 43 41 43 41 41 41 00 20 46 43 45 42 46   ACACACAAA. FCEBF
0060:  4A 45 44 45 42 46 44 46 45 43 41 43 41 43 41 43   JEDEBFDFECACACAC
0070:  41 43 41 43 41 43 41 43 41 42 4F 00 FF 53 4D 42   ACACACACABO..SMB
0080:  25 00 00 00 00 00 00 00 00 00 00 00 00 00 00 00   %...............
0090:  00 00 00 00 00 00 00 00 00 00 00 00 11 00 00 3A   ...............:
00A0:  00 00 00 00 00 00 00 00 00 00 00 00 00 00 00 00   ................
00B0:  00 00 00 3A 00 56 00 03 00 01 00 01 00 02 00 4B   ...:.V.........K
00C0:  00 5C 4D 41 49 4C 53 4C 4F 54 5C 42 52 4F 57 53   .\MAILSLOT\BROWS
00D0:  45 00 0F 07 C0 D4 01 00 44 52 4F 4E 45 32 00 00   E.......DRONE2..
00E0:  00 00 00 00 00 00 00 00 04 00 03 20 45 00 15 04   ........... E...
00F0:  55 AA 76 69 64 65 6F 2F 6E 65 74 77 6F 72 6B 20   U.video/network
0100:  65 6E 67 69 6E 65 65 72 69 6E 67 00               engineering.
```

802.3 [0000:000D]
  0000:0005   Destination Address: FFFFFFFFFFFF (Broadcast)
  0006:000B   Source Address: 00C0F0250B2A (Kingston250B2A)
  000C:000D   Ethernet Type: DOD Internet Protocol (IP)
IP [000E:0021]
  000E:000E   Version: 4, Header Length: 20
  000F:000F   TOS, Precedence: Routine, Delay: Normal, Throughput: Normal,
             Reliability: Normal
  0010:0011   Packet Length: 254
  0012:0013   Identification: 0x3900
  0014:0014   Fragment Flag (bit 6..5): Undefined
  0014:0015   Fragment Offset: 0x0000
  0016:0016   Time to Live: 128
  0017:0017   Transport: User Datagram
  0018:0019   Header Checksum: 0xDD95
  001A:001D   Source Address: 200.200.200.200
  001E:0021   Destination Address: 200.200.200.255
UDP [0022:0029]
  0022:0023   Source Port: NETBIOS Datagram Service
  0024:0025   Destination Port: NETBIOS Datagram Service
  0026:0027   Packet Length: 234
  0028:0029   Checksum: 0x9CCD
NETBIOS [002A:007B]
  002A:002A   Type: Direct Group Datagram
  002B:002B   Flags: 0x02
  002C:002D   ID: 62
  002E:0031   Source IP: 200.200.200.200

```
0032:0033   Source Port: 0x008A
0034:0035   Length: 212
0036:0037   Packet Offset: 0
0038:0059   Source Name: DRONE2
005A:007B   Destination Name: RAYCAST
SMB [007C:009B]
007C:007F   ID: 0xFF, 'SMB'
0080:0080   Command Code: Transaction (Client Command)
0081:0081   Error Class: Success
0082:0082   Reserved: 0
0083:0084   Error Code: Success
0085:0085   Flag: 0x00
0086:0087   Flag2: 0x0000
0088:0093   Reserved: Not Used
0094:0095   Tree ID: 0x0000
0096:0097   Process ID: 0x0000
0098:0099   User ID: 0x0000
009A:009B   Multiplex ID: 0x0000
```

The plain-text encryption used by NetBIOS is plainly illustrated. The encoded text beginning at address 0039 is EEFCEPEOEFDCCACACACACACACACAAA. To decode this text string, we find the difference between each letter and "A." Each pair of difference values makes an ASCII code representing the original symbol encoded. For example, the "EE" codes become 44 (E minus A is 4), which is the hexadecimal code for an ASCII "D." The next two characters, "FC," become 52, which is the hex code for an ASCII "R." Figure 11–3 illustrates this process for the entire string, which encodes the NetBIOS name DRONE2. All of the "CA" codes represent blanks used to pad out the 15 character NetBIOS name field. Verify for yourself that the encoded text beginning at address 005B represents the name RAYCAST.

Though not difficult to crack, the NetBIOS plain-text encryption provides an easy way to provide a small measure of security to your networked resources. A

Figure 11–3
Decoding NetBIOS names.

|EE|FC|EP|EO|EF|DC|CA|CA|···|CA|AA|

EE becomes 44, which is an ASCII D.
FC becomes 52, which is an ASCII R.
EP becomes 4F*, which is an ASCII O.
EO becomes 4E*, which is an ASCII N.
EF becomes 45, which is an ASCII E.
DC becomes 32, which is an ASCII 2.
CA becomes 20, which is a blank.
AA becomes 00, which signifies the end of the name.

*Note that P–A = 15, which is a hexadecimal F.
O–A = 14, which is a hexadecimal E.

more reliable method to allow access is based on authentication services that are available on some operating systems.

Kerberos

Kerberos is an authentication service developed at the Massachusetts Institute of Technology. Kerberos uses secret-key ciphers for encryption and authentication. Kerberos was designed to authenticate requests for network resources rather than to authenticate ownership of documents.

In a Kerberos environment, there is a designated site on each network, called the Kerberos server, that performs centralized key management and administrative functions. The server maintains a database containing the secret keys of all users, authenticates the identities of users, and distributes session keys to users and servers who want to authenticate one another. Kerberos requires trust in a third party (the Kerberos server). If the server is compromised, the integrity of the whole system is lost. Public-key cryptography was designed precisely to avoid the necessity to trust third parties with secret information. Kerberos is generally considered adequate within an administrative domain; however, across domains the more robust functions and properties of public-key systems are preferred. There has been some developmental work to incorporate public-key cryptography into Kerberos.

Public-Key Encryption

As the name indicates, *public-key encryption* uses a public key. Public-key encryption actually uses two keys: one public key and one private key. The public key is used to encrypt the data to be transmitted. The public key cannot be used to decrypt the data. Instead, the private key is used to decrypt the data. This eliminates the problem with other encryption technologies in which the same key is used to encrypt and decrypt the data. Public-key encryption is a more secure method to encrypt and decrypt the data, since the public key can be posted for public access. Only the private key must be guarded very carefully and protected from disclosure.

Using public-key encryption, the public keys for individuals are stored on a public key ring. As messages are created, the public key ring can be accessed and the appropriate public key used to encrypt the message so that only the receiver of the message (with the corresponding private key) can decode the message and read it. This procedure is shown in Figure 11–4. Notice that Jim's key ring contains entries for Ken and Jeff. When a message is composed and sent to Ken, Ken's public key is used to encrypt the message. While the encrypted message is transmitted on the network, the message contents cannot be examined. Only Ken, the receiver of the message, can decrypt and read the message text.

Certificates of Authority

A *certificate of authority* is a method to help guarantee the sender of an e-mail message is who they say they are. Certificates of authority for enterprise, small business, and home use are available through Verisign.com.

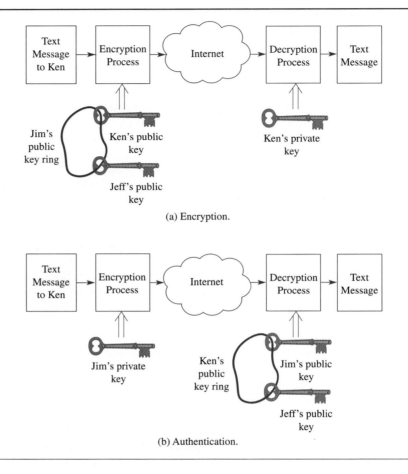

Figure 11–4
Information exchange using public-key encryption.

(a) Encryption.

(b) Authentication.

Certificates of authority are necessary because it is important to know who it is that you are dealing with. This provides an opportunity to

- Manage Web site domain names and server certificates
- Safeguard network resources using public-key encryption
- Secure network applications such as e-mail and messaging
- Enable e-commerce applications that support online payments and purchases

Certificates of authority are a necessary element in virtual private networks, business-to-business communications, secure e-mail, Web server certificates, wireless server certificates, and application security.

PGP

PGP stands for Pretty Good Privacy, a security application produced by Phil Zimmermann. PGP provides confidentiality and authentication services that can be used with electronic messages as well as file storage applications. PGP has gained significant popularity due to the following important elements:

- Uses the best cryptographic algorithms as basic building blocks, including public-key encryption and certificates of authority
- Unlimited distribution of source code and documentation
- Not controlled by a government or other standards organization

Specifically, PGP provides support mechanisms for digital signatures, message encryption, compression, and transparent compatibility with many application programs.

PGP provides an easy method to begin corresponding with a person who prefers to use encrypted messaging. The PGP freeware can be downloaded from the MIT Web server using the following address:

http://web.mit.edu/network/pgp.html

After the PGP software has been downloaded and installed, it is necessary to generate the key pair (one public key and one private key), publish the keys to the PGP server and create a public and private key ring. Depending on the type of e-mail software in use, the appropriate plug-in is installed. Figure 11–5 shows the PGP key generation process during the installation procedure.

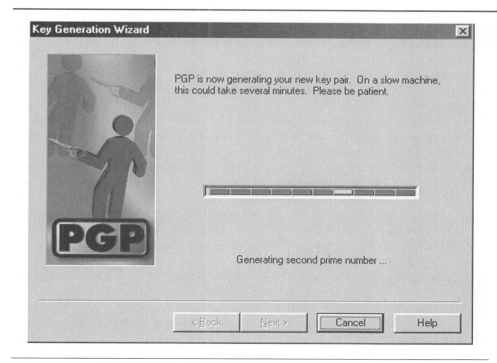

Figure 11–5
PGP key pair
generation process.

Figure 11–6
PGP tools menu icons.

The PGP tools program menu shown in Figure 11–6 is the launching pad for most PGP-related activities. Actions that can be selected directly are the PGP keys program, encrypt a file or message, sign a message, encrypt and sign a message, decrypt and verify a message, and wipe file or free information from a disk.

Masquerading

Masquerading takes on several different forms in computer networking and networking security. As a threat or attack, also known as *spoofing attacks*, masquerading can be used to enable one party to masquerade as another party without authority. This may be done by obtaining and using another principal's identity and password or by using a token after the authorization to use it has expired.

Another form of masquerading called *IP masquerading* or *IP spoofing* is a technique used in a network or system attack in which the attacking computer assumes the identity of a computer already in the internal network. The attacking computer spoofs or imitates the IP address of the internal computer to either send data as if they were on the internal network or to receive data intended for the machine being spoofed.

Yet another form of masquerading involves the use of one computer with an assigned IP address to forward information from a computer such as a LAN that uses an IP address not officially assigned by the network authority. Figure 11–7 shows how a computer that has two NIC cards installed can be configured to transmit network traffic from one network to another using a masqueraded IP address. This type of masquerade is used on networks where IP addresses are restricted or limited, such as a broadband network. For example, on the Road Runner system, the monthly service fee buys one IP address. If more than one IP address is required because there is more than one computer, an additional monthly fee is assessed for each additional address.

But to avoid purchasing additional IP addresses, another solution is available, which is to use IP masquerading. IP masquerading is available for the Windows platform using the Wingate product, as well as the Internet Connection Sharing feature of Windows 98 SE and Windows ME. It is also available in the Linux operating system as a built-in feature. Several companies such as Linksys and NetGear offer a hardware solution in products called *broadband routers*. These devices act as an intermediary between the broadband service provider and a local LAN.

Figure 11–7
IP masquerading.

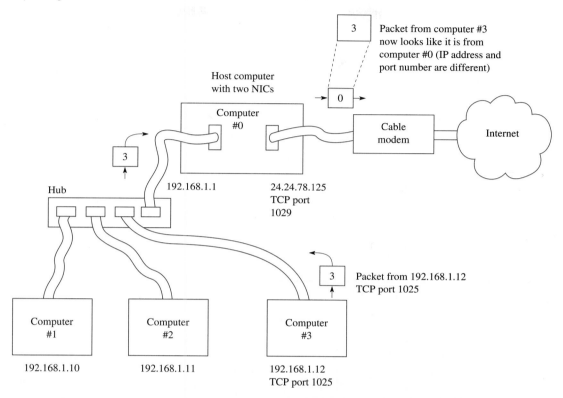

Firewalls

A *firewall* is a software program that examines packets of information to determine whether or not to allow the communication exchange to occur. Figure 11–8 shows how a firewall is used to protect an intranet from external access. Notice that some network traffic may be blocked from passing through the firewall in either direction, whereas other traffic passes freely.

When a firewall is used within an organization, it must be placed in a strategic location to prevent access to the private information but at the same time allowing access to the public. As you can see from Figure 11–9, the firewall is placed between the public and private networks and allows for packets to be exchanged based on rules determined by the network/security administrator.

A new firewall product (a software program called ZoneAlarm) has been created for users in broadband network environments, such as the Time Warner Road Runner system and the Digital Subscription Line (DSL) offered

Figure 11–8
Communication networks connected to a firewall.

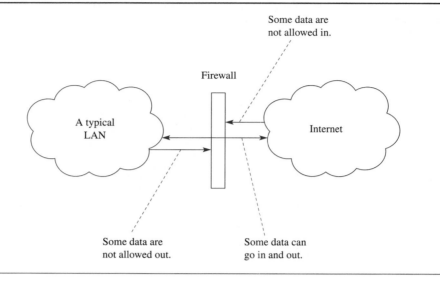

Figure 11–9
Placement of a firewall in a networked environment.

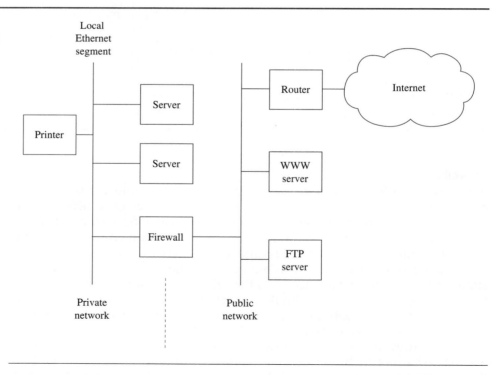

by many local phone companies. A computer attached to the Road Runner or DSL network is susceptible to probing and access from remote devices. Several new programs are available to restrict access to the personal computer resources that are connected to a cable or DSL modem. To see how vulnerable a particular computer is, visit Gibson Research Corporation at www.grc.com for a friendly interrogation using the Shields Up program.

One of the firewall programs is called ZoneAlarm, which is available for free for noncommercial use. Visit www.zonelabs.com for more information about ZoneAlarm.

IP Security

IPSec, or IP security, provides the capability to secure communications across a LAN, between public and private networks, and across the Internet. IPSec can be used to secure the transmission of data in the following situations:

- Secure branch office connectivity using the Internet
- Secure remote access to a user connected by an any Internet service provider
- Provide secure access to business partners

IPSec is incorporated into the TCP/IP protocol stack below the UDP and TCP transport protocols. This means that there is no need to modify the software on a system or user computer.

The Computer Emergency Response Team provides a centralized resource to collect and disseminate information regarding security issues on the Internet. You are encouraged to visit the CERT Web site at http://www.cert.org. The CERT Coordination Center provides incident response services to sites that have been the victims of attack, publishes a variety of security alerts, research security, and survivability reports in wide area networked computing, and develops information to help improve network security.

Tunneling

Tunneling is a security measure that uses the public network infrastructure, such as the Internet, as part of a private network. When data is transmitted on the network, it is encapsulated in such a way that the original source address, destination address, and payload data are encrypted. This is illustrated in Figure 11–10. A user who captures these encrypted packets cannot determine any information about the packet contents other than the source and destination address of the captured packet header, which provides no additional insight.

Denial-of-Service Attacks

A *denial-of-service attack* is characterized by an attempt to prevent legitimate users of a service from using that service. Examples include attempts to "flood" a network, thereby preventing legitimate network traffic; attempts to disrupt connections between two machines, thereby preventing access to a service; attempts to prevent a particular individual from accessing a service;

Figure 11–10
Tunnel-mode
encryption and
authentication.

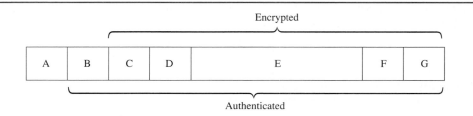

A—New IP header
B—Encapsulating Security Payload (ESP) headers
C—Original IP header
D—TCP header
E—Data
F—ESP trailer
G—ESP authentication data

and attempts to disrupt service to a specific system or person. Illegitimate use of resources also may result in denial of service. For example, an intruder may use your anonymous ftp area as a place to store illegal copies of commercial software, consuming diskspace and generating network traffic. Denial-of-service attacks can essentially disable your computer or your network. Some denial-of-service attacks can be executed with limited resources against a large, sophisticated site.

Denial-of-service attacks come in a variety of forms and aim at a variety of services. There are three basic types of attack:

1. Consumption of limited resources
2. Destruction or alteration of configuration files
3. Physical destruction or modification of network components

Denial-of-service attacks can result in significant loss of time and money for many organizations. The following steps can be taken to reduce the likelihood of a denial-of-service attack:

- Implement a firewall or filters on the router traffic
- Guard against TCP SYN flooding
- Disable any unneeded or unused network services
- Establish baselines for normal activity on the network

TROUBLESHOOTING TECHNIQUES

Network Management

Troubleshooting a network management problem requires patience and determination. Depending on the type of problem, there may be several different possible choices to choose from. Each of the choices may provide a workable solution, but one choice may be better than the others. For some problems it may be possible to choose the cheapest solution, but other problems may require the most complete solution, one that costs more than there is available in the budget.

Network Security

Troubleshooting a network security issue may involve a significant amount of research. It is best to have established a good baseline of normal system activity on which to start the investigative process. One of the most important tools available to the network/security administrator is a log of the system activities. By default, many activities are not written to a log file, but they probably should be. Examine what type of information is available, log the events to a file on a daily basis, and back up the log file information on a regular basis. Do not recycle the backups, because it may be necessary to review the contents of a log file long after the event originally occurred.

SELF-TEST

This self-test is designed to help you check your understanding of the background information presented in this chapter.

True/False
Answer *true* or *false*.

1. Users perform most network management functions.

2. A managed switch supports SNMP.

3. Firewalls prevent outside information from coming into a private LAN.

4. Kerberos uses plain-text encryption.

5. Tunneling utilizes encrypted data over a private network.

Multiple Choice
Select the best answer.

6. LanExplorer is a
   a. Sniffer.
   b. SNMP manager.
   c. SNMP agent.

7. This SNMP operation is used to capture network events of interest:
   a. GET.
   b. SET.
   c. TRAP.

8. Which is not a property of a virus?
   a. Can modify the boot sector.
   b. Replication.
   c. Safe to send via e-mail.

9. What ASCII symbol is represented by the NetBIOS plain-text encoded characters EN?
   a. 5.
   b. M.
   c. G.

10. PGP can be used to encrypt both e-mail messages and
    _____.
    a. Files.
    b. Modem connections.
    c. NIC data.

Completion
Fill in the blank or blanks with the best answers.

11. SMI stands for structure of _____
    _____.

12. A denial-of-service attack _____ normal network activity.

13. Kerberos is a(n) _____ service.

14. Public-key encryption uses _____ key(s).

15. IPSec stands for IP _____.

QUESTIONS/ACTIVITIES

1. Research three different denial-of-service attacks. Explain the methods used and the damage caused.

2. Search the Web for switches and routers that use SNMP.

3. What was the controversy surrounding PGP? Has the controversy been resolved?

REVIEW QUIZ

Under the supervision of your instructor

1. Discuss the various elements of network management and security.

2. Explain various encryption and authentication techniques.

3. Describe the purpose of IP masquerading and tunneling.

Networking Concepts Laboratory

Experiment #11

Network Security

Objectives

1. To examine encrypted passwords used by NetBIOS.
2. To experiment with a firewall.

Required Equipment

The following equipment is required for this experiment:

- Two or more computers connected by a network, with access to the Internet

Procedure

Perform each of the following steps. Record your observations, results, and any difficulties you encounter. You will use this information when you develop your conclusions about the experiment.

1. Use LanExplorer to capture NetBIOS passwords while users are logging in or sharing drives that are password protected.
2. Find an encrypted NetBIOS password and decode it.
3. Download and install a copy of a firewall application such as ZoneAlarm from www.zonelabs.com.
4. Try to PING the machine running the firewall. What kind of response do you get?
5. Let one computer executing the firewall software run overnight. What kind of attacks or attempts at access are found in the log the following day?

Discussion and Conclusion

Using a word processor, write your own detailed explanations of the results and observations made during the experiment. To begin, try to say something about each procedure step.
   In addition, provide answers to the following questions:

1. How secure is the network at your location?
2. What policies are in effect for network security violations at your location?
3. What is the occurrence of virus attacks on the network at your location?

12

Electronic Mail

PERFORMANCE OBJECTIVES

Upon completion of this chapter, you will be able to

- Describe the features of e-mail communication software.
- Configure an electronic mail client.
- Send and receive electronic mail.
- Discuss the protocols SMTP, POP3, and IMAP.

Joe Tekk checked his e-mail for the fifth time in 10 minutes. He was getting impatient, having gotten used to the quick turn around at his favorite software download site.

He checked it for a sixth time and was excited to see the e-mail he had been waiting for, an account verification response. The e-mail came with a small attachment containing a custom client application used with the software download site. Joe installed the client software and connected to the site to verify its operation.

Then Joe scanned several recent photographs and e-mailed their images to his sister, sent copies of a new network application he wrote to several friends, and finally handled the nine e-mail messages waiting in RWA Software's help desk mailbox.

Satisfied, Joe went to lunch. When he returned 45 minutes later, he had 18 additional e-mails to go through.

INTRODUCTION

Communications software is at the heart of the personal computer revolution. In this chapter, we will explore electronic mail (commonly referred to as *e-mail*), one of the most common communication tools available. This chapter will cover the basic features of electronic mail, how to configure client software, how to send and receive electronic mail, and how to organize e-mail messages on a computer that is connected to the Internet.

WHAT IS E-MAIL?

In the early days of computer networking, a simple electronic mail program was used to exchange plain-text messages. Since then, electronic mail has evolved into personal communication tool that can be used to

- Send a message to several recipients
- Send a message that contains text, graphics, and even multimedia audio and video files
- Send a message that a computer program will respond to such as a mailing list program or mail exploder
- Send messages that are encrypted for security purposes

Electronic mail combines the speed of electronic communication with features similar to the postal mail service. The major difference between the postal mail service and e-mail is that a computer can transmit a message across a computer network almost instantly.

When using electronic mail, several common features are available to the computer user. For example, it is possible for every user to

- Compose an e-mail message
- Send an e-mail message
- Receive notification that an e-mail message has arrived
- Read an e-mail message
- Forward a copy of an e-mail message
- Reply to an e-mail message

Let us begin our examination of e-mail by looking at the Simple Mail Transport Protocol (SMTP) to show how e-mail actually works on the Internet.

SIMPLE MAIL TRANSPORT PROTOCOL

The Simple Mail Transport Protocol specifies how electronic messages are exchanged between computers using the Transmission Control Protocol, or TCP. Recall that using TCP provides for a reliable exchange of data on the Internet without any possibility for loss of data. SMTP is used to exchange messages between servers or between a client and a server. Basically, SMTP is used to deliver electronic mail messages. The messages are retrieved through the use of an e-mail client program.

In order for a computer to use e-mail, it is necessary to install software on each system. Electronic mail uses the client-server method to allow mail to be exchanged. Client computers exchange messages with a server that is ultimately responsible for delivering the e-mail messages to the destination.

On the server computer each user is assigned a specific mailbox. Each electronic mailbox or e-mail address has a unique address. It is divided into two parts, a mailbox name and a computer host name, which are separated using an "at" sign (@) such as

mailbox@computer

Together, both of these components provide for a unique e-mail address.

The mailbox portion of the address is often made from a user's name. The host name part of the address is chosen by a network administrator. For example, Joe Tekk has the e-mail address joetekk@stny.rr.com. From the example, this indicates that joetekk is the mailbox name and stny.rr.com is the computer name. Notice that Joe Tekk's e-mail address ends in .com. The .com indicates that stny.rr is a commercial organization. You will observe that the last three characters of an e-mail address will normally end with a limited number of domain name categories. These categories are shown in Table 12–1. E-mail messages are actually exchanged using the client-server environment illustrated in Figure 12–1. Note that both of the computers in Figure 12–1 are called e-mail servers. When the mail message is exchanged, the mail transfer program on the sending computer temporarily becomes a client and connects to the mail transfer program running as a server on the receiving computer. In this way, whether mail is being sent or received will determine if the mail transfer program acts as a client or a server.

Domain Name*	Assigned Group
com	A company or commercial organization
edu	An educational institution
gov	A government organization
mil	A military organization
net	Network service provider
org	Other organizations
country code	A country code, for example, .us for United States, .ca for Canada, and .jp for Japan

Table 12–1
Common domain names.

*In November 2000, .biz, .info, .name., .pro, .aero, .museum and .coop were initially approved as additional domain types.

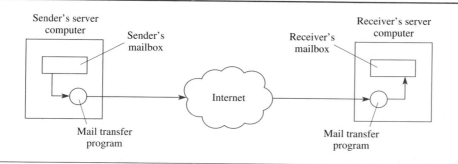

Figure 12–1
How e-mail is exchanged betwen servers.

Table 12–2
Typical e-mail
header keywords.

Header Keyword	Description
To	The mail recipient's e-mail address
From	The sender's e-mail address
Cc	List of carbon copy addresses
Bcc	List of blind carbon copy addresses
Date	The date when the message was sent
Subject	The subject of the message
Reply-to	The address to which a reply should be sent

FORMAT OF E-MAIL MESSAGES

The format of an e-mail message exchanged between the servers is quite simple. Each message consists of ASCII text that is separated into two parts. A blank line is used as the separator between the parts. The first part of the message is called a *header*. A header consists of a keyword followed by a colon and additional information. Some of the most common header keywords are shown in Table 12–2.

The second part of the message is called the *body* and contains the actual text of the message.

Recall that the body of a mail message first consisted of a plain-text message. In effect, the text that followed the blank line was the actual text of the message. A special scheme called Multipurpose Internet Mail Extensions (*MIME*) was developed to provide the ability to send many different file types as an attachment to an e-mail message. Information about MIME is provided later in this chapter.

E-MAIL CLIENT SOFTWARE

One of the most popular client software e-mail programs is Microsoft Outlook Express. It is installed as a part of the Windows operating system. There are usually several different ways to access the Outlook Express program. For example, there may be an icon on the desktop that can be double-clicked, a small Outlook Express icon may be found on the taskbar, or it may be a program that can be selected from the Windows Start menu. In any case, after the Outlook Express program is started, the computer user is presented with a screen display similar to Figure 12–2.

In order to use the Outlook Express program, it must be configured properly. This configuration consists of providing user information such as the user name, organization, e-mail address, and reply address. These items are located on the General Mail Properties tab, as shown in Figure 12–3. It is also

Figure 12–2

Microsoft Outlook Express displaying a message.

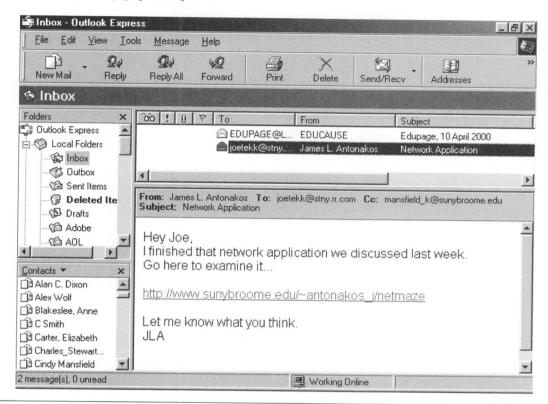

necessary to identify the server computer to which the client will connect to send and receive mail. This information is found on the Servers tab of the Mail Properties window shown in Figure 12–4. There is a server associated with both incoming and outgoing mail.

Incoming mail uses *POP3*, the Post Office Protocol, whereas the outgoing mail server uses SMTP, the Simple Mail Transport Protocol. Notice that the Servers tab is where the user enters an Incoming Mail Server account name and password. As an added convenience, it is possible for Outlook Express to save or remember the password for future use.

Sometimes it is necessary to change some of the mail parameters. For example, it may be necessary to change the server timeout value of the mail program or change the setting that determines if a copy of a mail message is to be left on the server computer after it has been transferred to the client. As you can see from Figure 12–5, there are several different settings that can be modified. It is always a good idea to leave the settings alone unless there is a good reason to change them, however.

Figure 12–3
Outlook Express
General E-mail
Properties tab.

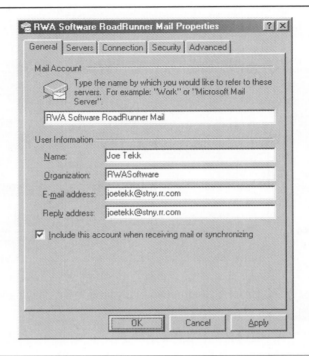

Figure 12–4
Outlook Express mail
servers.

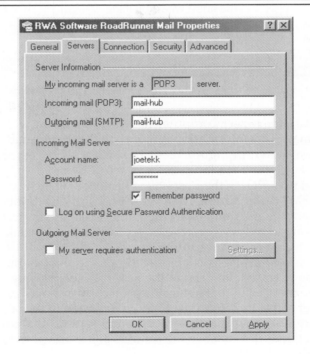

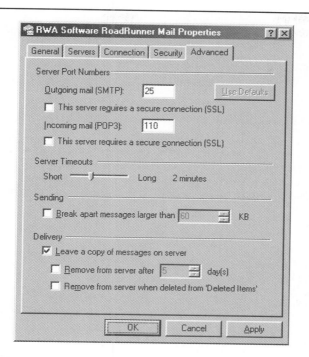

Figure 12–5
Outlook Express
Advanced Mail
Properties.

SENDING AN E-MAIL MESSAGE

Let us consider an example in which Joe Tekk creates the e-mail message shown in Figure 12–6. Joe uses the e-mail client to send a message to windy@alpha.com. The message is sent by Joe to the e-mail server at stny.rr.com. The mail server at stny.rr.com forwards the message to the e-mail server at alpha.com, where the user Windy can read that message. Figure 12–7 illustrates how the e-mail message is sent using the Microsoft Outlook Express client program. Notice that the SMTP protocol is used to transfer the message everywhere except for the client connection at the destination, which uses POP3.

RECEIVING AN E-MAIL MESSAGE USING THE POST OFFICE PROTOCOL

E-mail messages are received by the server and stored in the Inbox inside of a user's mailbox until it is read. For example, Figure 12–8 shows a message from the Java Developer Connection mailing list that was downloaded using the Post Office Protocol. After the message has been read, it can be deleted or saved. If a message is saved, it is normally moved to a folder other than the Inbox. This allows for mail to be stored in user-defined categories.

Figure 12–6
Creating a new
e-mail message.

Figure 12–7
Sending and
receiving e-mail.

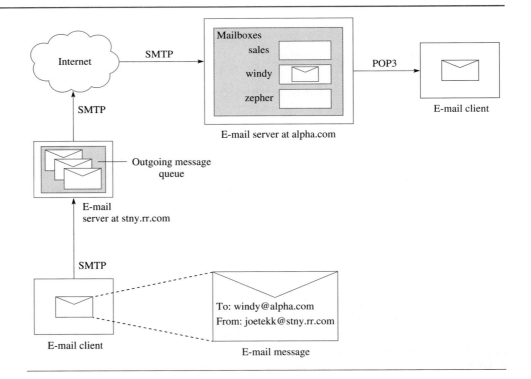

Figure 12–8
Reading a message in the Outlook Express Inbox.

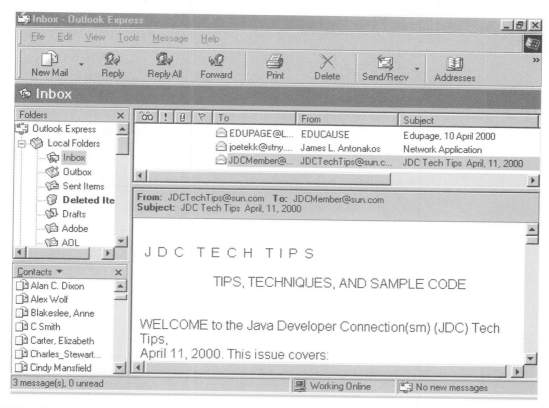

To create a new folder for the Java Developer Connection message, simply right-click on the Local Folders in the folder list and select New Folder. To move the message into the folder, drag it from the Inbox message list to the appropriate folder. This provides for an easy way to keep track of all related messages.

Note that Outlook Express provides the capability to store as many messages as necessary (as long as there is enough disk space available), although it is a good idea to keep the mailbox clean.

E-MAIL ERROR MESSAGES

There are several reasons why an error message may be generated when trying to send e-mail. Two of the most common errors stem from the user incorrectly specifying either the mailbox name or the computer name. In either

Figure 12–9
E-mail message indicating an invalid recipient.

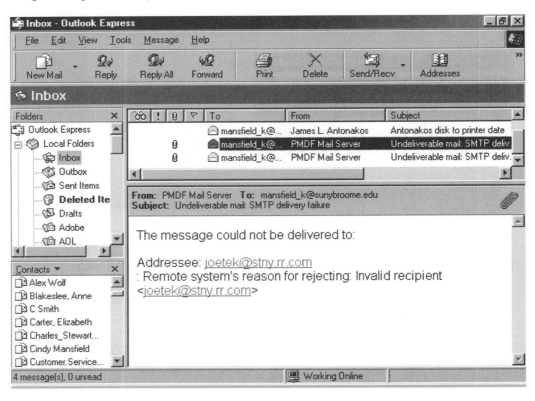

case, a message will be sent back to the sender indicating what type of error has occurred. Figure 12–9 illustrates an error with the mailbox portion of the address, whereas Figure 12–10 indicates a problem with the computer portion. Other problems with the mail will have their own specific message, which may help to resolve the problem.

ACCESS TO E-MAIL USING THE WEB

Some e-mail servers allow access to the mail system using a World Wide Web browser. The browser acts the same as an e-mail client that allows a user to send and receive e-mail messages. Figure 12–11 shows the opening screen of the Microsoft Outlook Web Access program, which uses the Microsoft Exchange Server. Note that a user name and password are required in order to access any mail files.

Figure 12–10
E-mail message indicating an invalid host-domain name.

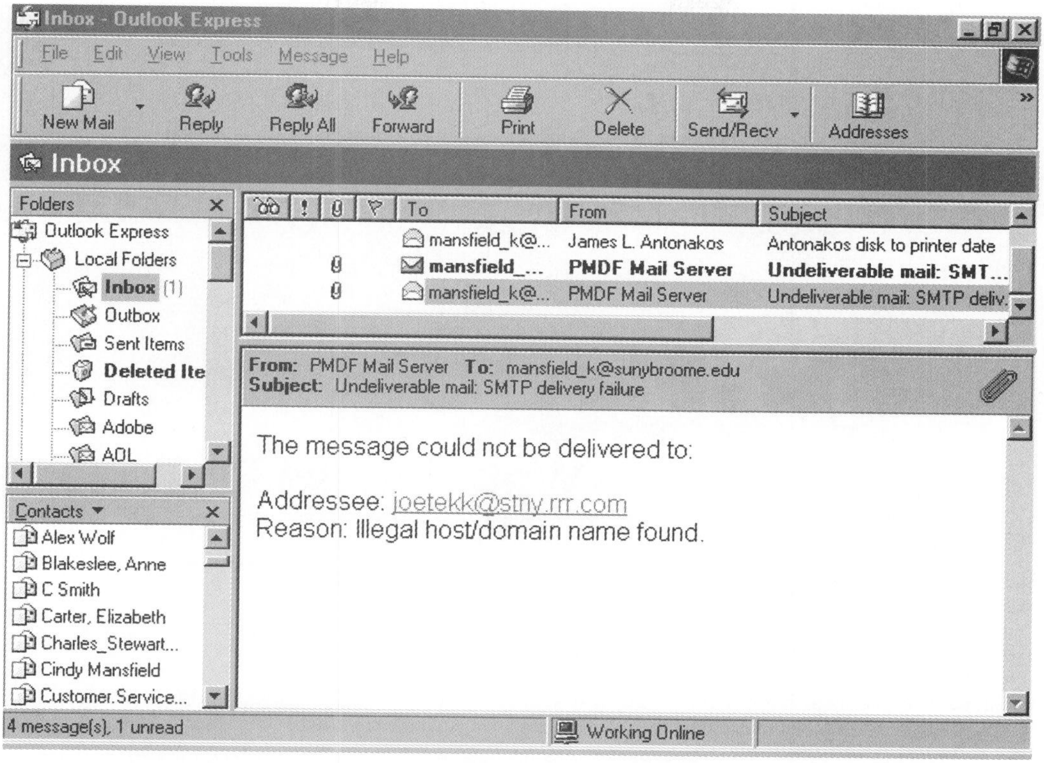

MULTPURPOSE INTERNET MAIL EXTENSIONS

Multipurpose Internet Mail Extensions, or MIME, provide a way for binary programs, graphical images, or other types of files to be attached to an e-mail message. Before the introduction of MIME, there were only a few methods to send electronic mail messages that contained anything other than plain ASCII text. Two of the most popular are uuencode and uudecode, available in the Unix environment.

The MIME standard provides several important features such as

- Specifications for other character sets
- Definitions for content types such as applications, images, and other multimedia file types
- A method to include several different objects within a single message
- An extended set of possible headers
- Standard encoding methods such as base64 and quote printable

Figure 12–11
Accessing the e-mail server using the Web.

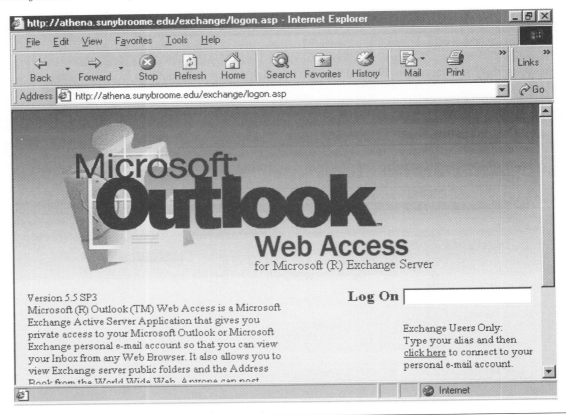

Note that although MIME was designed for electronic mail, Web browsers also use MIME to specify the appropriate plug-ins to handle the specified MIME data type. Table 12–3 shows a list of some of the common MIME data types. The MIME data type is associated to a file by the file extension. There are currently several hundred different MIME types. Additional MIME types are added as necessary.

The standard encoding methods used by MIME include base64 and quote printable. The base64 encoding method is used primarily to transfer binary attachments. Figure 12–12 illustrates how an e-mail message is displayed as a text file. Figure 12–12(a) shows the beginning of an e-mail message that contains the address information and all of the message headers. Notice that in order to continue reading the message as a text file, it is necessary to press the Return (or Enter) key as indicated at the bottom of the display. Examine the separator lines

MIME Type	Description
.au	Audio file
.bin	Binary file
.exe	Binary executable application file
.gif	GIF image file
.htm	HTML file
.java	Java text source file
.jpg	JPEG image file
.mid	MIDI Audio file
.mime	Message/RFC822 format
.mov	QuickTime movie file
.mpg	MPEG video file
.ra	Real audio file
.rtf	Rich text file
.tif	TIFF file
.uu	Uuencoded file
.wav	WAV file
.zip	ZIP file

Table 12–3
Common MIME data types.

and Content-type lines in the message displayed in Figure 12–12(b). This is where the base64 encoding method is specified for the message attachment. The string of characters that follows is the ZIP file shown in base64 encoded form.

The quote printable encoding method is used to encode 8-bit text codes such as those used in a foreign language character set into 7-bit U.S. ASCII characters. This quote printable format creates documents that are readable even in encoded form. Note that all MIME-compliant applications are capable of working with these standard encoding methods.

 INTERNET MESSAGE ACCESS PROTOCOL

The Internet Message Access Protocol, or **IMAP**, is a newer protocol designed to provide access to electronic messages that are stored on a mail server. IMAP was developed at Stanford University in 1986. IMAP is designed to eliminate the typical problems that are caused by downloading the electronic messages to a client computer using the Post Office Protocol. Instead, IMAP provides direct access to the messages that are stored on the server. This allows for mail messages to be managed from any computer at any time.

Figure 12–12
Text-based e-mail message with a binary attachment.

(a) Header

(b) Base64 Encoding

IMAP provides full compatibility with the Internet and MIME standards. In addition, IMAP includes several other new features such as concurrent access to shared mailboxes, online and offline access to messages, and management from any computer. With all of the benefits that IMAP provides, it is only a matter of time before its use is commonplace.

E-MAIL PACKET CAPTURE USING LANEXPLORER

Using a protocol analyzer such as LanExplorer, it is possible to capture all of the activity associated with sending a electronic mail message. For example, let us consider sending the following text message:

```
To: mansfield_k@sunybroome.edu
From: "James L. Antonakos" <antonakos_j@mail.sunybroome.edu>
Subject: Test message
Cc:
Bcc:

Ken,
Just wanted to capture this.


JLA
```

As you can see from the message text, it contains less than 40 characters. Examine each of the entries in Table 12–4 which shows the sequence of exchanges between the client and server to deliver the message. To help understand this exchange of packets, a list of the SMTP commands is shown in Table 12–5 and a list of possible server responses are provided in Table 12–6.

Three packet captures are provided here to illustrate how a mail message is exchanged. First, let us examine the contents of packet number 8, which contains the HELO message to waveguide:

```
Packet 8

Destination Source      Protocol        Summary    Size   Time Tick
-----------------------------------------------------------------------
192.203.130.2     24.94.41.254          Simple Mail Transfer Protocol TCP 70
        04/27/99 15:05:04.998

Addr.  Hex. Data                                       ASCII
0000:  08 00 3E 02 00 DD 00 60 97 2B E6 0F 08 00 45 00  ..>....'.+....E.
0010:  00 38 98 E5 40 00 80 06 DC B0 18 5E 29 FE C0 CB  .8..@......^)...
0020:  82 02 04 94 00 19 05 7C C6 43 01 A3 EC 43 50 18  .......|.C...CP.
0030:  21 3E E8 3E 00 00 48 45 4C 4F 20 77 61 76 65 67  !>.>..HELO waveg
0040:  75 69 64 65 0D 0A                                 uide..

802.3 [0000:000D]
```

Table 12–4
Electronic mail packet captures using LanExplorer.

Message	Packet	Destination	Source	Protocol	Summary	Size	Tick (msec.)
	1	Broadcast	Waveguide	ARP	Request	60	0
	2	Waveguide	bgm-41-1.stny.rr.com	ARP	Reply	60	20
	3	sbccab.cc.sunybroome.edu	Waveguide	SMTP	TCP (SYN)	62	0
	4	Waveguide	sbccab.cc.sunybroome.edu	SMTP	TCP (ACK,SYN)	60	45
	5	sbccab.cc.sunybroome.edu	Waveguide	SMTP	TCP (ACK)	60	0
	6	Broadcast	bgm-144-1.stny.rr.com	ARP	Request	60	1910
220	7	Waveguide	sbccab.cc.sunybroome.edu	SMTP	TCP (ACK,PSH)	120	165
HELO	8	sbccab.cc.sunybroome.edu	Waveguide	SMTP	TCP (ACK,PSH)	70	5
250	9	Waveguide	sbccab.cc.sunybroome.edu	SMTP	TCP (ACK,PSH)	112	70
RSET	10	sbccab.cc.sunybroome.edu	Waveguide	SMTP	TCP (ACK,PSH)	60	15
250	11	Waveguide	sbccab.cc.sunybroome.edu	SMTP	TCP (ACK,PSH)	63	40
MAIL FROM:	12	sbccab.cc.sunybroome.edu	Waveguide	SMTP	TCP (ACK,PSH)	99	5
250	13	Waveguide	sbccab.cc.sunybroome.edu	SMTP	TCP (ACK,PSH)	71	40
RCPT TO:	14	sbccab.cc.sunybroome.edu	Waveguide	SMTP	TCP (ACK,PSH)	92	5
	15	Waveguide	sbccab.cc.sunybroome.edu	SMTP	TCP (ACK)	60	95
250	16	Waveguide	sbccab.cc.sunybroome.edu	SMTP	TCP (ACK,PSH)	87	205
DATA	17	sbccab.cc.sunybroome.edu	Waveguide	SMTP	TCP (ACK,PSH)	60	0
354	18	Waveguide	sbccab.cc.sunybroome.edu	SMTP	TCP (ACK,PSH)	94	50
<text>	19	sbccab.cc.sunybroome.edu	Waveguide	SMTP	TCP (ACK,PSH)	488	40

Table 12–4
(continued)

Message	Packet	Destination	Source	Protocol	Summary	Size	Tick (msec.)
	20	Waveguide	sbccab.cc.sunybroome.edu	SMTP	TCP (ACK)	60	105
	21	sbccab.cc.sunybroome.edu	Waveguide	SMTP	TCP (ACK,PSH)	60	0
	22	Waveguide	sbccab.cc.sunybroome.edu	SMTP	TCP (ACK)	60	205
250	23	Waveguide	sbccab.cc.sunybroome.edu	SMTP	TCP (ACK,PSH)	63	155
QUIT	24	sbccab.cc.sunybroome.edu	Waveguide	SMTP	TCP (ACK,PSH)	60	5
221	25	Waveguide	sbccab.cc.sunybroome.edu	SMTP	TCP (ACK,PSH)	82	55
	26	sbccab.cc.sunybroome.edu	Waveguide	SMTP	TCP (ACK,FIN)	60	5
	27	Waveguide	sbccab.cc.sunybroome.edu	SMTP	TCP (ACK,FIN)	60	25
	28	sbccab.cc.sunybroome.edu	Waveguide	SMTP	TCP (ACK)	60	0
	29	Waveguide	sbccab.cc.sunybroome.edu	SMTP	TCP (ACK)	60	20
	30	Broadcast	bgm-135-1.stny.rr.com	ARP	Request	60	180

Table 12–5
SMTP commands.

Command	Parameter
HELO	<domain>
MAIL	FROM:<reverse-path>
RCPT	TO:<forward-path>
DATA	(none)
RSET	(none)
SEND	FROM:<reverse-path>
SOML	FROM:<reverse-path>
SAML	FROM:<reverse-path>
VRFY	<string>
EXPN	<string>
HELP	[<string>] (optional)
NOOP	(none)
QUIT	(none)
TURN	(none)

Table 12–6
SMTP reply codes.

Reply Code	Meaning
211	System status, or system help reply
214	Help message
220 <domain>	Service ready
221 <domain>	Service closing transmission channel
250	Requested mail action okay, completed
251	User not local; will forward to <forward-path>
354	Start mail input; end with <CRLF>
421 <domain>	Service not available, closing transmission channel
450	Requested mail action not taken: mailbox unavailable
451	Requested action aborted: local error in processing
452	Requested action not taken: insufficient system storage
500	Syntax error, command unrecognized
501	Syntax error in parameters or arguments
502	Command not implemented
503	Bad sequence of commands
504	Command parameter not implemented
550	Requested action not taken: mailbox unavailable
551	User not local; please try <forward-path>
552	Requested mail action aborted: exceeded storage allocation
553	Requested action not taken: mailbox name not allowed
554	Transaction failed

```
 0000:0005   Destination Address: 08003E0200DD
 0006:000B   Source Address: 0060972BE60F
 000C:000D   Ethernet Type: DOD Internet Protocol (IP)
IP [000E:0021]
 000E:000E   Version: 4, Header Length: 20
 000F:000F   TOS, Precedence: Routine, Delay: Normal, Throughput: Normal,
Reliability: Normal
 0010:0011   Packet Length: 56
 0012:0013   Identification: 0x98E5
 0014:0014   Fragment Flag (bit 6..5): Don't Fragment
 0014:0015   Fragment Offset: 0x0000
 0016:0016   Time to Live: 128
 0017:0017   Transport: Transmission Control
 0018:0019   Header Checksum: 0xDCB0
 001A:001D   Source Address: 24.94.41.254
 001E:0021   Destination Address: 192.203.130.2
TCP [0022:0035]
 0022:0023   Source Port: 0x0494
 0024:0025   Destination Port: Simple Mail Transfer Protocol
 0026:0029   Sequence Number: 92063299
 002A:002D   Acknowledgment Number: 27520067
 002E:002E   Header Length (bit 7..4): 20
 002F:002F   Control Bit - Acknowledgment; Push function;
 0030:0031   Window Size: 8510
 0032:0033   Checksum: 0xE83E
 0034:0035   Urgent Pointer: 0x0000
```

Notice that LanExplorer automatically decodes each packet and labels each item accordingly.

Next, packet number 12 shows the MAIL FROM: header, which identifies antonakos_j@mail.sunybroome.edu as the sender of the message.

```
Packet 12

Destination Source      Protocol        Summary        Size  Time Tick
-------------------------------------------------------------------------------
192.203.130.2     24.94.41.254          Simple Mail Transfer Protocol   TCP   99
         04/27/99 15:05:05.128

Addr.  Hex. Data                                          ASCII
0000:  08 00 3E 02 00 DD 00 60 97 2B E6 0F 08 00 45 00   ..>....'.+....E.
0010:  00 55 9A E5 40 00 80 06 DA 93 18 5E 29 FE C0 CB   .U..@......^)...
0020:  82 02 04 94 00 19 05 7C C6 59 01 A3 EC 86 50 18   .......|.Y...P.
0030:  20 FB 9F C0 00 00 4D 41 49 4C 20 46 52 4F 4D 3A    .....MAIL FROM:
0040:  3C 61 6E 74 6F 6E 61 6B 6F 73 5F 6A 40 6D 61 69   <antonakos_j@mai
0050:  6C 2E 73 75 6E 79 62 72 6F 6F 6D 65 2E 65 64 75   l.sunybroome.edu
0060:  3E 0D 0A                                          >..
```

```
802.3 [0000:000D]
  0000:0005   Destination Address: 08003E0200DD
  0006:000B   Source Address: 0060972BE60F
  000C:000D   Ethernet Type: DOD Internet Protocol (IP)
IP [000E:0021]
  000E:000E   Version: 4, Header Length: 20
  000F:000F   TOS, Precedence: Routine, Delay: Normal, Throughput: Normal,
Reliability: Normal
  0010:0011   Packet Length: 85
  0012:0013   Identification: 0x9AE5
  0014:0014   Fragment Flag (bit 6..5): Don't Fragment
  0014:0015   Fragment Offset: 0x0000
  0016:0016   Time to Live: 128
  0017:0017   Transport: Transmission Control
  0018:0019   Header Checksum: 0xDA93
  001A:001D   Source Address: 24.94.41.254
  001E:0021   Destination Address: 192.203.130.2
TCP [0022:0035]
  0022:0023   Source Port: 0x0494
  0024:0025   Destination Port: Simple Mail Transfer Protocol
  0026:0029   Sequence Number: 92063321
  002A:002D   Acknowledgment Number: 27520134
  002E:002E   Header Length (bit 7..4): 20
  002F:002F   Control Bit - Acknowledgment; Push function;
  0030:0031   Window Size: 8443
  0032:0033   Checksum: 0x9FC0
  0034:0035   Urgent Pointer: 0x0000
```

Lastly, examine the contents of packet number 19, which shows a large block of data that contains the actual text of the original message. Notice that the message consists of the mail headers as well as the mail message body.

Packet 19

```
Destination Source        Protocol       Summary      Size  Time Tick
-------------------------------------------------------------------------
192.203.130.2    24.94.41.254           Simple Mail Transfer Protocol TCP   488
        04/27/99 15:05:05.563

Addr.   Hex. Data                                          ASCII
0000:   08 00 3E 02 00 DD 00 60 97 2B E6 0F 08 00 45 00   ..>....'.+....E.
0010:   01 DA 9D E5 40 00 80 06 D6 0E 18 5E 29 FE C0 CB   ....@......^)...
0020:   82 02 04 94 00 19 05 7C C6 B2 01 A3 EC E0 50 18   .......|......P.
0030:   20 A1 A5 BC 00 00 4D 65 73 73 61 67 65 2D 49 64    .....Message-Id
0040:   3A 20 3C 33 2E 30 2E 31 2E 33 32 2E 31 39 39 39   : <3.0.1.32.1999
0050:   30 34 32 37 31 35 30 35 30 32 2E 30 30 36 65 62   0427150502.006eb
0060:   64 33 63 40 61 74 68 65 6E 61 2E 73 75 6E 79 62   d3c@athena.sunyb
```

```
0070:   72 6F 6F 6D 65 2E 65 64 75 3E 0D 0A 58 2D 53 65    roome.edu>..X-Se
0080:   6E 64 65 72 3A 20 61 6E 74 6F 6E 61 6B 6F 73 5F    nder: antonakos_
0090:   6A 40 61 74 68 65 6E 61 2E 73 75 6E 79 62 72 6F    j@athena.sunybro
00A0:   6F 6D 65 2E 65 64 75 0D 0A 58 2D 4D 61 69 6C 65    ome.edu..X-Maile
00B0:   72 3A 20 57 69 6E 64 6F 77 73 20 45 75 64 6F 72    r: Windows Eudor
00C0:   61 20 4C 69 67 68 74 20 56 65 72 73 69 6F 6E 20    a Light Version
00D0:   33 2E 30 2E 31 20 28 33 32 29 0D 0A 44 61 74 65    3.0.1 (32)..Date
00E0:   3A 20 54 75 65 2C 20 32 37 20 41 70 72 20 31 39    : Tue, 27 Apr 19
00F0:   39 39 20 31 35 3A 30 35 3A 30 32 20 2D 30 34 30    99 15:05:02 -040
0100:   30 0D 0A 54 6F 3A 20 6D 61 6E 73 66 69 65 6C 64    0..To: mansfield
0110:   5F 6B 40 73 75 6E 79 62 72 6F 6F 6D 65 2E 65 64    _k@sunybroome.ed
0120:   75 0D 0A 46 72 6F 6D 3A 20 22 4A 61 6D 65 73 20    u..From: "James
0130:   4C 2E 20 41 6E 74 6F 6E 61 6B 6F 73 22 20 3C 61    L. Antonakos" <a
0140:   6E 74 6F 6E 61 6B 6F 73 5F 6A 40 6D 61 69 6C 2E    ntonakos_j@mail.
0150:   73 75 6E 79 62 72 6F 6F 6D 65 2E 65 64 75 3E 0D    sunybroome.edu>.
0160:   0A 53 75 62 6A 65 63 74 3A 20 54 65 73 74 20 6D    .Subject: Test m
0170:   65 73 73 61 67 65 0D 0A 4D 69 6D 65 2D 56 65 72    essage..Mime-Ver
0180:   73 69 6F 6E 3A 20 31 2E 30 0D 0A 43 6F 6E 74 65    sion: 1.0..Conte
0190:   6E 74 2D 54 79 70 65 3A 20 74 65 78 74 2F 70 6C    nt-Type: text/pl
01A0:   61 69 6E 3B 20 63 68 61 72 73 65 74 3D 22 75 73    ain; charset="us
01B0:   2D 61 73 63 69 69 22 0D 0A 0D 0A 4B 65 6E 2C 0D    -ascii"....Ken,.
01C0:   0A 4A 75 73 74 20 77 61 6E 74 65 64 20 74 6F 20    .Just wanted to
01D0:   63 61 70 74 75 72 65 20 74 68 69 73 2E 0D 0A 0D    capture this....
01E0:   0A 4A 4C 41 0D 0A 0D 0A                            .JLA....
```

802.3 [0000:000D]
  0000:0005   Destination Address: 08003E0200DD
  0006:000B   Source Address: 0060972BE60F
  000C:000D   Ethernet Type: DOD Internet Protocol (IP)
IP [000E:0021]
  000E:000E   Version: 4, Header Length: 20
  000F:000F   TOS, Precedence: Routine, Delay: Normal, Throughput: Normal,
Reliability: Normal
  0010:0011   Packet Length: 474
  0012:0013   Identification: 0x9DE5
  0014:0014   Fragment Flag (bit 6..5): Don't Fragment
  0014:0015   Fragment Offset: 0x0000
  0016:0016   Time to Live: 128
  0017:0017   Transport: Transmission Control
  0018:0019   Header Checksum: 0xD60E
  001A:001D   Source Address: 24.94.41.254
  001E:0021   Destination Address: 192.203.130.2
TCP [0022:0035]
  0022:0023   Source Port: 0x0494
  0024:0025   Destination Port: Simple Mail Transfer Protocol
  0026:0029   Sequence Number: 92063410

```
002A:002D   Acknowledgment Number: 27520224
002E:002E   Header Length (bit 7..4): 20
002F:002F   Control Bit - Acknowledgment; Push function;
0030:0031   Window Size: 8353
0032:0033   Checksum: 0xA5BC
0034:0035   Urgent Pointer: 0x0000
```

Recall that the original message contained less than 40 bytes of data. Consider that each of these packet exchanges is required to send the message.

You are encouraged to study all of these packets to gain a deeper appreciation and understanding of the underlying processes involved in sending an e-mail message.

 TROUBLESHOOTING TECHNIQUES

One reason it might be helpful to know a few basic POP3 commands has to do with a real-world situation in which several e-mail messages were queued up behind an e-mail with a very large (over 4MB) attachment. Unfortunately, a network router problem creating frequent packet losses prevented the e-mail with the attachment from being properly transferred to the recipient's e-mail client. To get at the queued-up e-mail messages, the user used Telnet to connect to the POP3 server and delete the e-mail message containing the large attachment. This allowed the remaining messages to transfer to the e-mail client. Since the messages were small, they transferred quickly, with only a slight delay introduced by the router problem.

A Telnet session to a POP3 server is accomplished by choosing the Start, Run menu and entering a command similar to

```
telnet athena.sunybroome.edu 110
```

This instructs the Telnet application to connect to port 110 on the athena.suny-broome.edu computer system. Port 110 is the location where the POP3 server is installed. An actual interaction with the POP3 server follows:

```
+OK Microsoft Exchange POP3 server version 5.5.2650.23 ready
user antonakos_j
+OK
pass
-ERR Logon failure: unknown user name or bad password.
user antonakos_j
+OK
pass ********
+OK User successfully logged on
list
+OK
1 11605
2 14542
```

```
3 28602
4 28088
5 674
6 272530
.
.
.
40 12107
41 16549
42 42543
43 15640
.
retr 43
+OK
```

Received: from sbccab.cc.sunybroome.edu by athena.sunybroome.edu with SMTP
(Microsoft Exchange Internet Mail Service Version 5.0.1457.7) id CLT5Z7QR;
Mon, 2 Mar 1998 08:31:48 -0500
Received: from sunybroome.edu by sunybroome.edu (PMDF V5.0-3 #8051)
 id <01IU6NDXNT1C984NDS@sunybroome.edu>; Mon, 02 Mar 1998
08:34:11 -0500 (EST)
Date: Mon, 02 Mar 1998 08:34:11 -0500 (EST)
From: "ALAN C. DIXON" <DIXON_A@sunybroome.edu>
Subject: T1 Discussion
To: BCC002407@acad.sunybroome.edu, BleeF@worldnet.att.net,
dixon_a@mail.sunybroome.edu
Message-id: <01IU6NDXPAPU984NDS@sunybroome.edu>
X-VMS-To: @EET252,@DEPT
X-VMS-Cc: DIXON_A
MIME-version: 1.0
Content-type: TEXT/PLAIN; CHARSET=US-ASCII
Content-transfer-encoding: 7BIT

The Bell System's Digital Signal Hierachy

        To improve signal/noise ratio on multi-line phone trunks, Bell began
converting some frequency division multiplexing (FDM) lines to time division
multiplexing (TDM) back in the 1960s.
        The digitization technique chosen was pulse code modulation (PCM),
taking 8000 samples/second of the analog waveform and quantizing it to 8 bit
precision with an analog to digital (A/D) converter. When the bits are
serially shifted out, the signal source is called a "DS0" by the phone
company.
        Including several DS0 channels in one TDM bit stream requires the
addition of framing bits, so the individual channels can be identified on
recovery. A "DS1" is composed of 24 byte-wise interleaved 8-bit samples
(from 24 different DS0s) and one framing bit. The total bit rate is:

```
total rate = 8000 samples/sec * [(8 bits/sample * 24 samples) + 1 frame bit]
= 1.544 Mbps


a1 a2 a3 a4 a5 a6 a7 a8 b1 b2 b3 b4 b5 b6 b7 b8 ... x6 x7 x8 f0
 |                              |                      |              |
    sample from 1st DS0      sample from 2nd DS0 .....    frame
                                                           bit
                         Sample Bit Frame
```

Four DS1s can be combined into a DS2; 7 DS2s compose a DS3. There
are also DS4s and DS5s, used for long-distance trunks often running on
optical fiber.

```
.
del 43
-ERR Protocol Error
dele 43
+OK
stat
+OK 42 4116756


.
quit
+OK Microsoft Exchange POP3 server version 5.5.2650.23 signing off
```

You are encouraged to connect to a POP3 server to try a few of these commands on your own.

SELF-TEST

This self-test is designed to help you check your understanding of the background information presented in this chapter.

True/False
Answer *true* or *false*.

1. An e-mail address consists of three parts.

2. The header and body of an e-mail message are separated by a blank line.

3. MIME provides a way to send binary attachments to an e-mail message.

4. Microsoft Outlook Express is an e-mail server program.

5. E-mail messages can be read using a World Wide Web browser.

6. E-mail is always delivered to its destination.

7. E-mail messages are sent from the client directly to the destination e-mail server.

Multiple Choice
Select the best answer.

8. In order to keep all related e-mail messages together
   a. Create a message bucket.
   b. Create a message folder.
   c. Keep all messages in the Outbox.

9. The mailbox portion of an e-mail address is typically
   a. A server.
   b. A client.
   c. A user name.

10. Outlook Express is a _____ e-mail program.
    a. Client.
    b. Server.
    c. Both a and b.

11. E-mail messages are delivered on the Internet using the
    a. POP3 protocol.
    b. SMTP protocol.
    c. Both a and b.

12. To create a folder, it is necessary to right-click on the
    a. Inbox folder.
    b. Outbox folder.
    c. Local Folders folder.

13. What is user xyz's e-mail address at abcde.com?
    a. xyz@abcde.com
    b. abcde.com@xyz
    c. Either a or b.

14. POP3 servers operate on port
    a. 25.
    b. 77.
    c. 110.

Completion
Fill in the blank or blanks with the best answers.

15. MIME stands for _____ _____ _____ _____.

16. The Telnet application can be used to connect to a _____ server.

17. The _____ header keyword is used to send a carbon copy of an e-mail message.

18. After reading an e-mail message, it may be saved or _____.

19. The _____ is ultimately responsible for delivering e-mail messages to their destination.

20. The first message sent to an e-mail server is the _____.

QUESTIONS/ACTIVITIES

1. Why is it necessary to organize e-mail messages into folders?

2. Search the Web to locate information on POP3 commands. Make a detailed list.

3. Search the Web for free E-mail client programs. Are there any limitations or restrictions on using the software?

REVIEW QUIZ

Under the supervision of your instructor

1. Describe the features of e-mail communication software.

2. Configure an electronic mail client.

3. Send and receive electronic mail.

4. Discuss the protocols SMTP, POP3, and IMAP.

Networking Concepts Laboratory

Experiment #12
Electronic Mail

Objectives

1. To become more familiar with the processes of using e-mail.
2. To study the packets exchanged while sending and receiving e-mail.

Required Equipment

The following equipment is required for this experiment:

- A networked computer with access to the Internet
- A valid e-mail account
- LanExplorer software

Procedure

Perform each of the following steps. Record your observations, results, and any difficulties you encounter. You will use this information when you develop your conclusions about the experiment.

1. Create and send an e-mail message to an invalid mailbox. What type of error message is generated?
2. Create and send an e-mail message to an invalid computer. What type of error message is generated?
3. Identify the name of the server computer for your e-mail address.
4. Capture an electronic message delivery using LanExplorer. Review each of the packets for SMTP commands and server responses.
5. Repeat step 4, but attach a small file to the e-mail message.
6. Have your instructor arrange an e-mail session between your class and a class at a different school. Measure how long it takes to send and receive e-mail in both directions.

Discussion and Conclusion

Using a word processor, write your own detailed explanations of the results and observations made during the experiment. To begin, try to say something about each procedure step.
    In addition, provide answers to the following questions:

1. Why do you think an unreliable protocol can be used to read e-mail but not to send it?
2. With regard to mail servers, there are *open relays* and *closed relays*. What is the difference?

FTP and Telnet

PERFORMANCE OBJECTIVES

Upon completion of this chapter, you will be able to

- Describe the purpose of the File Transfer and Telnet protocols.
- Explain how File Transfer Protocol clients and servers are configured.
- Discuss the various FTP and Telnet commands.

Joe Tekk sat back in his chair waiting very impatiently for one of several file transfers to complete. "Just three more files," he thought to himself, "before I can check out my new web site."

When the transfer was complete, Joe quickly opened the Internet Explorer and Netscape Navigator browsers and began to examine each one of the pages. As he reviewed each page, he made some notes about the minor differences that he noticed.

After he examined each of the pages Joe made some additional changes to each of the HTML documents and then he FTPed them to the server again. After he changed the last document, he reviewed the pages with both of the browsers one last time. Satisfied with the results, Joe's mind began to wander. He became concerned about the other Web-related activities he wanted to accomplish.

INTRODUCTION

The FTP and Telnet applications presented in this chapter have many practical applications. Some of these are

- Authors exchanging manuscript files
- A faculty member hosting class notes and files
- Using Telnet to connect to a POP3 mail server
- Using FTP to update pages on a Web server

Let us examine the details of each application (and associated protocols).

FTP CLIENTS AND SERVERS

The capability to copy a file between computers is provided by the File Transfer Protocol, or FTP. FTP uses connection-oriented TCP as the underlying transport protocol providing guaranteed reliability. The File Transfer Protocol can transmit or receive text or binary files as described in RFC 959. The primary function of FTP is defined as transferring files efficiently and reliably among host computers and allowing the convenient use of remote file storage capabilities. Essentially, FTP is a client-server application that uses two ports on both the client and the server. One port is used to exchange FTP control or command information and the other port is used to transfer the data. This is illustrated in Figure 13–1.

On the FTP server computer, port 20 is used for data transfer and port 21 is used for control by default. The FTP client can use any port numbers greater than 1023. Recall that the port numbers less than or equal to 1023 are reserved for server applications. Note that FTP uses the Telnet protocol on the control connection. Telnet will be discussed later in this chapter.

FTP Commands

An FTP exchange of information consists of *requests* sent by the client and *responses* sent by the server. After the client connects, the server sends a response to the client either *accepting* or *rejecting* the connection. This initial response is called the *greeting*. If the server accepts the connection, the client sends requests to the server for processing. The server sends one or more responses back to the client. The last response from the server for a specific request indicates whether the request was accepted or rejected by the server.

An FTP request consists of a command or an action to be performed. A list of FTP commands is shown in Table 13–1. Note that a command may optionally include parameters. The command and parameters are separated by one space. The FTP command STAT (short for *status*) does not require any parameters, whereas a GET command does require a parameter, the name of the file to get, such as GET TEST.DAT.

Figure 13–1
FTP client-server interaction.

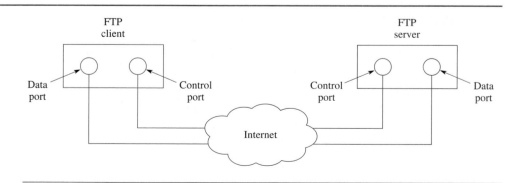

Command	Meaning
!	Escape to a DOS shell
delete	Delete remote file
literal	Send arbitrary FTP command
prompt	Force interactive prompting on multiple command
send	Send one file
?	Print local help information
debug	Toggle debugging mode
ls	List contents of remote directory
put	Send one file
status (or stat)	Show current status
append	Append to a file
dir	List contents of remote directory
mdelete	Delete multiple files
pwd	Print working directory on remote machine
trace	Toggle packet tracing
ascii	Set ASCII transfer type
disconnect	Terminate FTP session
mdir	List contents of multiple remote directories
quit	Terminate FTP session and exit
type	Set file transfer type
bell	Beep when command completed
get	Receive file
mget	Get multiple files
quote	Send arbitrary FTP command
user	Send new user information
binary	Set binary transfer type
glob	Toggle metacharacter expansion of local file names
mkdir	Make directory on the remote machine
recv	Receive file
verbose	Toggle verbose mode
bye	Terminate FTP session and exit
hash	Toggle printing '#' for each buffer transferred

Table 13–1
File Transfer
Protocol Windows
client commands

(continued on next page)

Table 13–1
(continued)

Command	Meaning
mls	List contents of multiple remote directories
remotehelp	Get help from remote server
cd	Change remote working directory
help	Print local help information
mput	Send multiple files
rename	Rename file
close	Terminate FTP session
lcd	Change local working directory
open	Connect to remote FTP
rmdir	Remove directory on the remote machine

A server response from a request consists of one or more lines. The client can identify the last line of the response because it begins with three ASCII digits and a space, whereas the previous response lines do not. The three digits form a *code*. Codes between 100 and 199 indicate marks; codes between 200 and 399 indicate acceptance; codes between 400 and 599 indicate rejection. Typical FTP response codes are shown in Table 13–2. Many other response codes are defined and may be displayed during an FTP exchange.

Table 13–2
Common FTP server
response codes.

FTP Response Code	Response Meaning
125	Data connection already open; transfer starting
150	File status okay; about to open data connection
200	Command okay
221	Service closing control connection
220	Service ready for new user
226	Closing data connection
230	User logged in, proceed
250	Requested file action okay, completed
331	User name okay, need password
421	Service not available, closing control connection
450	Requested file action not taken
500	Syntax error, command unrecognized
501	Syntax error in parameters or arguments
550	Requested action not taken

Now that the ground rules for communication have been laid, we can examine how FTP works from both the client and server side. Let us begin by looking at the client-side application program.

FTP Clients

An FTP client is provided for almost every type of hardware and operating system platform available. On a Windows computer, an FTP client is installed when the TCP/IP protocol is installed. Generally, there are two types of access to a FTP server. The first type of access is called *anonymous FTP*. This is a mode of operation which allows public access to files stored on an FTP server. This type of access is very useful in many different circumstances. For example, a manufacturer may provide free updates to device drivers or an easy method to distribute shareware applications.

The FTP client program can be started on a Windows computer through the Run option on the Start menu. Figure 13–2 shows the Run dialog box specifying the FTP program name and an Internet host to connect to. Note that the FTP client can also be run directly from the DOS prompt.

A sample anonymous FTP session run from the DOS prompt is as follows:

```
C:> ftp kcm.dyndns.org
Connected to kcm.dyndns.org.
220 server Microsoft FTP Service (Version 3.0).
User (kcm.dyndns.org:(none)): anonymous
331 Anonymous access allowed, send identity (e-mail name) as password.
Password:
230 Anonymous user logged in.
ftp> dir
200 PORT command successful.
150 Opening ASCII mode data connection for /bin/ls.
-r-xr-xr-x   1 owner    group        4487 Jul 24  1999 cgi_perl.c
-r-xr-xr-x   1 owner    group        4509 Oct  4  1997 client.c
-r-xr-xr-x   1 owner    group       62907 Nov 16  1998 cppsrc.zip
-r-xr-xr-x   1 owner    group        1287 Feb 22  5:16 getpost.pl
-r-xr-xr-x   1 owner    group    42755470 Oct 15  1999 itc.zip
```

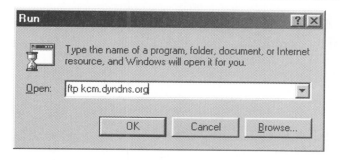

Figure 13–2
Running FTP on a Windows client.

```
-r-xr-xr-x   1 owner     group            3363 Feb  2  1:03 lab3.c
-r-xr-xr-x   1 owner     group          933851 Oct 30  1998 mgc115eq.zip
-r-xr-xr-x   1 owner     group           16452 Nov 13  1997 pdp10.jpg
-r-xr-xr-x   1 owner     group            4429 Oct  4  1997 server.c
226 Transfer complete.
ftp: 629 bytes received in 0.05Seconds 12.58Kbytes/sec.
ftp> stat
Connected to kcm.dyndns.org.
Type: ascii; Verbose: On ; Bell: Off ; Prompting: On ; Globbing: On
Debugging: Off ; Hash mark printing: Off .
ftp> binary
200 Type set to I.
ftp> get cppsrc.zip
200 PORT command successful.
150 Opening BINARY mode data connection for cppsrc.zip(62907 bytes).
226 Transfer complete.
ftp: 62907 bytes received in 3.90Seconds 16.13Kbytes/sec.
ftp> close
221 Goodbye
ftp> quit
```

In this example, the FTP server we want to connect to is running on a computer called kcm.dyndns.org. The first message shown is the connect message. Following the connect message, a message is displayed that identifies itself as a Microsoft FTP Service. The version number is typically displayed for informational or debugging purposes.

When the user is prompted to provide a user name, the word anonymous is entered. The following message from the server

```
331 Anonymous access allowed, send identity (e-mail name) as password.
```

indicates that anonymous access to the server is allowed and furthermore instructs the user to enter his or her e-mail name as the password. On some systems, simply entering the word *guest* is allowed.

After the connection is established, the client can enter any of the commands from Table 13–1. In the example, the first command entered is dir (short for directory) and the server returns several responses. The first response

```
200 PORT command successful.
```

indicates that the command was accepted by the server. The server continues by opening an ASCII connection and then proceeds to list each of the files in the directory as follows:

```
150 Opening ASCII mode data connection for /bin/ls.
-r-xr-xr-x   1 owner     group            4487 Jul 24  1999 cgi_perl.c
-r-xr-xr-x   1 owner     group            4509 Oct  4  1997 client.c
-r-xr-xr-x   1 owner     group           62907 Nov 16  1998 cppsrc.zip
-r-xr-xr-x   1 owner     group            1287 Feb 22  5:16 getpost.pl
```

```
-r-xr-xr-x   1 owner     group      42755470 Oct 15  1999 itc.zip
-r-xr-xr-x   1 owner     group          3363 Feb  2  1:03 lab3.c
-r-xr-xr-x   1 owner     group        933851 Oct 30  1998 mgc115eq.zip
-r-xr-xr-x   1 owner     group         16452 Nov 13  1997 pdp10.jpg
-r-xr-xr-x   1 owner     group          4429 Oct  4  1997 server.c
```

For each file displayed, several of the file properties are shown in a Unix-style format. From left to right, the first item is the file permissions (-r-xr-xr-x), followed by the file owner and group, the file size, the file date, and lastly, the name of the file. The format of the file permission codes are shown in Table 13–3. The file permissions determine whether or not a file can be accessed. For an anonymous login, it is necessary for the file to contain world read access. The file owner determines the file permissions. When the directory listing is complete, an informational message is displayed indicating that the transfer is complete, followed by the number of bytes transmitted and the amount of time necessary to complete the transfer.

```
226 Transfer complete.
ftp: 629 bytes received in 0.05Seconds 12.58Kbytes/sec.
```

To transfer files, it is necessary to select the appropriate type of file transfer mode. The `stat` command is used to show the status of the connection. For example,

```
ftp> stat
Connected to kcm.dyndns.org.
Type: ascii; Verbose: On ; Bell: Off ; Prompting: On ; Globbing: On
Debugging: Off ; Hash mark printing: Off .
```

indicate that a session is currently established, the current type of transfer is ASCII, the verbose flag is set to On, and so on. Of particular importance here

Table 13–3
Unix-style file permission codes.

Position Number	Permission Type	Meaning	
1	File Type	d = Directory	– = Regular file
2	Owner Read	r = Read Access	– = no Read Access
3	Owner Write	w = Write Access	– = no Write Access
4	Owner Execute	x = Execute	– = no Execute Access
5	Group Read	r = Read Access	– = no Read Access
6	Group Write	w = Write Access	– = no Write Access
7	Group Execute	x = Execute	– = no Execute Access
8	World Read	r = Read Access	– = no Read Access
9	World Write	w = Write Access	– = no Write Access
10	World Execute	x = Execute	– = no Execute Access

is the "Type," which is set to ASCII. To transfer a ZIP file (a binary file) it is necessary to change the mode to binary. This is accomplished by entering the command

```
ftp> binary
200 Type set to I.
```

The server response indicates that the Type is now set to "I," which stands for Image, or binary. After setting the mode, the cppsrc.zip file may be transferred as follows:

```
ftp> get cppsrc.zip
200 PORT command successful.
150 Opening BINARY mode data connection for cppsrc.zip(62907 bytes).
226 Transfer complete.
ftp: 62907 bytes received in 3.90Seconds 16.13Kbytes/sec.
```

Again, notice that informational responses are sent by the server to indicate the progress of the file transfer using binary mode. When the transfer is complete, the number of bytes and transfer time are displayed.

When the FTP session is complete, the connection can be closed and the program terminated using the following commands:

```
ftp> close
221 Goodbye
ftp> quit
```

The second mode of FTP operation (not anonymous) requires an account and password on the particular computer. In this mode of operation, access to files is restricted and not available for public access. The commands used for both modes of operation are the same. A sample FTP exchange using a valid computer account follows:

```
C:\>ftp ftp.sunybroome.edu
Connected to sbccab.cc.sunybroome.edu.
220 sbccab.cc FTP Server (Version V4.1-12) Ready.
User (sbccab.cc.sunybroome.edu:(none)): mansfield_k
331 Username MANSFIELD_K requires a Password.
Password:
530 Login incorrect.
Login failed.
ftp> close
425 Session is disconnected.
ftp> open ftp.sunybroome.edu
Connected to sbccab.cc.sunybroome.edu.
220 sbccab.cc FTP Server (Version V4.1-12) Ready.
User (sbccab.cc.sunybroome.edu:(none)): mansfield_k
331 Username MANSFIELD_K requires a Password.
Password:
230 User logged in.
```

```
ftp> cd cgi
250 CWD command succesful.
ftp> put getpost.c
200 PORT command successful.
150 Opening data connection for GETPOST.C (24.24.78.124,1168)
226 Transfer complete.
ftp: 5350 bytes sent in 0.00Seconds 5350000.00Kbytes/sec.
ftp> quit
221 Goodbye.
```

In this FTP session, the first attempt to log in was unsuccessful. This was because an invalid password was entered. Because of this error situation, it is necessary to disconnect the current session using the close command and then open another connection using the open command as shown. Following the successful login, the private directory tree can be navigated and files transferred as necessary.

In addition to the built-in Windows FTP client program, many other clients are available. One of the most popular FTP client programs is WS_FTP, produced by Ipswitch Incorporated. WS_FTP LE (Limited Edition) is available at no charge to qualified nonbusiness users at www.ipswitch.com. The WS_FTP program is written as a Windows application rather than as a DOS application, allowing us to use the mouse instead of the keyboard for many of the controls.

After WS_FTP is installed and run, the Session Profile window is displayed to the user, as shown in Figure 13–3. The session profile allows for the FTP client to be configured for each server to which the client connects. As shown in Figure 13–3, the profile name may be used to indicate the host name. For each profile, it is necessary to enter a host name and a user ID. Notice that the Anonymous Login box is checked and the user ID is set to *anonymous* and the password is set to *guest*. This information is entered automatically by checking the Anonymous Login checkbox. After the profile information is entered, the profile should be saved by clicking on the Save button.

The FTP session is established by clicking OK and the user is presented with the window shown in Figure 13–4. Notice that the left side of the window displays the contents of the local system and the right side of the window displays the contents of the remote system. For each of the systems (local and remote), the currently selected directory name is displayed as well as all of the files contained in the directory. On the local system, the wsftp32 directory contents are displayed and the root directory "/" is displayed on the remote system.

For each system, it is possible to perform the following operations by selecting the appropriate button on the display:

- Change to a different directory
- Make a new directory
- Remove a directory
- Refresh the current display
- Obtain directory information

Figure 13–3
WS_FTP Session
Profile window.

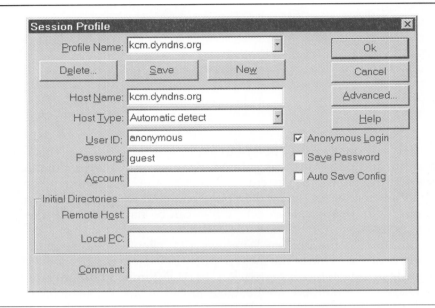

Figure 13–4
WS_FTP Main
window.

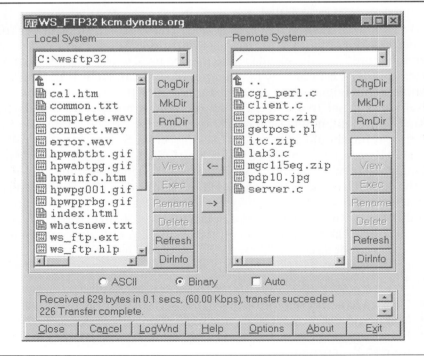

In addition, if a file is selected in one of the windows, it is possible to

- View the file
- Execute the file
- Rename the file
- Delete the file

Between the windows, two arrows are used to indicate the direction of the transfer. Below the local and remote system windows, notice that the two file transfer options plus an Auto check box are displayed. The Auto selection determines the file type by using the files extension. For example, an .exe or .com file will be set to binary and a file with a .txt extension would automatically be set to ASCII. The binary file type is selected by default, but it can be set to any of the three values using one of the WS_FTP configuration screens. Below the file transfer type fields, a status window is displayed that contains a complete list of the text messages exchanged by the client and server. Lastly, along the bottom of the screen, buttons are provided to perform the following:

- Close the current session
- Cancel an operation
- Open the message log window
- Obtain online help
- Change the program options
- Review the About program information
- Exit the program

Let us perform the same file transfer operation completed earlier with the DOS-based client using the WS_FTP program.

To duplicate the transfer in WS_FTP, it is necessary to select the file to be transferred (cppsrc.zip) and then click on the left arrow between the local and remote system windows to indicate which direction the file is being transferred. In this case the transfer is from the remote system to the local system. During the transfer, an informational window is displayed to show the progress of the exchange. This is illustrated in Figure 13–5. During the transfer, the cancel option may be selected and the transfer aborted if necessary. Note that it might be necessary to abort a transfer if it is taking an excessive amount of time or you notice that the wrong file or file type was selected. When the file

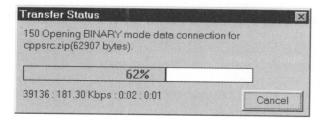

Figure 13–5
WS_FTP file transfer status.

Figure 13–6
WS_FTP main window
after file transfer.

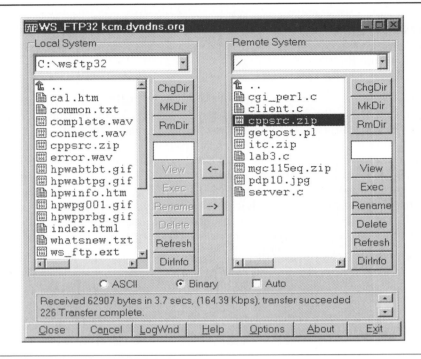

Figure 13–6
WS_FTP main window
after file transfer.

transfer is complete, the new file is displayed in the directory listing on the local computer as shown in Figure 13–6. Now a copy of the cppsrc.zip file is located on both the local and remote computer systems.

Obviously, the Windows user interface for the WS_FTP program has many advantages over the DOS-based client. It is worth mentioning that the same steps or processing is performed by each of the clients. We can prove this by examining the contents of the WS_FTP status window (also contained in the Message Log) with the exchange of messages observed during the DOS exchange. A complete copy of the WS_FTP Message Log is shown in Figure 13–7 for comparison purposes. Do you notice any similarities or differences? You will probably find that the WS_FTP message log contains more information.

The Options button at the bottom of the WS_FTP window allows the user to customize many of the features available in WS_FTP. The Options window shown in Figure 13–8 identifies each of the categories for customization. Two of these categories, Program Options and Session Options, contain the fields that are updated most often.

In the Program options configuration screen, the look and feel of the WS_FTP program can be changed. For example, it is possible to display the buttons at the top of the screen instead of the bottom, change the action of a double-click on the mouse, specify a different Log filename, and specify an e-mail address to be used

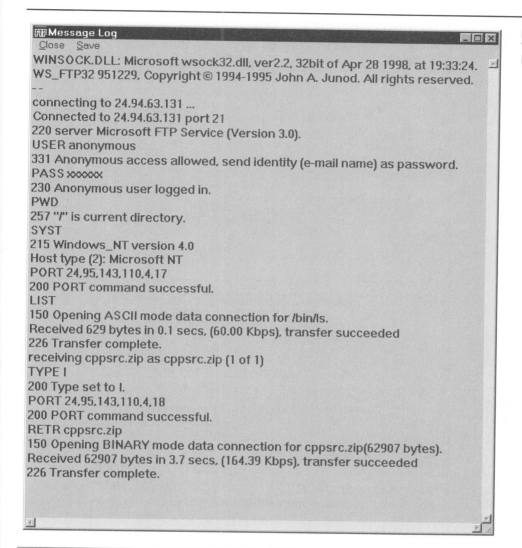

Figure 13–7
WS_FTP Message Log.

during anonymous FTP, to name just a few of the options. The Program Options window is shown in Figure 13–9.

The Session Options window (illustrated in Figure 13–10) provides the ability to

- Customize settings for file name differences that are commonly found between different server computers
- Control whether or not WS_FTP will use sounds to indicate successful transfers
- Set the default transfer mode shown on the main WS_FTP screen

Figure 13–8
WS_FTP Options
window.

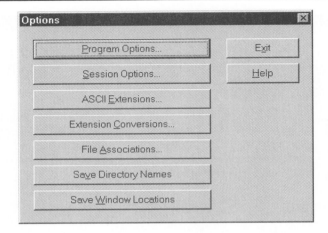

Figure 13–9
WS_FTP Program
Options.

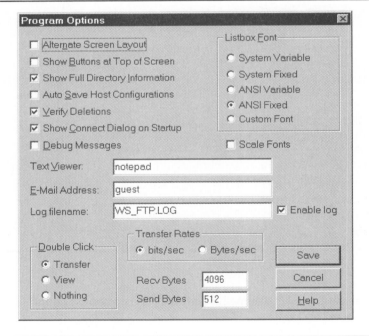

You are encouraged to explore each of the WS_FTP configuration screens. It is a good idea to make a hard copy of the default settings in case the new settings cause problems.

There are many different FTP clients to choose from. Many times, a college-level network programming class will assign each student the job of writing an

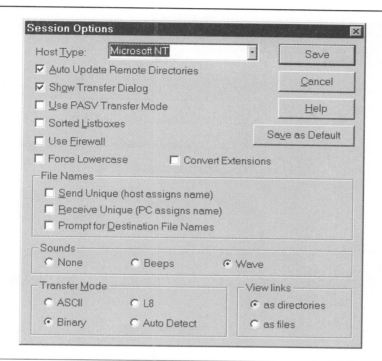

Figure 13–10
WS_FTP Session
Options.

FTP client as an exercise. A search of the Web might identify a dozen or so clients
that can be downloaded and installed for free or for a nominal fee.

Built-In FTP Clients

Many different application programs that use the Internet provide their own
FTP capability. For example, most HTML editing programs contain a built-in
FTP client to upload the HTML documents to the Web server. One such program is Softquad's HoTMetaL. For each stage of a Web page project, HTML
files (or any other type of file) stored in the project can be uploaded very
easily. Figure 13–11 shows a typical setup window for a specific destination.
The host name, user name, password, and path provide enough parameters to
perform an FTP exchange. The HTML files are published, or uploaded, to the
site as needed. Figure 13–12 shows several files selected for upload to the
server. As the files are FTPed to the server, a status window is shown to indicate the progress of the transfer, as illustrated in Figure 13–13. Note that it is
possible to stop the transfer at any time by clicking the Stop button.

FTP Servers

FTP servers operate on server class computers using operating systems such
as Windows NT, Unix, and many others. FTP servers are installed as a service
on ports 20 and 21 by default. Port 20 is used as the channel to transfer data

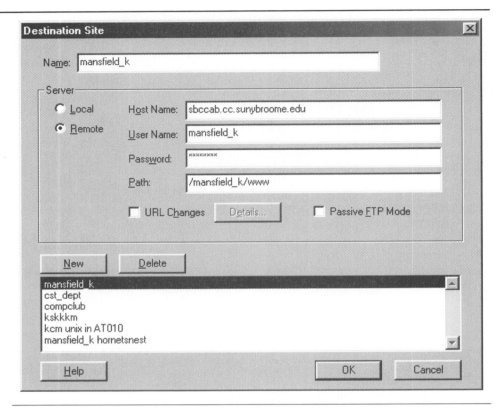

and port 21 is used to control the FTP session. A minimum implementation is required for all FTP servers so that each server, regardless of the underlying platform, can be used to reliably exchange information. These minimum requirements are specified in RFC 959. All hosts must operate using the standard settings specified in the RFC.

An FTP server is responsible for allowing access to the server and mechanisms are provided to authenticate users, access the server file structure, and set file transfer parameters. Authentication is accomplished by means of an account and a password. A user is permitted to transfer files only after entering a correct account name and associated password. Accessing the server file structure provides the user with the ability to navigate to a particular directory and store and/or retrieve a file.

On a Windows NT computer, the Microsoft Internet Information Server program, or IIS, provides the FTP service. During the installation of Windows NT, the system administrator is given the opportunity to install IIS. The Microsoft IIS provides three Internet services, WWW, Gopher, and FTP. Notice in Figure 13–14 that all three of the services are running. Each of the services can be controlled (stopped, paused, or started) using the buttons underneath the pull-down menus.

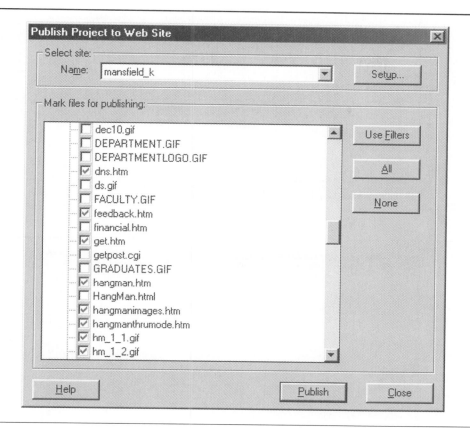

Figure 13–12
HoTMetaL selection
of files to publish.

Figure 13–13
HoTMetaL
Publishing Progress
status window.

The FTP server properties can be examined by double-clicking on the FTP service or selecting the FTP service and clicking on the Properties button. Figure 13–15 shows the FTP Service Properties window. The Services tab provides access to the TCP port, which is set by default to 21. In addition, the connection time-out value and the maximum connections supported by the

Figure 13–14
Microsoft Internet
Service Manager
services.

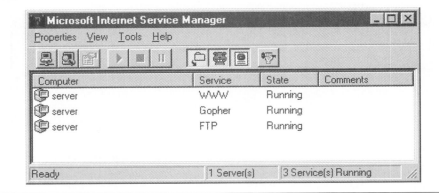

Figure 13–15
Microsoft IIS FTP
Service Properties
window.

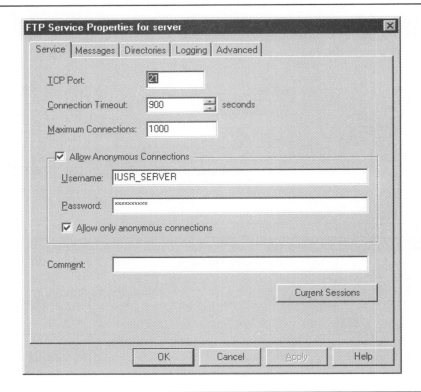

server can also be set. A check mark in the box for "Allow anonymous connections" indicates that anonymous connections are enabled. In fact, the second check box is set to allow only anonymous connections. This is a restriction that is useful in certain situations in which higher security is required. Notice that

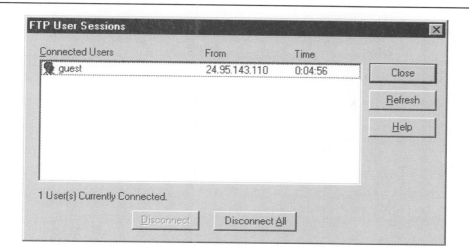

Figure 13–16
Microsoft IIS current
FTP sessions.

the current FTP sessions can be displayed by selecting the Current Sessions button. This causes the window shown in Figure 13–16 to be displayed. It is possible to disconnect any or all of the active sessions by pressing the appropriate button on the FTP Users Display window.

The FTP Service Properties Messages tab provides the ability for the server administrator to change the default message text. This includes the greeting, the maximum connections reached, and the connection termination messages. The Directories tab provides a mechanism to create additional directories to be used by the FTP server. The server administrator may add an unlimited number of directories for use by the FTP server.

The Logging tab is used to capture the FTP activity of the server. It is possible to log the information to a file or to a database. Information stored in a log file would be useful when examining FTP server usage or instances of abuse. As indicated in Figure 13–17, it is possible to have a log file created on a daily, weekly, or monthly basis, or when the size of the log file reaches a user specified limit. A database log would provide additional information that might be useful for a business or other organization that wants to track how the FTP server is used.

Lastly, the Advanced tab provides the ability to control who can access the FTP server. By default, all computers will be granted access to the FTP service, as shown in Figure 13–18. It is also possible to limit usage by specifying the type of access to be associated with individual IP addresses. This particular FTP server will allow access to all computers with no restrictions.

In addition to the Windows-based management screens that we have just examined, it is possible to manage the IIS services using a Web browser. The address of the management interface is http://localhost/iisadmin/default.htm. Note that `localhost` refers to the users computer (running IIS), and not a site

Figure 13–17
Microsoft IIS FTP
service logging.

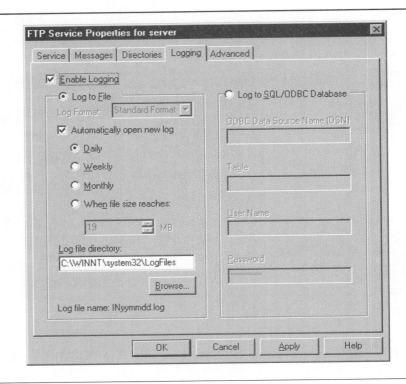

Figure 13–18
Microsoft IIS FTP
Service Advanced
Properties.

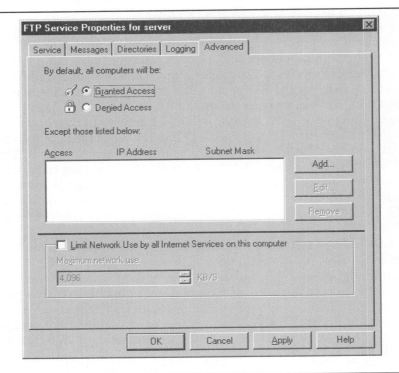

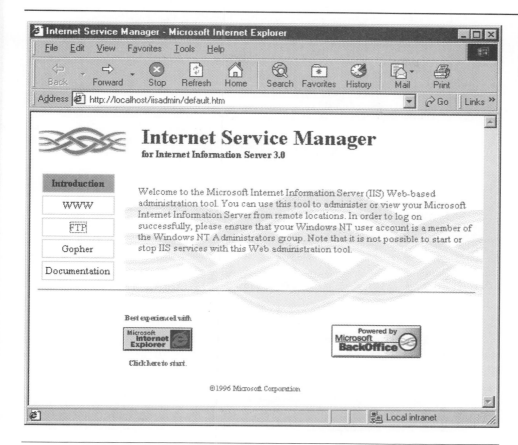

Figure 13–19
Microsoft IIS configuration using a browser.

on the Web. `localhost` uses the loopback address available for testing purposes. The default page is displayed in Figure 13–19. The Web management interface provides access to exactly the same information and configuration options. The main documentation for the Microsoft IIS is shown in Figure 13–20. It is well worth the time to read over all of the documentation provided.

Just as there are many different FTP clients, there are also many different FTP servers. Depending on the operating system platform that is selected, an FTP server is generally available.

TELNET CLIENTS AND SERVERS

The provision of remote terminal access was the very first service implemented. The goal was to allow a user with an interactive terminal session attached to one mainframe computer to remotely connect to and use another mainframe computer as though it were directly connected. The Telnet protocol

Figure 13–20
Microsoft IIS
Web-based help.

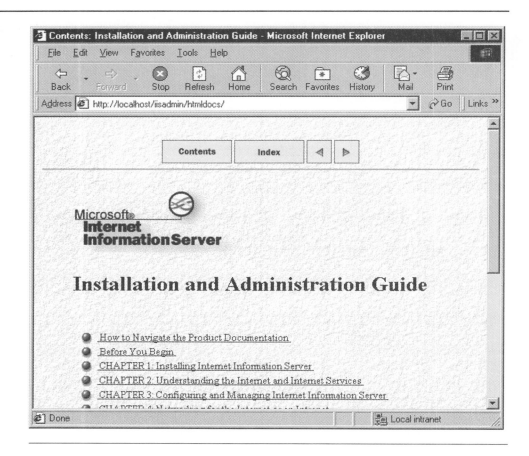

(RFC 854) provides for a bidirectional, byte-oriented service using TCP as the transport to reliably deliver messages. To provide remote terminal access, it is once again necessary to use the client-server model.

Telnet defines a Network Virtual Terminal, or NVT. The NVT is an imaginary reference terminal written to a set of standards. It is necessary for Telnet to translate the characteristics of a NVT to a real terminal device and vice versa. The Telnet NVT Implementation is shown in Figure 13–21. Typically, an NVT will have fewer features than a real physical terminal. For example, a DEC VT320 terminal has many features that are not implemented in the NVT. Similarly, in an IBM environment, an IBM 3270 terminal also has features that are not implemented in the NVT. In addition, the DEC terminal and IBM terminal are not compatible. This scenario in which the systems are not compatible describes a lot of the problems that most users experience when using Telnet.

The Telnet protocol officially calls for only certain codes to be recognized and processed. The NVT defines standard control codes and nonprinting character

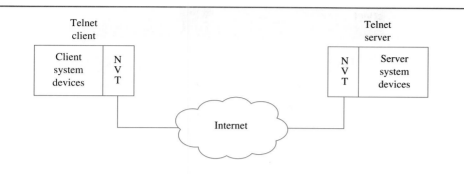

Figure 13–21
Telnet NVT
implementation.

Table 13–4
Telnet Network
Virtual Terminal
control codes.

Name	Code	Meaning
ABORT	238	Abort process
AO	245	Abort output
AYT	246	Are you there
BRK	243	Break
DO	253	Request support of option code
DONT	254	Request termination of option code
EC	247	Erase character
EL	248	Erase line
EOF	236	End of file
EOR	239	End of record
GA	249	Go ahead signal
IAC	255	Interpret the following octet(s) as controls
IP	244	Interrupt process
NOP	241	No operation code
SE	240	End of sub-negotiation parameters
SUSP	237	Suspend process
WILL	241	Will support option code
WONT	242	Will not support option code

functions. Table 13–4 shows a list of the control codes that must be recognized by Telnet clients and servers. Table 13–5 shows a list of the nonprinting characters. Due to these requirements, other manufacturer-specific codes are not supported.

Because of the differences between manufacturers, the Telnet protocol specifies how differences are dealt with between a Telnet server and a client.

Table 13–5
Telnet Network
Virtual Terminal
nonprinting
characters.

Name	Code	Meaning
BEL	7	Produce a sound
BS	8	Move one character toward the left margin
CR	13	Move to left margin of current line
FF	12	Move to the top of the next page
HT	9	Move to the next horizontal tab stop
LF	10	Move to the next line
NUL	0	No operation
VT	11	Move to the next vertical tab stop

This means that Telnet provides for the use of features not defined in the basic NVT using negotiated options. The negotiation process allows for the Telnet applications to either accept or reject a specific option. These options are implemented in the commands DO, DONT, WILL, and WONT. These commands are interpreted as follows:

DO   You please begin performing the option.
DONT   You please stop performing or do not begin performing the option.
WILL   I will begin performing the option.
WONT   I will stop performing or will not begin performing the option.

The first 20 NVT options that can be negotiated are shown in Table 13–6. Both Telnet servers and clients use this negotiation strategy to offer additional features to the user. A negotiation exchange between two NVTs is shown in Figure 13–22. In Figure 13–22(a), an offer to use an option (WILL) is sent to the remote NVT. If the remote NVT can use the option, it will respond with a DO. An offer to use an option that cannot be used is shown in Figure 13–22(b). The response to the offer to use an option is rejected with a DONT response. The local NVT acknowledges the rejection with a WONT.

Figure 13–22(c) shows a request for the other side to begin an option that can be accommodated. A WILL response is returned. Figure 13–22(d) shows a request for an option that cannot be accommodated and a WONT response is returned. The negative response is acknowledged by a DONT. A client or server NVT performs this process for every option that is requested.

Let us look at an example to illustrate how the negotiation for an ECHO option is negotiated. First, an IAC is sent to alert the receiving side that an option command is coming. Following the IAC, the command (WILL, WONT, DO, or DONT) is specified followed by the option number. The request to indicate an ECHO would look like the following, since an ECHO option is number 1:

```
<IAC> WILL 1
```

Table 13–6
NVT option codes.

Option	Description
0	Binary transmission
1	Echo
2	Reconnection
3	Suppress go ahead
4	Approximate message size
5	Status
6	Timing mark
7	Remote-controlled transmission and echo
8	Output line width
9	Output page size
10	Output carriage return disposition
11	Output horizontal tab stops
12	Output horizontal tab disposition
13	Output form feed disposition
14	Output vertical tab stops
15	Output vertical tab disposition
16	Output line feed disposition
17	Extended ASCII
18	Logout
19	Byte macro
20	Data entry terminal

The codes to represent this request are as follows:

```
<255> <251> <1>
```

In response to this request, a WILL or WONT message is expected. By default, no echoing is done over a Telnet connection.

Telnet Clients

A Telnet client is provided when the TCP/IP protocol suite is installed. On a Windows computer, the Telnet client is a DOS-based program that can be run from the DOS prompt or through the Run option on the Start menu. To begin a Telnet session, it is necessary to specify the Telnet program followed by the host to connect to. For example, the Run dialog box specifying a Telnet connection to sbccab.cc.sunybroome.edu is shown in Figure 13–23. After the Telnet program

Figure 13–22
NVT negotiation.

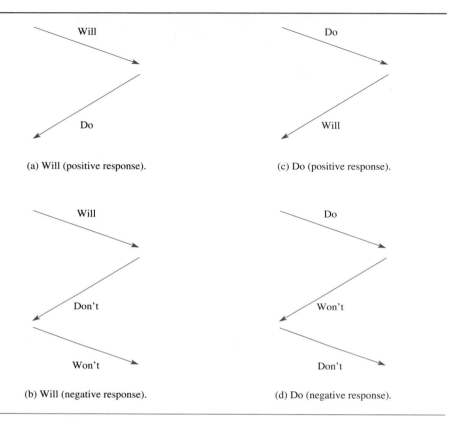

(a) Will (positive response).

(c) Do (positive response).

(b) Will (negative response).

(d) Do (negative response).

Figure 13–23
Starting a Telnet
session.

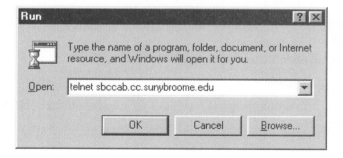

begins execution, the window shown in Figure 13–24 is displayed. The first activity to be tackled is authenticating the Telnet session. Before any interactive commands can be entered on the remote host, it is necessary for a user to enter a valid user name and password in order to gain access to the remote system. Once this is complete, the user can enter any valid operating system command

Figure 13–24
Authenticating a Telnet session with a user name and password.

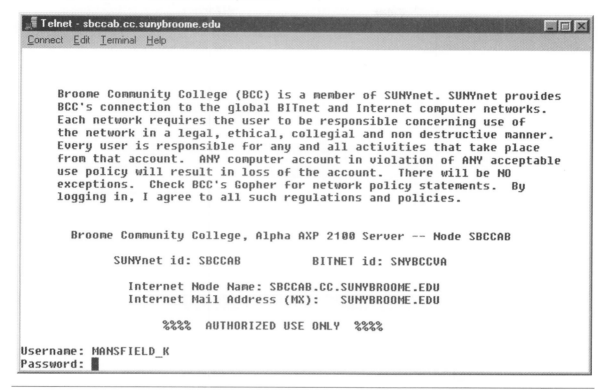

```
Telnet - sbccab.cc.sunybroome.edu                                    _ □ ×
Connect  Edit  Terminal  Help


     Broome Community College (BCC) is a member of SUNYnet. SUNYnet provides
     BCC's connection to the global BITnet and Internet computer networks.
     Each network requires the user to be responsible concerning use of
     the network in a legal, ethical, collegial and non destructive manner.
     Every user is responsible for any and all activities that take place
     from that account.  ANY computer account in violation of ANY acceptable
     use policy will result in loss of the account.  There will be NO
     exceptions.  Check BCC's Gopher for network policy statements.  By
     logging in, I agree to all such regulations and policies.


       Broome Community College, Alpha AXP 2100 Server -- Node SBCCAB

          SUNYnet id: SBCCAB              BITNET id: SNYBCCVA

             Internet Node Name: SBCCAB.CC.SUNYBROOME.EDU
             Internet Mail Address (MX):   SUNYBROOME.EDU

                  %%%%  AUTHORIZED USE ONLY  %%%%

Username: MANSFIELD_K
Password: █
```

on the remote computer. The computer system used in Figure 13–24 is a DEC/Compaq Alpha computer running the Open-VMS operating system.

A typical terminal display window consists of 24 lines, each of which can hold 80 characters. The NVT display may be larger or smaller than the physical device. As the screen is used for an interactive terminal session, new data is entered at the bottom of the display, and the older information scrolls off the top of the display. Because the information that scrolls off the top of the display is lost, the Telnet client offers the user an option to log the session activity to a file. Figure 13–25 shows the Open log file dialog box. The logging option is enabled on the Terminal pull-down menu.

When using the Telnet services, it is important to remember that there is a need to perform some type of remote interactive access. This may involve connecting to a mainframe computer (see Figure 13–26) to read mail, update records in a database, or update a CGI application on a Web server.

Suppose that the C source code file that was transferred to the server using the FTP protocol earlier in this chapter must be compiled and moved to

Figure 13–25
Specifying the file
name for a Telnet log.

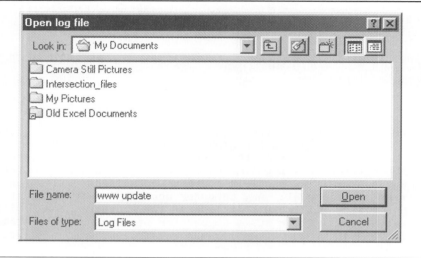

Figure 13–26
Windows Telnet client Connect menu.

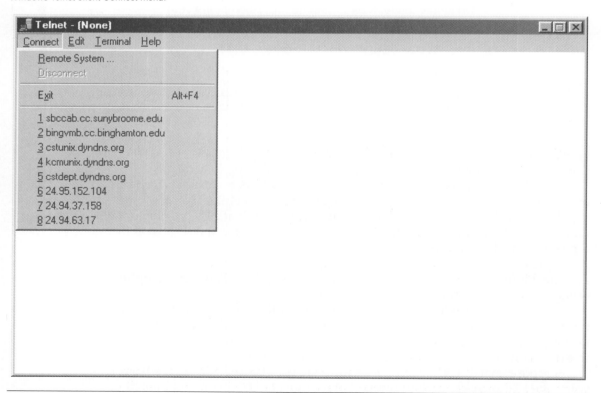

a different location. The Telnet protocol may be used to accomplish this. The following Telnet dialog implements a procedure that is necessary to update a CGI application on a Web server. The Telnet client is running under the Windows operating system and the Telnet server is running under the Open-VMS operating system.

```
Username: MANSFIELD_K
Password:

    Welcome to OpenVMS 6.2 running on a Digital Alpha-2100 Server.

    Last interactive login on Monday, 19-JUN-2000 17:11:13.67
    Last non-interactive login on Thursday, 22-JUN-2000 20:53:45.46
        2 failures since last successful login


SBCCAB>  set def [.cgi]
SBCCAB>  dir/since=today


Directory DSKB:[MANSFIELD_K.CGI]


GETPOST.C;14              11/12        22-JUN-2000 20:57:01.37   (RWED,RWED,RWE,)


Total of 1 file, 11/12 blocks.
SBCCAB>  cc getpost.c
SBCCAB>  link getpost, scriptlib, cgilib
SBCCAB>  copy getpost.exe [-.htbin]
SBCCAB>  dir [-.htbin]getpost.exe


Directory DSKB:[MANSFIELD_K.HTBIN]


GETPOST.EXE;8            58/60        22-JUN-2000 23:39:01.16   (RWED,RWED,RWE,)
GETPOST.EXE;7            57/60        12-FEB-2000 01:25:19.14   (RWED,RWED,RWE,)
GETPOST.EXE;6            56/56        12-FEB-2000 01:17:50.62   (RWED,RWED,RWE,)


Total of 3 files, 171/176 blocks.
SBCCAB>  lo
  MANSFIELD_K  logged out at 22-JUN-2000 23:40:31.98


  Accounting information:
  Buffered I/O count:           477      Peak working set size:   12048
  Direct I/O count:             304      Peak page file size:     50960
  Page faults:                 1265      Mounted volumes:             0
```

In this example, the complete session was logged to a file. The log file was closed when the session was complete.

The file GETPOST.C (FTPed to sbccab.cc.sunybroome.edu earlier) was compiled and linked into an executable image GETPOST.EXE. This file

GETPOST.EXE must be copied to the proper location on the server so that the HTTP server application can find it when needed. Without the Telnet client and server applications, this process would be much more difficult to accomplish.

When a Telnet session is complete, it is necessary to disconnect it. This option is available on the Connect pull-down menu, as shown in Figure 13–26. A session is automatically disconnected if the client program is terminated.

Telnet Servers

Telnet servers are available for most hardware and operating system platforms. On a Windows computer, it is necessary to locate a third party Telnet server because Microsoft does not provide a Telnet server program. Fortunately, there are many companies that produce Windows Telnet server application programs. Most other server class operating systems have a built-in Telnet server that is installed when the TCP/IP protocol is installed. By default, the Telnet server service is installed on port number 23.

You are encouraged to search the Web for Telnet server applications that can be run on a Windows platform. It is useful to compare the features and cost of each product.

Telnet 3270

A different version of Telnet clients and servers are required for use on most IBM mainframe computers. The Telnet 3270 protocol (commonly called TN3270) is described by RFC 1576. The architecture of the IBM operating system does not easily allow for a standard NVT to work properly. In fact, if you use a regular Telnet client to connect to an IBM mainframe, the session is not established and the server appears not to have a Telnet server application running at all. Instead, IBM provides 3270 server and client applications. The IBM client application called Host on Demand can be used to connect to an IBM mainframe. Previously, the Host on Demand application program was distributed as a part of the Netscape Navigator product, but now it must be purchased separately.

 TROUBLESHOOTING TECHNIQUES

FTP File Types

Many of the problems experienced when using the File Transfer Protocol stem from the differences between the text and binary files that a user wants to transfer. By default, an FTP client will transfer a file using the ASCII mode. The only type of file that can be transferred without corruption in ASCII mode is an ASCII file. Any other type of file such as an executable or a ZIP file will be modified during the transfer and corrupted. Similarly, a binary file must be transferred using FTP binary mode or it too will be corrupted. Since FTP does not know what type of file a user is transferring, it requires the user to set the transfer mode accordingly. Use of an application like WS_FTP (which provides the automatic ability to determine the type of file being processed based on the files extension) makes using the FTP program easier. You are encouraged to experiment with FTP.

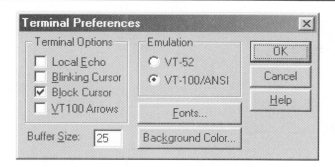

Figure 13–27
Telnet Terminal Preferences.

Telnet Keyboard Mapping

One of the most frustrating experiences with the Telnet protocol involve keyboard mapping. The first step in solving a keyboard mapping problem is to understand what keys are supported by Telnet and then be able to locate those keys on your particular keyboard. As an example, the Backspace key on most keyboards will back up one character to the left each time the key is pressed until the beginning of the line is reached. When using a Telnet client, the Backspace key may move the cursor to the left margin on the very first press. This makes it much more difficult to correct or edit a typing mistake. A quick solution can be found by pressing a left arrow key instead of the Backspace key.

Depending on the type of computer system that is being connected to, a lot of different keyboard mapping issue arise. Approach the situation from the standpoint that some solution or compromise probably exists and then try to locate it. The Terminal Preferences option, which is also available on the Terminal pull-down menu on the Windows client, is displayed in Figure 13–27. There are very few preferences that actually can be set. The emulation mode specifies the type of physical terminal that is used. Note that a VT-100/ANSI terminal offers more features than a VT-52. Different Telnet clients may offer more or less preference options. You are encouraged to explore the many other features of the Telnet protocol.

SELF-TEST

This self-test is designed to help you check your understanding of the background information presented in this chapter.

True/False

Answer *true* or *false*.

1. The File Transfer Protocol uses the UDP transport protocol.

2. Telnet uses a Network Virtual Terminal.

3. FTP can transfer files in both directions.

4. FTP uses one port for both data and control.

5. Telnet negotiates options between the client and a server.

6. FTP clients are included in many HTML editors.

7. Telnet provides a mechanism to use all of a physical terminal features.

Multiple Choice

Select the best answer.

8. The File Transfer Protocol uses _____ for the control communication.
    a. UDP.
    b. ICMP.
    c. Telnet.

9. The Telnet protocol is defined in RFC _____.
    a. 276.
    b. 627.
    c. 854.

10. _____ transfer mode is selected by default when using FTP.
    a. Text.
    b. Binary.
    c. ASCII.

11. The file permission needed to allow access to a file for FTP is _____.
    a. Write.
    b. Read.
    c. Execute.

12. An NVT is a(n) _____ device.
    a. Real.
    b. Imaginary.
    c. Physical.

13. The image FTP transfer mode will perform a _____ file transfer.
    a. Text.
    b. ASCII.
    c. Binary.

14. A Telnet option negotiation begins with a(n) _____.
    a. Carriage return and line feed.
    b. IAC.
    c. EL.

Completion

Fill in the blank or blanks with the best answers.

15. A FTP _____ code of 331 indicates that a password is required.

16. Telnet uses a _____ _____ _____ on both the client and server.

17. A(n) _____ and _____ both implement no operation codes in Telnet.

18. The _____ FTP command is used to show the status of a connection.

19. The _____ and _____ FTP commands will retrieve a file.

20. A _____ session uses port 23 on the server.

QUESTIONS/ACTIVITIES

1. Search the Web to find places to download FTP clients free of charge. How many clients did you find?

2. Search the Web to locate Telnet servers for the Windows operating system. Make a chart of features and pricing.

3. Search the Web to locate RFCs associated with the Telnet protocol.

4. Search the Web to locate RFCs associated with the FTP protocol.

REVIEW QUIZ

Under the supervision of your instructor

1. Describe the purpose of the File Transfer and Telnet protocols.

2. Explain how File Transfer Protocol clients and servers are configured.

3. Discuss the various FTP and Telnet commands.

Networking Concepts Laboratory

Experiment #13
FTP and Telnet

Objectives

1. To use FTP to exchange files between computers.
2. To use Telnet to connect to a host computer.

Required Equipment

The following equipment is required for this experiment:

- A networked computer with access to the Internet
- LanExplorer software

Procedure

Perform each of the following steps. Record your observations, results, and any difficulties you encounter. You will use this information when you develop your conclusions about the experiment.

1. Contact your local computer center and ask if there is FTP and Telnet service available. Record the corresponding network addresses for each service.
2. Use the Windows FTP client (or another FTP client of your choosing) to connect to an FTP site.
3. Transfer a text file using the ASCII transfer mode. *Optional:* Capture the entire file transfer using LanExplorer.
4. Examine the size of the original text file and the size of the transferred file. Are they the same?
5. Repeat steps 3 and 4, except transfer the text file using the binary mode.
6. Transfer a binary file using both the ASCII and binary transfer modes. Examine the size of the original and the sizes of both transferred files. Note any differences.
7. Quit the FTP client.
8. Run the FTP client again and enter a STAT command before, during, and after a FTP session is established. What information is different? What information stays the same?
9. Use Telnet to connect to your computer center's mainframe. Log all session activity to a file. *Optional:* Capture the session using LanExplorer.

Discussion and Conclusion

Using a word processor, write your own detailed explanations of the results and observations made during the experiment. To begin, try to say something about each procedure step.

In addition, provide answers to the following questions:

1. Why use FTP to transfer files rather than e-mail?
2. What advantages does a Telnet session have over using an ordinary ASCII data terminal?

14

Multimedia Networking

Joe Tekk was excited. It was close to midnight, but he was wide awake, adjusting the view from a small color video camera mounted above his monitor. His e-mail pal from Japan, Fumiko Sawa, would contact him at 2 P.M., her time. She also had a color camera, so they agreed to try a video connection over the Internet, since they had never met in person.

At three minutes past midnight the speakers on Joe's monitor said, "You have a call." Joe clicked on the answer button in the virtual videophone application window, and Fumiko appeared in a small window, her voice coming clearly from the speakers.

By the end of the conversation Joe had used the Web to book a flight to Japan to visit Fumiko.

INTRODUCTION

Multimedia, or multiple types of media, has become a large part of the computing experience. Computers of the past were basically number crunchers and word processors. With the acceptance and widespread use of the Internet and the World Wide Web, multimedia has become an important form of communication. Processor and PC designers now design their products with multimedia applications in mind, to improve performance.

In this chapter we will examine several important multimedia components, including images, sound, and video.

🖥️🖥️ IMAGE FILES

Web browsers accept two different types of image files: .GIF images and .JPG (or JPEG) images. *GIF* stands for Graphics Interchange Format. *JPEG* stands for Joint Photographic Experts Group. .GIF files were created by CompuServe as a method to exchange graphical information. The features of a .GIF file are as follows:

- Maximum of 256 colors
- Lossless compression using LZW (Lempel-Ziv-Welch) algorithm
- Support for animation and transparency built in

Lossless compression means none of the original data is lost during compression. When the image data is decompressed for display purposes, an exact copy of the original data is reproduced.

Compare the properties of a .GIF file with those of a JPEG file:

- 24-bit color
- Lossy compression using the DCT (Discrete Cosine Transform) algorithm on 8-by-8 blocks of pixels
- No animation or transparency available

JPEG files are preferred for their photographic-quality color. In addition, the lossy compression provides better compression, in general, than the lossless compression used in .GIF files, with little noticeable effect on image quality. For example, consider the image shown in Figure 14–1(a). The image contains 190 × 128, or 24,320 pixels. Without compression, a total of 24,320 bytes would be needed to store 8-bit pixel values, and 72,960 bytes would be required for 24-bit pixel values. Examine Table 14–1, which shows the results of saving the image in .GIF and JPEG formats. The JPEG compression is clearly superior to the .GIF compression. Viewing each image side by side also illustrates why JPEG is the better format for high-quality images.

To get a better feel for the differences between lossless and lossy compression, try the following experiment:

1. Create a new .GIF image using an image editor. Make the background of the image white.
2. Add a text message to the image, using black lettering.
3. Save the .GIF image.
4. Convert the .GIF image into a JPEG image and save it as well.
5. Open the .GIF image and zoom into it several times so that the pixels making up the text can be easily seen (a zoom factor of 8:1 should work fine). You should only see black pixels on a white background. This is shown in Figure 14–1(b).
6. Open the JPEG image and zoom in on the same area you examined in the .GIF image. You should notice pixels of an off-white color hovering around the text. This is the result of the lossy compression applied to the

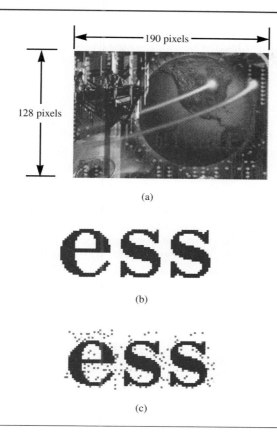

(a)

ess

(b)

ess

(c)

Property	EARTH.JPG	EARTH.GIF
Bits/pixel	24	8
Unique colors	20089	256
Possible colors	16777216	256
File size (bytes)	10097	24557

Table 14–1
Comparing
EARTH.JPG and
EARTH.GIF files.

JPEG image. Figure 14–1(c) shows this effect. Note that the off-white pixels have been changed to a darker color to make them more visisble for the publishing process. In actuality, the off-white pixels are close to the color of the white background, and may not be noticeable when the image is viewed at its normal size. This is why we can get away with lossy compression in the JPEG image. Our eyes are not sensitive enough to see the effects of the lossy compression.

SOUND FILES

Three types of sound files are popular on the Web. These are .WAV, .MID, and .MP3. Let us examine the features of each sound file.

.WAV Files

The *.WAV* (WAVE) file is the standard audio file format used by Windows. All the little sounds Windows makes are stored in .WAV files. The Sound Recorder found in the Entertainment folder of Accessories can be used to play, record, and even edit WAV files. Figure 14–2 shows the Sound Recorder window with the BLAST.WAV file loaded and displayed. The waveform window is updated as the file is played.

The Sound Recorder provides editing features such as cut, paste, and delete, and special effects, such as adding echo, reversing the audio (playing the file backwards), and adjusting the playback speed.

Figure 14–3 shows the properties of the BLAST.WAV file. The 0.30 seconds of audio require 6786 bytes of sample data. Note that the audio was recorded in 8-bit stereo, at a sampling rate of 11,025 Hz (11,025 samples/second). The sampling method is PCM, or pulse code modulation. PCM is one of many different techniques for encoding audio into digital form.

CD-quality sound is sampled at 44,100 Hz and uses 16-bit stereo samples. The Sound Recorder allows you to choose the sampling properties. Select the Recording formats entry in the 'Choose from' drop-down menu in the Properties window. This will open the Sound Selection window shown in Figure 14–4. Here you are able to specify the sound quality in the Name box (CD, Radio, or Telephone), the encoding format (PCM, uLaw, ADPCM, plus others), and the sampling attributes (sampling rate, bits per channel, number of channels). The Attributes entry also indicates the data rate of the bitstream. In this case, two 16-bit channels being sampled 44,100 times per second requires $2 \times 16 \times 44,100$ or 1,411,200 bits per second. Dividing by 8, we get 176,400 bytes/second (which is just over 172 KB/second).

.MID Files

.MID is the file extension used on MIDI (Musical Instrument Digital Interface) files. A .MID file contains information (commands for the MIDI *sequencer*) on

Figure 14–2
Sound Recorder
displaying portion of
BLAST.WAV.

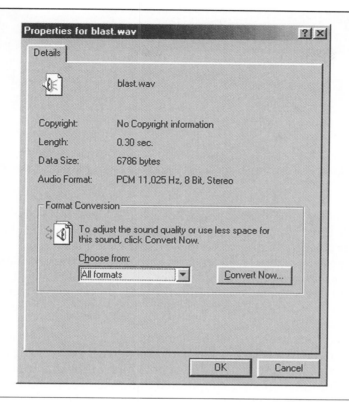

Figure 14–3
BLAST.WAV
properties.

Figure 14–4
Changing the
sampling properties.

what notes to play and how to play them. A total of 128 pitched instruments can generate 24 notes in 16 channels. The sound card in the PC uses the MIDI-information to reproduce the notes, using techniques such as frequency modulation and wave table synthesis. The attack, delay, sustain, and release portions of each note can be controlled.

Table 14–2
MPEG audio layer
differences.

MPEG Audio Layer	Encoder Complexity	Compression	Typical Bit Rate
1	Low	Low (4:1)	384 Kbps
2	Medium	Medium (8:1)	192 Kbps
3	High	High (12:1)	112 Kbps

.MID files are capable of producing very complex sounds with a small amount of data. For example, an 18KB .MID file has a playing time of 3 minutes.

.MP3 Files

.MP3 files get their name from the MPEG Audio Layer 3 specification. **MPEG** (Moving Picture Experts Group) audio and video are popular encoding methods for creating high-quality, low-bit rate multimedia files.

There are three audio layers defined in the MPEG standard. Table 14–2 lists some of their features. As indicated, Layer 2 is superior to Layer 1, and Layer 3 is superior to Layer 2. Layer 3 requires the most processing power, Layer 1 the least. Layer 3 encoding did not get popular until the speed of the PC was able to support its calculations.

All three layers use the same basic techniques for encoding audio and compressing the data. These techniques, called *perceptual audio coding* and *psychoacoustic compression*, utilize knowledge of how humans hear and process sounds to eliminate information that is duplicated or masked out by other sounds.

.MP3 files can be used to burn an audio CD-ROM or can be downloaded into a portable MP3 player.

 THE DIGITAL CONVERSATION

Before we examine a method for transmitting voice data over a network, let us take a look at how an analog voice waveform, such as one representing your voice when you are speaking, is sampled and converted into digital data.

Figure 14–5(a) shows the basic process of analog-to-digital (A/D) conversion. An analog waveform, such as the signal from a microphone, is sampled at regular intervals. Each sample voltage is input to an analog-to-digital converter (ADC), which outputs an 8-bit binary number associated with the sample voltage.

The telephone company samples your phone conversation 8000 times each second. Using 8-bit samples gives a bit rate of 64,000 bits/second. This is a high enough bit rate to provide a reasonable amount of quality when the bit-stream is converted back into an audio waveform. This process, called digital-to-analog (D/A) conversion, is shown in Figure 14–5(b). Each 8-bit sample is converted back into a corresponding voltage. The 8000 voltage samples generated by the digital-to-analog converter (DAC) each second are smoothed out using a low-pass filter.

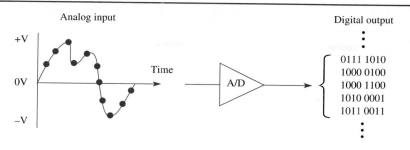

(a) Analog-to-Digital conversion.

Figure 14–5
A/D and D/A
conversion.

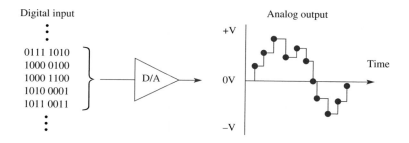

(b) Digital-to-Analog conversion.

TRANSMITTING DATA OVER A NETWORK

Imagine having to send each of the 8000 digital samples from the A/D converter over a network connection. At first, this would seem a reasonable thing to do. The 64,000 bits required each second is only 6.4% of the bandwidth of a 10baseT connection (ignoring overhead). Packing 1500 samples (the same as 1500 bytes) into a TCP message (for reliability) would require only six messages per second to support the audio stream. Of course, if even one message is lost, a large part of the conversation will be missing. The delay required to retransmit the missing message may affect the audio quality of the conversation.

Making the messages smaller (sending 80 bytes at a time for a total of 100 messages) would reduce the effect of a missing packet but also would require more bandwidth for transmission. Why? When only six 1500-byte messages are used, the network overhead is not significant. The network overhead consists, in this case, of the following:

- 26 bytes of Ethernet framing
- 24 bytes of IP header
- 24 bytes of TCP header

Table 14–3
Transmitting 8000
bytes (64,000 bits)
of data using
multiple packets.

Data Length (Bytes)	74-Byte Overhead (%)	Number of Packets	Total Bytes	Total Bits
1500	4.93	6	9444	75552
1400	5.28	6	8844	70752
1200	6.16	7	8918	71344
1000	7.4	8	8592	68736
500	14.8	16	9184	73472
250	29.6	32	10368	82944
150	49.33	54	12096	96768
100	74	80	13920	111360
80	92.5	100	15400	123200
64	115.62	125	17250	138000

These 74 bytes of overhead are only 4.93% of the 1500 bytes of data in each message. Thus, only 4.93% more bandwidth is required to transmit the data stream. Compare this to the situation in which only 80 bytes of data are sent in a message. The 74 bytes of overhead now represents 92.5% of the 80-byte data block. This almost doubles the bandwidth required and increases the time required to transmit the data stream. So, a balance must be found between packet size and overhead. Table 14–3 provides a number of examples for comparison. The numbers in Table 14–3 suggest that a packet containing 1000 bytes of data requires the least amount of bandwidth.

In actual practice, UDP datagrams are preferred over TCP streams, to eliminate the overhead of TCP. Reliability is maintained by protocols in use above UDP, such as those utilized by Voice-over-IP.

VOICE-OVER-IP

The difficulties of transmitting voice data (IP telephony) over a network are weighed against the growing need to move all communication technologies onto the network. Voice-over-IP (VoIP) is a method for sending voice and fax data using the IP protocol. VoIP interfaces with the public service telephone network (PSTN) and attempts to provide the same quality of service.

Figure 14–6 shows the architecture of VoIP and its associated gateway/terminal. Several different IP protocols are used in VoIP. These are RTP (Real-Time Transfer Protocol), RTCP (Real-Time Control Protocol), and RSVP (Resources Reservation Protocol). RTP handles reliable delivery of real-time data. RTCP monitors the VoIP session to maintain the quality of service. RSVP manages network resources during the connection.

The voice processing and gateway/terminal operation are specified by the H.323 standard, which also supports video over IP.

Figure 14–6
VoIP architecture.

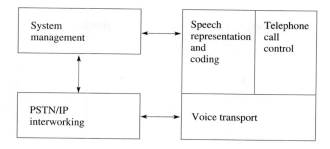

(a) Overall structure.

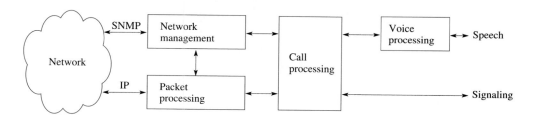

(b) VoIP gateway/terminal.

VIDEO

The problems associated with networked audio are worse for networked video, since greater bandwidth is required and it is easy to visually spot problems with the video stream. Real-time video, both live (streaming) and through playback (from an MPEG file), requires a powerful processor and a fast network connection. As with VoIP, the RTP, RTCP, and RSVP protocols are used to manage the information stream.

It is now affordable for any PC owner to purchase an inexpensive (under $100) color camera that connects to the printer port or USB port and allows real-time capture of video. Figure 14–7 shows the video camera window, showing a view of a certain author's home office. Applications such as CU-SeeMe use live camera video to establish a video conference between two or more individuals. Windows NetMeeting provides similar features. Bear in mind that any camera connected to the printer port will require plenty of processing power to capture and frame the image. The frame rate possible with this type of interface is based on the image resolution (smaller images allow a faster frame rate).

Figure 14–7
Video capture using
QuickPict.

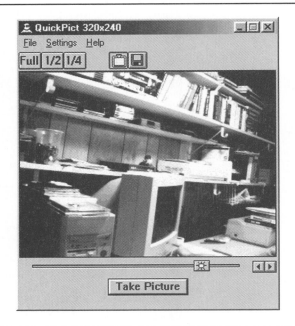

MPEG Files

As we saw earlier in this exercise, the MPEG standard specifies methods used to encode CD-quality audio in a compressed format. MPEG also defines a set of digital video parameters, such as bit rate, resolution, and compression techniques. MPEG video compression is lossy, using the Discrete Cosine Transform (also found in JPEG compression). MPEG video is processed in three types of frames:

- I (Intra) frames; a standalone video frame
- P (Predicted) frames; frames generated using the most recent I or P frame
- B (Bidirectional) frames; frames generated based on past and future frames

Frames are generated in a sequence similar to this:

```
...BPIBBPBBPBBPBBIBBP...
```

with an I frame every 12 frames (0.4 seconds of time when the frame rate is 30 frames per second). Skipping through the I frames allows you to view the video in fast-forward or rewind.

To reduce the require bandwidth, MPEG utilizes *motion vectors* that identify movement of blocks of pixels between frames. For example, suppose a 16-by-16 block of pixels in frame 10 appears in frame 11 in a slightly different position. Instead of coding the block a second time in frame 11, a motion vector is used to identify where the block has moved to in frame 11. This requires less data and helps reduce the bandwidth. A frame resolution of 352 by 240, at 30 frames per second, typically requires a 1.5 M bps stream, although higher resolutions are possible that push the bandwidth up to 6 M bps.

MPEG files can be played through the Microsoft Media Player.

MULTICASTING

It is not difficult to imagine a network getting bogged down when multiple video streams are being transmitted to numerous clients. For example, consider Figure 14–8(a), which shows a server sending identical copies of a video packet to 30 clients. The main switch receives and forwards the 30 copies to three additional switches, each of which forwards 10 copies to their respective clients. Clearly, the server and first switch are kept very busy.

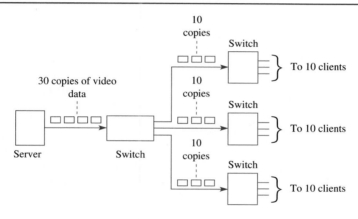

(a) Unicasting video stream to 30 clients.

Figure 14–8
Unicasting versus multicasting.

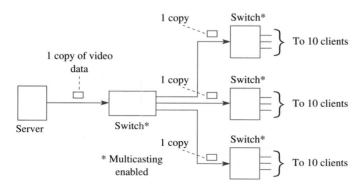

(b) Multicasting video stream to 30 clients.

Figure 14–8(b) shows how multicasting eliminates a large portion of the duplicated information. The server sends one copy of the video data to a multicasting-enabled switch, which in turn forwards a single copy to each of the other three multicasting-enabled switches, which replicate the video data and forward copies to each client. The bandwidth required by the server and the first switch has been significantly reduced.

IP multicasting is possible through the use of IGMP, the Internet Group Management Protocol, which is defined in RFC 1112. Class D addresses are used for all group members.

An experimental multicasting backbone, called *MBone*, supports multicasting over the Internet. For more information on MBone, look through the Mbone FAQ located at http://www.cs.columbia.edu/~hgs/internet/mbone-faq.html.

 ## GAMES

Computer games that have networking capabilities have steadily grown in popularity. Typically, one machine runs the game in server mode, with multiple game client machines connected to it at the same time. The game programmers must take many factors into account when designing the network components of the game, such as available bandwidth, communication delay, and processing speed. Care must be taken to provide each player with a real-time game environment.

Chapter 16 provides the details behind the development and operation of a two-player network game called NETMAZE. An excellent source of network game source code can be found at http://cg.cs.tu-berlin.de/~ki/engines.html. This site is the 3-D Engines List, a Web site containing 643 different game engines (at the time of this writing). Thirty-five games contain network support.

 ## TROUBLESHOOTING TECHNIQUES

Sometimes a little math can save you a great deal of time and effort. For example, a small college wants add an .MP3 audio server to their internal network. The administrators think that their thickwire college network infrastructure is fast enough to handle the additional digital audio bandwidth, since there are only 76 employees, and in the words of one administrator, "How many employees will be listening to music at the same time?"

Well, a worst-case scenario does involve all 76 employees listening to .MP3 audio at the same time. Figure 14–9(a) shows the bandwidth calculations, assuming 12:1 compression and 15 Ethernet frames/second for each audio stream. A total of 9,612,480 bits are needed each second. Even though this is less than the 10 Mbps available with thickwire, consider these important factors:

- Collisions will lower the available bandwidth.
- The college's Internet connection accounts for 22% of the total bandwidth.

1,411,200 bps	CD-quality bit rate	**Figure 14–9**
÷ 12	Compression factor	Bandwidth
117,600 bps	Compressed bit rate	calculations.
+ 8,880 bps	Overhead for 15 Ethernet frames	
126,480 bps	Total bits for single user	
× 76	Users	
9,612,480 bps	Total bits required	

(a) Bits required for all streams.

1,000,000 bits	Allocated bandwidth
÷ 126,480 bps	Bit rate for one stream
7.9	Number of streams possible

(b) Number of streams possible.

- Network activity (NetBIOS sessions, printing, user authentication) accounts for 15% of the total bandwidth.
- The 9.6-microsecond interframe gap after every frame is equivalent to 96 bits of lost bandwidth.

It should not be difficult to see that the 9,612,480 bps needed for the audio streams will not be available.

Looking at this problem from a different perspective, suppose the administrators decide to allocate a fixed bandwidth for the digital audio equal to 1 Mbps. How many streams can be supported? As shown in Figure 14–9(b), only seven users can be supported with a 1-Mbps bandwidth allocation.

With these simple calculations, it is clear the college administration must upgrade their existing network before adding any more traffic from the audio server.

SELF-TEST

This self-test is designed to help you check your understanding of the background information presented in this chapter.

True/False
Answer *true* or *false*.

1. JPEG images utilize lossy compression.

2. MP3 is an abbreviation for MPEG Layer 3.

3. Ethernet framing overhead can be ignored when transmitting large blocks of data.

4. VoIP provides IP telephony.

5. MPEG I frames are based on previous frames.

Multiple Choice

Select the best answer.

6. GIF compression uses the _____ algorithm.
   a. LZW.
   b. DCT.
   c. GIF.

7. JPEG compression uses the _____ algorithm.
   a. LZW.
   b. DCT.
   c. PAL.

8. CD-quality sound has an uncompressed bit rate of
   a. 64,000 bps.
   b. 1,411,200 bps.
   c. 10,000,000 bps.

9. The resolution of a video frame
   a. Is not a factor in the frame rate.
   b. Affects the frame rate.
   c. Increases as the frame rate increases.

10. The protocol used in IP multicasting is
    a. IGMP.
    b. IPMP.
    c. IMCT.

Completion

Fill in the blank or blanks with the best answers.

11. LZW is a _____ compression technique.

12. MIDI stands for Musical Instrument _____ _____.

13. Phone conversations are sampled _____ times per second.

14. MPEG video compression utilizes _____ vectors to reduce bandwidth.

15. MBone stands for _____ _____.

QUESTIONS/ACTIVITIES

1. Create a table similar to Table 14–3 showing the packets required for a CD-quality bit stream with no compression.

2. Repeat step 1 for compression ratios of 2:1, 5:1, and 10:1.

3. Find an .MP3 file on the Web containing one of your favorite songs. Use the file length and playing time to estimate the compression ratio.

REVIEW QUIZ

Under the supervision of your instructor

1. Explain the basic properties of .GIF and .JPG image files.

2. Discuss the various sound file formats, such as .WAV, .MID, and .MP3.

3. Describe MPEG, Voice-over-IP, and multicasting.

Networking Concepts Laboratory

Experiment #14
Multimedia Networking

Objectives

1. To investigate the differences between .JPG and .GIF files.
2. To compare .WAV and .MP3 sound files.
3. To examine an MPEG file and its characteristics.

Required Equipment

The following equipment is required for this experiment:

- A networked computer with access to the Internet

Procedure

Perform each of the following steps. Record your observations, results, and any difficulties you encounter. You will use this information when you develop your conclusions about the experiment.

1. Find an interesting .JPG file on the Web. Use a paint program to convert it to .GIF format.
2. Compare the size of each file and their image quality.
3. Use the Sound Recorder in the Entertainment folder of Accessories to record 5-second, 10-second, and 30-second .WAV files.
4. Compare the .WAV file lengths. Can you determine the average bit rate during recording?
5. Download a WAV-to-MP3 converter. Convert the 30-second .WAV file into .MP3 format.
6. Compare the size of each file and their playback quality.
7. View an MPEG movie using Windows Media Player. Compare the file size to the playback time.

Discussion and Conclusion

Using a word processor, write your own detailed explanations of the results and observations made during the experiment. To begin, try to say something about each procedure step.
   In addition, provide answers to the following questions:

1. The steps used to compress a .JPG file are as follow: (1) convert an 8-by-8 group of pixels into a corresponding 8-by-8 matrix of DCT values, (2) quantize the DCT values, (3) read the DCT values out of the matrix using the zigzag method, and (4) run-length encode the DCT

zigzag elements. Each step is repeated for all 8-by-8 groups in the image. What does each step actually do?

2. Two additional multimedia file formats are .AVI and .MOV. What are they and what are their features?

15

The Internet

PERFORMANCE OBJECTIVES

Upon completion of this chapter, you will be able to

- Describe the basic organization of the Internet.

- Explain the purpose of a browser and its relationship to HTML.

- Discuss the usefulness of CGI and Java applications.

- Identify the elements of a Virtual Private Network.

- List the steps involved in setting up a Web server.

It was 2:45 A.M. Joe Tekk was awake, sitting in his darkened living room. The only light in the room was coming from the monitor of his computer. Joe was exhausted, but he didn't want to stop browsing the Web. He had stumbled onto a Web page containing links to computer graphics, game design, and protected-mode programming. For three hours, Joe had been going back and forth from one page to another, adding some links to his bookmarks and ignoring others. When he finally decided to quit, it was not because of lack of interest, but simply because it was time to go to sleep.

"From now on, I'm only browsing for 30 minutes," Joe vowed to himself. But he knew he would have another late-night browsing session that would last much longer. It was too much fun having so much information available instantly.

INTRODUCTION

The Internet started as a small network of computers connecting a few large mainframe computers. It has grown to become the largest computer network in the world, connecting virtually all types of computers. The Internet offers a method to achieve *universal service,* or a connection to virtually any computer, anywhere in the world, at any time. This concept is similar to the use of a telephone, which provides a voice connection anywhere at any time. The Internet provides a way to connect all types of computers together regardless of their manufacturer, size, and resources. The *one* requirement is a connection to the network. Figure 15–1 shows how several networks are connected together.

Figure 15–1
Concept of Internet
connections.

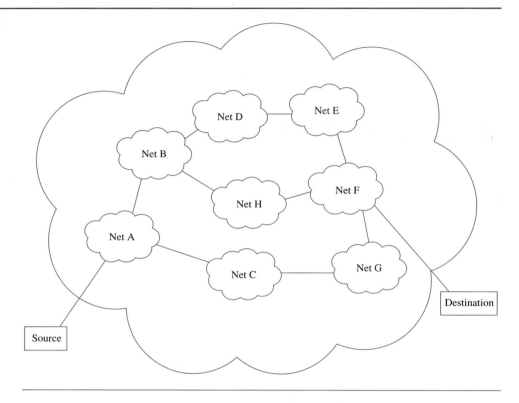

The type of connection to the Internet can take many different forms, such as a simple modem connection, a cable modem connection, a T1 line, a T3 line, or a frame relay connection.

THE ORGANIZATION OF THE INTERNET

The current version of the Internet (V4) is organized into several categories, as shown in Table 15–1. The name of an Internet host shows the category to which it is assigned. For example, the rwa.com domain is the name of a company, and the bcc.edu domain is an educational institution. Each domain is registered on the appropriate root server. For example, the domain rwa.com is known by the com root server. Then, within each domain, a locally administered Domain Name Server allows for each host to be configured.

WORLD WIDE WEB

The World Wide Web, or **WWW** as it is commonly referred to, is actually the Hypertext Transport Protocol (HTTP) in use on the Internet. The HTTP

Domain Type*	Organization Type
edu	Educational institution
com	Commercial organization
gov	Government
mil	Military
net	Network providers and support
org	Other organizations not listed above
country code	A country code, for example, .us for United States, .ca for Canada, .jp for Japan

Table 15–1
Organization of the
Internet.

*In November 2000, .biz, .info, .name, .pro, .aero, .museum, and .coop were initially approved as additional domain types.

protocol allows for hypermedia information to be exchanged, such as text, video, audio, animation, Java applets, images, and more. The hypertext markup language, or HTML, is used to determine how the hypermedia information is to be displayed on a WWW browser screen.

The WWW *browser* is used to navigate the Internet by selecting *links* on any WWW page or by specifying a uniform resource locator, or *URL*, to point to a specific *page* of information. There are many different WWW browsers. The two most popular are Microsoft Internet Explorer and Netscape Navigator, shown in Figures 15–2 and 15–3, respectively. Both of these browsers are

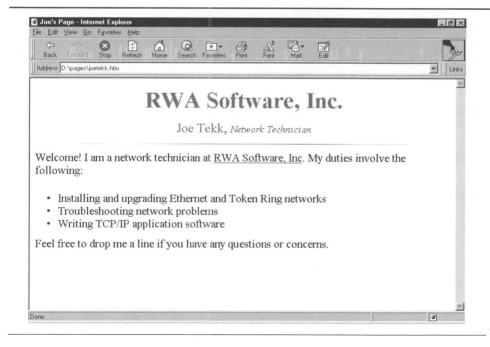

Figure 15–2
Sample home page
displayed using
Internet Explorer.

Figure 15–3
Sample home page
displayed using
Netscape Navigator.

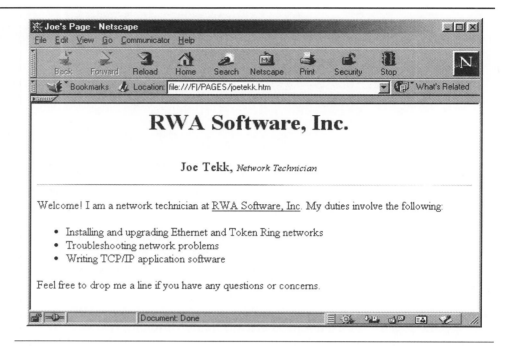

available free over the Internet and contain familiar pull-down menus and graphical toolbars to access the most commonly used functions such as forward, backward, stop, print, and reload.

Note the differences in page layout between Figures 15–2 and 15–3. Individuals who design Web pages must take into account the different requirements of each browser so that the page looks acceptable in both browsers.

 HTML

HTML stands for hypertext markup language. HTML is the core component of the information that composes a Web page. The HTML *source code* for a Web page has an overall syntax and structure that contains formatting commands (called *tags*) understood by a Web browser. Following is a sample HTML source (JOETEKK.HTM). The actual Web page for this HTML code was shown in Figure 15–3.

```
<HTML>

<HEAD>
<TITLE>Joe's Page</TITLE>
</HEAD>

<BODY BGCOLOR="#FFFF80">
```

```
<P ALIGN="CENTER">
<B><FONT SIZE="+3" COLOR="#FF0000">RWA Software, Inc.</FONT></B>
</P>

<P ALIGN="CENTER">
<FONT SIZE="+1"><FONT COLOR="#008000">Joe Tekk</FONT>,
<FONT SIZE="-1"><I>Network Technician</I></FONT></FONT>
</P>

<P ALIGN="CENTER">
<IMG SRC="bar.gif" ALT="Color Bar">
</P>

<P ALIGN="LEFT">
Welcome! I am a network technician at
<A HREF="http://www.rwasoftware.com">RWA Software, Inc</A>. My duties
 involve the following:
</P>

<UL>
<LI>Installing and upgrading Ethernet and Token Ring networks</LI>
<LI>Troubleshooting network problems</LI>
<LI>Writing TCP/IP application software </LI>
</UL>

<P ALIGN="LEFT">
Feel free to drop me a line if you have any questions or
concerns.
</P>

</BODY>
</HTML>
```

The HTML source consists of many different tags that instruct the browser what to do when preparing the graphical Web page. Table 15–2 shows some of the more common tags. The main portion of the Web page is contained between the BODY tags. Note that BGCOLOR= "#FFFF80" sets the background color of the Web page. The six-digit hexadecimal number contains three pairs of values for the red, green, and blue color levels desired.

Pay attention to the tags used in the HTML source and what actually appears on the Web page in the browser (Figure 15–3). The browser ignores white space (multiple blanks between words or lines of text) when it processes the HTML source. For example, the anchor for the RWA Software link begins on its own line in the source, but the actual link for the anchor is displayed on the same line as the text that comes before and after it.

Many people use HTML editors, such as HoTMetaL or Front Page, to create and maintain their Web pages. Options to display the page in HTML format or in *WYSIWYG* (what you see is what you get) are usually available, along with

Table 15–2
Assorted HTML
tags.

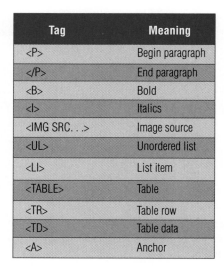

Tag	Meaning
<P>	Begin paragraph
</P>	End paragraph
<B>	Bold
<I>	Italics
<IMG SRC. . .>	Image source
<UL>	Unordered list
<LI>	List item
<TABLE>	Table
<TR>	Table row
<TD>	Table data
<A>	Anchor

sample pages, image editing, and conversion tools that convert many different file types (such as a Word document) into HTML. Demo versions of these HTML editors and others can be downloaded from the Web. Figure 15–4 shows HoTMetaL's graphical page editor with Joe Tekk's page loaded.

Figure 15–4
HoTMetaL PRO with
sample page.

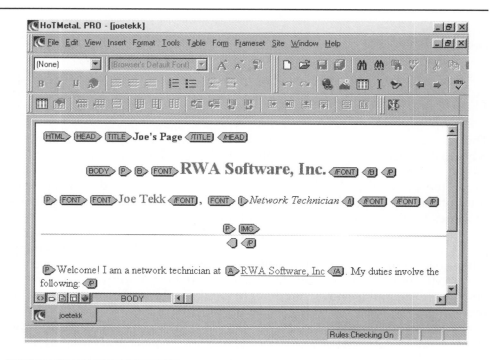

WWW pages are classified into three categories: static, dynamic, and active. The easiest to make are static and involve only HTML code. The page content is determined by what is contained in the HTML code. Dynamic WWW pages contain a combination of HTML code and a "call" to a server using a Common Gateway Interface (*CGI*) application. In this scenario, information supplied by the user into an HTML form is transferred back to a host computer for processing. The host computer then returns a dynamic customized WWW page. Active pages contain a combination of HTML code and applets. Therefore, the WWW page is not completely specified during the HTML coding process. Instead, using a Java applet, it is specified while being displayed by the WWW browser.

 ## CGI

The Common Gateway Interface (CGI) is a software interface that allows a small amount of interactive processing to take place with information provided on a Web page. For example, consider the Web page shown in Figure 15–5. The Web page contains a FORM element, which itself can contain many different types of inputs, such as text boxes, radio buttons, lists with scroll bars, and other types of buttons and elements. The user browsing the page

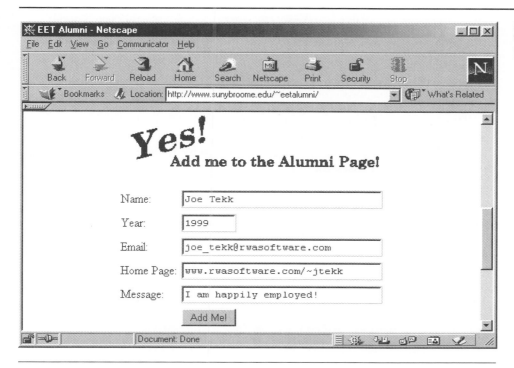

Figure 15–5
Web page with FORM element.

enters his or her information and then clicks the Add Me! button. This begins the following chain of events:

1. The form data entered by the user is placed into a message.
2. The browser POSTs the form data (sends message to CGI server).
3. The CGI server application processes the form data.
4. The CGI server application sends the results back to the CGI client (Netscape or Internet Explorer).

Let us take a closer look. The HTML code for the alumni page form looks like this:

```
<FORM ACTION="/htbin/cgi-mailto/eetalumni" METHOD="POST">
<P ALIGN="CENTER"><IMG SRC="yes.gif"></P>
<CENTER>
<TABLE WIDTH="50%" ALIGN="CENTER">
<TR><TD>Name:</TD>
<TD><INPUT TYPE="TEXT" NAME="name" SIZE="32"></TD></TR>
<TR><TD>Year:</TD>
<TD><INPUT TYPE="TEXT" NAME="year" SIZE="8"></TD></TR>
<TR><TD>Email:</TD>
<TD><INPUT TYPE="TEXT" NAME="email" SIZE="32"></TD></TR>
<TR><TD>Home Page:</TD>
<TD><INPUT TYPE="TEXT" NAME="home" SIZE="32"></TD></TR>
<TR><TD>Message:</TD>
<TD><INPUT TYPE="TEXT" NAME="msg" SIZE="32"></TD></TR>
<TR><TD></TD>
<TD><INPUT TYPE="SUBMIT" VALUE="Add Me!"></TD></TR>
</TABLE>
</CENTER>
</FORM>
```

The first line of the form element specifies POST as the method used to send the form data out for processing. The CGI application that will receive the POSTed form data is the cgi-mailto program in the *htbin* directory. Specifically, cgi-mailto processes the form data and sends an e-mail message to the *eetalumni* account. The e-mail message looks like this:

```
From:   SBCCVA::WWWSERVER
To:     eetalumni
CC:
Subj:

REMOTE_ADDRESS: 204.210.159.19
name: Joe Tekk
year: 1998
email: joe_tekk@rwa.software.com
home: www.rwasoftware.com/~jtekk
msg: I am happily employed!
```

Note that the identifiers (name, year, email, home, and msg) match the names used to identify the text input elements in the form.

Instead of e-mailing the form data, another CGI application might create a Web page on the fly containing custom information based on the form data submitted. CGI applications are written in C/C++, Visual BASIC, Java, Perl, and many other languages. The Web is full of sample forms and CGI applications available for download and inclusion in your own Web pages.

JAVA

The Java programming language is the method used to create active WWW pages using Java applets. An active WWW page is specified by the Java applet when the WWW page is displayed rather than during the HTML coding process. A Java applet is actually a program transferred from an Internet host to the WWW browser. The WWW browser executes the Java applet code on a Java virtual machine (which is built into the WWW browser). The Java language can be characterized by the following nonexhaustive list:

- General purpose
- High level
- Object oriented
- Dynamic
- Concurrent

Java consists of a programming language, a run-time environment, and a class library. The Java programming language resembles C++ and can be used to create conventional computer applications or applets. Only an applet is used to create an active WWW page. The run-time environment provides the facilities to execute an application or applet. The class library contains prewritten code that can simply be included in the application or applet. Table 15–3 shows the Java class library functional areas.

The following Java program MYSW.JAVA is used to switch from one image to a second image (and back) whenever the mouse moves over the Java applet

Class	Description
Graphics	Abstract window tool kit (AWT)
Network I/O	Socket level connnections
File I/O	Local and remote file access
Event capture	User actions (mouse, keyboard, etc.)
Run-time system calls	Access to built-in functions
Exception handling	Method to handle any type of error condition
Server interaction	Built-in code to interact with a server

Table 15–3
Java class library categories.

window. Furthermore, a mouse click while the mouse is over the applet window causes a new page to load.

```java
import java.awt.Graphics;
import java.awt.Image;
import java.awt.Color;
import java.awt.Event;
import java.net.URL;
import java.net.MalformedURLException;

public class myswitch extends java.applet.Applet implements Runnable
{
    Image swoffpic;
    Image swonpic;
    Image currentimg;
    Thread runner;

public void start()
{
    if (runner == null)
    {
        runner = new Thread(this);
        runner.start();
    }
}

public void stop()
{
    if (runner != null)
    {
        runner.stop();
        runner = null;
    }
}

public void run()
{
    swoffpic = getImage(getCodeBase(), "swoff.gif");
    swonpic = getImage(getCodeBase(), "swon.gif");
    currentimg = swoffpic;
    setBackground(Color.red);
    repaint();
}

public void paint(Graphics g)
{
    g.drawImage(currentimg, 8, 8, this);
}
```

```java
public boolean mouseEnter(Event evt, int x, int y)
{
    currentimg = swonpic;
    repaint();
    return(true);
}

public boolean mouseExit(Event evt, int x, int y)
{
    currentimg = swoffpic;
    repaint();
    return(true);
}

public boolean mouseDown(Event evt, int x, int y)
{
    URL destURL = null;
    String url = "http://www.sunybroome.edu/~eet_dept";

    try
    {
        destURL = new URL(url);
    }
    catch(MalformedURLException e)
    {
        System.out.println("Bad destination URL: " + destURL);
    }
    if (destURL != null)
        getAppletContext().showDocument(destURL);
    return(true);
}

}
```

Programming in Java, like any other language, requires practice and skill. With its popularity still increasing, now would be a good time to experiment with Java yourself by downloading the free Java compiler and writing some applets.

VIRTUAL PRIVATE NETWORKS

A virtual private network (VPN) allows for remote private LANs to communicate securely through an untrusted public network such as the Internet. This technique is shown in Figure 15–6. This technique is in contrast to the traditional approach in which a large corporation or organization used private or leased lines to communicate between different sites in order to provide privacy of data. Using a VPN, only authorized members of the network are allowed ac-

Figure 15–6
RWA Software VPN
(physical view).

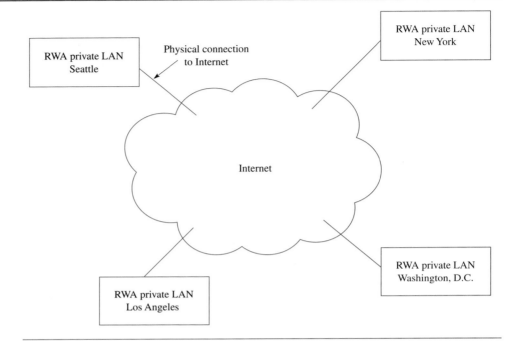

cess to the data. A VPN uses an IP tunneling protocol and security services that are transparent to the private network users.

Using a VPN, a private LAN connected to the Internet can be connected to other LANs using a combination of tunneling, encryption and authentication. *Tunneling* means that data that is transferred through the public network in an encapsulated form. This is illustrated in Figure 15–7.

All of the data, including the addresses of the sender and destination, are enclosed within a packet. Although tunneling is sufficient to create a VPN, it does not ensure complete data security.

Complete security is accomplished when the data communication is also encrypted and authenticated. Packets that are protected by tunneling, encryption, and authentication (certified by an agreed-on certification authority such as verisign.com) offer the highest level of security. The IP Security (IPSec) standards provide a security protocol for tunneling as well as for data privacy, integrity, and authentication, creating a truly secure VPN.

IPSec is a set of protocols developed by the Internet Engineering Task Force that adds additional security solutions to TCP/IP networking. IPSec currently supports several encryption algorithms such as DES, 3DES, and public-key encryption and is designed to incorporate new algorithms as they are created. IPSec offers a solution to data privacy, integrity, and authentication that is network independent, application independent, and supports all

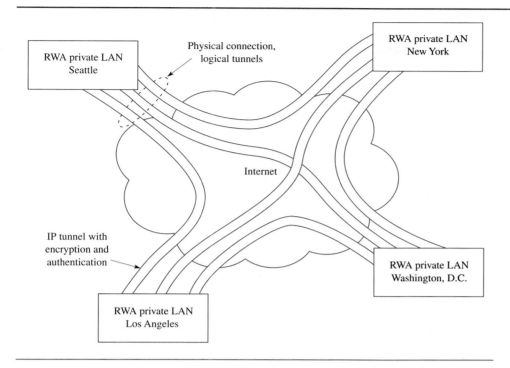

Figure 15–7
RWA Software VPN
(logical view).

IP services (e.g., HTTP, FTP, SNMP, etc.). Note that protocols such as PPTP (Point-to-Point Tunneling Protocol) and L2TP (Layer 2 Tunneling Protocol) used to create a VPN support only tunneling, whereas IPSec includes tunneling, encryption, and authentication.

INSTANT MESSAGING

One of the latest tools to communicate with on the Internet is instant messaging. Many different companies provide software to enable users to send electronic messages. Instant messaging is an application that provides the capability for a user to send and receive instant messages, which are delivered to the recipient *instantly*—even faster than electronic mail. Some of the most popular instant messaging applications are AOL's Instant Messenger and Microsoft's NetMeeting. Both of these programs allow for a user to send or receive instant messages.

Figure 15–8 shows the instant messaging screen for AOL's Instant Messenger program. Figure 15–9 shows a similar screen for Microsoft's NetMeeting.

There are many additional choices available for instant messaging. You are encouraged to search for, download, and test other instant messaging applications.

Figure 15–8
AOL Instant Message
window.

Figure 15–9
Microsoft NetMeeting.

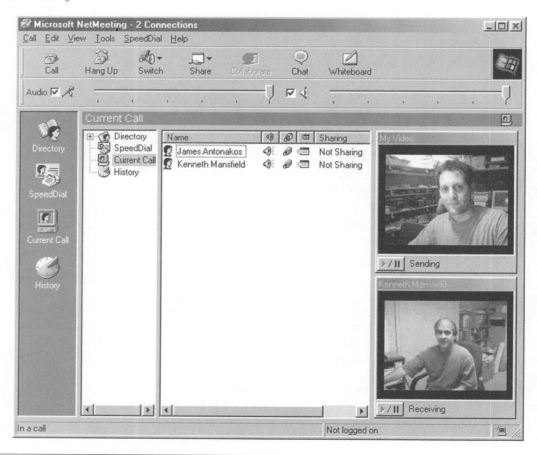

SETTING UP A WEB SERVER

Setting up a Web server to host WWW pages on the Internet is becoming a commonplace activity for business and personal use. Although a Web server is typically installed on large computer systems running Unix or Windows NT, a Web server can also be installed on most personal computers. The first step in setting up a Web server is to choose the Web server software.

One of the most popular Web server programs is the Apache Server from the Apache Software Foundation. Apache currently holds over 50% of the entire Web server market. Two of the reasons why the Apache Server is the most popular are because it is *free* and *fully featured*. The Apache Web server is available for many operating systems, including Windows, Unix, and many others. Figure 15–10 shows the Web page at apache.org where the Apache server can be downloaded. Figure 15–11 shows the status of the Apache server during the installation process. Figure 15–12 shows the default home page on a computer that is running the Apache Server Web server software.

Figure 15–10
Downloading Apache Server.

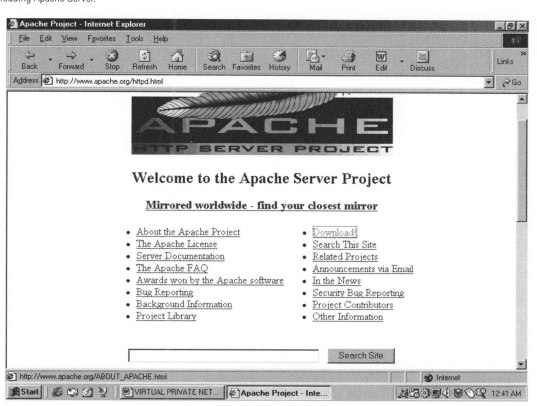

Figure 15–11
Apache installation
process.

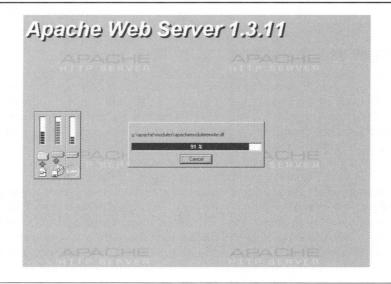

Figure 15–12
Apache Web server default home page.

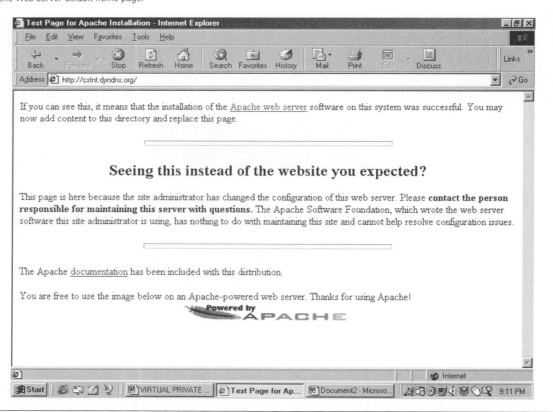

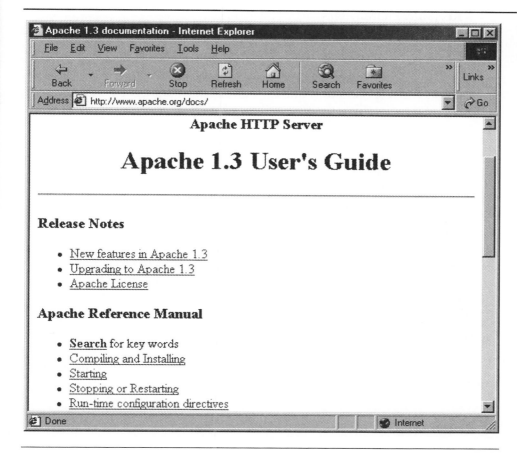

Figure 15–13
Apache HTTP server
documentation.

The built-in features of a Web server are best explored by viewing the Apache User's Guide. By selecting the Apache documentation link, the output shown in Figure 15–13 is displayed. From this page, all of the Apache Web server features can be explored.

Typically, after the Web server is installed, it is necessary to update the configuration file to provide a server name, e-mail contact, and several other items. When configuring the Apache Web server, it is necessary to update the httpd.conf file. This file describes

1. Directives that control the "global" operation of the Apache Server process. Directives that are configured at the global level include
   - Server type
   - Server root
   - Scoreboard file
   - Timeout value

- Keep-alive parameters
- Server pool size
- Max clients
- Extended status settings

2. Directives that define the parameters of the *main* or *default server*. The default server responds to requests that are not handled by virtual hosts. Some of the directives defined at the default level include
   - Port number
   - Server administrator
   - Server name
   - Document root
   - Default permissions
   - Override parameters
   - Accesses file name
   - CGI script aliases
   - Cache settings

3. Settings for all virtual hosts that allow Web requests to be sent to different IP addresses or host names. The typical settings for virtual hosts include virtual host addresses, names, and directives (with similar entries used in the main or default server listed in step 2).

 Each of these settings is described in detail within the httpd.conf file. A sample copy of `httpd.conf` is located on the companion CD-ROM.

All that remains after the installation is to create the HTML documents and accompanying CGI applications to be served.

RELATED SITES

Following are a number of service, reference, and technology-based sites that may be of interest:

• www.prenhall.com	Engineering and technology textbooks
• www.yahoo.com	Search engine
• www.internic.net	Internet authority
• www.intel.com	Intel Corporation
• www.microsoft.com	Microsoft Corporation
• www.sunybroome.edu/~mansfield_k	Author's home page
• www.sunybroome.edu/~antonakos_j	Author's home page
• www.netscape.com	Netscape corporation

The Internet is full of information about every aspect of the Web page development process. Many people put a tremendous amount of information on their own Web pages. You are encouraged to learn more about Web pages and Web programming.

🖥️ TROUBLESHOOTING TECHNIQUES

The Internet and the World Wide Web are not the same thing. The Internet is a physical collection of networked computers. The World Wide Web is a logical collection of information contained on many of the computers comprising the Internet. To download a file from a Web page, the two computers (client machine running a browser and server machine hosting the Web page) must exchange the file data along with other control information. If the download speed is slow, what could be the cause? A short list identifies many suspects:

- Noise in the communication channel forces retransmission of many packets.
- The path through the Internet introduces delay.
- The server is sending data at a limited rate.
- The Internet service provider has limited bandwidth.

So, before buying a new modem or upgrading your network, determine where the bottleneck is. The Internet gets more popular every day. New home pages are added, additional files are placed on FTP sites for downloading, news and entertainment services are coming online and broadcasting digitally, and more and more machines are being connected. The 10- and 100-Mbit Ethernet technology is already hard-pressed to keep up with the Internet traffic. Gigabit networking is coming but will only provide a short respite from the ever-increasing demands of global information exchange.

SELF-TEST

This self-test is designed to help you check your understanding of the background information presented in this chapter.

True/False
Answer *true* or *false*.

1. The hypertext markup language is used to encode .GIF images.

2. CGI stands for Common Gateway Interchange.

3. HTML contains formatting commands called tags.

4. The main portion of a Web page is contained between the HEADER tags.

5. Java is a Web browser produced by Microsoft Corporation.

Multiple Choice
Select the best answer.

6. CGI applications can be written using
   a. Perl, Java, C, C++, and Visual BASIC.
   b. Only the Javascript language.
   c. An HTML editor.

7. The three different categories of Web pages are
   a. Large, medium, and small.
   b. Active, passive, and neutral.
   c. Static, dynamic, and active.

8. When the network is slow,
   a. Turn off all power to the computer and perform a reset.
   b. Try to determine where the bottleneck is located.
   c. Immediately upgrade to the newest, most expensive hardware available.

9. CGI applications use FORMs to
   a. Receive the input required for processing.
   b. Post the data to an e-mail application.
   c. Send information to the browser display.

10. The concept of universal service and the Internet involves
    a. Being able to connect to a universal router on the Internet.
    b. Being able to exchange information between computers at any time or place.
    c. Allowing all users to access the universal Internet database.

Completion

Fill in the blank or blanks with the best answers.

11. The same _____ code is displayed differently using different Internet browsers.

12. A CGI application provides the ability to create _____ _____ on the fly.

13. Java is used to create _____ Web pages.

14. _____ information includes text, video, audio, Java applets, and images.

15. The _____ protocol is used to exchange hypermedia information.

QUESTIONS/ACTIVITIES

1. Determine how to clear the browser's cache memory.

2. Determine the current allocation settings for the browser cache.

3. Search the Web to locate some useful resources related to active Web page development.

REVIEW QUIZ

Under the supervision of your instructor

1. Describe the basic organization of the Internet.

2. Explain the purpose of a browser and its relationship to HTML.

3. Discuss the usefulness of CGI applications.

Networking Concepts Laboratory

Experiment #15
The Internet

Objectives

1. To compare the features of two Web browsers.
2. To experiment with CGI applications.

Required Equipment

The following equipment is required for this experiment:

- A networked computer with access to the Internet

Procedure

Perform each of the following steps. Record your observations, results, and any difficulties you encounter. You will use this information when you develop your conclusions about the experiment.

The Web
1. Examine each of the pull-down menu items in Netscape Navigator or Internet Explorer.
2. Read the online help to learn about browser features.
3. Identify similarities between Netscape Navigator and Internet Explorer.
4. Identify differences between the two browsers.

CGI
1. Search the Web to locate information about Perl.
2. Locate a source for Perl, available free of charge.
3. Download Perl.
4. Install Perl.
5. Run some sample Perl scripts.

Java
1. Search the Web to locate information about the Java language.
2. Locate a source of a Java compiler, available free of charge.
3. Download the Java compiler.
4. Install the Java compiler.
5. Compile some sample Java applets.
6. Execute a sample Java applet.

Discussion and Conclusion

Using a word processor, write your own detailed explanations of the results and observations made during the experiment. To begin, try to say something about each procedure step.

In addition, provide answers to the following questions:

1. Which language (Perl, Java, C++) would be your choice for an Internet CGI application? Why?
2. How many different ways can you think of to communicate over the Internet?

Writing a Network Application

PERFORMANCE OBJECTIVES
Upon completion of this chapter, you will be able to

- Discuss the client-server model.
- Explain the basic features of a socket.
- Summarize the various network programming languages.
- Show examples of both connectionless and connection-oriented network applications.

Joe Tekk was experimenting with a simple network game he was developing with his friend Ken Koder. He was using a small network consisting of two Windows 98 computers and a 10baseT hub to host the game. He had just completed the code to exchange player position information over the network. When he moved the player on the server machine, the player figure on the client computer also moved, but at a slower pace and always lagging behind the server. As a test, he quickly moved the mouse forward and backward 10 times. He watched with surprise as it took the client computer an extra 4 seconds to process the player moves.

Comparing the clock speeds of the two computers, Joe found that the server was running at 400 MHz and the client at only 166 MHz. This caused messages to queue up in the client computer while the program was busy rendering the graphical game environment. Joe changed the message handling code to compensate for speed differences and reran the game. The player position now updated properly in real time.

INTRODUCTION

In this chapter we will examine the operation of client-server network applications. We will see how clients and servers communicate and study several working networking applications. We will also examine the various programming languages that are used to develop network applications.

Our study begins with the details of the client-server model.

▄,▄ CLIENT-SERVER MODEL

Figure 16–1 shows the basic idea behind the client-server model of network communication. The *client* sends messages to the server requesting service of some kind. The *server* responds with messages containing the desired information or takes other appropriate action.

The message containing the client request is encapsulated inside a network packet and transmitted over a physical connection to the server. Conceptually, a logical connection also exists between the client and server (through the use of their respective network addresses).

Following are some sample client-server interactions:

Echo Server
Client: Hello there 123.
Server: Hello there 123.

Time Server
Client: What time is it?
Server: 12:08:00 p.m.

Web Server
Client: Send the Web page http://www.rwasoftware.com/apps
Server: OK (lots of messages follow as page is transferred).

Game Server
Client: My move is 7.
Server: You win!

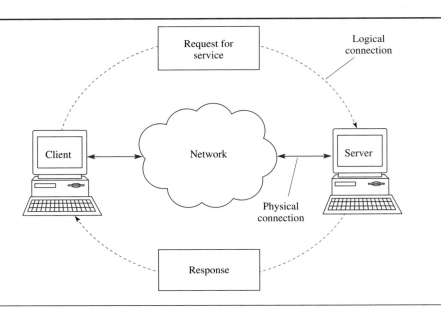

Figure 16–1
Client-server network model.

What may be surprising is that the client-server messages can easily be text based and look just like the examples. Or they can contain data (a portion of an image file, an e-mail attachment, or even system information).

The server must already be running for the client to communicate with it. In addition, the client must know the IP address or domain name of the server to initiate communication.

CONNECTION-ORIENTED VERSUS CONNECTIONLESS COMMUNICATION

Clients and servers exchange messages two ways: through connection-oriented or connectionless communication. Connection-oriented communication requires a session to be established between the client and server. This guarantees reliable, error-free delivery of messages in both directions and is accomplished through the use of TCP. Sessions are typically established when the connection must exist for an extended period of time, such as during a file download or an e-mail exchange. Connection-oriented communication is also used for streaming applications, such as *streaming* audio and video.

Connectionless communication, accomplished through the use of UDP datagrams, eliminates the session overhead. The client and server send messages to each other with the *hope* that they arrive correctly. If they do not, the application is not severely affected. For example, in a network game in which the client and server constantly exchange player position information, if a position packet gets lost or corrupted now and then, the game can still be played. Compare this with a connection-oriented session in which an e-mail message with attachments is being exchanged. It would certainly be bad if a packet was lost or corrupted.

Eliminating the session overhead is important when speed is a consideration in the network application. For example, in a network game, most of the processor time will be spent performing all the graphical rendering. Network communication must be as quick and easy as possible.

In addition, why set up and maintain a session if the number of messages exchanged is small? In the time server application mentioned previously, there is one client message (What time is it?) and one server message (12:08:00 p.m.). Establishing a session just to get the time from the server would be overkill.

Table 16–1 summarizes connectionless and connection-oriented communication.

	Connectionless	Connection-Oriented
Protocol	UDP	TCP
Reliable?	No	Yes
Overhead	Low	High
Session?	No	Yes

Table 16–1
Communication types.

🖥️ SOCKETS

In this section we examine the basic operation and use of network *sockets*. A socket is an input/output mechanism for network messages. Every network application uses a socket to communicate. We will examine how to create, initialize, use, and tear down a socket. Although the code samples presented here are written in Visual C++, the bulk of the code is easily portable to other network environments (Unix, etc.).

In the Windows environment, network functions are provided through the Winsock API (**Windows Sockets** Application Programming Interface). To use any kind of socket, a certain amount of initialization is required (to set up various data structures and other parameters). This is performed automatically with a single function call:

```
WORD VersionRequest = MAKEWORD(1,1);
WSADATA WSData;
int stat;

stat = WSAStartup(VersionRequest, &WSData);
if (WSData.wVersion != VersionRequest)
{
      FatalError("Cannot start Winsock.");
      return FALSE;
}
```

This code requests Winsock version 1.1, the first version of Winsock. Version 2.0 may also be requested. All version 1.1 code works with version 2.0, but not vice versa.

Once Winsock has been started it is useful to know the name of the host machine running Winsock. This can be determined with the following statements:

```
int sockerr;
char HostName[18];

sockerr = gethostname(HostName, sizeof(HostName));
if (sockerr == SOCKET_ERROR)
{
      FatalError("Cannot read host name.");
      return FALSE;
}
```

To create a UDP socket in the Windows environment we use the `socket()` function as follows:

```
SOCKET SocketID;

SocketID = socket(AF_INET, SOCK_DGRAM, IPPROTO_UDP);

if (SocketID == INVALID_SOCKET)
```

```
{
        FatalError("Cannot create socket.");
        return FALSE;
}
```

The parameters passed to the `socket()` function have the following meanings:

- AF_INET   Address Family, Internet
- SOCK_DGRAM   Socket Type, Datagram
- IPPROTO_UDP   IP Protocol, UDP

A TCP socket type is created by using IPPROTO_TCP.

By default, sockets are blocking when they are created. Recall that in blocking mode, when a read type of function is called, the program will stop and wait for a packet to be received. In nonblocking mode, the program accepts a packet if one is available but will not stop and wait for a new packet to arrive. Instead, the program continues to execute. To make a socket nonblocking, use the following code after the socket has been created. This will change the socket mode from blocking to nonblocking.

```
u_long tempvar = TRUE;

sockerr = ioctlsocket(SocketID, FIONBIO, (u_long FAR *)&tempvar);
if (sockerr == SOCKET_ERROR)
{
        FatalError("Cannot switch to non-blocking socket.");
        return FALSE;
}
```

Client sockets and server sockets require slightly different initialization. For the client, the initialization code looks like this:

```
LPHOSTENT HostEntry;
SOCKADDR_IN ServerInfo;

HostEntry = gethostbyname("www.rwasoftware.com");
if (HostEntry == NULL)
{
        FatalError("Cannot find the server.");
        return FALSE;
}

ServerInfo.sin_family = AF_INET;
ServerInfo.sin_addr = *((LPIN_ADDR)*HostEntry->h_addr_list);
ServerInfo.sin_port = htons(7500);
```

This tells the client socket that the server is running on port 7500 at rwa.software.com. Note that you may use an IP address or Windows machine name with `gethostbyname()`. The port number of the server must be known in advance.

Server initialization does not require the call to `gethostbyname()`, since the server is the host.

```
ServerInfo.sin_family = AF_INET;
ServerInfo.sin_addr.s_addr = INADDR_ANY;
ServerInfo.sin_port = htons(7500);
```

where `INADDR_ANY` causes the IP address of the server to be stored.

In addition, the server must *bind* the address information to the socket. This is a necessary step, since the IP address and port number of the socket will be used to uniquely identify it. Perhaps another application is already using the same port for communication. This will be discovered by the `bind()` function. These statements handle the socket binding:

```
sockerr = bind(SocketID, (LPSOCKADDR)&ServerInfo, sizeof(struct sockaddr));

if (sockerr == SOCKET_ERROR)
{
      FatalError("Cannot bind to the socket.");
}
```

Now, if the socket communication is session oriented (TCP), the server calls the `listen()` function to wait for a connection. The client calls the `connect()` function to initiate a session, which is acknowledged by the server function `accept()`. Then the `send()` and `recv()` functions are used by both the client and server to exchange messages.

This process is simpler with connectionless (UDP) communication. After initializing the address structures, the client and server simply exchange messages using the `sendto()` and `recvfrom()` functions. Sample functions used to send and receive UDP datagrams are as follows:

```
int SendNetMessage(char *Message)
{
      int stat;

      stat = sendto(SocketID, Message, strlen(Message), 0,
            (LPSOCKADDR)&ServerInfo, sizeof(struct sockaddr));

      if (stat == SOCKET_ERROR)
      {
            FatalError("Cannot send message.");
            Return FALSE;
      }
      return TRUE;
}

int ReadNetMessage(char *Message)
{
      int BuffLength;
      int BytesRecd;
```

```
BuffLength = sizeof(struct sockaddr);

BytesRecd = recvfrom(SocketID, Message, sizeof(Message), 0,
        (LPSOCKADDR)&ServerInfo, &BuffLength);

if (BytesRecd == SOCKET_ERROR)
{
        Fatal Error ("Cannot read message.");
        return FALSE;
}
    return TRUE;
}
```

When we are through using the socket it must be properly closed. This housecleaning is performed by calling these two functions:

```
closesocket(SocketID);
WSACleanup();
```

Putting everything together, we get the client-server flowcharts shown in Figures 16–2 and 16–3. Figure 16–2 shows the basic sequence of operations required to establish and use a TCP socket. All of the functions are summarized in Table 16–2.

Notice the similarities between Figure 16–2 and Figure 16–3, which illustrates the requirements of UDP communication. Significantly, the `listen()` function is not present. In addition, different functions are used to exchange messages.

All of the network applications on the companion CD-ROM use the socket code presented in this section. Written using Microsoft Visual C++, the network functions are located in its wsock32 library.

🖥️ NETWORK PROGRAMMING LANGUAGES

Network applications may be written in one of several programming languages. In this section we will examine four of the most popular programming languages and their networking capabilities.

C/C++
We have just seen how the popular C and C++ languages contain networking functions that support both connectionless and connection-oriented communications. From Unix boxes like Sun workstations to Windows 98 machines, anyone with a C/C++ compiler and a networking library can develop a network application.

Visual BASIC
Visual BASIC code comes in two forms: compiled executable programs and scripts. Visual BASIC 6.0 provides many ways to create applications for use with the Internet. Two of these are

- IIS Applications
- DHTML Applications

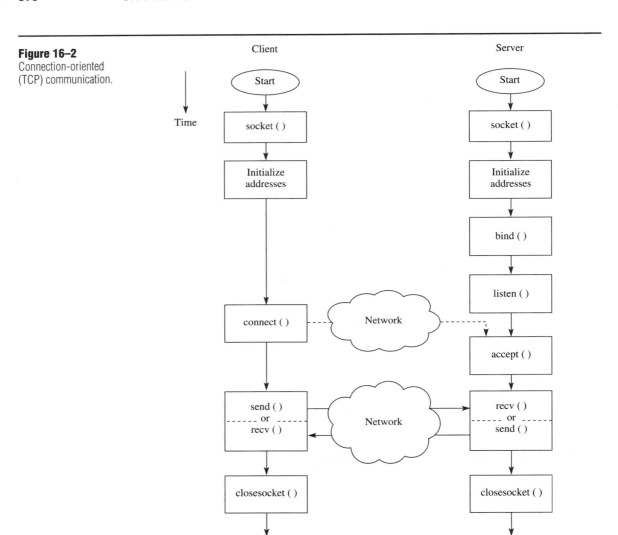

Figure 16–2
Connection-oriented
(TCP) communication.

IIS applications are server applications that run on the Microsoft Internet
Information Server. A compiled Visual BASIC IIS application receives and
processes requests for service from a Web browser.

DHTML (Dynamic HTML) applications are client applications that interface directly with the browser. DHTML applications are able to create new or
updated Web pages on the fly, based on user interaction.

Visual BASIC comes complete with many sample applications to help get
you started in Internet programming right away.

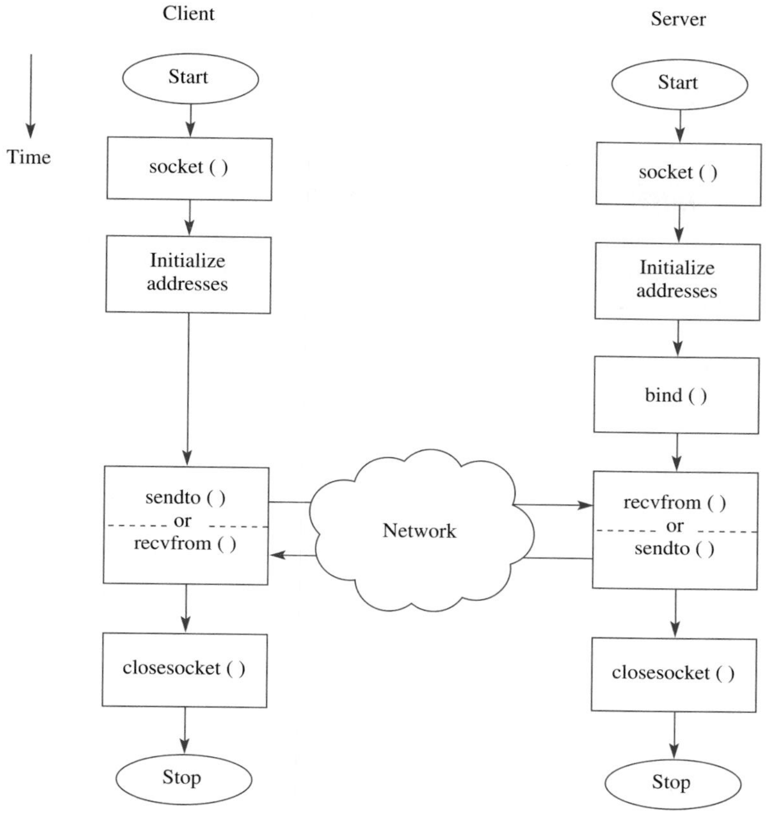

Figure 16–3
Connectionless (UDP) communication.

Function	Description
socket()	Create a socket
bind()	Bind name to socket
listen()	Listen for a connection request
connect()	Begin a connection
accept()	Accept a connection
send()	Send data on connected socket
sendto()	Send data on connectionless socket
recv()	Receive data from connected socket
recvfrom()	Receive data from connectionless socket
closesocket()	Close socket (connection)
gethostbyname()	Get host information using name
gethostname()	Get host name of local machine
ioctlsocket()	Check/set I/O mode of socket

Table 16–2
Winsock functions.

Perl

Perl (Practical Extraction and Reporting Language) is an *interpreted* language useful for CGI applications. Perl programs, called *scripts*, are not precompiled and stored in binary form, as C/C++ programs are. Instead, they are processed upon demand. Because Perl scripts are not precompiled, they can be easily ported to other computing environments. The host machine must provide a Perl interpreter.

A sample Perl script called VIEW.PL is used to generate a Web page on the fly, containing an image and the current time and date. Examine VIEW.PL:

```
#Perl script to generate a Web page

print "Content-type: text/html\n\n";

#Use mainframe TIME command to get local time
$today = 'time';

#Generate web page
print <<"end-of-html-text";
<html>
<head>
<title>Perl Web-page Generator</title>
</head>
<body bgcolor="F5E39A">
<center>
<p><font size="+2">The view from my office window</font>
<br>
<font size="+1"><i>at Broome Community College</i></font></p>
<img src="http://www.sunybroome.edu/~antonakos_j/view.jpg">
<p>It is now $today
<br>
in Binghamton, NY</p>
</center>
</body>
</html>
end-of-html-text
```

Figure 16–4 shows the Web page returned by the VIEW.PL script running on a DEC Alpha mainframe. Note that the URL in the Location field specifies the VIEW.PL script. The current time and date displayed in the page is obtained by the statement

```
$today = 'time';
```

where 'time' is a mainframe command. The output of the time command on the mainframe is stored in the $today variable and subsequently used to place the time and date into the HTML document.

Figure 16–4
Web page generated by VIEW.PL.

Perl is able to work with text and binary files and is equipped with the standard programming elements found in other languages, such as conditional statements, arithmetic and logical operations, loops, and subroutines.

Java

Recall from Chapter 15 that Java uses *applets* transferred from the server to the browser client. The applets are executed on a Java *virtual machine* contained within the browser.

Java supports both stream (TCP) and datagram (UDP) sockets through its `java.net` package. Additional networking capabilities are provided by the `java.rmi` package. RMI stands for remote method invocation, a technique used to allow distributed Java objects to communicate with each other.

A third networking component available in Java is the *servlet*. A servlet is an applet that runs on a WWW server. Servlets provide additional capabilities beyond that of an ordinary Web server. The packages `javax.servlet` and `javax.servlet.http` contain the associated classes and interfaces.

NETWORK APPLICATIONS

All of the network applications presented here will work on machines running Windows 95/98/NT. Each application is written in Visual C/C++. Source and executable files can be found on the companion CD-ROM. It is not the intent to show hundreds of program statements to illustrate how each application works. Instead, we will concentrate on sample executions of each network application and the messages passed between the client and server in each case. It would be worthwhile, however, to spend some time looking through the source code for each application. You will notice many similarities between each application.

Echo Server

The Echo server is a connectionless application that simply returns the same message back to the client that it receives from the client. The echo server, called ECHOSRVR, must be started first, with a user-supplied port number. For example, the command line

```
F:\echo-server> echosrvr 7500
```

will launch a copy of ECHOSRVR and bind it to port 7500. The port number is important and must be used by the ECHOCLNT (echo client) program in order to communicate with the server.

ECHOSRVR then displays this message:

```
Echo server [waveguide] waiting on port 7500
```

Notice that ECHOSRVR has determined the name of the machine it is running on.

ECHOSRVR will wait until it receives a message. Then it will create a reply message containing the same data from the received message and send it back.

To send a message using ECHOCLNT, start up the application using this command:

```
F:\echo-server> echoclnt 192.168.1.105 7500
```

where 192.168.1.105 is the IP address of the machine the echo server is running on.

ECHOCLNT will display a greeting and ask for the message to send:

```
F:\echo-server> echoclnt 192.168.1.105 7500
Echo client [drone2] sending to server [192.168.1.105] on port 7500...
Enter message:
```

Here we see the name of the client computer. If the user enters "Hello there" for the message, the echo server displays the following:

```
F:\echo-server> echosrvr 7500
Echo server [waveguide] waiting on port 7500
Message received: [drone2] Hello there
```

Although this client-server application is not very practical, it is a good starting point on which to build more complex network applications.

Time Server

The time server is a connectionless application that replies to a message from the client with a message containing the current time and date. The time server application is called TIMESRVR and the time client is called TIMECLNT. TIMESRVR must be started with a user-supplied port number. The TIMECLNT application must be started with the address of the server (machine name or IP address) and the same port number. A sample execution is as follows:

Time Server

```
F:\time-server> timesrvr 7500
Server [waveguide] waiting on port 7500
Message received: [drone2] What time is it?
```

Time Client

```
F:\time-server> timeclnt 192.168.1.105 7500
Time client [drone2] sending to server [192.168.1.105] on port 7500...
From the [waveguide] Server: The time is Fri Jun 16 09:56:53 AM.
```

The waveguide server is located at IP address 192.168.1.105. The format of each message is as follows:

Client Message: [<client name>] What time is it?

Server Message: From the [<server name>] Server: The time is <date and time>.

Tic-Tac-Toe

As in the previous applications, two programs are used to handle the client and server tasks. These are TTTCLNT and TTTSRVR. No port number is required on the command line (the default is 7500), but the client still requires the machine name or IP address of the server. UDP datagrams exchange the game information.

The server is responsible for the following:

- Checking the legality of the clients move
- Making its own countermove
- Testing for win, lose, or tie after each move

The server is extremely easy to beat, since its entire strategy for choosing its next move is to go in the first free board position. This point is proved by the sample execution shown in Figure 16–5.

Figure 16–5
Tic-tac-toe sample game.

```
TicTacToe Network Client, V1.0
TTTCLNT [drone2] connecting to server [192.168.1.105]

1 | 2 | 3
---------
4 | 5 | 6
---------
7 | 8 | 9

What is your move? 5
192.168.1.105> My move is 1.

O | 2 | 3
---------
4 | X | 6
---------
7 | 8 | 9

What is your move? 2
192.168.1.105> My move is 3.

O | X | O
---------
4 | X | 6
---------
7 | 8 | 9

What is your move? 8
192.168.1.105> My move is ?. I lose.

O | X | O
---------
4 | X | 6
---------
7 | X | 9
```

(a) Client execution.

```
TTTSRVR [waveguide] waiting on port 7500

1 | 2 | 3
---------
4 | 5 | 6
---------
7 | 8 | 9

drone2> Play?
drone2> I choose 5.

1 | 2 | 3
---------
4 | X | 6
---------
7 | 8 | 9

My move is 1.

O | 2 | 3
---------
4 | X | 6
---------
7 | 8 | 9

drone2> I choose 2.

O | X | 3
---------
4 | X | 6
---------
7 | 8 | 9

My move is 3.

O | X | O
---------
4 | X | 6
---------
7 | 8 | 9

drone2> I choose 8.

O | X | O
---------
4 | X | 6
---------
7 | X | 9

My move is ?. I lose.
```

(b) Server execution.

The first message sent from the client to the server is "Play?," to which the server automatically responds "Yes." Note that the client will wait for this reply, since blocking sockets are used. A series of messages are then sent back and forth as the client and server exchange moves. This continues until there is a win or a tie. The server sends a final message to the client indicating who won or lost (or that there was a tie). Part of your lab activity for this chapter is to discover the actual messages that go back and forth.

Some improvements that could be made to the tic-tac-toe programs are

- Let the client choose X or O
- Flip a coin (so to speak) to see who goes first
- Add some intelligence to the server so it makes better moves
- Have the server respond "No" to a new client if a game is in progress
- Combine both programs into a single application that runs in client mode or in server mode

NETMAZE

This application is the most complex of all the client-server examples we have seen. The NETMAZE program contains both client code and server code, using command line parameters to enter one mode or the other. If neither mode is specified, NETMAZE operates as a stand-alone game, not using the network at all.

To get a decent frame rate (number of screens drawn per second), NET-MAZE should be run on a computer with a clock speed of at least 166 MHz. In addition, the DirectX package must be installed, since NETMAZE uses portions of DirectX to handle its graphics, mouse, and sound processing. DirectX can be downloaded free from Microsoft.

The goal of the game is to walk around the maze and find the exit.

Following are the various command line parameters:

Server Mode: `netmaze -server`

Client Mode: `netmaze -client <server address>`

Standalone: `netmaze`

In addition, other parameters can be used to change the game operation. Slower machines can boost their performance by not drawing the floor patterns. Use `"-nofloor"` on the command line to enable this mode.

It is also possible to log all of the game activity to a file. Use `-log` on the command line to enable this feature. All information will be written to a file called MAZE.LOG.

The default port for NETMAZE is 7500 but this can be changed using the parameter `-port <port number>`.

There are five game levels. Level 1 is the default starting level, but this can be changed using the parameter `-level <level number>`.

While playing the game, several keys provide additional features. These features are as follow:

T   Talk: Send a text message to the other player.

Figure 16–6
Simplified NETMAZE
flowchart for two-
player mode.

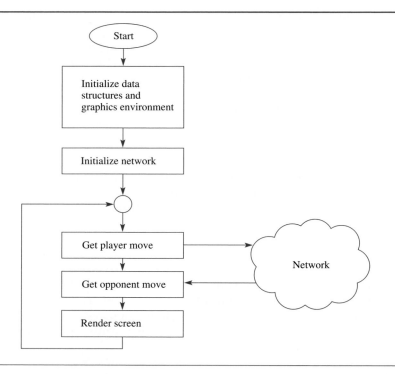

M	Map: Display a map of the game level. Causes map to be displayed on other player's screen also.
\<spacebar\>	Fire energy burst.
Q	Quit.
\<esc\>	Quit.

The UDP socket communication used by NETMAZE is nonblocking. The previous three applications all used blocking communication (try to determine why on your own). If blocking sockets were used in NETMAZE, the game would synchronize to the speed of the slower computer. This is not desirable in a real-time game environment. Furthermore, the server makes all the decisions. For example, when the client player wants to move, the request is sent to the server, which decides if the move is valid. The updated player position is sent back to the client. This basic process is illustrated in Figure 16–6.

The following code is a sample of the statements used to process and generate network messages during the game:

```
gotpkt = ReadNetMessage();
if(gotpkt)
{
        LogFile(netBuff);
```

```
if ('P' == netBuff[0])
{
     player2.r = atof(&netBuff[5]);
     player2.c = atof(&netBuff[14]);
     player2.dir = atof(&netBuff[23]);
}
else
if ('T' == netBuff[0])
{
     statmsg = TRUE;
     strcpy(statstr,&netBuff[4]);
     msg_die = frames + MSGTIME;
     sndBeep();
     LogFile(netBuff);
}
else
if ('J' == netBuff[0])
{
     waiting = FALSE;
     strcpy(statstr,&netBuff[4]);
     strcat(statstr," has joined the game");
     statmsg = TRUE;
     msg_die = frames + MSGTIME;
     sprintf(playerinfo,"Ack. Level %d",gameLevel);
     WriteNetMessage(playerinfo);
}
else
if (('E' == netBuff[0]) && !waiting)
{
     if (CheckParm("-server"))
          waiting = TRUE;
     strcpy(statstr,&netBuff[4]);
     strcat(statstr," has left the game");
     statmsg = TRUE;
     msg_die = frames + MSGTIME;
}
else
if ('V' == netBuff[0])
{
     strcpy(statstr,&netBuff[4]);
     strcat(statstr," has won the game");
     gameover = TRUE;
     statmsg = TRUE;
     msg_die = frames + MSGTIME;
     ShowStats();
}
```

Table 16–3
NETMAZE
messages.

Message Type	Meaning
Talk	Message to other player
Exit	Leave the game
MapOn	Turn map on
Blst	Server blast-ball control
Fire	Client blast-ball control
Ppos	Player position
Join	Request to join game
Ack	Acknowledge Join request
Vict	Victory—someone found the exit

The first letter of a received message (found in `netBuff[0]`, the first message character) is used to identify the message type. Table 16–3 lists the various message types. The exact format of each message is left for you to discover using LanExplorer.

A number of interesting problems occurred during development of NET-MAZE. The Joe Tekk scenario at the beginning of this chapter was an actual problem encountered with NETMAZE. Initially, only one network message was read and processed between frames. This caused messages to queue up on the slower computer. This problem was eliminated by changing the code so that all queued messages are processed between frames.

A number of improvements to NETMAZE are possible. These include

- Adding sequence numbers to the messages to allow detection of out-of-order messages
- Supporting more than two players
- Timing out when there is no response from the server
- Combining all messages into a single message containing fields for all game activity, which would reduce the number of messages exchanged and shorten the message processing time

Before attempting any of these modifications, spend time carefully examining all of the source files for the NETMAZE game.

CGI IP ADDRESS CALCULATOR

The IP Address Calculator is an example of a CGI (Common Gateway Interface) application. Recall from Chapter 15 that a FORM element contained in a Web page allows the user to enter data that is POSTed in a message to a CGI

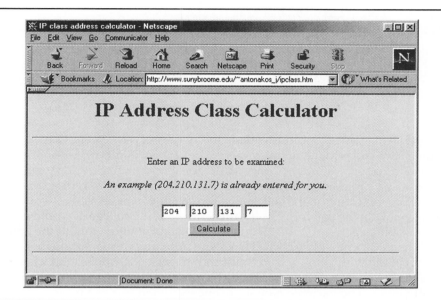

Figure 16–7
IPCLASS CGI
application
Web page.

server application for processing. The IP Address Calculator CGI application uses its FORM data to determine what class of IP address was supplied.

There are two versions of the IP Address Calculator. The first, IPCLASS, uses data POSTed from the FORM element to generate text-only output back to the browser. The second version, IPCLASS2, returns HTML output, allowing WYSIWYG formatting. Let us examine IPCLASS first.

Figure 16–7 shows the start page for the IP address calculator. A default IP address of 204.210.131.7 is automatically entered into the FORM INPUT boxes. The user can change the numbers before clicking on the Calculate button. The purpose of the IPCLASS program is to examine the input numbers, determine the corresponding network and host IDs, and return the results.

The FORM element for the start page is as follows:

```
<FORM ACTION="http://www.sunybroome.edu/jla-bin/ipclass.exe" METHOD="POST">
<P align="center">Enter an IP address to be examined:</P>
<p align="center">
<i>An example (204.210.131.7) is already entered for you.</i></p>
<center>

<TABLE BORDER="0" WIDTH="25%">
<TR>
<TD><INPUT TYPE="TEXT" NAME="ip1" VALUE="204" SIZE="4"></TD>
<TD><INPUT TYPE="TEXT" NAME="ip2" VALUE="210" SIZE="4"></TD>
```

```
<TD><INPUT TYPE="TEXT" NAME="ip3" VALUE="131" SIZE="4"></TD>
<TD><INPUT TYPE="TEXT" NAME="ip4" VALUE="7" SIZE="4"></TD>
</TR>
</TABLE>
<INPUT TYPE="SUBMIT" VALUE="Calculate">
</center>
</FORM>
```

The ACTION value indicates that the CGI server application is called `ipclass.exe` and is found in the `jla-bin` directory at www.sunybroome.edu. The `jla-bin` directory is a symbolic name for the actual directory where the `ipclass.exe` program is located. This directory is the `htbin` directory in the `antonakos_j` account on the college mainframe. It was necessary to work details like this out with the network/Web administrator at the college. It would not have been possible to get the IPCLASS program up and running without the administrator's help. Other institutions will have similar requirements, so you must expect to work closely with your own administrator to get a CGI application working.

Note the names of the four INPUT variables (`ip1` through `ip4`) and their default values. The variable names are encapsulated into the message POSTed from the FORM, along with their values. Figure 16–8, which shows the results of the IPCLASS application execution, indicates the POSTed data.

Variable values follow the = signs and are separated by the & sign. The same variable names are used in the CGI server program to search for and extract the user information. A sample of the IPCLASS.C source program is shown here to show how this is done:

```
getvar("ip1",dest1,cgidata);
a = atoi(dest1);

getvar("ip2",dest2,cgidata);
b = atoi(dest2);
```

Here, the `getvar()` function scans the POSTed data (stored in the character array named `cgidata`) for the desired variable name. `getvar()` returns the associated value of the variable (as a string of characters). The `atoi()` function then converts the variable value into an actual number.

The `cgidata` array is loaded with the POSTed data using these statements:

```
result = cgi_init_env(argc, argv);
length = atoi(cgi_info("CONTENT_LENGTH"));
cgidata = (char *) malloc(sizeof(char) * (length + 1));
result = cgi_read(cgidata, length);
*(cgidata + strlen(cgidata)) = '&';
```

The `cgi_init_env()` and `cgi_read()` functions take care of initializing the input data stream and reading the POSTed data. These functions are specific to the VAX/Alpha mainframe environment.

Figure 16–8
Output of IPCLASS program.

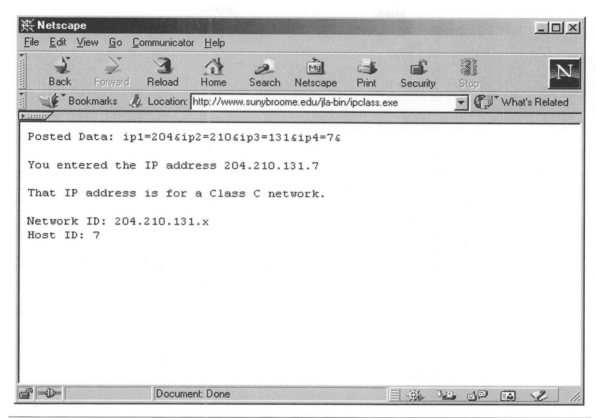

After the four input numbers have been converted, these statements generate the text-only output back to the browser:

```
cgi_begin_output(1);
cgi_printf("Content-type: text/plain\n\n");
cgi_printf("Posted Data: %s\n\n",cgidata);
cgi_printf("You entered the IP address %d.%d.%d.%d\n\n",
      a,b,c,d);
if (!inrange(a) || !inrange(b) || !inrange(c) || !inrange(d))
{
      cgi_printf("One or more values is incorrect.\n");
      cgi_printf("Enter 0 to 255 only in each box.\n");
}
else
{
```

```
        ipclass = show_class(a);
        show_netid(ipclass,a,b,c,d);
        show_hostid(ipclass,a,b,c,d);
    }
    free(cgidata);
```

The `cgi_printf()` function is used to send text results back to the browser. The first information sent back is the `"Content-type: text/plain"` message. The `text/plain` portion indicates to the browser that the format of the page is plain ASCII text. Assuming that the input numbers are all in range, the `show_class()`, `show_netid()`, and `show_hostid()` functions are called to output the proper network information.

Take another look at Figure 16–8. The URL for the page is

http://www.sunybroome.edu/jla-bin/ipclass.exe

which, significantly, does not end with an .HTM or .HTML extension. The Web page is actually the output of the IPCLASS program (indicated by `ipclass.exe` in the URL). This page can not be bookmarked and returned to at a later time, because it only exists whenever the IPCLASS program has been executed.

Everything we have seen regarding the IPCLASS application applies to the IPCLASS2 application, except the Web page returned contains HTML formatting tags to allow for things like bold text, italics, and links. Figure 16–9 shows the Web page returned by IPCLASS2.

Again, note the URL ends with the name of the CGI application (`ipclass2.exe`), and that the page contains extra formatting not possible with the text-only IPCLASS application. Compare the code for IPCLASS previously shown with these statements from IPCLASS2:

```
cgi_begin_output(1);
cgi_printf("Content-type: text/html\n\n");
cgi_printf("<html><head><title>IP class"
    "calculator</title></head>\n");
cgi_printf("<body bgcolor=\"#f5e39a\">\n");
cgi_printf("<p>Posted Data: <b>%s</b></p>\n",cgidata);
cgi_printf("<p>You entered the IP address"
    "%d.%d.%d.%d</p>\n",a,b,c,d);
if (!inrange(a) || !inrange(b) || !inrange(c) || !inrange(d))
{
    cgi_printf("<p>One or more values is incorrect.<hr>\n");
    cgi_printf("Enter 0 to 255 only in each box.<hr>\n");
    cgi_printf("<a href=\"http://www.sunybroome.edu/");
    cgi_printf("~antonakos_j/ipclass2.htm\">Try again?");
    cgi_printf("</a> <i>Back to the form...</i></p>\n");
}
else
```

Figure 16–9
Output of IPCLASS2 program.

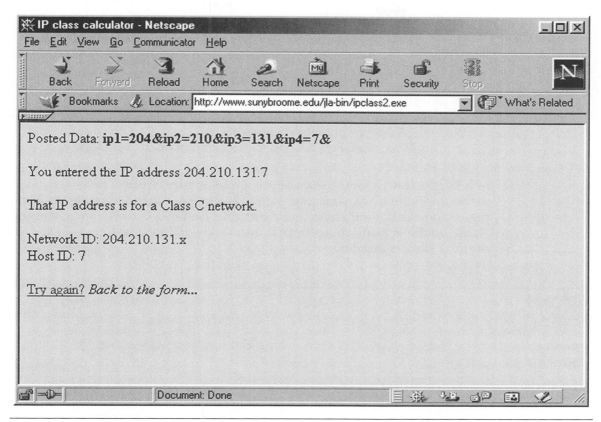

```
{
        ipclass = show_class(a);
        show_netid(ipclass,a,b,c,d);
        show_hostid(ipclass,a,b,c,d);
        cgi_printf("<p><a href=\"http://www.sunybroome.edu/");
        cgi_printf("~antonakos_j/ipclass2.htm\">Try again?");
        cgi_printf("</a> <i>Back to the form...</i></p>\n");
}
cgi_printf("</body></html>\n");
```

The only additions are the HTML formatting tags required by the browser and
the `text/html` (instead of `text/plain`) indicator in the first `cgi_printf()`.
The `show_class()`, `show_netid()`, and `show_hostid()` functions contain
similar modifications.

TROUBLESHOOTING TECHNIQUES

Troubleshooting a network application requires time and patience. Here are a few points to keep in mind:

- Never assume anything regarding the operation of the network. Test your connection by PINGing the server machine from the client (or vice versa) to make sure the machines are able to communicate.
- Check the network properties to verify the protocol is installed properly and bound to the network adapter.
- Verify that the problem is not operating system–related (works on Windows 95/98 but not on Windows NT).
- Check for correct Winsock version number, IP address, and port number.

In addition, how many networked computers are required to test a client-server application? One may be enough is some cases. For example, the echo server and client, time server and client, and Tic-Tac-Toe server and client can all run on the same machine (in their own DOS windows), as long as a TCP/IP protocol stack is installed.

SELF-TEST

This self-test is designed to help you check your understanding of the background information presented in this chapter.

True/False

Answer *true* or *false*.

1. In the client-server model, the server contacts the client first.

2. Connection-oriented communication is reliable.

3. Connectionless communication is accomplished using UDP datagrams.

4. Both client and server applications utilize sockets.

5. Visual BASIC code may be written in script form.

6. Blocking sockets are used in the Tic-Tac-Toe application.

Multiple Choice

Select the best answer.

7. Which communication type requires a session?
   a. Connectionless.
   b. Connection-oriented.
   c. Both a and b.

8. Which programming language is interpreted?
   a. C/C++.
   b. Perl.
   c. Both a and b.

9. Servlets are part of what network programming language?
   a. C/C++.
   b. Perl.
   c. Java.

10. NETMAZE uses _____ to communicate.
    a. TCP.
    b. UDP.
    c. Both a and b.

11. CGI applications use the _____ element to POST data.
    a. HTML.
    b. FORM.
    c. POST.

12. Multiple TCP and UDP applications running on the same machine are selected through their
    a. Port numbers.
    b. I/O address.
    c. IP address.

Matching
Match the application on the left with the connection type on the right.

13. E-mail transfer
14. Web page transfer
15. TIMECLNT
16. TCP

a. Connectionless
b. Connection-oriented

Completion
Fill in the blank or blanks with the best answers.

17. Client-server communication is both physical and _____.

18. Perl programs are not compiled, they are _____.

19. Reliable, error-free delivery is guaranteed by the _____ protocol.

20. In Java, RMI stands for remote method _____.

QUESTIONS/ACTIVITIES

1. Search the Web for examples of Perl, Java, and C/C++ CGI applications. If possible, find an application that is implemented in all three languages.

2. Design a set of messages that can be used to implement a client-server telephone directory for a small business. The server contains the telephone database, which can be queried by phone number (4-digit extension) or by a person's last name. You must determine how to handle invalid extensions and duplicate matches on the last names.

REVIEW QUIZ

Under the supervision of your instructor

1. Discuss the client-server model.

2. Explain the basic features of a socket.

3. Summarize the various network programming languages.

4. Show examples of both connectionless and connection-oriented network applications.

Networking Concepts Laboratory

Experiment #16
Network Programming

Objectives

1. To examine the operation of client-server applications interacting with each other.
2. To use a Web-based CGI application.

Required Equipment

The following equipment is required for this experiment:

- A working networking laboratory containing two or more computers running Windows, connected with a network
- LanExplorer software

Procedure

Perform each of the following steps. Record your observations, results, and any difficulties you encounter. You will use this information when you develop your conclusions about the experiment.

1. Use LanExplorer to capture the packets exchanged while playing Tic-Tac-Toe.
2. Decode one example of each type of packet captured in step 1.
3. Draw a diagram showing the timeline of the game.
4. Repeat steps 1 through 3 for the NETMAZE game. There are several scenarios to test, such as client wins, server wins, client quits early, and server quits early. The use of the T and M commands should also be captured.
5. Run five tests with the IP Address Calculator, using a different IP address class each time.

Discussion and Conclusion

Using a word processor, write your own detailed explanations of the results and observations made during the experiment. To begin, try to say something about each procedure step.

In addition, provide answers to the following questions:

1. Based on your exposure to network programming languages, which one would you choose when beginning a new project?

2. Compare the following two-player client-server game scenarios:
   Scenario #1: Each player runs a client/server program.
   Scenario #2: One player runs a server program; the other player runs a client program.
   Scenario #3: Each player runs a client program. A server program runs on a different computer.
   a. Does any scenario have an advantage?
   b. If the number of players is not two, but from three to eight, does any scenario have an advantage?

17

An Introduction to Networking with Windows

PERFORMANCE OBJECTIVES

Upon completion of this chapter, you will be able to

- Identify hard disk resources available on a network computer.
- Identify printer resources available on a network computer.
- Create a Dial-Up Networking connection.

"That's the computer right there."

Those were the first words Joe Tekk heard when he entered a high school laboratory maintained under contract by RWA Software. "Pardon me?" Joe asked.

The laboratory technician was a senior, ready to graduate in a few months, with little patience for computers that did not work.

"It's that one right there. It won't connect to the network." He pointed at the computer until Joe got to it. Joe walked around to the back of the computer, pulled the T-connector off the back of the network card, and looked at it closely.

"Here's your problem," he said, to the surprise of the student. "The metal pin is missing from the center of the connector."

The student looked at the connector and then back at Joe. "How did you know to look for that?"

"I always pull the connector out first. I've seen this happen before. Now, it's just a habit."

INTRODUCTION

Windows offers many different ways to connect your machine to one or more computers and plenty of applications to assist you with your networking needs. In this chapter we will examine the basics of networking in Windows.

🖳🖳 MICROSOFT NETWORKING

Although Windows supports many different types of common networking protocols, the backbone of its network operations is NetBEUI (NetBIOS Extended User Interface), a specialized Microsoft protocol used in Windows for Workgroups, Windows 95/98, Windows NT, and Windows 2000. NetBEUI allows small (up to 200 nodes) networks of users to share resources (files and printers).

🖳🖳 THE NETWORK NEIGHBORHOOD

The Network Neighborhood is a hierarchical collection of the machines capable of communicating with each other over a Windows network. Note that systems running Windows for Workgroups have the ability to connect to the network as well.

Figure 17–1 shows a typical Network Neighborhood. The three small PC icons named At213_tower, Nomad, and Waveguide all represent different machines connected to the network. Each machine is also a member of a *workgroup* or *domain* of computers that share a common set of properties.

Double-clicking on Waveguide brings up the items being shared by Waveguide. As indicated in Figure 17–2, Waveguide is sharing two folders: pcx and pub.

Figure 17–1
Network Neighborhood window.

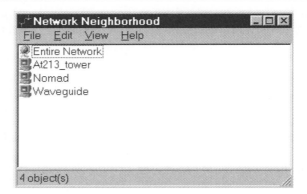

Figure 17–2
Items shared by Waveguide.

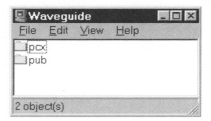

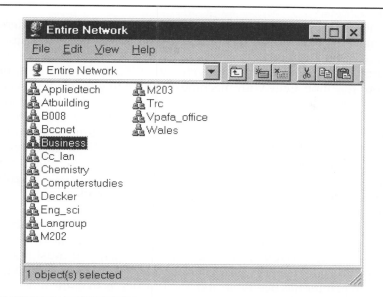

Figure 17–3
A large network
depicted graphically
on Network
Neighborhood.

The Network Neighborhood gives you a way to graphically navigate to shared resources (files, CD-ROM drives, printers). Figure 17–3 shows an Entire Network on a large Windows network.

NETWORK PRINTING

A network printer is a printer that a user has decided to share. For the user's machine it is a local printer. But other users on the network can map to the network printer and use it as if it were their own printer. Figure 17–4 shows a shared printer offered by a computer named Nomad. Nomad is offering an hp 890c.

It is necessary to install the printer on your machine before you can begin using it over the network.

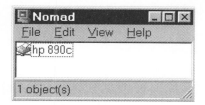

Figure 17–4
A printer shared by
Nomad.

Adding a New Printer

To add a new printer, double-click the Add Printer icon in the Printers folder. This will start the Add Printer Wizard, an automated process that guides you through the installation process.

The first choice you must make is shown in Figure 17–5. A local printer is local to your machine. Only your machine can print to your printer, even if your computer is networked. A network printer can be printed to by anyone on the network who has made a connection to that printer. A network printer is also a local printer to the machine that hosts it. If you are installing a network printer, the next window will look like that shown in Figure 17–6. The printer being mapped is an HP LaserJet II (named "hplaserii" on the network) connected to the machine "deepspace." You can also browse the Network Neighborhood to select a network printer. DOS accessibility to the network printer is controlled from this window as well.

Next, the manufacturer and model of your printer must be chosen. Windows has a large database of printers to choose from. Figure 17–7 shows the initial set of choices. If your printer is not on the list, you must insert a disk with the appropriate drivers (usually supplied by the printer manufacturer).

Once the printer has been selected, the last step is to name it (as in the network printer "hplaserii").

If only one printer is installed, it is automatically the default printer for Windows. For two or more printers (including network printers), one must be set as the default. This can be done by right-clicking on the Printer's icon and selecting Set As Default. You can also access printer properties and change the default printer from inside the printer status window, using the Printer pull-down menu.

Figure 17–5
Choosing local/
network printing.

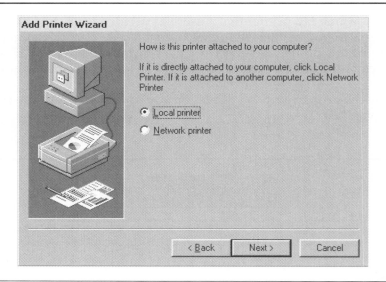

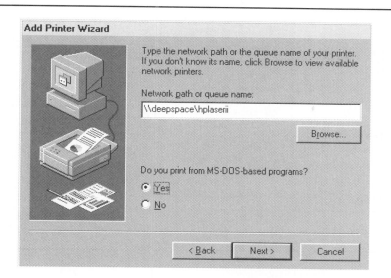

Figure 17–6
Mapping a network printer.

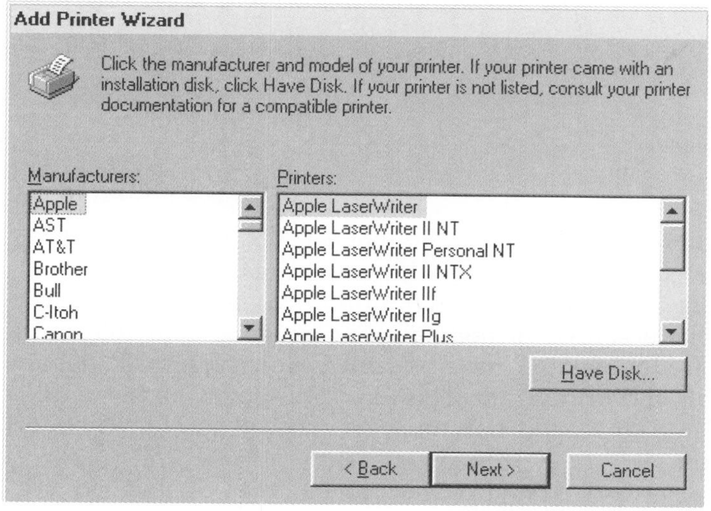

Figure 17–7
Choosing a printer manufacturer/model.

If the printer has been installed correctly, left-clicking the Print Test Page button will cause the printer to print a test page. The test page contains a graphical Windows logo and information about the printer and its various drivers. A dialog box appears asking whether the test page printed correctly. If the answer is no, Windows starts a printer help session. Figure 17–8 shows the initial Help window.

Figure 17–8
Built-in printer help.

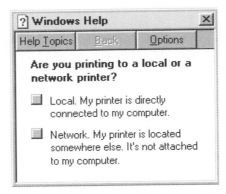

Figure 17–9
Giving network access
to your printer.

Windows will ask several printer-related questions to help determine why the printer is not working. The causes are different for network printers, so Windows provides two different troubleshooting paths (network vs. local).

To make a shared printer on your machine available to the network, you need to double-click the Network icon in Control Panel and then left-click the File and Print Sharing buttons. This opens up the window shown in Figure 17–9. The second box must be checked to allow network access to your printer.

After a network printer connection has been established, you may use it like an ordinary local printer. Windows communicates with the network printer's host machine using NetBEUI. What this means is that jobs sent to a network printer are sent in small bursts (packets) and typically require additional time to print due to the network overhead. In a busy environment, such as an office or college laboratory, printer packets compete with all the other data flying around on the network and thus take longer to transmit than data traveling over a simple parallel connection between the computer and the printer.

SHARING FILES OVER A NETWORK

A computer can share its disks with the network and allow remote users to map them for use as an available drive on a remote computer. The first time a disk is shared and a connection is established, it may be necessary to provide a password to gain access to the data. The password is typically provided by the network administrator. This password is usually stored in the password file for subsequent access to the disk if it is reconnected after a reboot. Figure 17–10 shows the contents of My Computer. The small hand holding drive D: (Fireballxl5) indicates the drive is shared.

The user sharing the drive controls the access others will have to it over the network. Figure 17–11 shows the sharing properties for drive D: (right-click on the drive icon and select Properties). Clearly, the user has a good deal of control over how sharing takes place.

Finding a Networked Computer

If you do not know the name of a computer that is sharing files, one way to locate it is to use the "Find. . . Computer" selection in the Tools menu of Windows Explorer. Figure 17–12 shows how a machine called "Waveguide" is found using this method.

Working with Network Drives

If you have a connection to a network (dial-up PPP or network interface card), you can use Explorer to *map* a network drive to your machine. This is done by selecting Map Network Drive on the Tools menu. Figure 17–13 shows the menu window used to map a network drive.

Figure 17–10
Indicating a shared drive.

Figure 17–11
Sharing Properties
window for drive D:.

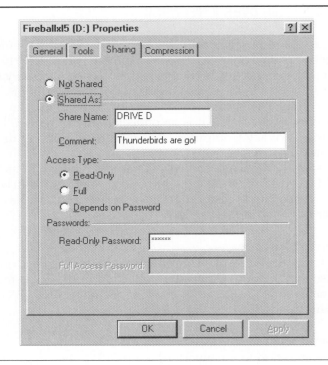

Figure 17–12
Searching for a
computer on a
network.

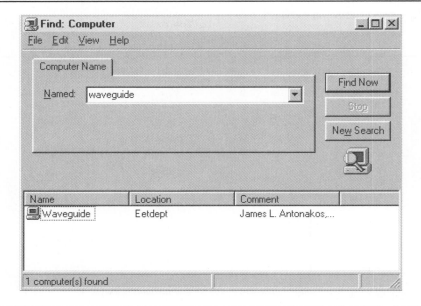

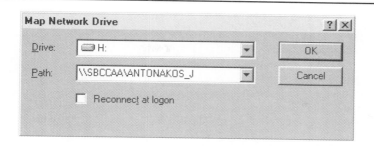

Figure 17–13
Mapping a network drive.

Figure 17–14
Supplying a network password.

The computer automatically picks the first free drive letter (you can pick a different one) and requires a path to the network drive. In Figure 17–13 the path is \\SBCCAA\ANTONAKOS_J. The general format is \\machinename\username.

Access to the network drive may require a password, as indicated in Figure 17–14. If an invalid password is entered, the drive is not mapped.

If the drive is successfully mapped, it will show up in Explorer's folder display window. Figure 17–15 shows the contents of the mapped drive. Note that drive H: has a different icon from the other hard drives.

When you have finished using the network drive, you can disconnect it (via the Tools menu). This is illustrated in Figure 17–16.

 DIAL-UP NETWORKING

Dial-Up Networking is designed to provide reliable data connections using a modem and a telephone line. Figure 17–17 shows two icons in the Dial-Up Networking folder (found in Accessories on the Start menu). Double-clicking the Make New Connection icon will start the process of making a new connection as shown in Figure 17–18. The name of the connection and the modem for the connection are specified.

Figure 17–15
Contents of network
drive H:.

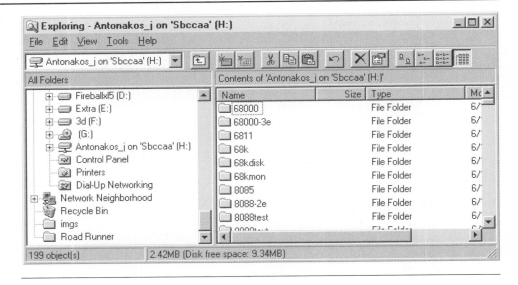

Figure 17–16
Disconnecting a
network drive.

Figure 17–17
Dial-Up Networking
icons.

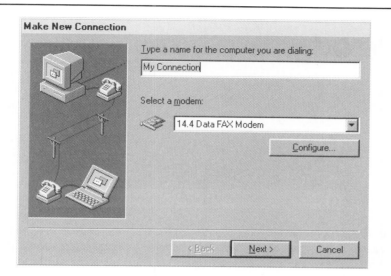

Figure 17–18
Make New Connection window.

It is also necessary to provide an area code and telephone number during the configuration process. This number must be for a machine capable of supporting a PPP (point-to-point protocol) connection.

Once the connection has been created, it is activated by double-clicking it. To connect to a remote host, it is necessary to supply a user name and a password. This can be done automatically by the Dial-Up Networking software. Figure 17–19 shows the connection window for the My Office icon.

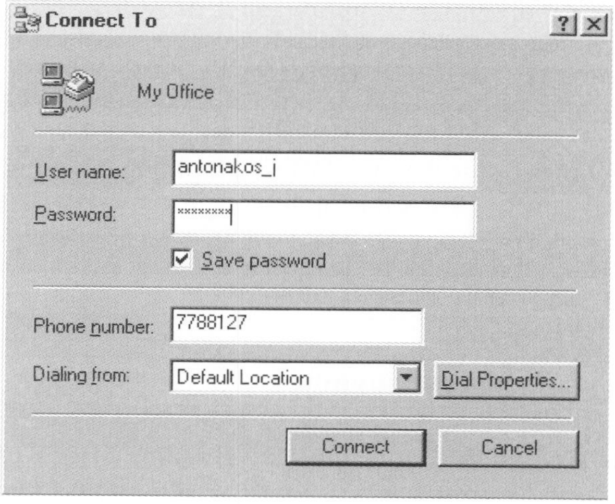

Figure 17–19
Information required to access host.

Figure 17–20
Active Dial-Up
Networking
connection.

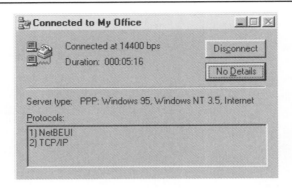

After the information has been entered, the Connect button is used to start up a connection. When the connection has been established, Windows displays a status window showing the current duration of the connection and the active protocols. Figure 17–20 shows the status for the My Office connection. Left-clicking the Disconnect button shuts the connection down and hangs up the modem.

CONNECTING TO THE INTERNET

Besides a modem or a network interface card and the associated software, one more piece is needed to complete the networking picture: the *Internet service provider* (ISP). An ISP is any facility that contains its own direct connection to the Internet. For example, many schools and businesses now have their own dedicated high-speed connection (typically a T1 line, which provides data transfers of more than 1.5 million bits/second).

Many users sign up with a company (such as AOL or MSN) and then dial in to these companies' computers, which themselves provide the Internet connection. The company is the ISP in this case.

Even the local cable company is an ISP now, offering high-speed cable modems that use unassigned television channels for Internet data. The cable modem is many times faster than the fastest telephone modems on the market.

Once you have an ISP, the rest is up to you. You may design your own Web page (many ISPs host Web pages for their customers), use e-mail, browse the Web, Telnet to your school's mainframe and work on an assignment, or download a cool game from an FTP site.

TROUBLESHOOTING TECHNIQUES

Troubleshooting a network connection requires familiarity with several levels of operation. At the hardware level, the physical connection (parallel cable, modem, network interface card) must be working properly. A noisy phone line, the wrong interrupt selected during setup for the network interface card, incompatible parallel ports, and many other types of hardware glitches can prevent a good network connection.

At the software level there are two areas of concern: the network operating system software and the application software. For example, if Internet Explorer will not open any Web pages, is the cause of the problem Internet Explorer or the underlying TCP/IP protocol software?

Even with all of the built-in functions Windows automatically performs, there is still a need for human intervention to get things up and running in the world of networking.

Remember that the Network menu allows you to add, modify, or remove various networking components, such as protocols (NetBEUI, TCP/IP), drivers for network interface cards, and Dial-Up Networking utilities. You can also specify the way your machine is identified on the network, as well as various options involving file and printer sharing and protection. Figure 17–21 shows a sample Network menu. Selecting any of the network components allows its properties to be examined.

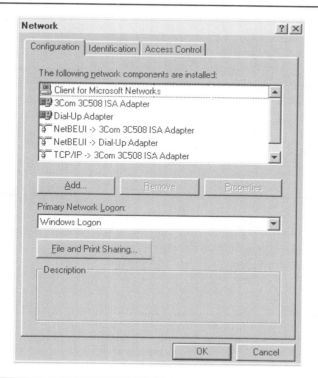

Figure 17–21
Network menu.

SELF-TEST

This self-test is designed to help you check your understanding of the background information presented in this chapter.

True/False

Answer *true* or *false*.

1. NetBEUI is a protocol only used by Windows NT.

2. Dial-up connections work with ordinary dial-up phone numbers.

3. The cable company is an example of an ISP.

4. Network printers can be used as soon as you map them.

5. Anyone who wants to can delete all the files on a shared drive.

Multiple Choice

Select the best answer.

6. NetBEUI is a protocol used
   a. Only for network printers.
   b. Only for file sharing.
   c. For sharing files and printers.

7. A workgroup is a set of users that
   a. Share common properties.
   b. Use the same printer.
   c. Work as a team on projects.

8. The Network Neighborhood shows
   a. The networked computers within 20 meters of your machine.
   b. Every computer on the entire network.
   c. Machines sharing resources.

9. What is required for Dial-Up Networking?
   a. A modem.
   b. A network interface card.
   c. A direct cable connection.

10. The Network Neighborhood shows
    a. Every computer on the network at the same time.
    b. Hierarchical groups of networked computers.
    c. All the computers on the Internet.

Completion

Fill in the blank or blanks with the best answers.

11. NetBEUI stands for NetBIOS _____

    _____ _____.

12. Another term for workgroup is _____.

13. Dial-Up Networking is accessed via the _____ folder in the Start menu.

14. The Dial-Up Networking connection uses the _____ protocol.

15. ISP stands for _____ _____

    _____.

QUESTIONS/ACTIVITIES

1. Go to a local business that advertises on the Web. Ask them to describe their network connection. Do they have Dial-Up service? What is the cost? Who maintains their systems?

2. Search the Web for information about how satellites are used in Internet connections.

REVIEW QUIZ

Under the supervision of your instructor

1. Identify hard disk resources available on a network computer.

2. Identify printer resources available on a network computer.

3. Create a Dial-Up Networking connection.

Networking Concepts Laboratory

Experiment #17
Networking with Windows

Objectives

1. To configure a modem to use Dial-Up Networking.
2. To share and use network resources.

Required Equipment

The following equipment is required for this experiment:

- Two or more computers connected with modems and a network
- Phone connections
- Network printer
- Cables

Procedure

Perform each of the following steps. Record your observations, results, and any difficulties you encounter. You will use this information when you develop your conclusions about the experiment.

1. Establish a Dial-Up Networking session using information provided by your instructor.
2. Share a disk or folder on your hard drive.
3. Map a network resource available in the lab.
4. Transfer several files.
5. Perform steps 1 through 4 using a network connection. Is there a difference in speed for the transfers?

Optional Procedure (if a network printer is available)

6. Add a network printer according to manufacturer instructions.
7. Map the network printer.
8. Capture network printer traffic using LanExplorer.

Discussion and Conclusion

Using a word processor, write your own detailed explanations of the results and observations made during the experiment. To begin, try to say something about each procedure step.

In addition, provide answers to the following questions:

1. How long would it take to transfer the file BIGFILE.DAT (25 MB) using a modem? Estimate your answer; do not actually transfer the file.
2. What are the advantages of a modem connection?
3. How does the operation of a modem connection compare to a network connection?

18

Windows NT Domains

PERFORMANCE OBJECTIVES

Upon completion of this chapter, you will be able to

- Describe the benefits of creating a Windows NT domain.
- Explain some different types of Windows NT domains.
- Discuss the different types of clients able to join a Windows NT domain.
- Describe RAS and DHCP.

Joe Tekk was very excited. He was finally given the opportunity to set up the new Windows NT domain for RWA Software, Inc. Joe thought that a Windows NT network was necessary because it was becoming harder and harder to maintain the workgroup that was originally installed several years ago.

Joe told Don, his manager, "RWA has grown so much since I started working here. The NT Server operating system is going make it so much easier to administer the network."

Don replied, "If you say so, Joe. I'll leave the network administration up to you." He continued, "Joe, please let me know what you are planning before we make any big changes. We don't want to make any avoidable mistakes."

Joe responded, "I'm glad you mentioned that, Don. I laid out the plan on paper so everyone can understand how the new network will operate. I have also set up a timetable to get everyone up and running."

Don smiled and said, "Great job, Joe. Keep it up!"

Joe spent most of his spare time reading about Windows NT. When he finally received his copy of the Windows NT Server CD-ROM, he could not wait to get started.

INTRODUCTION

Any group of personal computers can be joined together to form either a workgroup or a domain. In a workgroup, each computer is managed independently but may share some of its resources with the other members of the network, such as printers, disks, or a scanner. Unfortunately, as the

413

Table 18–1
Comparing a work-group and a domain.

Workgroup	Domain
Small networks	Large networks
Peer-to-peer	Client–server
No central server	Central server
Low cost	Higher cost
Decentralized	Centralized

number of computers in the workgroup grows, it becomes more and more difficult to manage the network. This is exactly the situation in which a Windows NT domain can be used. A domain offers a centralized mechanism to relieve much of the administrative burden commonly experienced in a workgroup. A domain requires at least one computer running the Windows NT Server operating system. Table 18–1 illustrates the characteristics of a workgroup and a domain.

DOMAINS

Each Windows NT domain can be configured independently or as a group in which all computers are members of the same domain. Figure 18–1 shows two independent domains. Each domain consists of at least one Windows NT primary domain controller (PDC) and any number of backup domain controllers (BDC). One shared directory database is used to store user account information and security settings for the entire domain.

A BDC can be promoted to a PDC in the event the current PDC on the network becomes unavailable for any reason. A promotion can be initiated manually, causing the current PDC to be demoted to a backup. Figure 18–2 shows a domain containing two Windows NT server computers. One computer is the PDC, and the other computer is the BDC.

Windows NT can administer the following types of domains:

- Windows NT Server domains
- Windows NT Server and Lan Manager 2.x domains
- LAN Manager 2.x domains

Figure 18–1
Independent Windows NT domains.

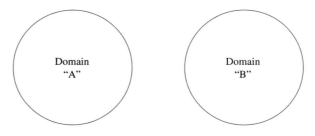

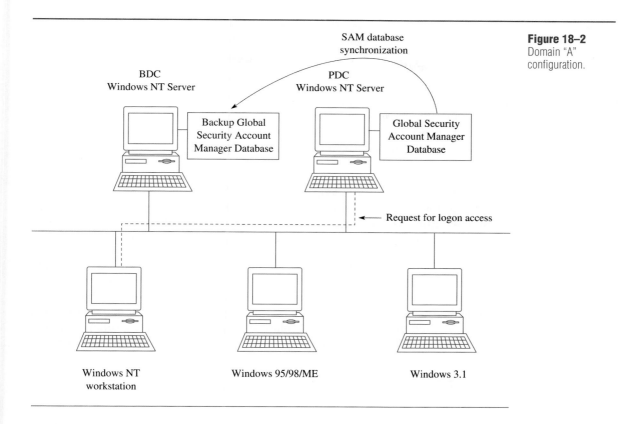

Figure 18–2
Domain "A"
configuration.

A LAN Manager 2.x domain is a previous version of Microsoft networking software used by older MS-DOS and Windows computers.

The different types of activities that can be performed on a domain include the following:

- Create a new domain
- Modify an existing domain
- Join a domain
- Add a computer to a domain
- Remove a computer from a domain
- Synchronize files in a domain
- Promote a BDC to a PDC
- Establish trust relationships

When a system is set up as a PDC, the new domain name is required in order to proceed through the Windows NT installation process. This domain name is required by all other computer users who want to join the domain. Note that each domain can contain only one primary domain controller. All other Windows NT Server computers can be designated as backups or ones that do not participate in the domain control process at all.

A computer can be configured to join a domain during the Windows NT installation process by using the Network icon in the system Control Panel or by using the Server Manager tool. A computer can be removed using the Network icon in the system Control Panel or the Server Manager tool.

Synchronizing a domain involves exchanging information between a primary domain controller and any secondary or backup domain controllers as previously shown in Figure 18–2. The synchronization interval for a Windows NT computer is 5 minutes. This means account information entered on the primary domain controller takes only 5 minutes to be exchanged with all secondary computers. This synchronization is performed automatically by Windows NT.

Domains can also be set up to offer *trust relationships.* A trust relationship involves either providing or receiving services from an external domain, as shown in Figure 18–3. A trust relationship can permit users in one domain to use the resources of another domain. A trust relationship can be a one-way trust or a two-way trust, offering the ability to handle many types of requirements.

A one-way trust relationship as shown in Figure 18–3(a) identifies domain "B" as a trusted source for domain "A." A two-way trust, shown in Figure 18–3(b), involves two separate domains sharing their resources with each other. Each domain considers the other to be a trusted source. Extreme caution must be exercised when setting up trust relationships. If the trusted domain is really untrustworthy, valuable information can be lost using the "trusted" accounts.

Figure 18–3
Domain trust
relationships.

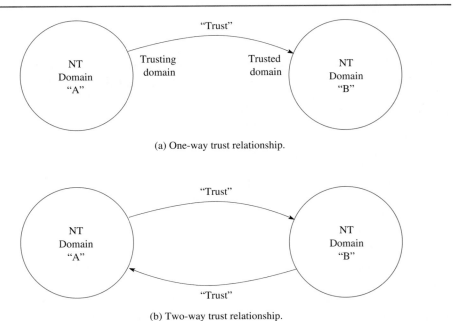

(a) One-way trust relationship.

(b) Two-way trust relationship.

DOMAIN CLIENTS

A Windows NT domain can support many different types of clients, such as

- Windows NT servers
- Windows NT workstations
- Windows 95/98/ME clients
- Windows 3.11 clients
- Windows 3.1 clients
- MS-DOS clients
- OS/2 workstations

LOGGING ONTO A NETWORK

When a computer is configured to run in a network, each user must be authorized before access to the computer can be granted. Figure 18–4 shows a typical Windows 95/98 logon screen. Each user must supply a valid user name and a valid password in order to gain access to the computer and any network resources. In a *workgroup* setting, all password information is stored locally on each computer in PWL files. The PWL files are named using the following format: the first eight letters of the user name entered in the logon screen followed by the .PWL file extension. The PWL files contain account and password information stored in encrypted form. These files are typically stored in the Windows directory. Figure 18–5 shows the concept of a workgroup in which each computer is administered independently.

In a *domain* setting, a centralized computer running Windows NT is contacted to verify the user name and password. If the information provided to the server is valid, access is granted to the local machine. If either the user name or password is invalid, access to the local computer is denied. As you might think, this method offers tremendously more flexibility as far as the administration is concerned. This concept is illustrated in Figure 18–6.

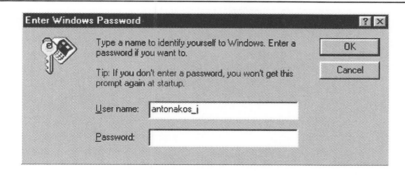

Figure 18–4
Windows 95/98 logon screen.

Figure 18–5
Workgroup concept in which each computer is administered independently.

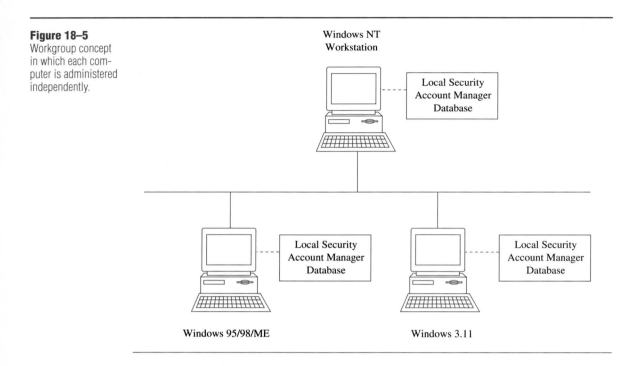

Figure 18–6
Domain concept.

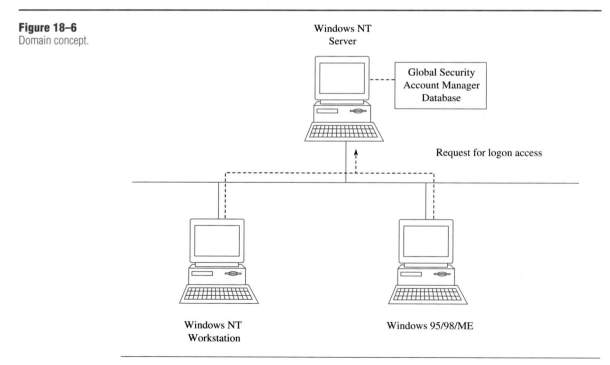

RUNNING A NETWORK SERVER

Running a network server involves installing the Windows NT operating system and then configuring it to run as a primary or secondary domain controller during the installation process. After a PDC is created during the installation, the domain exists on the network. Windows NT computers can then join the domain by changing the Member of domain as shown in Figure 18–7. Windows computers join the domain by changing individual settings on each computer. Figure 18–8 shows the Primary Network Logon selecting the Client for Microsoft Networks option. Then, by selecting the properties for Client for Microsoft Networks, the specific domain can be identified as illustrated in Figure 18–9. After making these changes, a system reset is necessary to make the changes active.

Network server computers are also assigned the task of running more applications to manage both the server and network. For example, a Windows NT Server may be used to add fault tolerance to disks using Redundant Array of Inexpensive Disks (*RAID*) technology. *Fault tolerance* means the system can recover from a fault (such as a hard-drive failure). A server may also run the WWW server application, Windows Internet Naming System (WINS), Dynamic Host Configuration Protocol (DHCP), and Remote Access Server (RAS). These services are usually required 24 hours a day, 7 days per week.

Windows NT Server computers are designed to handle the computing workload for entire organizations, corporations, or any other type of enterprise.

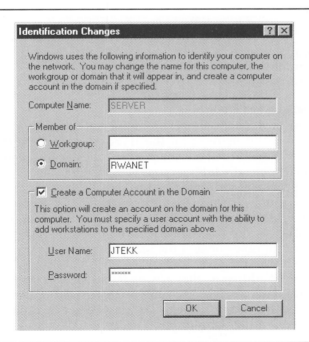

Figure 18–7
Configuring a
Windows NT Server.

Figure 18–8
Windows 95/98
Network settings.

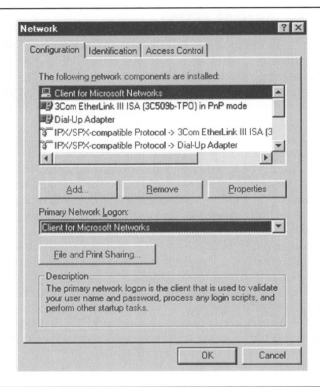

In these cases, many servers (including a PDC and several BDCs) are made available to guarantee the availability of any required services.

Let us take a closer look at two of these services, DHCP and RAS.

Dynamic Host Configuration Protocol

One nice feature of a Windows NT domain is the ability for Windows NT Server to automatically manage all the IP addresses in the domain. IP addresses may be assigned to client machines statically (by manually entering the address) or dynamically (at boot time) via DHCP.

The DHCP service is controlled by the DHCP Manager application found in Administrative Tools. Figure 18–10 shows the DHCP Manager window, indicating a DHCP server running at IP address 206.210.24.2. The highlighted entry (206.210.24.0) is the *scope*, or range of IP addresses managed by the DHCP server. Left double-clicking the scope entry brings up the Scope Properties windows shown in Figure 18–11.

The range of IP addresses that are available for use via DHCP begins at 206.210.24.10 and ends at 206.210.24.253, with two subranges excluded. Addresses are leased for 3 days, but could also be set to unlimited duration. Clearly, the network administrator has a great deal of control over the allocation of IP addresses within the domain.

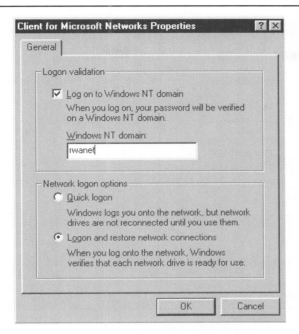

Figure 18–9
Configuring
Windows 95/98 to
log on to a domain.

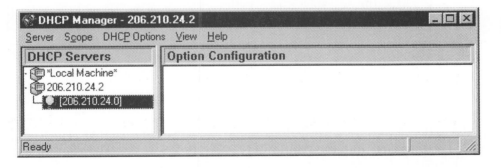

Figure 18–10
DHCP Manager
Window.

DHCP provides a time-saving, practically hands-off solution to the problem of managing IP addresses for a large number of clients.

Remote Access Service

There are many reasons why remote access to a domain, via a modem, is useful to a user. A short list includes the following:

- Employee access to company information and personal account
- Remote control of network by administrator
- Customer access

Figure 18–11
DHCP Scope
Properties.

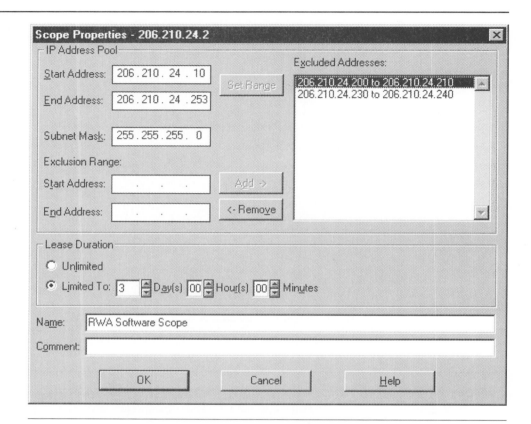

- Company used as gateway to the Internet
- System can be available 24 hours a day

Using the Windows NT operating system, a dial-in user can be granted access to the network resources using the Remote Access Service, or *RAS*. The RAS is added as a service from the Windows NT Network Services tab. After the service is added, Remote Access Services can be configured by selecting the item and clicking on the Properties button as shown in Figure 18–12.

Using one or more modems, the Remote Access Service may be configured to provide each modem up to three different types of network protocol connections: NetBEUI, TCP/IP, and IPX. This is accomplished using the Remote Access Setup program. All three protocols, and many others, are transported over the modem connection using PPP (Point-to-Point Protocol). PPP is built in to Dial-Up Networking, enabling Windows 95 and 98 clients to connect to an NT domain.

If a modem has not been installed, Remote Access Service can automatically set up and detect a modem on a specified port. A modem installed on COM2 is shown in the Remote Access Setup screen in Figure 18–13. From this

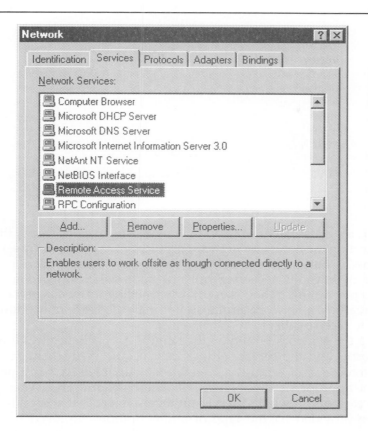

Figure 18–12
Windows NT
Network Services.

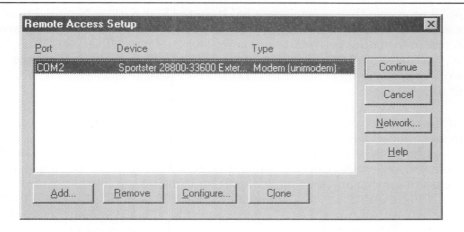

Figure 18–13
Remote Access
Setup window.

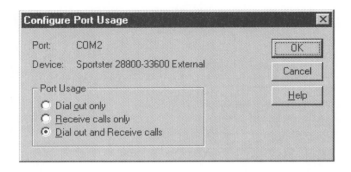

Figure 18–14
Remote Access
Service port
configuration.

screen it is also possible to add, remove, configure, or clone (copy) the modem ports, or set up the necessary network protocols. For example, by selecting the Configure . . . button, it is possible to specify how each modem port will be used (for dialing out, receiving calls, or both, as shown in Figure 18–14). Cloning a port configuration is useful when setting up a bank of modems. For security reasons, a network administrator may choose to only allow the RAS modems to receive calls.

Using the Network button on the Remote Access Setup window, the dial out protocols and the server settings may be specified as shown in Figure 18–15. Protocols and settings are enabled or disabled by selecting or deselecting the appropriate check boxes. Clicking the appropriate Configure buttons sets each of the selected server protocols. Note that several levels of security are provided by the type of authentication employed by RAS. For example, user passwords may be encrypted to help prevent detection.

The RAS Server NetBEUI Configuration is used to specify the level of access you want to grant all users who dial in to this computer using the NetBEUI protocol. This option is selected from the RAS Service NetBEUI Configuration menu, as shown in Figure 18–16. Notice that a client may be granted access to the entire network or one computer only (the NT server).

Similarly, the TCP/IP properties can be set to allow access to the entire network or this computer only. In addition, it is necessary to select a method in which IP addresses are assigned to the dial-up user. This is shown in Figure 18–17.

The RAS Server supports dynamic allocation and static allocation of IP addresses. You can even specify the range of static addresses available for the modem pool if DHCP is not used.

After each of the properties has been specified, the operation of the Remote Access Services can be examined as shown in Figure 18–18. At a glance it is easy to see that only one modem port is available, and it is not in use.

All of the RAS services within a domain may be controlled using the Remote Access Admin screen. Together with the dial-up options available to each user, RAS provides a secure way to allow remote access to the domain and its resources.

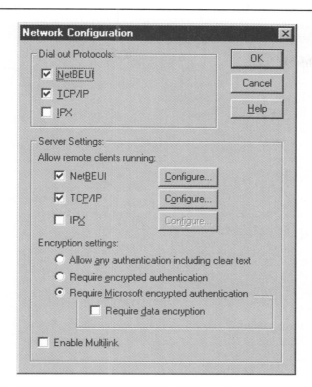

Figure 18–15
Remote Access
Service Network
Configuration.

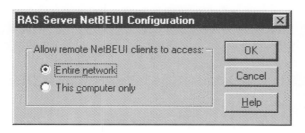

Figure 18–16
Configuring the
NetBEUI protocol
for RAS.

USER PROFILES

In a domain, the primary domain controller maintains all user profiles. This allows for centralized control of the Security Accounts Manager (SAM) database. Two programs are provided to update the SAM database. One of the programs is used in a stand-alone (no domain) environment and the other is for use if a domain is specified. Otherwise the programs operate in the same way. Let us examine what is involved when setting up a user account as illustrated in Figure 18–19.

Figure 18–17
Configuring the
TCP/IP protocol
for RAS.

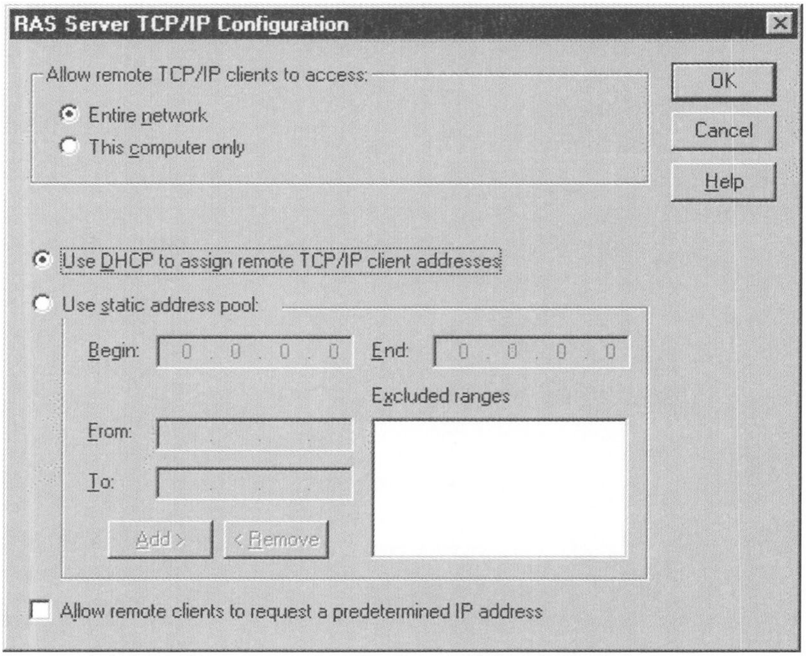

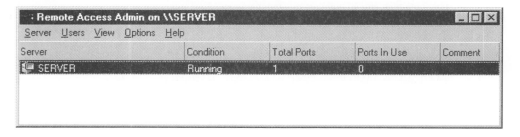

Figure 18–18
Remote Access Server Administration window.

Information must be specified about each user account including user name, full name, a description of the account, and the password setting. The check boxes are used to further modify the account, such as requiring a password change during the first logon, restricting changing the password, extending the life of a password, and, lastly, disabling the account.

The three buttons at the bottom of the New User window (Figure 18–19) allow for each new account to be added to different *groups*, as shown in Figure 18–20. It

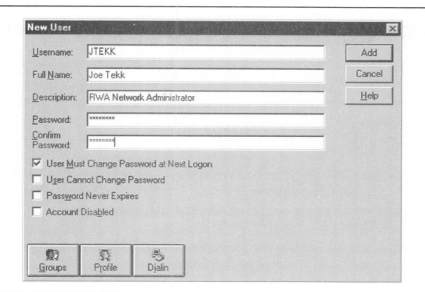

Figure 18–19
New User dialog box

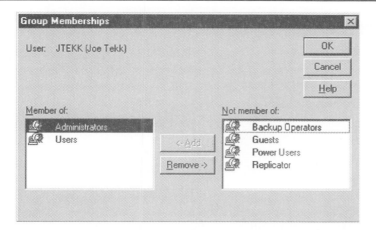

Figure 18–20
Group Memberships selection screen.

is a good idea to grant access to groups on an individual basis as certain privileges are granted by simply belonging to the group, such as administrator.

The User Environment Profile screen specifies the path to an individual profile and any required logon script name. Additionally, the home directory may be specified as shown in Figure 18–21.

Lastly, the Dialin Information window determines if a Windows NT account has access to Dial-Up Networking. The Call Back option may also be configured

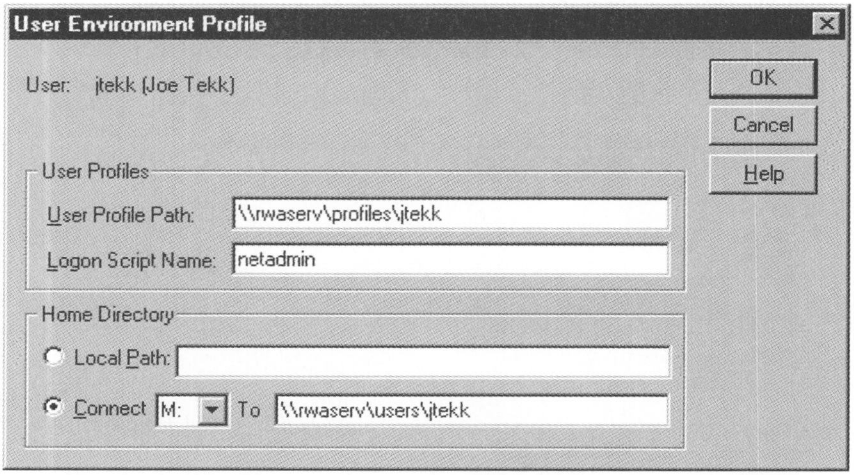

Figure 18–21
User Environment
configuration screen.

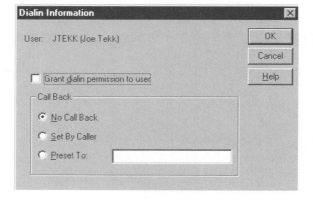

Figure 18–22
Dialin Information
settings.

to require the computer to call the user back. This is an additional security feature that may be implemented if necessary. Figure 18–22 shows these settings.

SECURITY

Windows NT is a C2-compliant operating system, when it is configured properly as defined by the National Computer Security Center (NCSC). C2 compliance involves properly configuring Windows NT to use the built-in safeguards. An application tool supplied with the operating system (C2CONFIG.EXE) examines the operating system setting against a recommended setting. Any exceptions are noted.

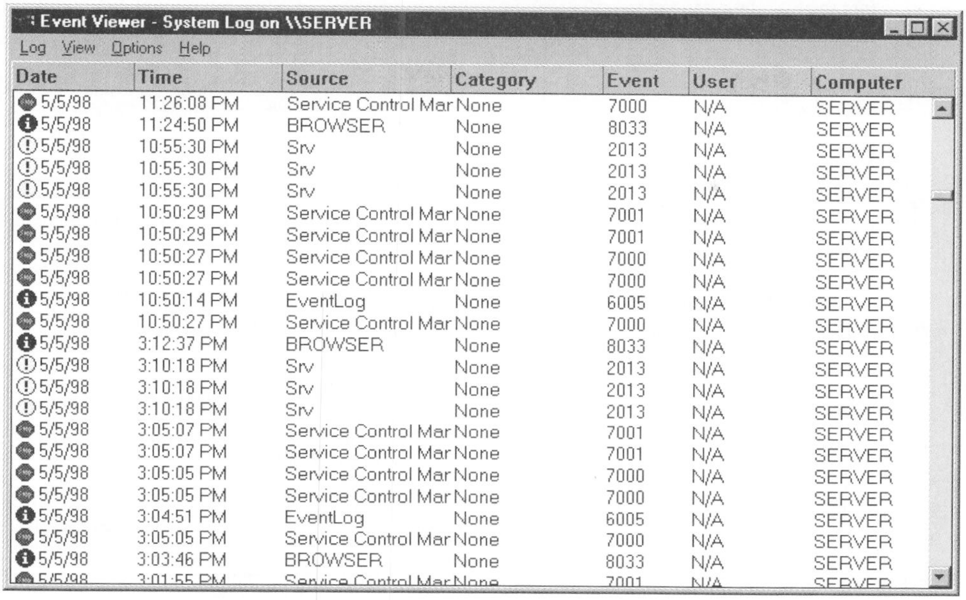

Date	Time	Source	Category	Event	User	Computer
5/5/98	11:26:08 PM	Service Control Mar	None	7000	N/A	SERVER
5/5/98	11:24:50 PM	BROWSER	None	8033	N/A	SERVER
5/5/98	10:55:30 PM	Srv	None	2013	N/A	SERVER
5/5/98	10:55:30 PM	Srv	None	2013	N/A	SERVER
5/5/98	10:55:30 PM	Srv	None	2013	N/A	SERVER
5/5/98	10:50:29 PM	Service Control Mar	None	7001	N/A	SERVER
5/5/98	10:50:29 PM	Service Control Mar	None	7001	N/A	SERVER
5/5/98	10:50:27 PM	Service Control Mar	None	7000	N/A	SERVER
5/5/98	10:50:27 PM	Service Control Mar	None	7000	N/A	SERVER
5/5/98	10:50:14 PM	EventLog	None	6005	N/A	SERVER
5/5/98	10:50:27 PM	Service Control Mar	None	7000	N/A	SERVER
5/5/98	3:12:37 PM	BROWSER	None	8033	N/A	SERVER
5/5/98	3:10:18 PM	Srv	None	2013	N/A	SERVER
5/5/98	3:10:18 PM	Srv	None	2013	N/A	SERVER
5/5/98	3:10:18 PM	Srv	None	2013	N/A	SERVER
5/5/98	3:05:07 PM	Service Control Mar	None	7001	N/A	SERVER
5/5/98	3:05:07 PM	Service Control Mar	None	7001	N/A	SERVER
5/5/98	3:05:05 PM	Service Control Mar	None	7000	N/A	SERVER
5/5/98	3:05:05 PM	Service Control Mar	None	7000	N/A	SERVER
5/5/98	3:04:51 PM	EventLog	None	6005	N/A	SERVER
5/5/98	3:05:05 PM	Service Control Mar	None	7000	N/A	SERVER
5/5/98	3:03:46 PM	BROWSER	None	8033	N/A	SERVER
5/5/98	3:01:55 PM	Service Control Mar	None	7001	N/A	SERVER

Figure 18–23 System events display.

Windows NT provides security-logging features designed to track all types of system activities, such as logon attempts, file transfers, Telnet sessions, and many more. Typically the System Administrator will determine which types of events are logged by the system. Figure 18–23 shows the system log. The icons along the left margin are color coded to draw attention to more serious events. Event logs should be reviewed daily.

TROUBLESHOOTING TECHNIQUES

A networked computer environment (especially when using Windows NT) can become somewhat complex, requiring the system or network administrator to have many technical skills. Fortunately, Windows NT also provides many resources designed to tackle most networking tasks. For example, the Administrative Tools menu contains the Administrative Wizards option shown in Figure 18–24. Most of these wizards perform the activities that are necessary to get a domain up and running.

It is also a good idea to examine the online help system to get additional information, which may simplify any task. Figure 18–25 shows a Help screen that contains a total of 8383 topics, many of which contain information about networking. Figure 18–26 shows the initial RAS help window. Plenty of details are provided.

Figure 18–24
Administrative Wizards
display.

Figure 18–25
Windows NT Help
display.

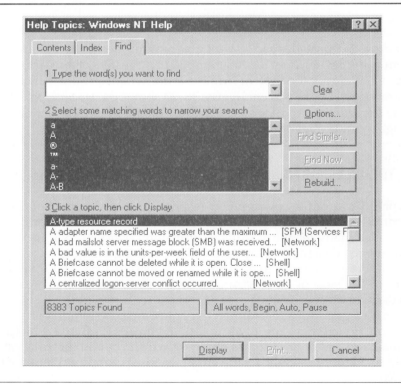

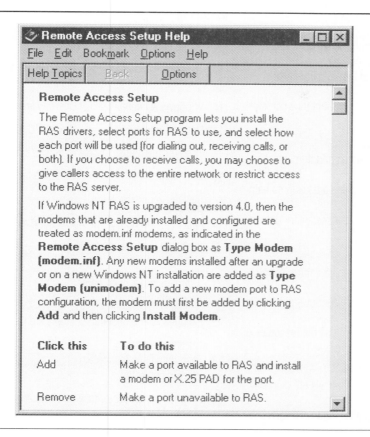

Figure 18–26
Remote Access
Services Setup Help.

SELF-TEST

This self-test is designed to help you check your understanding of the background information presented in this chapter.

True/False
Answer *true* or *false*.

1. A workgroup uses a centralized server to administer the network.

2. Each Windows NT domain can be configured independently.

3. A primary domain controller can be demoted to a backup domain controller.

4. A backup domain controller is updated every 10 minutes.

5. Windows 95 computers function only marginally in a Windows NT domain.

6. Windows NT only provides static IP addressing.

7. RAS only works with a single modem.

Multiple Choice
Select the best answer.

8. A Windows NT server can administer
   a. Windows NT domains.
   b. Windows NT and TCP/IP domains.
   c. Windows NT and LAN Manager domains.

9. Windows computers are added to a Windows NT domain by
   a. Double-clicking on the Windows NT computer in the Network Neighborhood.
   b. Modifying the properties of the TCP/IP network settings.
   c. Modifying the properties of the Client for Microsoft Network settings.

10. A Windows NT Server can be a
   a. Parent domain controller and a child domain controller.
   b. Secondary domain controller and a backup domain controller.
   c. Primary domain controller and a secondary domain controller.

11. A trusted domain
   a. Contains only one primary domain controller and no secondary controller.
   b. Is granted special access to all Windows computers in the trusted domain.
   c. Permits users in one domain to use the resources of another domain.

12. Running a network server involves
   a. Installing and configuring a Windows NT Workstation computer.
   b. Installing and configuring a Windows NT Server computer.
   c. Connecting Windows 95 computers to Windows NT workstation computers.

13. The range of IP addresses managed by the DHCP Manager is called a
   a. Scope.
   b. Subnet.
   c. Pool.

14. RAS supports the following protocols:
   a. TCP/IP and NetBEUI.
   b. IPX.
   c. Both a and b.

Matching
Match a description of the networking topic on the right with each item on the left.

15. Windows NT client   a. Windows NT and LAN Manager

16. Windows NT server   b. One way and two way

17. Domain types   c. PDC, BDC, none

18. Trust relationships   d. DOS, OS/2, Windows 95/98

19. Domain activity   e. Establish trust relationships

Completion
Fill in the blank or blanks with the best answers.

20. A backup domain controller is _____ to a primary domain controller.

21. A large number of computers cannot be managed effectively in a(n) _____ setting.

22. Computers administered centrally are part of a(n) _____.

23. Each domain must contain _____ primary domain controller.

24. A Windows NT Server may be either a(n) _____, _____, or not involved in the domain controller process.

25. DHCP stands for _____ _____ _____ _____.

26. The _____ protocol is used over the RAS modem connection.

QUESTIONS/ACTIVITIES

1. Under what circumstances can a Windows NT workstation computer become a primary domain controller? A Windows NT Server computer?

2. When should a Windows NT domain be used instead of a workgroup?

3. What is necessary for an operating system to become a network client?

4. What is C2 security?

5. Where can additional C2 information be found?

REVIEW QUIZ

Under the supervision of your instructor

1. Describe the benefits of creating a Windows NT domain.

2. Explain some different types of Windows NT domains.

3. Discuss the different types of clients able to join a Windows NT domain.

4. Describe RAS and DHCP.

Networking Concepts Laboratory

Experiment #18
Windows NT

Objectives

1. To become familiar with the operation of Windows NT Server and its associated domain operations.
2. *Optional:* To install Windows NT Server.
3. *Optional:* To install and configure RAS and DHCP services.
4. *Optional:* To add users and computers to the new Windows NT domain.

Required Equipment

The following equipment is required for this experiment:

- A copy of the Windows NT Server installation CD-ROM and two or more computers connected by a network
- If no NT Server CD-ROM is available, a previously configured NT Server system connected to a network

Procedure

Perform each of the following steps. Record your observations, results, and any difficulties you encounter. You will use this information when you develop your conclusions about the experiment.

1. Invite the Windows NT expert on your campus to demonstrate some of the following features of the Windows NT operating system:
   - PDC Windows NT Installation
   - BDC Windows NT Installation
   - Add users to the domain
   - Add computers to the domain
   - Configure DHCP
   - Configure RAS
   - Demonstrate various security features (file protection, event viewer, etc.)
   - Add/configure other Windows NT services (DNS, WINS, SNMP)
2. Call five local companies and ask what operating system they use.
3. Search the Web for security issues related to Windows NT.

Discussion and Conclusion

Using a word processor, write your own detailed explanations of the results and observations made during the experiment. To begin, try to say something about each procedure step.

In addition, provide answers to the following questions:

1. What are the advantages of using the Windows NT operating system?
2. What role does RAS play in Dial-Up Networking?
3. How does a program like LanExplorer threaten the security of a Windows NT domain? Explain how the use of switches in a LAN reduces this threat.

19

Linux

PERFORMANCE OBJECTIVES
Upon completion of this chapter, you will be able to

- Explain the differences between the Unix and Linux operating systems.
- Discuss the built-in Linux network applications.
- Describe the open source licensing for the Linux operating system.

Joe Tekk was busy making final preparations to install Linux on a computer he had just picked up from his friend Ken Koder. He was interested in setting it up to be a Web server to host his new Web pages.

Joe Tekk recalled talking to Ken's wife Suzanne about the Web courses she was taking at the local community college. She was in the process of searching for free Web services that offer CGI capabilities to their customers. Joe learned that many companies offer free Web serving including CGI to their customers and that many of them use the Apache Web server on the Linux operating system.

Joe downloaded a copy of Red Hat Linux off the Web. Before the afternoon was over, the installation was complete. He was surprised to learn that it came with the Apache server preinstalled. For the rest of the evening, Joe figured out how to run his own CGI applications.

INTRODUCTION

The Unix and Linux operating systems comprise a growing segment in the operating systems market. The Unix operating system has been available since the 1970s. The Unix operating system was originally developed by Ken Thompson, Dennis Ritchie, and others at AT&T labs. Unix is a trademark of the Open Systems Group. Because the source code was sold to many businesses and organizations, many different versions are available. The source code was also given to colleges and universities. One of the most popular versions of Unix to come out of the education market was created at the University of California at Berkeley.

437

The Linux operating system is a free version of Unix that was created by Linus Torvalds. Linux was originally released in 1991. The source code for Linux was available for free and users were encouraged to add additional features. There are many different versions of the Linux operating system available. A few of the most notable are from Red Hat, Caldera, and Corel Linux. All versions of the Linux operating system offer similar core capabilities, with the differences being various add-on features and custom services. Because the Linux operating system is so popular, many computer vendors (IBM, Dell, etc.) make their products available with Linux preinstalled. In this chapter, we will examine the Red Hat version of the Linux operating system.

RED HAT LINUX ENVIRONMENT

The Red Hat Linux operating system environment provides many features commonly found on large mainframes and mini-computers running Unix. Some of these features found on the latest version of the Red Hat Linux operating system include

- True multiuser, multitasking operating system
- Virtual memory
- Built-in network support
- OpenSSL with 128-bit encryption for secure communication
- Easy graphical installation with autodetection of hardware
- Software RAID support for RAID 0 through RAID 5
- USB support for mice and keyboards
- Graphical firewall configuration tool
- GUI interface
- POSIX compliant

Because of the many features available in Linux, it is commonly used as a server on the Internet. Linux contains all of the TCP/IP network applications that are necessary to offer a full range of Internet and networking services including

- DHCP
- FTP
- Telnet
- DNS
- HTTP Server
- PING
- Traceroute
- Nslookup
- Network File System
- Network Information System
- Firewall

The software for Linux is distributed free of charge. The Linux operating system is based on the open-source software model and is distributed freely under the GNU GPL (general public license). Under the GNU GPL, users of any type (home, education, business, or commercial) have the ability to update the source code in any way and to contribute to the ongoing development. In essence, the users are encouraged to add features that are then turned back to the community at large. Many software programs are available for Linux under the open-source agreement.

Many of the programs available in Linux can be run from the command prompt. Table 19–1 lists many of the most frequently used programs. Note

Program Name	Purpose
cat	Display file contents
cd	Change directory
chmod	Change file protection
chown	Change file owner
cp	Copy file(s)
df	Show free disk space
find	Locate files
ftp	File transfer
ifconfig	Network interface configuration
kill	Terminate process
ls	List files (directory)
man	Display online manual pages
mkdir	Create new directory
mv	Move file(s)
netstat	Display network connection status
pine	Internet news and email application
ping	Test network connectivity
ps	Display current system processes
rm	Remove file(s)
shutdown	Initiate system shutdown procedure
su	Temporarily become a different user
tar	Disk backup/archival tool
telnet	Remote communication tool
traceroute	Trace route to destination
vi	Invoke text editor
who	List current system users

Table 19–1
Common commands and utility programs.

that the input and output for these use only text. For example, entering the `df` command on a Linux system produces the following output:

```
# df
Filesystem            1k-blocks        Used Available Use% Mounted
/dev/hda8                256667       74168    169247  30% /
/dev/hda1                 23302        2647     19452  12% /boot
/dev/hda5               3541904       15920   3346060   0% /home
/dev/hda6               3541904     1266324   2095656  38% /usr
/dev/hda7                256667       34079    209336  14% /var
#
```

The `df` command produces a list of the currently mounted disks. For each disk, the `df` command shows the filesystem (disk partition), how large each disk is, how much of the disk is used, a percentage of disk utilization, and the disk name under which it is mounted. The names `/`, `/boot`, `/home`, `/usr`, and `/var` are typical mount points. The `df` command is useful to determine the amount of free space on each disk. Table 19–2 lists the purpose of each mounted disk. Figure 19–1 shows the layout and structure of a typical Linux disk.

Note that although each of the programs in Table 19–1 can be run from the command prompt, most people prefer to use a graphical interface to interact with the operating system.

 LINUX GRAPHICAL USER ENVIRONMENT

Aside from the original character-based interface, the Linux environment contains a GUI interface based on the X11 standard. On the Intel hardware platform, the latest version of X11 is release 6. Using X Windows, software developers have written several window manger programs. Two of the most popular are Gnome (http://www.gnome.org) and KDE (http://www.kde.org), the K Desktop Environment. Both of these window managers are available on Red Hat Linux. Basically, the window manager provides the user interface, using X Windows as the foundation.

Table 19–2
Common Linux disk/directory structure.

Disk Mount Point	Purpose
/	Root disk directory
/boot	Files necessary to boot Linux
/home	User directories
/usr	Installed software directories
/var	Variable disk information such as logs and temp files

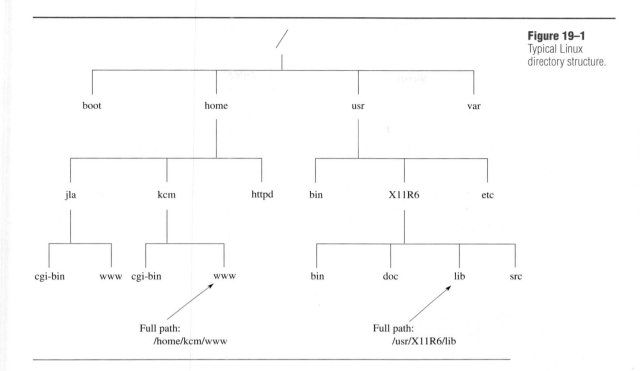

Figure 19–1
Typical Linux
directory structure.

Two of the most popular window managers are shown in Figure 19–2. Figure 19–2(a) shows a view of the Linux operating system running Gnome. The Gnome interface is provided by the GNU project. Similar to the Windows operating system, the desktop contains icons that are shortcuts to commonly used programs. At the bottom of the window, the taskbar contains the Gnome footprint that provides access to a menu system, similar to the function of the Start button in Windows. The task bar also contains several shortcuts to open the help system, the Gnome configuration tool, a terminal emulation program, and Netscape Navigator. Next to the Netscape Navigator icon is the desktop selection tool that allows the user to select from one of four desktop views, each of which can contain any number of programs. The outline of windows inside of the desktop view shows which desktops are currently active. The remainder of the taskbar is devoted to the current application list and the date and time display. Notice that the desktop being displayed contains three windows, the outlines of which are viewable in the desktop selection display. The Terminal window shown in the forefront is running the Pine program, a mail utility.

The KDE interface shown in Figure 19–2(b) is currently displaying the Javasoft.com home page using Netscape Navigator. Similar to the Gnome desktop, KDE provides a taskbar to allow fast access to the commonly used features, four desktop views, and a list of currently running applications that are displayed along the top of the screen. The K button operates similar to the Start button that allows access to all installed operating system and window manager features. Red Hat Linux provides a desktop switching tool to allow a user to choose between the Gnome and KDE desktops.

INSTALLATION AND CONFIGURATION

The installation and configuration of the Linux operating system varies from manufacturer to manufacturer. The Red Hat distribution allows the system administrator to select the type of installation to perform. Figure 19–3 shows the menu that is presented during the installation process. Depending on the requirements, a user can choose a Workstation, Server, or custom installation type setting. An upgrade option is used to perform an upgrade from a pre-

Figure 19–2
(a) The Linux operating system running the Gnome desktop interface.

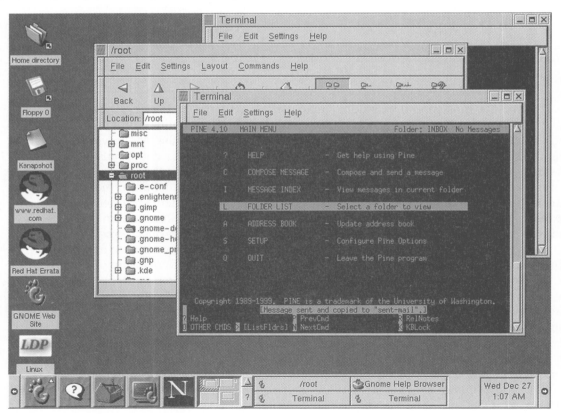

Figure 19–2
(continued) (b) The Linux operating system running the KDE desktop interface.

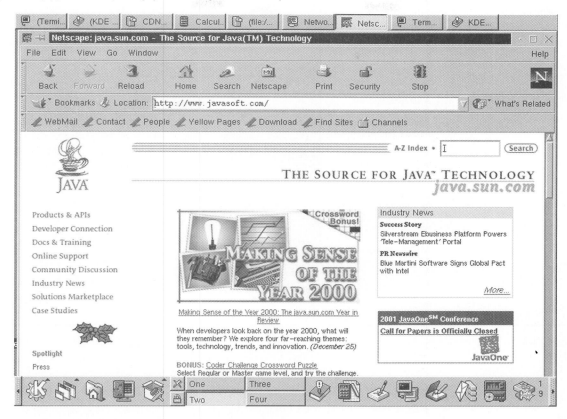

vious version. Due to the variety of hardware components available, the installation process will interrogate the system hardware to determine the correct drivers to load. After selecting the type of installation to perform, the user can also select the various packages to be installed, as shown in Figure 19–4.

After the installation type and selection of packages has been completed, the Linux installer partitions and formats the hard drive as necessary, and copies all of the files selected by the user. At the end of the operating system installation, the X Windows configuration tool, called `Xconfigurator`, is run to configure the optimum settings for the installed video card. When X Windows has been properly configured, the installation of the operating system is complete, and the system must be rebooted.

After installation, most of the system configuration that will need to be performed is done using the `linuxconf` (Linux Configuration) program.

Figure 19–3
Red Hat Linux
installation options.

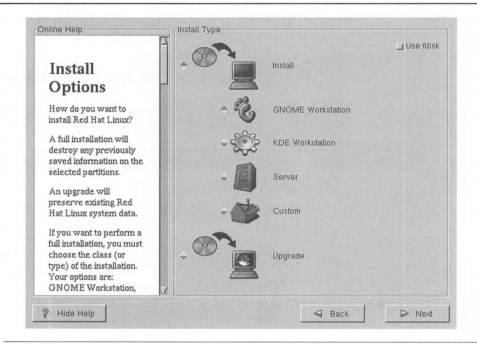

Figure 19–4
Red Hat Linux
packages.

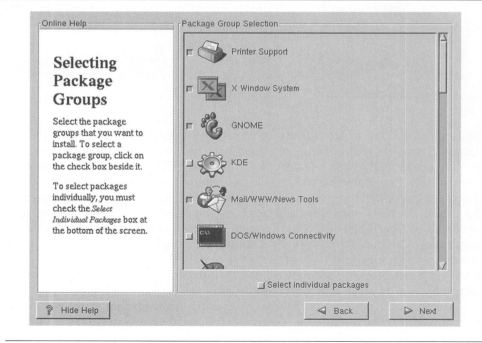

The Linux Configuration program is used to automate the process to add or maintain all of the critical system applications to keep the system running properly. You may want to visit the Linux Configuration Project home page located at http://www.solucorp.qc.ca/linuxconf/ for additional information about `linuxconf`.

🖥️🖥️ APPLICATION SOFTWARE

Depending on which window manager is chosen, a variety of application software is available. For example, using the KDE interface, a mail client program (shown in Figure 19–5) allows for e-mail to be managed by the user. Like any other mail client, there are ways for a user to organize the mail. The system will automatically use the default folders. For example, before a new mail message has been sent, it will be shown in the outbox. After it has been sent, it is automatically moved to the sent mail folder where it is stored for future reference. The user can also create new folders as necessary. The window shown in Figure 19–6 illustrates how easy it is to create a message that contains attachments in addition to a text message.

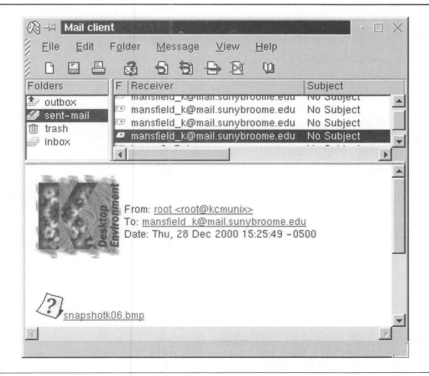

Figure 19–5
The KDE mail client.

Figure 19–6
KDE mail message
with attachments.

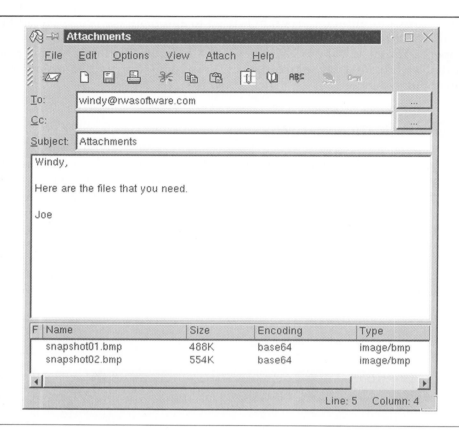

Another program from the KDE desktop environment is the network utilities program shown in Figure 19–7. It combines the functionality of PING, traceroute, host resolution (DNS), finger, and mtr in one application program. This application can be quite useful when setting up a TCP/IP based computer network.

Many programs are installed during the operating system installation process. If a program is not installed, it can be installed later as necessary using the Gnome RPM (Red Hat Package Manager). Each of the installed packages can be examined and new programs can be installed. Figure 19–8 shows the Internet category of packages currently installed. A query of the selected package (netscape-navigator-4.61-12) shows information about the installed package, as illustrated in Figure 19–9. The size, build host, distribution, group, install date, build date, vendor, and packager are available for examination. A description of the program and the local installation paths are also displayed. At the bottom of the Package Info screen, the application can be verified or uninstalled. If a package is not functioning properly, it may be useful to verify the installation. Figure 19–10 shows that no problems are found with the

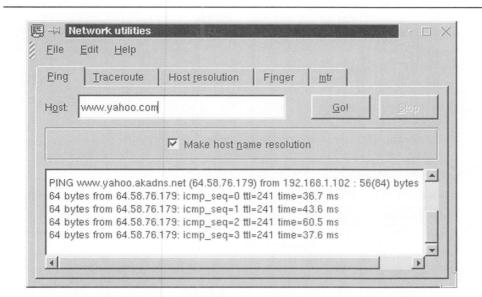

Figure 19–7
KDE network utilities program.

Figure 19–8
Gnome RPM Internet packages.

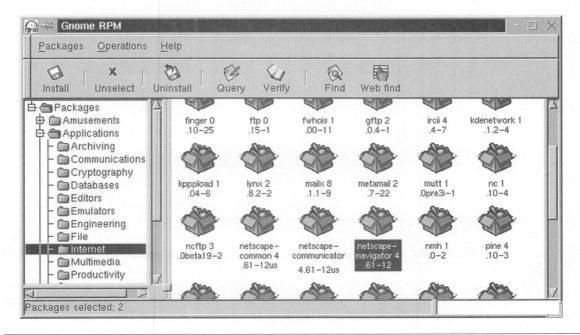

Figure 19–9
RPM Netscape
package information.

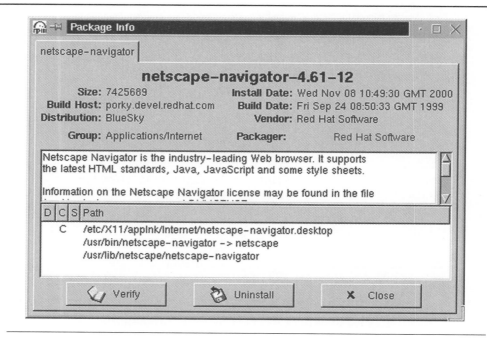

Figure 19–10
RPM package
verification of
Netscape.

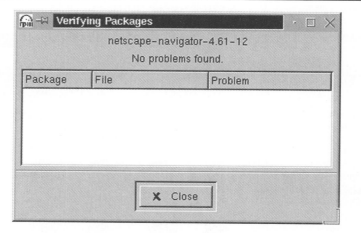

installation. The Gnome RPM program is also used to download and install
new packages as well. By clicking on the Web Find button, a list of additional
packages is displayed. Using Gnome RPM is probably the easiest method to
ensure that the latest versions of all software programs are installed. You are
encouraged to explore the Gnome RPM program in detail.

SYSTEM ADMINISTRATION, MANAGEMENT, AND SECURITY

The administration and management of a Linux system can be a complicated task, especially with a computer connected to the Internet. First and foremost, it is necessary for the system administrator to protect the root account. The system administrator is responsible for a wide variety of system tasks. For example, the following list of items would be reviewed regularly:

- Physical system security
- Disk backups
- Addition and removal of authorized users
- Verification of proper file permission settings
- Installation and configuration of server and client applications
- Examination and review of system resources (memory, disks, etc.)
- Setting up and maintaining printers
- Performance monitoring and tuning
- System start-up and shut-down options
- System log files review

The security of a Linux system must be treated as a very important task. It is necessary to review the list of users periodically to ensure that no accounts have been added that would indicate a breach of security. For the system administrator, the management of a Linux system may be a full-time activity.

TCP/IP NETWORK MANAGEMENT

The management of the TCP/IP network on a Linux system is performed using `linuxconf`. Linuxconf is used to perform many different types of system configuration. Figure 19–11 shows basic host information in the `linuxconf` window. Notice that the left side of the window shows the various categories that may be configured. The right side of the display shows the current settings for each of the categories. The host name is entered during the installation of the operating system. It can be modified later using `linuxconf`. The Adaptor tabs (labeled 1–4) are used to identify each of the NIC cards that are installed. Figure 19–12 shows that Adaptor 1 is enabled using the DHCP configuration mode. The network device specifies eth0 with the eepro100 kernel module or driver. By enabling the DHCP configuration, a DHCP server must be available to assign TCP/IP network parameters when the system is booted. These are the only parameters that are necessary to get a Linux system up on a TCP/IP network. Figure 19–13 shows the name server specifications assigned to the computer. Note that each of the nameserver fields has been assigned a value by the DHCP server for the current network. If a DHCP server is not available, a valid IP address, network mask, and nameserver addresses must be specified.

Figure 19–11
Linux Configuration
utility program.

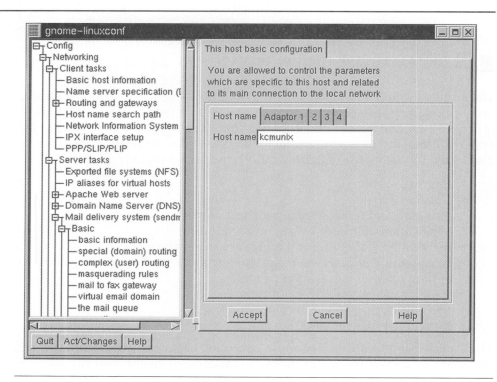

Figure 19–12
Configuration options
for Ethernet Adaptor 1.

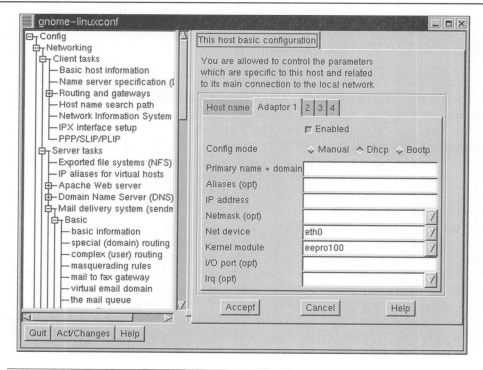

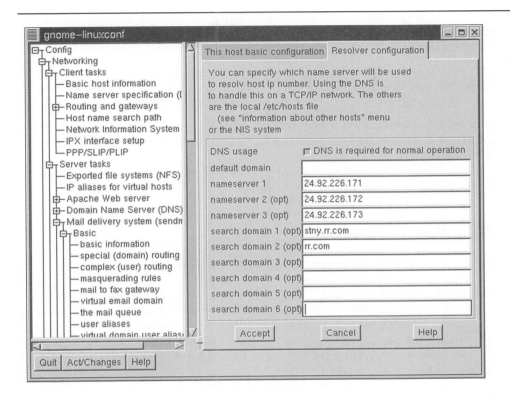

Figure 19–13
Setting for the name servers assigned by DHCP.

There are also many other tools that are used in Linux to verify correct network operations. A list of built in applications includes

- ifconfig
- PING
- traceroute
- tcpdump
- nslookup

For example, a sample execution of `tcdump` utility with the output redirected to the file TCP.TXT looks like the following:

```
# tcdump >> tcp.txt
Kernel filter, protocol ALL, datagram packet socket
tcpump: listening on all devices

100 packets received by filter

#
```

The `tcpdump` execution was terminated by pressing Ctrl + C. As noted, the contents of the TCP.TXT file contain 100 packets. The first captured packet in the file contains:

```
13:08:51.176746 eth0 < bgm-24-95-142-58.stny.rr.com.1028 > bgm-24-
94-63160.stny.rr.com.telnet: . 4486926:4486926(0) ack 3337880229
win 65505 (DF)
```

This information may be useful when examining network traffic. You are encouraged to review the online manual pages to help examine the output from the `tcpdump` program.

In addition to these built-in applications, there are many other programs that can be downloaded from the Internet.

SAMBA

The Samba (http://www.samba.org) program allows for a Linux system to participate in a Windows network by sharing files and printers using SMB (Server Message Blocks) and CIFS (Common Internet File System) protocols.

SMB is a client-server, request-response protocol for sharing files and printers. All Windows for Workgroups, Windows 95/98, and Windows NT systems are (or are capable of) running SMB as a client, a server, or both. CIFS is a new specification for a file access designed for the Internet. CIFS is based on the existing SMB protocol.

Using Samba, it is possible to connect to Unix disks and printers from

- LAN Manager clients
- Windows for Workgroups 3.11 clients
- Windows 95/98 clients
- Windows NT clients
- Linux clients
- OS/2 clients

Figure 19–14 shows the `linuxconf` windows used to configure directories to be shared using Samba.

Notice that the window contains several different tabs, allowing the system administrator to enter many different parameters to customize the operating of Samba. Samba provides a replacement for Windows NT, Warp, NFS, or Netware servers.

NETWORK INFORMATION SERVICES

The Network Information Service (NIS) is a method used on Unix and Linux systems to share passwords and group file access within a computer network. NIS was created by Sun Microsystems as a part of the Sun operating systems.

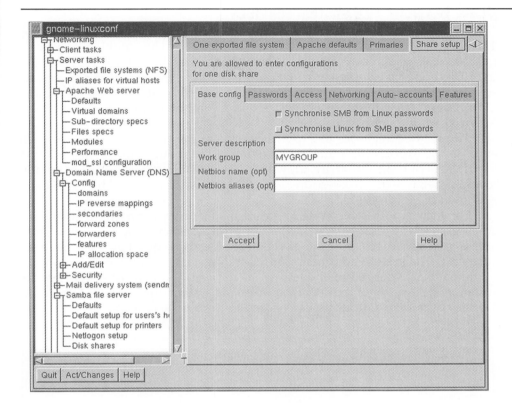

Figure 19–14
Samba configuration options.

Originally these services were called YP (short for Yellow Pages), but due to a lawsuit the name was eventually changed to NIS.

NIS domains are created to allow for servers and clients to communicate. The servers and clients must be in the same domain in order to communicate. NIS domains are supported by master NIS servers and slave NIS servers. A master NIS server contains the actual resource information to be shared on the network and the NIS clients are used to distribute the load across the network.

There is much talk about the security of NIS resources. Security and system administrators make recommendations on how the resources may be guarded to offer maximum protection. You are encouraged to read about what types of problems there are and the solutions that are available, if any.

A newer version of NIS called NIS+ stands for Network Information Service Plus. It was designed to replace NIS and is a default naming service for the Sun Microsystems Solaris operating system. Using YP-compatibility mode, NIS+ can provide limited support to NIS clients. One important thing to note is that there is no relation between NIS+ and NIS. NIS+ was designed from scratch and the overall structure and commands of NIS+ are different from NIS.

NETWORK FILE SYSTEM SERVICES

The Network File System (NFS) is the method used by Unix and Linux systems to share disk resources. NFS was originally designed by Sun Microsystems in the 1980s and was adopted as a standard method to create shared network resources. The file systems that are exported using NFS can be imported by any Linux computer within the network. A Linux computer can import and export NFS disks at the same time.

The list of directories to export is stored in the file /etc/exports. Each entry in the exports file contains the name of the mount point followed by a list of users or groups that are allow to use it. This file can be edited manually to add or remove the disk resource. The file can also maintained by linuxconf as shown in Figure 19–15.

For each exported file system, the clients that may connect are given specific rights to the resource. Each client or group of clients may be given write access, root privileges, translate symbolic links, and request access from a secure port. The system administrator must determine what values are appropriate to use. When all of the entries have been updated, the exported file system will show up in the list of Exported file systems shown in Figure 19–16. These are the same entries that are stored in the file /etc/exports.

Figure 19–15
Configuration
window for exported
file system.

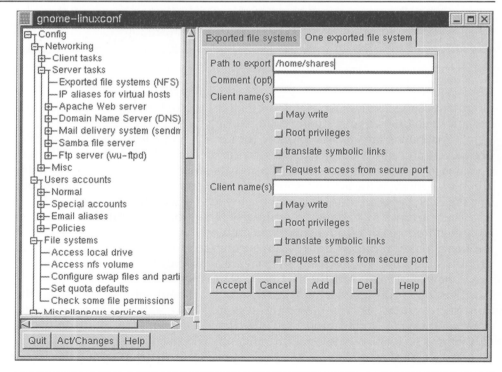

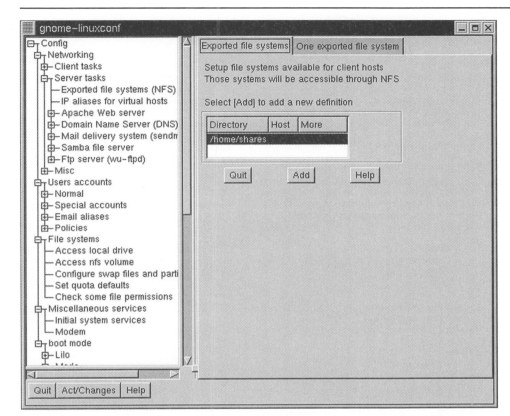

Figure 19–16
List of Exported file systems.

APACHE WEB SERVER

The Linux operating system also comes with the Apache Web server from http://www.apache.org. The Apache Server is an HTTP 1.1-compliant Web server offering the ability to use CGI scripting using Perl, Python, C/C++, plus many other compatible languages. Apache Server also provides complete Java compatibility. The Apache Server is the most popular HTTP server on the Internet, with almost 60% of the market share according to the statistics compiled at http://www.netcraft.com. The Apache Server on Linux provides commercial-grade service with all of the bells and whistles that are required, and it's free.

The `linuxconf` program can also be used to maintain the Apache Web server. Figure 19–17 shows the Apache default settings. Notice that on the left side of the window there are several different configuration categories.

Administering a Web server today is a very important task. Most businesses and organizations rely on a Web presence to provide services to their

Figure 19–17
Apache Web server
configuration options.

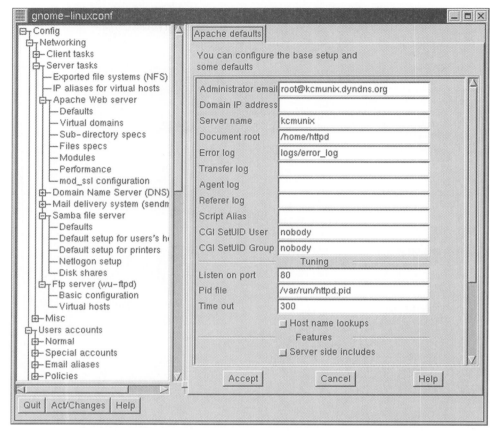

customers around the clock. Using the Apache Server, there are no restrictions in what can be provided to the end users.

LINUX DOCUMENTATION

When using the Unix or Linux operating systems, it is possible to experience many different types of problems. Unfortunately there are too many problems to even list. The good news is that there are many sources of information to help solve problems that are encountered. Figures 19–18 and 19–19 show a starting point for any investigation, depending on whether the Gnome or KDE interface is being used. In addition to these resources, the Linux documentation project provides extensive information about most of the applications that can be installed, configured, and used on a Linux system. The Linux documentation project provides access to electronic books, FAQs, man pages, HOWTOs,

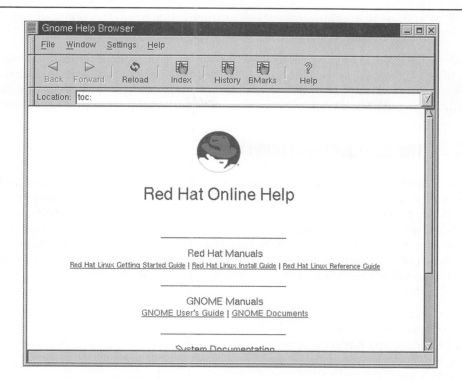

Figure 19–18
Red Hat Online Help for the Gnome desktop interface.

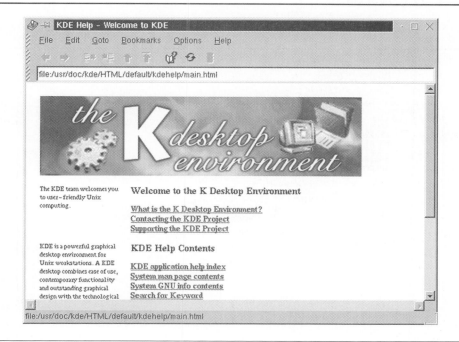

Figure 19–19
Red Hat Online Help for the KDE desktop interface.

plus much more. You are encouraged to visit the Linux documentation project at http://www.linuxdoc.org. All of the documentation available prepares a system administrator to maintain and enhance a Linux system with as few difficulties as possible. Don't reinvent the wheel unless it is absolutely necessary.

 TROUBLESHOOTING TECHNIQUES

When troubleshooting a Linux system, it is necessary to use all of the available tools that are provided. For example, if the network doesn't seem to be working properly, it may be necessary to make sure that the computer has a valid IP address. The ifconfig program is useful in this type of situation. For example, refer to Figure 19–20. Notice that there are two Ethernet adapters shown. The first, eth0, is the eepro100. The second, lo, is the loopback adapter that is useful for testing and debugging purposes. For the eth0 device the following items are listed:

- Hardware address
- Internet address
- Broadcast address
- Network mask
- Status (UP or DOWN)
- MTU
- Metric
- RX packet statistics

Figure 19–20.
Ethernet statistics shown using the ifconfig utility.

```
[root@kcmunix /root]# ifconfig
eth0        Link encap:Ethernet   HWaddr 00:D0:B7:68:2A:15
            inet addr:192.168.1.102  Bcast:192.168.1.255  Mask:255.255.255.0
            UP BROADCAST RUNNING  MTU:1500  Metric:1
            RX packets:6568 errors:1 dropped:0 overruns:0 frame:0
            TX packets:11137 errors:0 dropped:0 overruns:0 carrier:0
            collisions:0 txqueuelen:100
            Interrupt:11 Base address:0x6000

lo          Link encap:Local Loopback
            inet addr:127.0.0.1  Mask:255.0.0.0
            UP LOOPBACK RUNNING  MTU:3924  Metric:1
            RX packets:5931 errors:0 dropped:0 overruns:0 frame:0
            TX packets:5931 errors:0 dropped:0 overruns:0 carrier:0
            collisions:0 txqueuelen:0

[root@kcmunix /root]# 
```

- TX packet statistics
- Collision statistics
- NIC hardware settings

For the loopback adapter, the same information is listed, with the exception of the hardware references.

By reviewing the information on this screen to make sure that a valid IP address is displayed, it is clear whether or not the network is working properly. There are also many other programs available that can be used to diagnose problems. Read all of the available Linux documentation to determine what tools are available and how to use them.

SELF-TEST

This self-test is designed to help you check your understanding of the background information presented in this chapter.

True/False

Answer *true* or *false*.

1. The Unix operating system was created by Linus Torvalds.

2. The Gnome desktop interface is a part of the KDE.

3. Software programs installed in Linux are called packages.

4. `Linuxconf` is used to display IP addresses.

5. Network Information Services allow Linux to participate in a Windows network.

6. The Common Internet File Structure is used to share Yellow Page passwords.

7. The first Ethernet adapter is called eth1.

Multiple Choice

Select the best answer.

8. The Linux GUI environment is provided by the use of
   a. Microsoft Windows.
   b. X Windows.
   c. GNU Windows.

9. The two window managers provided by Red Hat Linux both provide _____ desktops.
   a. Two.
   b. Four.
   c. Eight.

10. When installing Linux, there are three types of basic software installation choices, called
    a. Client, server, and host.
    b. Workstation, server, and custom.
    c. Server, host, and upgrade.

11. To be sure that a software package has been installed properly, the system administrator performs a
    a. Check.
    b. Verify.
    c. Review.

12. Samba allows a Linux computer to participate in a _____ network.
    a. Linux.
    b. Unix.
    c. Windows.

13. The original name for Network Information Services was
    a. Yellow Pages.
    b. White Pages.
    c. Network Sharing Service.

14. The program used to verify the IP address on a Linux computer is called
    a. `ifconfig`.
    b. `ipconfig`.
    c. `netconfig`.

Completion

Fill in the blank or blanks with the best answers.

15. One of the most popular versions of Unix was created at the University of California at _____.

16. The GUI interface to Linux is provided through the use of a _____ manager.

17. The Gnome _____ button operates like the Start menu on a Microsoft Windows desktop.

18. The _____ program is run at the end of a Linux installation to configure the video card.

19. After Linux is installed, the _____ program is used to configure the Linux operating system.

20. The Red Hat _____ _____ is used to examine installed packages and add new packages.

QUESTIONS/ACTIVITIES

1. Search the Web to find places to download GNU application programs. How many programs did you find?

2. Search the Web to locate RPM packages for the Red Hat Linux. How many packages are available?

3. Search the Web to determine what other window managers are available to run under Linux. Are these window manager programs available as a package?

4. Research how the Linux operating system can be configured to operate as a firewall.

REVIEW QUIZ

Under the supervision of your instructor

1. Explain some of the differences between the Unix and Linux operating systems.

2. Discuss the built-in Linux network applications.

3. Describe the open source licensing for the Linux operating system.

Networking Concepts Laboratory

Experiment #19
Linux

Objectives

1. To examine the features and characteristics of programs available on the Linux operating system.
2. To create a network boot disk to begin the Linux installation process.

Required Equipment

The following equipment is required for this experiment:

- A networked computer with access to the Internet
- *(Optional:)* One floppy diskette

Procedure

Perform each of the following steps. Record your observations, results, and any difficulties you encounter. You will use this information when you develop your conclusions about the experiment.

1. Run the Linux configuration program and review the client network settings. What driver is used for your NIC card?
2. Visit the Red Hat Linux Web site to determine how to download and install the Linux operating system free of charge.
3. Run each of the following built-in programs. Review any system help resources as necessary.
   a. ping
   b. traceroute
   c. ftp
   d. telnet
   e. tcpdump
4. Visit another Linux operating system Web site and locate instructions on how to download and install the Linux operating system for free over the Web.
5. Download and review some of the source code available for the Linux operating system. Comment on anything interesting that you discover.

Optional Procedures

6. Create a bootable floppy disk with network support that can be used to install Linux on a computer with a supported NIC card installed.
7. Install the Linux operating system over the Internet using the floppy disk created in step 6.

Discussion and Conclusion

Using a word processor, write your own detailed explanations of the results and observations made during the experiment. To begin, try to say something about each procedure step.

In addition, provide answers to the following questions:

1. List several reasons why an organization may want to use the Linux operating system.
2. What are the advantages of using Linux compared to Windows?
3. What are the disadvantages of using Linux compared to Windows?

20

PERFORMANCE OBJECTIVES

Upon completion of this chapter, you will be able to

- Compare the features of NetWare with Windows NT.
- Discuss the file organization, protocols, and security available in NetWare.
- Briefly describe the VMS and MacOs operating systems.

Other Network Operating Systems

Joe Tekk visited his friend Marlene Hall, an educational planner for a high-technology consulting firm. Marlene was busy preparing color transparencies for a presentation.

"Hi, Joe," she said, handing him a thick pile of transparencies. "Look through these and tell me what you think."

Joe examined the transparencies with interest. Marlene had put together a detailed comparison of Windows NT and NetWare. "Who are these for?" he asked.

Marlene gave Joe a quick stare and then replied, "The president of our European division."

Two weeks later, Joe received a call from Marlene. The presentation had gone so well the president chose both operating systems and hired Marlene to oversee their integration in the European office.

INTRODUCTION

In this chapter we will examine several additional network operating systems. Let us start with a look at the features of Novell's NetWare operating system.

NETWARE

The NetWare operating system originated in the early days of DOS, allowing users to share information, print documents on network printers, manage a set of users, and so on. One important difference between NetWare and Windows is in the area of application software. NetWare does not provide the 32-bit preemptive multitasking environment found in Windows. Applications written for Windows will not run on NetWare. They may, however, communicate over the network using NetWare's proprietary IPX/SPX protocol. The following sections describe many of the main features of NetWare.

Installing/Upgrading Netware

Unlike Windows, the NetWare operating system runs on top of DOS (as Windows 3.x did). So before NetWare can be installed on a system, DOS must be up and running. NetWare 4.x and above provide a DOS environment as part of the installation process. Versions of NetWare older than 3.1x must be upgraded to 3.1x before they can be further upgraded to NetWare 4.x and above.

There are two ways to perform an upgrade: through *in-place migration* and through *across-the-wire migration*. In-place migration involves shutting down the NetWare server to perform the upgrade directly on the machine. Across-the-wire migration transfers all NetWare files from the current server to a new machine attached to the network. The new machine must already be running NetWare 4.x or above. This method allows the older 3.1x server to continue running during the upgrade.

Netware-Windows Timeline

Table 20–1 shows the NetWare and Windows operating system releases during the last decade. Both operating systems have matured to provide significant network support, management, and productivity features.

NDS

The Network Directory Service (NDS) is the cornerstone of newer NetWare networks. Network administrators can manage all users and resources from one location. NDS allows users to access global resources regardless of their

Table 20–1
NetWare–Windows timeline.

NetWare		Windows			
		3.x/95/98/ME		NT	
Version	Year	Version	Year	Version	Year
3.x	1989	3.0	1990	3.1	1993
4.x	1993	3.1	1992	3.5	1994
5	1998	3.11	1993	3.51	1995
5.1	1999	95	1995	4.0	1996
6	2001	98	1998	2000	2000
		ME	2000		

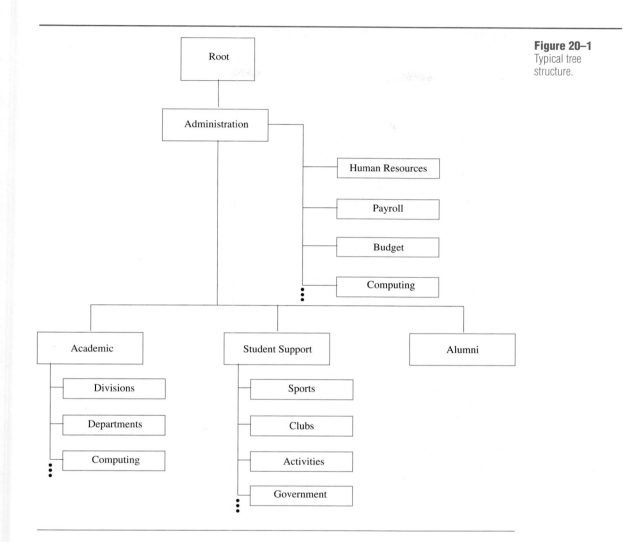

Figure 20–1
Typical tree
structure.

physical location using a single login. The NDS database organizes information on each object in the network. These objects are users, groups, printers, and disk volumes. Typically these objects are organized into a hierarchical tree that matches the internal structure of an organization. Figure 20–1 shows a typical tree structure for a small two-year college. Each major area of the organization (Administration, Academic, Student Support, and Alumni) has its own unique requirements. The requirements are applied to all the users who are associated with each specific area. Over time, as the requirements of the organization change, elements in the hierarchical tree are added, modified, or removed very easily.

NetWare uses *data migration* to move data from one location to another to maintain effective use of available hard drive space. Large files are moved to a secondary storage system (such as a *jukebox*) and copied back (demigrated) to the hard drive when needed. Files that have been migrated still show up in directory listings.

Accurate timekeeping plays an important role in the operation of NDS. Multiple servers must agree on the network time so that file updates are performed in the correct sequence. NetWare uses several kinds of time servers to maintain an accurate Universal Coordinated Time (UCT). These servers are called *reference*, *primary*, *secondary*, and *single-reference*. Reference servers use a connection to an accurate time source (such as the U.S. Naval Observatory's Atomic Clock) to provide the network time. Primary and reference servers negotiate with each other to determine the network time. Secondary servers provide the time to NetWare clients. Single-reference time servers are designed for use on small networks where one machine has total control over the network time.

NDS add-ons are also available for Windows NT and Unix environments, allowing those systems to fully participate in the NetWare environment.

HCSS

The High Capacity Storage System (HCSS) provided by NetWare allows for tremendously large volumes to be created that span up to 32 physical hard drives. When hard drives were quite small in comparison to the sizes available today, HCSS allowed for the creation of volumes up to 32GB in size. NetWare 5 introduced increased volume sizes up to 8 Terabytes (still much larger than disks typically available today). In conjunction with a configuration of RAID (Redundant Array of Inexpensive Disks), data is protected even if one of the disks in the volume fails.

Menus, Login Scripts, and Messaging

Several of the most important issues for the user involve the system menus, shared access to a common set of data, and electronic messaging capabilities. Access to the software located on each system is created using the menu generation program. Access to items in the menu is made available during the login process using a login script.

The login script contains a list of commands that are executed when each user logs in to the network. The commands are typically used to establish connections to network resources such as mapping of network drives. A login script is a property of a container, Profile, or User object. If a login script is defined for each of these objects, all associated login scripts will execute when a user logs in, allowing for a great deal of control over each user's environment.

Electronic messaging is provided for all users using information available through NDS. Each user's specific information is centrally maintained in the NDS database. The Message Handling Service (MHS) provides access to

Rights Name	Rights Description
Access Control	May control the rights of other users to access files and directories
Create	May create new file or subdirectory
Erase	May delete existing files or directories
File Scan	May list the contents of a directory
Modify	May rename and change file attributes
Write	May write data into an existing file

Table 20–2
NetWare rights.

the X.400 standard implementation for e-mail. FirstMail client software is provided with Novell NetWare 4.1 and above, which is used to access the X.400 messaging services. Add-on products such as GroupWise offer more sophisticated support for electronic messaging. GroupWise also provides document management, calendaring, scheduling, task management, workflow, and imaging.

Security
The security features of the NetWare operating system offer the system and/or network administrator the ability to monitor all aspects of the system operation from a single location. There are two types of security: file system security and NDS security.

File System Security   Table 20–2 shows the various types of rights that may be assigned to a NetWare user. Note that similar rights are available under Windows NT.

Rights are inherited and/or modified via filters or masks that designate permissible operations.

NDS Security   In addition to encryption of login passwords, NDS security provides auditing features that allow one user to monitor events caused by other users (changes to the file system, resource utilization).

Management
Management of any network involves many different activities to ensure quality control. Some of these items include

- Monitor network traffic to develop a baseline from which to make network-related decisions
- Unusual activity monitoring such as successive login failures, or file creation or file write errors
- Disk resource utilization issues
- Software and hardware installation and upgrades
- Backup scheduling

- Help desk support for problem resolution
- Short-range and long-range planning

Many other important items can be added to this list, depending on the organization. Some of these issues will be explored in the problems located at the end of this chapter.

Print Services

A core component of NetWare consists of the services available for managing and using printers. Print jobs are first sent to a printer queue, where they are temporarily stored until the assigned printer is available. Printers may be attached to workstations, print servers, or even directly connected to the network.

NetWare 5 expands print services to allow for notification of print job completion or status, enhanced communication between printers and clients (printer features are shared), and support for multiple operating systems. An online database of printer drivers is also provided to assist with new printer installations.

NetWare Client Software

In addition to one or more NetWare servers, there will be many NetWare clients on the network taking advantage of the services provided. Windows users can install NetWare client software and have access to the power of NetWare while still being part of a Windows network environment.

Figure 20–2 shows the new items found in the Network Neighborhood window after the NetWare client software has been installed. NetWare's folders exist side by side with Windows 98's icon for the Raycast machine.

Figure 20–3 shows the context-sensitive menu that appears after right-clicking on the NetWare icon (N) in the system tray. Note all the different

Figure 20–2
Network Neighborhood contents after NetWare installation.

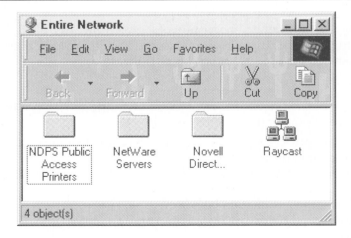

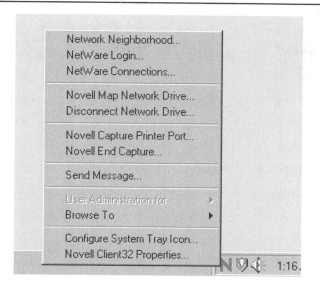

Figure 20–3
NetWare controls.

features accessible from the menu. Other NetWare properties can be examined and/or modified by selecting Novell NetWare Client properties in the Network window under Control Panel.

OpenVMS

The OpenVMS operating system was originally designed for VAX and Alpha computer systems manufactured by Digital Equipment Corporation (DEC, which was acquired by Compaq in 1997). The OpenVMS operating system is still a popular choice for many customers such as universities and businesses. Network services provided by OpenVMS include the ability to connect computers together to form clusters of computers that act as one computer. This allows for computers to be added and removed from the cluster without affecting the overall operation of the system.

The native network in a DEC environment is called DECnet. In a DECnet network, computers are assigned a node number and an area number. Node numbers can be in the range between 1 and 1023. Area numbers range between 1 and 63. A total of almost 65,000 nodes can participate in a DECnet network. A node can be of two types, a router or an end node. A router accepts and forwards messages from the end nodes and other routers to their destinations.

Most OpenVMS computer systems run the TCP/IP network protocols in addition to DECnet. Many different TCP/IP stacks are available for the OpenVMS operating system. Each provides the capability to connect OpenVMS to the

Internet. These packages generally include SMTP, FTP, and Telnet TCP/IP protocol application programs. Basic connectivity programs like PING, tracert, and nslookup are provided as well. A sample execution of nslookup on OpenVMS to review the MX type DNS records for sunybroome.edu and binghamton.edu looks like the following:

```
$ nslookup
Default Server:  ins1.milw.twtelecom.net
Address:  216.136.95.3

> set query=mx
> sunybroome.edu
Server:  ins1.milw.twtelecom.net
Address:  216.136.95.3

sunybroome.edu   preference = 30, mail exchanger = mail.iplt.twtelecom.net
sunybroome.edu   preference = 10, mail exchanger = sbccab.cc.sunybroome.edu
sunybroome.edu   preference = 20, mail exchanger = mail.milw.twtelecom.net
sunybroome.edu   nameserver = ins1.milw.twtelecom.net
sunybroome.edu   nameserver = ins1.iplt.twtelecom.net
mail.iplt.twtelecom.net inet address = 216.136.95.20
sbccab.cc.sunybroome.edu         inet address = 172.16.0.2
mail.milw.twtelecom.net inet address = 216.136.95.4
ins1.milw.twtelecom.net inet address = 216.136.95.3
ins1.iplt.twtelecom.net inet address = 216.136.95.19

> binghamton.edu
Server:  ins1.milw.twtelecom.net
Address:  216.136.95.3

binghamton.edu   preference = 0, mail exchanger = mail.binghamton.edu
binghamton.edu   nameserver = bingnet1.cc.binghamton.edu
binghamton.edu   nameserver = bingnet2.cc.binghamton.edu
mail.binghamton.edu      inet address = 128.226.1.18
bingnet1.cc.binghamton.edu        inet address = 128.226.1.11
bingnet2.cc.binghamton.edu        inet address = 128.226.1.18

> exit
```

In addition to the built-in TCP/IP applications like nslookup, both commercial and freeware Web servers are available for OpenVMS, allowing these computers to provide stable and reliable Web services. You may be surprised to find that many popular Web servers run the OpenVMS operating system.

MACINTOSH OS (MACOS)

The operating system for Apple Computers' Macintosh line of personal computers was first released in 1984. MacOS X (version 10) came out in 2000. Initially based on the Motorola 680x0 series microprocessors, MacOS has evolved to exploit the PowerPC CPU.

MacOS supports the use of multiple protocols, such as TCP/IP (through software called Open Transport) and Apple's own AppleTalk protocol, which enables Macintosh computers to share files and printers. AppleTalk running over Ethernet is called EtherTalk. A version of AppleTalk that operates over the serial port is called LocalTalk. Multiple Macintosh computers are daisy-chained through their serial ports when using LocalTalk.

Wireless networking is supported by MacOS and is handled by a device called the AirPort. The AirPort is based on the the IEEE 802.11 Direct Sequence Spread Spectrum standard and provides simultaneous connection for up to 10 users in a 150-foot radius from the AirPort. The maximum available bandwidth is 11 Mbps, with each channel having a 1 Mbps capacity.

The Web site http://www.threemacs.com provides an excellent networking tutorial for the Macintosh.

OS/2 WARP

IBM came out with the OS/2 operating system about the same time that early versions of Windows were available. The latest version of OS/2 is called OS/2 Warp and provides for a stable 32-bit multitasking operation on Intel-based computers. OS/2 Warp contains a built-in TCP/IP stack and Microsoft LAN Manager capability. OS/2 Warp provides the ability to communicate with several other network operating systems including

- Microsoft Windows
- Banyan Vines
- IBM LAN Server
- OS/2 Warp Server
- DECnet

OS/2 provides a stable scalable platform on which any business network can be built.

ADDITIONAL NETWORK OPERATING SYSTEMS

Table 20–3 lists several additional network operating systems and architectures. You are encouraged to discover more features through your own research.

Table 20–3
Features of some
additional network
operating systems
and architectures.

Operating System	Manufacturer	Features
BeOS	Be	• Enhanced for multimedia applications • Multiple file systems supported • Journaling to prevent loss of data
LANtastic	Artisoft	• Runs on most Windows platforms, OS/2, and DOS • Logs network resource accesses
SNA	IBM	• Systems Network Architecture • Enables different devices (mainframe, terminal, printer) to communicate with each other • Advanced Peer-to-Peer Networking (APPN) • Advanced Program-to-Program Computing (APPC)
Solaris	Sun Microsystems	• Unix-based environment • Runs on Sun systems and x86 machines
VINES	Banyan Systems	• Virtual Network System, based on Unix • Uses a global naming system called StreetTalk. Example: joetekk@helpdesk@rwasoftware • Communicates with SNA, TCP/IP, and AppleTalk networks
XNS	Xerox	• Xerox Network Services • Five-layer protocol

  ## TROUBLESHOOTING TECHNIQUES

Selecting a network operating system is based on many factors, including the features provided and the complexity of the installation and management procedures. Is the operating system centralized or distributed? Will the network be strictly TCP/IP or should multiple protocols be supported? What file system properties are desired?

Whatever the answers are, the end result is an operating system that will require specific troubleshooting methods to diagnose and repair problems.

SELF-TEST

This self-test is designed to help you check your understanding of the background information presented in this chapter.

True/False
Answer *true* or *false*.

1. NetWare is a distributed operating system.

2. NDS allows users global access to resources.

3. The source code for NetWare is provided on the installation CD-ROM.

4. NetWare runs on top of DOS.

5. DECnet is a suite of protocols for the VMS operating system.

6. The MacOs supports wireless networking.

Multiple Choice

Select the best answer.

7. Two ways to upgrade a NetWare server are in-place migration and
   a. Out-of-place migration.
   b. Across-the-wire migration.
   c. Parallel migration.

8. NetWare login passwords are
   a. Stored as plain text.
   b. Stored as encrypted text.
   c. Not stored.

9. Using a single login, each NetWare user
   a. Gains access to container files only.
   b. Gains access to all network resources.
   c. Gains access to local files only.

10. NetWare print services support
    a. Multiple operating systems.
    b. Notification of job completion.
    c. Both a and b.

11. Sharing files and printers with the MacOs is done using
    a. AppleTalk.
    b. ShareTalk.
    c. EtherTalk.

12. OS/2 Warp provides
    a. File and printer sharing.
    b. Internet connectivity.
    c. Both a and b.

Completion

Fill in the blank or blanks with the best answers.

13. Two types of security are file system security and _____ security.

14. NetWare can be upgraded using in-place _____.

15. The main protocol used for NetWare operations is _____.

16. RAID stands for _____ _____ _____ _____.

17. NetWare uses several types of _____ servers to synchronize network events.

18. VMS allows computers to be connected together using _____.

19. The _____ operating systerm can communicate with several other network operating systems.

QUESTIONS/ACTIVITIES

1. Find a local business that uses NetWare. How many users are supported? Why did they choose NetWare? What version are they running?

2. Can you purchase NetWare in your local computer software store?

3. What kinds of support does IBM offer for OS/2 Warp?

4. Research some basic details of AppleTalk.

REVIEW QUIZ

Under the supervision of your instructor

1. Compare the features of NetWare with Windows NT.

2. Discuss the file organization, protocols, and security available in NetWare.

3. Briefly describe the VMS and MacOs operating systems.

Networking Concepts Laboratory

Experiment #20
Other Network Operating Systems

Objectives

1. To examine the features of other network operating systems.
2. To explore the strengths and weaknesses of the network operating systems.

Required Equipment

The following equipment is required for this experiment:

- A networked computer with access to the Internet

Procedure

Perform each of the following steps. Record your observations, results, and any difficulties you encounter. You will use this information when you develop your conclusions about the experiment.

For this laboratory experiment, choose a non-Windows operating system from the list below and perform some research to determine the particular operating system's strengths and weaknesses. You may choose from any of the following operating systems:

- Netware
- BeOS
- OpenVMS
- Mac/Apple OS
- IBM MVS
- Any other operating system not listed

You can go to the following Web site to obtain information about the operating system that you chose from the list, or you may choose from the many other operating systems listed on this Web page:

http://directory.google.com/Top/Computers/Software/Operating_Systems

Or search the Web for your own list of operating systems.

For the operating system that you chose, try to answer all of the following questions:

1. What operating system did you choose?
2. What company is the producer of the operating system?
3. How much does the operating system cost?

4. What are the particular strengths?
5. What are the weaknesses?
6 What type of interface is available? Is it a GUI, text-based, or both?
7. What type of processor hardware does it run on?
8. What is the minimum amount of memory required?
9. What is the minimum hard disk storage required?
10. How many Web sites contain information about the operating system? Provide the number of hits and the search engine used.

Discussion and Conclusion

Using a word processor, write your own detailed explanations of the results and observations made during the experiment. To begin, try to say something about each procedure step.
   In addition, provide answers to the following questions:

1. How many different operating systems are you now aware of?
2. What features are common to most operating systems?
3. Where can support be obtained for most operating systems?

ARP. Address Resolution Protocol. A protocol used to discover the MAC address of a station based on its IP address.

ASCII. American Standard Code for Information Interchange. A 7-bit code representing all alphanumeric and special codes required for text-based communication.

Autonomous System. A single network or group of networks that is controlled by a single administrative authority.

Backbone Cable. Main cable used to distribute network signals.

Baseband System. A communication system in which a single carrier is used to exchange information. Ethernet is a baseband system.

BGP. Border Gateway Protocol. An RFC-based exterior gateway protocol.

Broadband System. A communication system in which multiple carrier signals are used to exchange information. Cable television is an example of a broadband system.

Broadcast Storm. An out-of-control flooding of the network with packets.

Broadcasting. Transmitting a frame that is meant to be received by all stations on a network, not one specific station.

Browser. An application capable of displaying Web pages in WYSIWYG format.

Bus Network. A network where all stations share the same media.

Cable Modem. A high-speed modem that provides the interface between television cable and a NIC.

Carrier Extension. Technique used in Gigabit Ethernet to extend the minimum length of an Ethernet frame.

CD-Quality Sound. CD-quality sound provides 44,100 samples per second. Each sample represents two channels (left and right) at 16-bits each.

CIDR. Classless Inter-Domain Routing. A routing protocol that extends IP addressing by using a variable length network mask.

CGI. Common Gateway Interface. A method for exchanging data between clients and servers over the World Wide Web.

Client. A network station that requests services from a network server.

Cloud. A graphic symbol used to describe a network without specifying the details of the internal connections.

Collision. Two or more stations transmitting at the same time within the same collision domain.

Collision Domain. A portion of a network where two or more stations transmitting at the same time will interfere with each other.

Combo Card. A NIC that contains both 10base2 and 10baseT connections.

Congestion. Too much traffic on a network, causing packets to be lost.

Convergence. The amount of time required for changes in a network topology to be propagated to all routers.

CRC. Cyclic redundancy check. An error detection scheme able to detect bit errors in streams of bits of varying length.

CSMA/CD. Carrier Sense Multiple Access with Collision Detection. An IEEE 802.3 standard access method used to share bandwidth among a maximum of 1024 stations. Two or more stations transmitting at a time will cause a collision, forcing random waiting periods before retransmission is attempted.

CSMA/CA. Carrier Sense Multiple Access with Collision Avoidance. An IEEE 802.11 standard access method for wireless Ethernet.

Cut-Through Switching. A switching technique in which retransmission of a received packet begins as soon as the destination MAC address is received. Faster than store-and-forward switching.

Datagram. A routable packet of data used in connectionless communication.

DHCP. Dynamic Host Configuration Protocol. A protocol used to allocate IP addresses dynamically.

Diameter. The total distance allowed in a collision domain.

Dijkstra's Algorithm. An algorithm developed by Edsger Dijkstra which is used to compute the shortest paths in a graph. It or a variation is used by most link-state routing algorithms.

Distance-Vector Routing. A routing algorithm used to compute the optimal route to a destination. Each router sends its complete routing table to each of its neighbors during each 30-second update period.

DNS. Domain Name System. Protocol used to resolve a domain name, such as www.rwasoftware.com, into an IP address.

Domain. A collection of networked computers managed by a central server.

Domain-Based Priority Access. The access method used by 100VG-AnyLAN to poll stations in a round-robin fashion.

Dotted Decimal Notation. This is another way to refer to an IP address.

EGP. Exterior Gateway Protocol. A routing protocol used between autonomous systems.

E-Mail. Electronic Mail. Method used to exchange mail (including attachments) over a network.

Encoding. A method of converting digital data into a different representation for transmission. Methods include Manchester, 8B6T, 4B5B, NRZI, PAM5x5, and 8B10B.

Ethernet. LAN technology employing CSMA/CD to share access to the available bandwidth.

Fast Ethernet. This is the term used for 100-Mbps Ethernet.

Fast Link Pulse. Beginning with Fast Ethernet, fast link pulses are used to perform autonegotiation on a hardware link (such as a UTP cable).

FCS. Frame check sequence. A 32-bit CRC value used to check the validity of a received frame.

FDDI. Fiber-distributed data interface. A fiber optic, 100-Mbps ring technology with a range of 200 kilometers (124 miles).

Firewall. A program designed to control/limit the traffic into and out-of a LAN.

Flooding Protocol. The method used by many link-state routers to propagate information between routers.

FOIRL. Fiber optic inter-repeater link. The original specification for Ethernet communication over fiber.

Frame. Structure used to transport data over a network. Contains source and destination addresses, data, and a 32-bit frame check sequence.

Frame Bursting. Technique used in Gigabit Ethernet to send multiple frames in a small window of time.

FTP. File Transfer Protocol. A protocol designed to enable reliable transfer of files between stations.

Fully Connected Network. This network contains a link from each station to every other station.

GIF. Graphics Interchange Format. A lossless image compression format allowing 256 colors.

Gigabit Ethernet. This is the term used for 1000-Mbps Ethernet.

Hierarchy. The number of levels in a network. Switches and routers add hierarchy to a network, hubs and repeaters do not.

HTML. Hypertext markup language. A specific set of tags and syntax rules for describing a Web page in WYSIWYG format.

HTTP. Hypertext Transport Protocol. The protocol used to exchange hypermedia (text, audio, video, images) over the Internet.

Hub. A multiport device that broadcasts frames received on one port to all other ports. All ports are in the same collision domain.

ICMP. Internet Control Message Protocol. A protocol used to report errors over the Internet.

IGP. Interior Gateway Protocol. A routing protocol used within an autonomous system.

IMAP. Internet Message Access Protocol. Another method for retrieving e-mail from a server.

Interframe Gap. A deliberate gap of 96 bit times between successive Ethernet frames.

Internet. A global collection of computer networks that allows any station to communicate with any other station.

IP. Internet Protocol. This is the base protocol for TCP/IP. It is used to carry TCP, UDP, and many other higher-level protocols.

IP Address. A 32-bit logical address of a station (host) on the network. An example IP address is 192.168.1.105.

IPSec. IP Security. A set of protocols used to establish security in a TCP/IP environment.

ISP. Internet service provider. A facility/organization that enables multiple users to connect to the Internet.

Jabber. An out-of-control station transmitting garbage.

Jam Sequence. A 32-bit sequence generated when a collision is detected, to guarantee all stations are notified of the collision.

JPEG. Joint Photographic Experts Group. A lossy image compression format allowing 24-bit color.

Kerberos. An authentication service that uses secret-key ciphers.

LAN. Local area network. A collection of computers in a small geographical area.

Latency. The delay between reception and retransmission of a packet that is associated with switches and routers.

Layer 3 Switching. A special, high-speed switching/routing combination used on a LAN.

Link-State Routing. A routing algorithm used to compute the optimal route to a destination. Each router broadcasts information about the cost of reaching each of its neighbors to all routers in the network.

LLC. Logical Link Control. IEEE 802.2 standard for providing connectionless and connection-oriented sessions between two stations. LLC is the first sublayer in the Data-Link layer.

Logical Topology. Describes the way logical addresses are allocated on a physical network and the routes used to transport information.

MAC Address. Media access control address. A 48-bit physical address associated with every network interface. An example MAC address is 00-C0-F0-27-64-E2.

Manchester Encoding. Technique used to encode 0s and 1s so that a signal transition occurs during every bit time. A 0 is represented by a low-to-high transition and a 1 is represented by a high-to-low transition.

MAU. Multistation access unit. Device used to connect multiple stations to the same network.

Mbone. Multicasting Backbone. A method for performing multicasting over the Internet.

MIME. Multipurpose Internet Mail Extensions. Standard method for attaching many different types of media to an e-mail message.

MPEG. Moving Picture Experts Group. Standard encoding method for audio and video.

MP3. MPEG Audio Layer 3. Encoding method allowing high-quality, low-bit rate audio encoding.

MTU. Maximum transmission unit. The maximum size of a frame on the network.

Multicasting. A method in which a single server stream is duplicated by routers and switches to multiple clients.

NAP. Network Access Point. A connection to the main Internet backbone.

NetBEUI. NetBIOS Extended User Interface. Protocol used to transport NetBIOS messages.

NetBIOS. Network Basic Input Output System. Low-level networking operations that enable network activities such as file and printer sharing.

Network Realization. The point in time at which a router is aware of the complete network topology.

NIC. Network interface card. Electronic circuit used to connect a computer to the network.

Node. An individual device connected to a network.

OSPF. Open Shortest Path First. An RFC-based link-state routing algorithm used by Interior and Exterior Gateways.

Parity. A bit indicating that the number of 1s contained in a block of data is even or odd. Used for error detection.

Peering Agreement. An agreement between two Internet providers that allows them to exchange traffic.

PGP. Pretty Good Privacy. A cryptographic utility that provides security to e-mail and files.

Physical Topology. Describes the actual hardware connections that make up the network.

Policy-Based Routing. Any type of routing that is based on factors other than the minimum number of hops or the shortest path.

POP. Point of presence. The location of an actual Internet connection.

POP3. Post Office Protocol. Used to receive e-mail from a mail server.

Port. A 16-bit number associated with a TCP or UDP application. Used to demultiplex the incoming packet stream.

PPP. Point-to-Point Protocol. A more advanced protocol than SLIP for serial connections.

Protocol. The rules for exchanging information between two objects (network devices, application programs).

Protocol Stack. A suite of protocols, such as TCP/IP.

RAID. Redundant Array of Inexpensive Disks. A technique for using multiple hard drives to implement fast, reliable data transfers.

RARP. Reverse Address Resolution Protocol. A protocol used to determine the IP address of a station based on its MAC address.

RAS. Remote Access Server. Dial-up server function provided by Windows NT/2000.

RFC. Request for Comments. Official standards for the Internet.

Ring Network. A network in which all stations are connected in a circular ring (each station has exactly two connections).

RIP. Routing Information Protocol. An RFC-based routing protocol based on a distance vector algorithm.

Route Aggregation. The method used by CIDR to extend the IP addressing scheme. Several routes are arranged in such a way that a single route is advertised by a router.

Router. A multiport device that forwards packets between ports based on their IP address. Each port connects to a different LAN, and possibly even different LAN technologies.

Routing Table. A table stored in the memory of a router that indicates the best route to use to forward a packet of data to the destination.

Runt. A frame that is smaller than the minimum frame size.

Segment. A portion of a network that may or may not contain nodes. Ethernet allows up to five segments to be connected in series.

Server. A network station that provides services to clients.

SLIP. Serial Line Interface Protocol. A protocol for exchanging TCP/IP over a serial connection such as a telephone modem.

Slot Time. The time required to transmit 512 bits of data.

SMB. Server Message Block. Main portion of a NetBIOS message.

SMTP. Simple Mail Transport Protocol. Method used to reliably exchange electronic mail between networks.

SNMP. Simple Network Management Protocol. A protocol used to manage network components.

Socket. A networking port connection asociated with a TCP/IP application.

Spanning Tree. An algorithm used to create non-looping paths between bridges, switches, and routers on a network.

Star Network. A network in which all stations connect to one or more central hubs.

Store-and-Forward Switching. A switching technique in which the entire frame is received and stored before it is retransmitted. Slower than cut-through switching.

Subnet. A small portion of a larger network.

Supernetting. A route made available through the use of CIDR.

Switch. A multiport device that forwards frames to a specific port based on their destination MAC address. Each port is in its own collision domain.

Tap. Used to make a connection with coaxial cable. The tap may be a BNC T-connector or a vampire tap.

TCP. Transmission Control Protocol. Connection (session or stream)-oriented communication. Reliable exchange of data.

TCP/IP. Suite of protocols that enable communication over LANs and WANs.

Telnet. A protocol used to emulate a network virtual terminal.

Thickwire. RG-11 coaxial cable used in 10base5 networks.

Thinwire. RG-58 coaxial cable used in 10base2 networks.

Token Ring. An IEEE 802.5 standard LAN technology in which information circulates in a closed ring of stations.

Topology. The manner in which network components are connected.

Transceiver. A device capable of transmitting and receiving data.

Tunnel. A logical connection between two nodes in a virtual private network.

UDP. User Datagram Protocol. Connectionless communication; unreliable exchange of data.

URL. Uniform resource locator. A path to a specific station on the Internet, such as

http://www.rwasoftware.com.

UTP. Unshielded twisted pair. Cable used in 10baseT Ethernet, as well as Fast and Gigabit Ethernet.

Virtual Circuit. A prearranged path through a network that is used for a single session.

VPN. Virtual private network. A network that uses public networking facilities to carry private data. The data is encrypted before transmission.

WAN. Wide area network. A collection of LANs connected via routers over a large geographical area.

WAV. Wave file. Windows standard audio encoding file format.

Windows Socket. Networking API for the Windows operating system.

Wireless Network. An IEEE 802.11 standard network using high-frequency radio signals or infrared lasers instead of wires. Typically, multiple mobile stations communicate with a single base station.

WWW. World Wide Web. A logical collection of computers on the Internet supported by HTTP.

WYSIWYG. What You See Is What You Get.

Internet
Milestones

1969
ARPAnet formed.
First RFC submitted.

1970
UNIX developed at Bell Labs.

1972
First e-mail program created.

1973
First Ethernet system up and running.

1975
Microsoft is formed.

1981
BITNET created.
IBM PC introduced.

1982
U.S. Department of Defense declares TCP/IP as its communication standard.

1983
TCP/IP enables global Internet.
10base5 standard ratified by the IEEE.

1984
More than 1000 computers connected.

1986
NSFNET created.

1987
1000th RFC (Request for Comments) submitted.
More than 10,000 computers connected.

1988
Internet worm virus affects 6000 computers.
CERT formed.

1989
More than 100,000 computers connected.

1990
ARPAnet shuts down.
10baseT standard ratified by the IEEE.

1991
WWW developed at CERN.

1992
More than 1,000,000 computers connected.

1993
InterNIC started by NSF.
10baseFP standard ratified by the IEEE.

1995
Sun Microsystems introduces Java.
IPv6 specification released.
100baseT Fast Ethernet standard is ratified by the IEEE.

1997
2000th RFC submitted.
More than 16,000,000 computers connected.

1998
Gigabit Ethernet standards approved by IEEE.

1999
The Melissa virus is released.

2000
Yahoo, eBay, and Amazon.com hit by denial-of-service attacks.

Web Resources

www.internet2.edu

www.patents.ibm.com

www.100vg.com

www.gigabit-ethernet.org

www.10gea.org

www.protocols.com

www.whatis.com

www.grc.com

www.ietf.org/rfc.html

www.music-ic.com

www.mplsrc.com

www.ietf.org/ids.by.wg/mpls.html

www.3com.com/technology/tech_net/white_papers/500660.html

www.internettrafficreport.com

www.caida.org

web.mit.edu/network/pgp.html

www.zonelabs.com

www.cert.org

www.ipswitch.com

www.cs.columbia.edu/~hgs/internet/mbone-faq.html

cg.cs.tu-berlin.de/~ki/engines.html

www.intel.com

www.microsoft.com

www.internic.net

www.apache.org

www.rwasoftware.com

www.sunybroome.edu/jla-bin/view.pl

www.sunybroome.edu/~antonakos_j/ipclass.htm

www.sunybroome.edu/~antonakos_j/ipclass2.htm

C

ASCII Character Set

DECIMAL VALUE → / HEXADECIMAL VALUE ↓		0	16	32	48	64	80	96	112	128	144	160	176	192	208	224	240
		0	1	2	3	4	5	6	7	8	9	A	B	C	D	E	F
0	0	BLANK (NULL)	►	BLANK (SPACE)	0	@	P	`	p	Ḉ	É	á				∝	≡
1	1	☺	◄	!	1	A	Q	a	q	ü	Æ	í				β	±
2	2	●	↕	"	2	B	R	b	r	é	FE	ó				γ	≥
3	3	♥	‼	#	3	C	S	c	s	â	ô	ú				π	≤
4	4	♦	¶	$	4	D	T	d	t	ä	ö	ñ				Σ	∫
5	5	♣	§	%	5	E	U	e	u	à	ò	Ñ				σ	∫
6	6	♠	▬	&	6	F	V	f	v	å	û	ª				μ	÷
7	7	•	↨	'	7	G	W	g	w	ç	ù	º				τ	≈
8	8	◘	↑	(	8	H	X	h	x	ê	ÿ	¿				Φ	°
9	9	○	↓	)	9	I	Y	i	y	ë	Ö	⌐				Θ	•
10	A	◎	→	*	:	J	Z	j	z	è	Ü	¬				Ω	·
11	B	♂	←	+	;	K	[	k	{	ï	¢	½				δ	√
12	C	♀	∟	,	<	L	\	l	|	î	£	¼				∞	η
13	D	♪	↔	–	=	M	]	m	}	ì	¥	¡				Ø	2
14	E	♫	▲	.	>	N	^	n	~	Ä	Pts	«				∈	■
15	F	☼	▼	/	?	O	_	o	△	Å	ƒ	»				∩	BLANK 'FF'

D

RFC Index

 RFCs

The Internet Engineering Task Force is located at www.ietf.org. It contains information about many different aspects of the Internet. One of the most important items stored there are the Request for Comments documents, or RFCs. These documents describe how each of the protocols contained in TCP/IP are implemented. Refer to Table D.1 for a list

Protocol	RFC	Name
Telnet	854	Remote Terminal Protocol
FTP	959	File Transfer Protocol
SMTP	821	Simple Mail Transfer Protocol
SNMP	1098	Simple Network Management Protocol
DNS	1034	Domain Name System
TCP	793	Transport Control Protocol
UDP	768	User Datagram Protocol
ARP	826	Address Resolution Protocol
RARP	903	Reverse Address Resolution Protocol
ICMP	792	Internet Control Message Protocol
BOOTP	951	Bootstrap Protocol
IP	791	Internet Protocol

Table D–1
Several important
TCP/IP RFCs.

489

of RFCs associated with some of the most popular TCP/IP protocols. You are encouraged to visit the IETF to become familiar with all the information and services offered, such as the RFCs.

A detailed listing of RFCs is shown in Listing D.1.

Listing D–1
Request for comments documents.

```
0001: Host Software
0002: Host software
0004: Network timetable
0005: Decode Encode Language (DEL)
0006: Conversation with Bob Kahn
0007: Host-IMP interface
0008: Functional specifications for the ARPA Network
0009: Host software
0012: IMP-Host interface flow diagrams
0013: Zero Text Length EOF Message
0015: Network subsystem for time sharing hosts
0017: Some questions re: Host-IMP Protocol
0018: IMP-IMP and HOST-HOST Control Links
0019: Two protocol suggestions to reduce congestion at swap
      bound nodes
0020: ASCII format for network interchange
0021: Network meeting
0022: Host-host control message formats
0023: Transmission of Multiple Control Messages
0024: Documentation Conventions
0025: No High Link Numbers
0027: Documentation Conventions
0028: Time Standards
0029: Response to 28
0030: Documentation Conventions
0031: Binary Message Forms in Computer
0032: Connecting M.I.T
0033: New Host-Host Protocol
0034: Some Brief Preliminary Notes on the Augmentation Research
      Center Clock
0035: Network Meeting
0036: Protocol Notes
0037: Network Meeting Epilogue, etc.
0038: Comments on Network Protocol from NWG/#36
0039: Comments on Protocol Re: NWG/#36
0040: More Comments on the Forthcoming Protocol
0041: IMP-IMP Teletype Communication
0042: Message Data Types
0043: Proposed Meeting
0044: Comments on NWG/33 and 36
0045: New Protocol Is Coming
0046: ARPA Network protocol notes
0047: BBN's Comments on NWG/#33
```

0100: Categorization and guide to NWG/RFCs
0101: Notes on the Network Working Group meeting, Urbana,
      Illinois, February 17, 1971
0102: Output of the Host-Host Protocol glitch cleaning
      committee
0103: Implementation of Interrupt Keys
0104: Link 191
0105: Network Specifications for Remote Job Entry and Remote
      Job Output Retrieval at UCSB
0106: User/Server Site Protocol Network Host Questionnaire
0107: Output of the Host-Host Protocol Glitch Cleaning
      Committee
0108: Attendance list at the Urbana NWG meeting, February 17-
      19, 1971
0109: Level III Server Protocol for the Lincoln Laboratory NIC
      360/67 Host
0110: Conventions for using an IBM 2741 terminal as a user
      console for access to network server hosts
0111: Pressure from the Chairman
0112: User/Server Site Protocol: Network host questionnaire
      responses
0113: Network activity report: UCSB Rand
0114: File Transfer Protocol
0115: Some Network Information Center policies on handling
      documents
0116: Structure of the May NWG Meeting
0117: Some comments on the official protocol
0118: Recommendations for facility documentation
0119: Network Fortran subprograms
0120: Network PL1 subprograms
0121: Network on-line operators
0122: Network specifications for UCSB's Simple-Minded File
      System
0124: Typographical error in 107
0125: Response to 86: Proposal for Network Standard Format for
      a Graphics Data Stream
0126: Graphics Facilities at Ames Research Center
0128: Bytes
0129: Request for comments on socket name structure
0130: Response to 111: Pressure from the Chairman
0131: Response to 116: May NWG meeting
0133: File Transfer and Recovery
0134: Network Graphics meeting
0135: Response to NWG/110
0136: Host accounting and administrative procedures
0137: Telnet Protocol: A proposed document
0138: Status report on proposed Data Reconfiguration Service
0139: Discussion of Telnet Protocol
0140: Agenda for the May NWG meeting
0141: Comments on 114: A File Transfer Protocol
0142: Time-Out Mechanism in the Host-Host Protocol

```
0203: Achieving reliable communication
0204: Sockets in use
0205: NETCRT: A character display protocol
0206: User Telnet: Description of an initial implementation
0208: Address tables
0209: Host/IMP interface documentation
0210: Improvement of Flow Control
0212: NWG meeting on network usage
0213: IMP System change notification
0214: Network checkpoint
0215: NCP, ICP, and Telnet: The Terminal IMP implementation
0216: Telnet access to UCSB's On-Line System
0217: Specifications changes for OLS, RJE/RJOR, and SMFS
0218: Changing the IMP status reporting facility
0219: User's view of the datacomputer
0222: Subject: System programmer's workshop
0223: Network Information Center schedule for network users
0224: Comments on Mailbox Protocol
0225: Rand/UCSB network graphics experiment
0227: Data transfer rates (Rand/UCLA)
0228: Clarification
0230: Toward reliable operation of minicomputer-based terminals
      on a TIP
0231: Service center standards for remote usage: A user's view
0232: Postponement of network graphics meeting
0233: Standardization of host call letters
0234: Network Working Group meeting schedule
0236: Standard host names
0238: Comments on DTP and FTP proposals
0239: Host mnemonics proposed in 226 (NIC 7625)
0241: Connecting computers to MLC ports
0242: Data Descriptive Language for Shared Data
0245: Reservations for Network Group meeting
0246: Network Graphics meeting
0247: Proffered set of standard host names
0249: Coordination of equipment and supplies purchase
0250: Some thoughts on file transfer
0251: Weather data
0253: Second Network Graphics meeting details
0254: Scenarios for using ARPANET computers
0256: IMPSYS change notification
0263: "Very Distant" Host interface
0268: Graphics facilities information
0269: Some Experience with File Transfer
0270: Correction to BBN Report No
0271: IMP System change notifications
0273: More on standard host names
0274: Establishing a local guide for network usage
0276: NIC course
0278: Revision of the Mail Box Protocol
0280: A Draft of Host Names
```

0471: Workshop on multi-site executive programs
0472: Illinois' reply to Maxwell's request for graphics
      information (NIC 14925)
0473: MIX and MIXAL?
0474: Announcement of NGWG meeting: Call for papers
0475: FTP and network mail system
0476: IMP/TIP memory retrofit schedule (rev 2)
0477: Remote Job Service at UCSB
0478: FTP server-server interaction: II
0479: Use of FTP by the NIC Journal
0480: Host-dependent FTP parameters
0482: Traffic statistics (February 1973)
0483: Cancellation of the resource notebook framework meeting
0485: MIX and MIXAL at UCSB
0486: Data transfer revisited
0487: Free file transfer
0488: NLS classes at network sites
0489: Comment on resynchronization of connection status
      proposal
0490: Surrogate RJS for UCLA-CCN
0491: What Is "Free"?
0492: Response to 467
0493: Graphics Protocol
0494: Availability of MIX and MIXAL in the Network
0495: Telnet Protocol specifications
0496: TNLS quick reference card is available
0497: Traffic statistics (March 1973)
0498: On mail service to CCN
0499: Harvard's network RJE
0500: Integration of data management systems on a computer
      network
0501: Un-muddling "free file transfer"
0504: Distributed resources workshop announcement
0505: Two solutions to a file transfer access problem
0506: FTP command naming problem
0508: Real-time data transmission on the ARPANET
0509: Traffic statistics (April 1973)
0510: Request for network mailbox addresses
0511: Enterprise phone service to NIC from ARPANET sites
0512: More on lost message detection
0513: Comments on the new Telnet specifications
0514: Network make-work
0515: Specifications for datalanguage: Version 0/9
0516: Lost message detection
0518: ARPANET accounts
0519: Resource evaluation
0520: Memo to FTP group: Proposal for File Access Protocol
0521: Restricted use of IMP DDT
0522: Traffic statistics (May 1973)
0523: SURVEY is in operation again
0524: Proposed Mail Protocol

0822: Standard for the format of ARPA Internet text messages
0823: DARPA Internet gateway
0824: CRONUS Virtual Local Network
0826: Ethernet Address Resolution Protocol: Or converting network protocol addresses to 48.bit Ethernet address for transmission on Ethernet hardware
0827: Exterior Gateway Protocol (EGP)
0828: Data communications: IFIP's international "network" of experts
0829: Packet satellite technology reference sources
0830: Distributed system for Internet name service
0831: Backup access to the European side of SATNET
0841: Specification for message format for Computer Based Message Systems
0844: Who talks ICMP, too?: Survey of 18 February 1983
0847: Summary of Smallberg surveys
0848: Who provides the "little" TCP services?
0849: Suggestions for improved host table distribution
0852: ARPANET short blocking feature
0853: Not Issued
0854: Telnet Protocol Specification
0855: Telnet Option Specifications
0856: Telnet Binary Transmission
0857: Telnet Echo Option
0858: Telnet Suppress Go Ahead Option
0859: Telnet Status Option
0860: Telnet Timing Mark Option
0861: Telnet Extended Options: List Option
0862: Echo Protocol
0863: Discard Protocol
0864: Character Generator Protocol
0865: Quote of the Day Protocol
0866: Active users
0867: Daytime Protocol
0868: Time Protocol
0869: Host Monitoring Protocol
0871: Perspective on the ARPANET reference model
0872: TCP-on-a-LAN
0873: Illusion of vendor support
0874: Critique of X.25
0875: Gateways, architectures, and heffalumps
0876: Survey of SMTP implementations
0878: ARPANET 1822L Host Access Protocol
0879: TCP maximum segment size and related topics
0881: Domain names plan and schedule
0885: Telnet end of record option
0886: Proposed standard for message header munging
0887: Resource Location Protocol
0888: "STUB" Exterior Gateway Protocol
0889: Internet delay experiments
0890: Exterior Gateway Protocol implementation schedule

```
0947: Multi-network broadcasting within the Internet
0949: FTP unique-named store command
0950: Internet Standard Subnetting Procedure
0951: Bootstrap Protocol
0952: DoD Internet host table specification
0953: Hostname Server
0954: NICNAME/WHOIS
0955: Towards a transport service for transaction processing
      applications
0956: Algorithms for synchronizing network clocks
0957: Experiments in network clock synchronization
0959: File Transfer Protocol
0962: TCP-4 prime
0963: Some problems with the specification of the Military
      Standard Internet Protocol
0964: Some problems with the specification of the Military
      Standard Transmission Control Protocol
0965: Format for a graphical communication protocol
0967: All victims together
0968: Twas the night before start-up
0970: On packet switches with infinite storage
0971: Survey of data representation standards
0972: Password Generator Protocol
0974: Mail routing and the domain system
0975: Autonomous confederations
0976: UUCP mail interchange format standard
0977: Network News Transfer Protocol
0978: Voice File Interchange Protocol (VFIP)
0979: PSN End-to-End functional specification
0980: Protocol document order information
0981: Experimental multiple-path routing algorithm
0982: Guidelines for the specification of the structure of the
      Domain Specific Part (DSP) of the ISO standard NSAP
      address
0992: On communication support for fault tolerant process
      groups
0994: Final text of DIS 8473, Protocol for Providing the
      Connectionless-mode Network Service
0995: End System to Intermediate System Routing Exchange
      Protocol for use in conjunction with ISO 8473
0996: Statistics server
0998: NETBLT: A bulk data transfer protocol
1000: Request for Comments reference guide
1001: Protocol standard for a NetBIOS service on a TCP/UDP
      transport: Concepts and methods
1002: Protocol standard for a NetBIOS service on a TCP/UDP
      transport: Detailed specifications
1003: Issues in defining an equations representation standard
1004: Distributed-protocol authentication scheme
1005: ARPANET AHIP-E Host Access Protocol (enhanced AHIP)
1006: ISO transport services on top of the TCP: Version 3
```

```
1058: Routing Information Protocol
1061: Not Issued
1068: Background File Transfer Program (BFTP)
1069: Guidelines for the use of Internet-IP addresses in the
      ISO Connectionless-Mode Network Protocol
1070: Use of the Internet as a subnetwork for experimentation
      with the OSI network layer
1071: Computing the Internet checksum
1073: Telnet window size option
1074: NSFNET backbone SPF based Interior Gateway Protocol
1075: Distance Vector Multicast Routing Protocol
1076: HEMS monitoring and control language
1077: Critical issues in high bandwidth networking
1078: TCP port service Multiplexer (TCPMUX)
1079: Telnet terminal speed option
1082: Post Office Protocol: Version 3: Extended service
      offerings
1085: ISO presentation services on top of TCP/IP based
      internets
1086: ISO-TP0 bridge between TCP and X.25
1087: Ethics and the Internet
1088: Standard for the transmission of IP datagrams over
      NetBIOS networks
1089: SNMP over Ethernet
1090: SMTP on X.25
1091: Telnet terminal-type option
1092: EGP and policy based routing in the new NSFNET backbone
1093: NSFNET routing architecture
1094: NFS: Network File System Protocol specification
1096: Telnet X display location option
1097: Telnet subliminal-message option
1098: SNMP
1099: Request for Comments Summary: Numbers 1000-1099
1101: DNS encoding of network names and other types
1102: Policy routing in Internet protocols
1104: Models of policy based routing
1106: TCP big window and NAK options
1107: Plan for Internet directory services
1108: U.S. Department of Defense Security Options for IP
1109: Report of the second Ad Hoc Network Management Review
      Group
1110: Problem with the TCP big window option
1112: Host extensions for IP multicasting
1118: Hitchhikers guide to the Internet
1121: Act one: The poems
1122: Requirements for Internet hosts: Communication layers
1123: Requirements for Internet hosts: Application and support
1124: Policy issues in interconnecting networks
1125: Policy requirements for inter Administrative Domain
      routing
```

1181: RIPE Terms of Reference
1182: Not Issued
1183: New DNS RR Definitions
1184: Telnet Linemode Option
1186: MD4 Message Digest Algorithm
1187: Bulk Table Retrieval with the SNMP
1188: Proposed Standard for the Transmission of IP Datagrams
      over FDDI Networks
1189: Common Management Information Services and Protocols for
      the Internet (CMOT and CMIP)
1191: Path MTU discovery
1192: Commercialization of the Internet summary report
1193: Client requirements for real-time communication services
1195: Use of OSI IS-IS for routing in TCP/IP and dual
      environments
1197: Using ODA for translating multimedia information
1198: FYI on the X window system
1199: Request for Comments Summary Notes: 1100-1199
1201: Transmitting IP traffic over ARCNET networks
1202: Directory Assistance service
1203: Interactive Mail Access Protocol: Version 3
1204: Message Posting Protocol (MPP)
1205: 5250 Telnet interface
1207: FYI on Questions and Answers: Answers to commonly asked
      "experienced Internet user" questions
1208: Glossary of networking terms
1209: Transmission of IP datagrams over the SMDS Service
1210: Network and infrastructure user requirements for
      transatlantic research collaboration: Brussels, July 16-
      18, and Washington, July 24-25, 1990
1211: Problems with the maintenance of large mailing lists
1212: Concise MIB definitions
1213: Management Information Base for Network Management of
      TCP/IP-based internets: MIB-II
1214: OSI internet management: Management Information Base
1215: Convention for defining traps for use with the SNMP
1216: Gigabit network economics and paradigm shifts
1217: Memo from the Consortium for Slow Commotion Research
      (CSCR)
1219: On the assignment of subnet numbers
1221: Host Access Protocol (HAP) specification: Version 2
1222: Advancing the NSFNET routing architecture
1223: OSI CLNS and LLC1 protocols on Network Systems
      HYPERchannel
1224: Techniques for managing asynchronously generated alerts
1226: Internet protocol encapsulation of AX.25 frames
1227: SNMP MUX protocol and MIB
1230: IEEE 802.4 Token Bus MIB
1234: Tunneling IPX traffic through IP networks
1235: Coherent File Distribution Protocol
1236: IP to X.121 address mapping for DDN

1638: PPP Bridging Control Protocol (BCP)
1639: FTP Operation Over Big Address Records (FOOBAR)
1640: The Process for Organization of Internet Standards
       Working Group (POISED)
1641: Using Unicode with MIME
1643: Definitions of Managed Objects for the Ethernet-like
       Interface Types
1644: T/TCP--TCP Extensions for Transactions Functional
       Specification
1646: TN3270 Extensions for LUname and Printer Selection
1648: Postmaster Convention for X.400 Operations
1649: Operational Requirements for X.400 Management Domains in
       the GO-MHS Community
1652: SMTP Service Extension for 8bit-MIMEtransport
1657: Definitions of Managed Objects for the Fourth Version of
       the Border Gateway Protocol (BGP-4) using SMIv2
1658: Definitions of Managed Objects for Character Stream
       Devices using SMIv2
1659: Definitions of Managed Objects for RS-232-like Hardware
       Devices using SMIv2
1660: Definitions of Managed Objects for Parallel-printer-like
       Hardware Devices using SMIv2
1661: The Point-to-Point Protocol (PPP)
1662: PPP in HDLC-like Framing
1663: PPP Reliable Transmission
1666: Definitions of Managed Objects for SNA NAUs using SMIv2
1667: Modeling and Simulation Requirements for IPng
1668: Unified Routing Requirements for IPng
1669: Market Viability as a IPng Criteria
1670: Input to IPng Engineering Considerations
1671: IPng White Paper on Transition and Other Considerations
1672: Accounting Requirements for IPng
1673: Electric Power Research Institute Comments on IPng
1674: A Cellular Industry View of IPng
1675: Security Concerns for IPng
1676: INFN Requirements for an IPng
1677: Tactical Radio Frequency Communication Requirements for
       IPng
1678: IPng Requirements of Large Corporate Networks
1679: HPN Working Group Input to the IPng Requirements
       Solicitation
1680: IPng Support for ATM Services
1681: On Many Addresses per Host
1682: IPng BSD Host Implementation Analysis
1683: Multiprotocol Interoperability In IPng
1684: Introduction to White Pages Services based on X.500
1685: Writing X.400 O/R Names
1686: IPng Requirements: A Cable Television Industry Viewpoint
1687: A Large Corporate User's View of IPng
1688: IPng Mobility Considerations

1933: Transition Mechanisms for IPv6 Hosts and Routers
1934: Ascend's Multilink Protocol Plus (MP+)
1935: What Is the Internet, Anyway?
1936: Implementing the Internet Checksum in Hardware
1937: "Local/Remote" Forwarding Decision in Switched Data Link
      Subnetworks
1939: Post Office Protocol: Version 3
1940: Source Demand Routing: Packet Format and Forwarding
      Specification (Version 1)
1941: Frequently Asked Questions for Schools
1942: HTML Tables
1943: Building an X.500 Directory Service in the US
1945: Hypertext Transfer Protocol--HTTP/1.0
1946: Native ATM Support for ST2+
1947: Greek Character Encoding for Electronic Mail Messages
1948: Defending Against Sequence Number Attacks
1949: Scalable Multicast Key Distribution
1950: ZLIB Compressed Data Format Specification version 3.3
1951: DEFLATE Compressed Data Format Specification version 1.3
1952: GZIP file format specification version 4.3
1953: Ipsilon Flow Management Protocol Specification for IPv4
      Version 1.0
1954: Transmission of Flow Labelled IPv4 on ATM Data Links
      Ipsilon Version 1.0
1955: New Scheme for Internet Routing and Addressing (ENCAPS)
      for IPNG
1956: Registration in the MIL Domain
1957: Some Observations on Implementations of the Post Office
      Protocol (POP3)
1958: Architectural Principles of the Internet
1961: GSS-API Authentication Method for SOCKS Version 5
1962: The PPP Compression Control Protocol (CCP)
1963: PPP Serial Data Transport Protocol (SDTP)
1964: The Kerberos Version 5 GSS-API Mechanism
1965: Autonomous System Confederations for BGP
1966: BGP Route Reflection: An alternative to full mesh IBGP
1967: PPP LZS-DCP Compression Protocol (LZS-DCP)
1968: The PPP Encryption Control Protocol (ECP)
1973: PPP in Frame Relay
1974: PPP Stac LZS Compression Protocol
1975: PPP Magnalink Variable Resource Compression
1976: PPP for Data Compression in Data Circuit-Terminating
      Equipment (DCE)
1977: PPP BSD Compression Protocol
1978: PPP Predictor Compression Protocol
1979: PPP Deflate Protocol
1980: A Proposed Extension to HTML: Client-Side Image Maps
1981: Path MTU Discovery for IP version 6
1982: Serial Number Arithmetic
1983: Internet Users' Glossary

2125: The PPP Bandwidth Allocation Protocol (BAP)/The PPP
      Bandwidth Allocation Control Protocol (BACP)
2126: ISO Transport Service on top of TCP (ITOT)
2127: ISDN Management Information Base Using SMIv2
2128: Dial Control Management Information Base Using SMIv2
2129: Toshiba's Flow Attribute Notification Protocol (FANP)
      Specification
2130: The Report of the IAB Character Set Workshop Held 29
      February: 1 March, 1996
2131: Dynamic Host Configuration Protocol
2132: DHCP Options and BOOTP Vendor Extensions
2134: Articles of Incorporation of Internet Society
2135: Internet Society By-Laws
2136: Dynamic Updates in the Domain Name System (DNS UPDATE)
2137: Secure Domain Name System Dynamic Update
2138: Remote Authentication Dial In User Service (RADIUS)
2139: RADIUS Accounting
2140: TCP Control Block Interdependence
2141: URN Syntax
2142: Mailbox Names for Common Services, Roles and Functions
2143: Encapsulating IP with the Small Computer System Interface
2144: The CAST-128 Encryption Algorithm
2145: Use and Interpretation of HTTP Version Numbers
2146: U.S. Government Internet Domain Names
2148: Deployment of the Internet White Pages Service
2149: Multicast Server Architectures for MARS-based ATM
      multicasting
2150: Humanities and Arts: Sharing Center Stage on the Internet
2151: A Primer on Internet and TCP/IP Tools and Utilities
2152: UTF-7: A Mail-Safe Transformation Format of Unicode
2153: PPP Vendor Extensions
2154: OSPF with Digital Signatures
2156: MIXER (Mime Internet X.400 Enhanced Relay): Mapping
      between X.400 and 822/MIME
2157: Mapping between X.400 and RFC-822/MIME Message Bodies
2158: X.400 Image Body Parts
2159: A MIME Body Part for FAX
2160: Carrying PostScript in X.400 and MIME
2161: A MIME Body Part for ODA
2162: MaXIM-11: Mapping between X.400/Internet mail and Mail-
      11 mail
2163: Using the Internet DNS to Distribute MIXER Conformant
      Global Address Mapping (MCGAM)
2164: Use of an X.500/LDAP directory to support MIXER address
      mapping
2165: Service Location Protocol
2166: APPN Implementer's Workshop Closed Pages Document DLSw
      v2.0 Enhancements
2167: Referral Whois (RWhois) Protocol V1.5
2168: Resolution of Uniform Resource Identifiers Using the
      Domain Name System

2903: Generic AAA Architecture
2904: AAA Authorization Framework
2905: AAA Authorization Application Examples
2906: AAA Authorization Requirements
2907: MADCAP Multicast Scope Nesting State Option
2908: The Internet Multicast Address Allocation Architecture
2909: The Multicast Address-Set Claim (MASC) Protocol
2910: Internet Printing Protocol/1.1: Encoding and Transport
2911: Internet Printing Protocol/1.1: Model and Semantics
2912: Indicating Media Features for MIME Content
2913: MIME Content Types in Media Feature Expressions
2914: Congestion Control Principles. S. Floyd. September 2000
2915: The Naming Authority Pointer (NAPTR) DNS Resource Record
2916: E.164 number and DNS
2917: A Core MPLS IP VPN Architecture
2918: Route Refresh Capability for BGP-4
2920: SMTP Service Extension for Command Pipelining
2921: 6BONE pTLA and pNLA Formats (pTLA)
2922: Physical Topology MIB
2923: TCP Problems with Path MTU Discovery
2924: Accounting Attributes and Record Formats
2925: Definitions of Managed Objects for Remote Ping,
      Traceroute, and Lookup Operations
2926: Conversion of LDAP Schemas to and from SLP Templates
2927: MIME Directory Profile for LDAP Schema
2928: Initial IPv6 Sub-TLA ID Assignments
2929: Domain Name System (DNS) IANA Considerations
2930: Secret Key Establishment for DNS (TKEY RR)
2931: DNS Request and Transaction Signatures (SIG(0)s)
2932: IPv4 Multicast Routing MIB
2933: Internet Group Management Protocol MIB
2934: Protocol Independent Multicast MIB for IPv4
2935: Internet Open Trading Protocol (IOTP) HTTP Supplement
2936: HTTP MIME Type Handler Detection
2937: The Name Service Search Option for DHCP
2938: Identifying Composite Media Features
2939: Procedures and IANA Guidelines for Definition of New DHCP
      Options and Message Types
2940: Definitions of Managed Objects for Common Open Policy
      Service (COPS) Protocol Clients
2941: Telnet Authentication Option
2942: Telnet Authentication: Kerberos Version 5
2943: TELNET Authentication Using DSA
2944: Telnet Authentication: SRP
2945: The SRP Authentication and Key Exchange System
2946: Telnet Data Encryption Option
2947: Telnet Encryption: DES3 64 bit Cipher Feedback
2948: Telnet Encryption: DES3 64 bit Output Feedback
2949: Telnet Encryption: CAST-128 64 bit Output Feedback
2950: Telnet Encryption: CAST-128 64 bit Cipher Feedback
2951: TELNET Authentication Using KEA and SKIPJACK

3080: The Blocks Extensible Exchange Protocol Core
3081: Mapping the BEEP Core onto TCP
3082: Notification and Subscription for SLP
3083: Baseline Privacy Interface Management Information Base for
        DOCSIS Compliant Cable Modems and Cable Modem Termination
        Systems
3084: COPS Usage for Policy Provisioning (COPS-PR)
3085: URN Namespace for NewsML Resources
3086: Definition of Differentiated Services per Domain Behaviors
        and Rules for Their Specification
3087: Control of Service Context Using SIP Request-URI
3088: OpenLDAP Root Service: An experimental LDAP referral
        service
3090: DNS Security Extension Clarification on Zone Status
3091: Pi Digit Generation Protocol
3092: Etymology of "Foo"
3093: Firewall Enhancement Protocol (FEP)
3094: Transport Adapter Layer Interface
3098: How to Advertise Responsibly Using E-Mail and Newsgroups or
        How NOT to $$$$ MAKE ENEMIES FAST! $$$$
3106: ECML v1.1: Field Specifications for E-Commerce
3115: Mobile IP Vendor/Organization-Specific Extensions

Modems

In order for computers to communicate, four items must be available, as shown in Figure E–1.

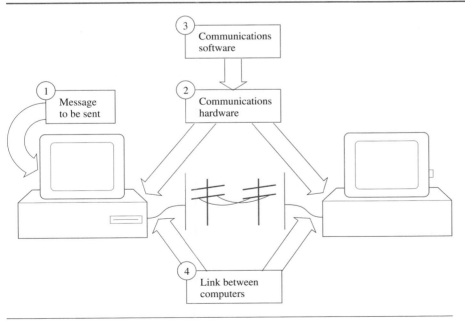

Figure E–2
Basic needs for the use of telephone lines in computer communications.

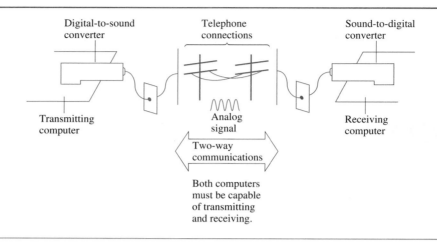

As shown in Figure E–1, there must be some kind of link between the computers. The most convenient link to use is the already established telephone system lines. Using these lines and a properly equipped computer allows communications between any two computers that have access to a telephone. This is a very convenient and inexpensive method of communicating between computers.

There is, however, one problem. Telephone lines were designed for the transmission of the human voice, not for the transmission of digital data. Therefore, in order to make use of these telephone lines for transmitting computer data, the ONs and OFFs of the computer must first be converted to an analog signal, sent over the telephone line, and then reconverted from analog back to the ONs and OFFs that the computer understands. This concept is shown in Figure E–2.

THE MODEM

The word *modulate* means to change. Thus an electronic circuit that changes digital data into analog data can be called a *modulator*. The word *demodulate* can be thought of as meaning "unchange," or restore to an original condition. Any electronic circuit that converts the analog signal used to represent the digital signals back to the ONs and OFFs understood by a computer can, therefore, be called a *demodulator*. Since each computer must be capable of both transmission and reception, each computer must contain an electrical circuit that can modulate as well as demodulate. Such a circuit is commonly called a <u>mo</u>dulator/<u>dem</u>odulator, or *modem*.

For personal computers, a modem may be an internal or an external circuit—both perform identical functions.

THE RS-232 STANDARD

The EIA (Electronics Industries Association) has published the EIA *Standard Interface Between Data Terminal Equipment Employing Serial Binary Data Interchange*—specifically, EIA-232-C. This is a standard defining 25 conductors that may be used in interfacing *data terminal equipment* (DTE, such as your computer) and *data communications equipment* (DCE, such as a modem) hardware. The standard specifies the function of each conductor, but it does not state the physical connector that is to be used. This standard exists so that different manufacturers of communications equipment can communicate with each other. In other words, the RS-232 standard is an example of an interface, essentially an agreement among equipment manufacturers on how to allow their equipment to communicate.

The RS-232 standard is designed to allow DTEs to communicate with DCEs. The RS-232 uses a DB-25 connector; the male DB-25 goes on the DTEs and the female goes on the DCEs. The RS-232 standard signals are shown in Figure E–3.

The RS-232 is a digital interface designed to operate at no more than 50 feet with a 20,000-bps bit rate. The *baud*, named after J. M. E. Baudot, actually indicates the number of *discrete* signal changes per second. In the transmission of binary values, one such change represents a single bit. What this means is that the popular usage of the term *baud* has become the same as bits per second (bps). Table E–1 shows the standard set of baud rates.

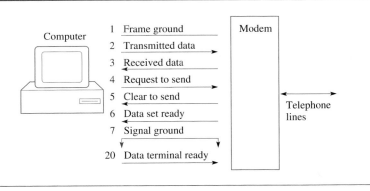

Figure E–3
The RS-232 standard signals.

Table E–1
Standard baud rates.

Low Speed	High Speed
300	
600	
1200	14,400
2400	28,800
4800	33,600
9600	56K

TELEPHONE MODEM SETUP

The most common problem with telephone modems is the correct setting of the software. There are essentially six distinct areas to which you must pay attention when using a telephone modem:

1. Port to be used
2. Baud rate
3. Parity
4. Number of data bits
5. Number of stop bits
6. Local echo ON or OFF

Most telephone modems have a default setting for each of these areas. However, as a user you should understand what each of these areas means. You will have to consult the specific documentation that comes with the modem in order to see how to change any of the six settings. For now it is important that you understand the idea behind each of these areas.

Port to Be Used

The most common ports to be used are COM1 and COM2. Other possible ports are COM3 and COM4. The port you select from the communications software depends on the port to which you have the modem connected. On most communications software, once you set the correct port number, you do not need to set it again.

Baud Rate

Typical values for the baud rate are between 9600 and 56K. Again, these values can be selected from the communications software menu. It is important that both computers be set at the same baud rate.

Parity

Parity is a way of having the data checked. Normally, parity is not used. Depending on your software, there can be up to five options for the parity bit, as follows:

Space: Parity bit is always a 0.
Odd: Parity bit is 0 if there is an odd number of 1s in the transmission and is a 1 if there is an even number of 1s in the transmission.
Even: Parity bit is a 1 if there is an odd number of 1s in the transmission and is a 0 if there is an even number of 1s in the transmission.
Mark: Parity bit is always a 1.
None: No parity bit is transmitted.

Again, what is important is that both the sending and receiving units are set up to agree on the status of the parity bit.

Number of Data Bits

The number of data bits to be used is usually set at 8. There are options that allow the number of data bits to be set at 7. It is important that both computers expect the same number of data bits.

Number of Stop Bits

The number of stop bits used is normally 1. However, depending on the system, the number of stop bits may be 2. Stop bits are used to mark the end of each character transmitted. Both computers must have their communications software set to agree on the number of stop bits used.

The subject of local echo is discussed later in this appendix, in the section about modem terminology.

WINDOWS MODEM SOFTWARE

Windows has built-in modem software, accessed through the Control Panel. Clicking on the Modem icon displays the window shown in Figure E–4. Notice that Windows indicates the presence of an external Sportster modem. To test the modem, click the Diagnostics tab. Figure E–5 shows the Diagnostics window.

Selecting COM2 (the Sportster modem) and then clicking More Info will cause Windows to interrogate the modem for a few moments and then display the results in a new window, shown in Figure E–6.

Specific information about the modem port is displayed, along with the responses to several AT commands. The *AT command set* is a standard set of commands that can be sent to the modem to configure, test, and control it. Table E–2 lists the typical *Hayes compatible* commands (first used by Hayes in its modem products). An example of an AT command is

ATDT 778 8108

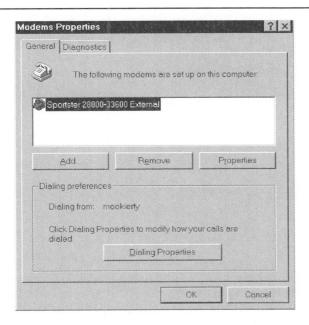

Figure E–4
Modems Properties window.

Figure E–5
Modem Diagnostics
window.

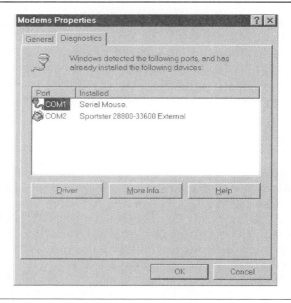

Figure E–6
Modem diagnostic
information.

which stands for AT (attention) DT (dial using tones). This AT command causes the modem to touch-tone dial the indicated phone number. Many modems require an initial AT command string to be properly initialized. This string is automatically output to the modem when a modem application is executed.

Table E–2
Selected AT commands.

Command	Function	Command	Function
A/	Repeat last command	Xn	Result code type
A	Answer	Yn	Long space disconnect
Bn	Select CCITT or Bell	Zn	Recall stored profile
Cn	Carrier control option	&Cn	DCD option
D	Dial command	&Dn	DTR option
En	Command echo	&F	Load factory defaults
Fn	Online echo	&Gn	Guard tone option
Hn	Switch hook control	&Jn	Auxiliary relay control
In	Identification/checksum	&M0	Communication mode option
Kn	SRAM buffer control	&Pn	Dial pulse ratio
Ln	Speaker volume control	&Q0	Communication mode option
Mn	Speaker control	&Sn	DSR option
Nn	Connection data rate control	&Tn	Self-test commands
On	Go online	&Vn	View active and stored configuration
P	Select pulse dialing	&Un	Disable Trellis coding
Qn	Result code display control	&Wn	Stored active profile
Sn	Select an S-register	&Yn	Select stored profile on power-on
Sn=x	Write to an S-register	&Zn=x	Store telephone number
Sn?	Read from an S-register	%En	Auto-retrain control
?	Read last accessed S-register	%G0	Rate renegotiation
T	Select DTMF dialing	%Q	Line signal quality
Vn	Result code form	-Cn	Generate data modem calling tone

 **TELEPHONE MODEM TERMINOLOGY**

In using technical documentation concerning a telephone modem, you will encounter some specialized terminology. Figure E–7 illustrates some of the ideas behind some basic communication methods. As you can see from the figure, *simplex* is a term that refers to a communications channel in which information flows in one direction only. An example of this is a radio or a television station.

Duplex

The *duplex* mode refers to two-way communication between two systems. This term is further refined as follows: *Full duplex* describes a communication link that can pass data in two directions at the same time. This mode is

Figure E–7
Some basic communication methods.

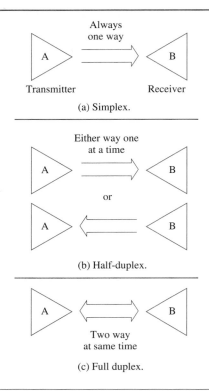

(a) Simplex.

(b) Half-duplex.

(c) Full duplex.

analogous to an everyday conversation between two people either face to face or over the telephone. The other mode, which is not commonly available with telephone modems, is the *multiplex* mode. Multiplex refers to a communications link in which multiple transmissions are possible.

Echo

The terminology used here has to do with how the characters you send to the other terminal are displayed on your monitor screen. The term *echo* refers to the method used to display characters on the monitor screen. First, there is a *local echo*. A local echo means that the sending modem immediately returns or echoes each character back to the screen as it is entered into the keyboard. This mode is required before transmission, so that you can see what instructions you are giving the communications software. Next there is *remote echo*. Remote echo means that during the communications between two computers, the remote computer (the one being transmitted to) sends back the character it is receiving. The character that then appears on your screen is the result of a transmission from the remote unit. This is a method of verifying what you are sending. To use the remote echo mode, you must be in the full duplex mode. This idea is illustrated in Figure E–8.

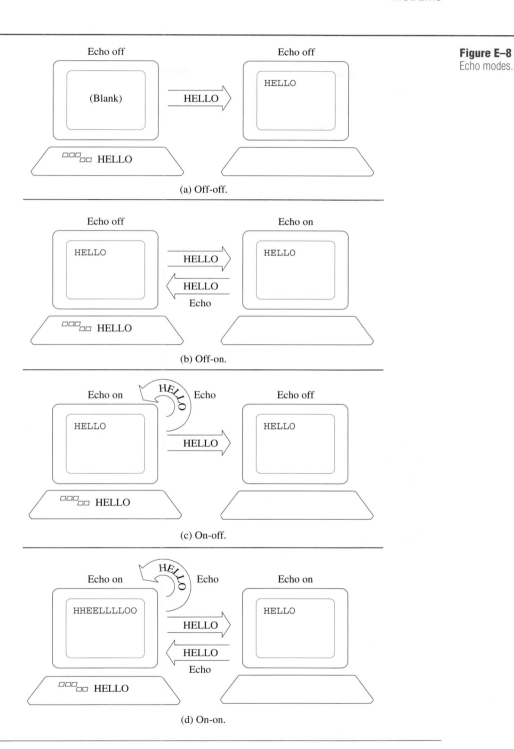

Figure E–8
Echo modes.

MODULATION METHODS

Many different techniques are used to encode digital data into analog form (for use by the modem). Several of these techniques are

- AM (amplitude modulation)
- FSK (frequency shift keying)
- Phase modulation
- Group coding

Figure E–9 shows how the first three of these techniques encode their digital data.

To get a high data rate (in bits per second) over ordinary telephone lines, group coding techniques are used. In this method, one cycle of the transmitted signal encodes two or more bits of data. For example, using *quadrature modulation*, the binary patterns 00, 01, 10, and 11 encode one of four different phase shifts for the current output signal. Thus, a signal that changes at a rate of 2400 baud actually represents 9600 bps!

Another technique, called *Trellis modulation*, combines two or more other techniques, such as AM and quadrature modulation, to increase the data rate.

MNP STANDARDS

MNP (Microcom Networking Protocol) is a set of protocols used to provide error detection and correction, as well as compression, to the modem data stream. Table E–3 lists the MNP classes and their characteristics.

MNP classes 4 and above are used with newer, high-speed modems. When two modems initially connect, they will negotiate the best type of

Figure E–9
Modulation techniques.

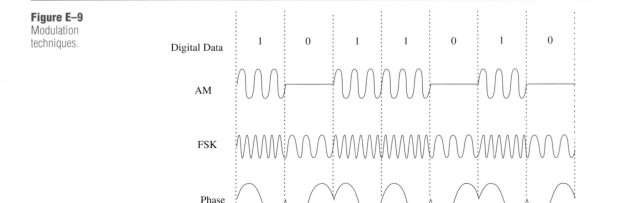

Class	Feature
1	Asynchronous, half duplex, byte oriented
2	Asynchronous, full duplex, byte oriented
3	Synchronous, full duplex, byte oriented
4	Error correction, packet oriented
5	Data compression
6	Negotiation
7	Huffman data compression
9	Improved error correction
10	Line monitoring

Note: There is no MNP-8 standard.

connection possible, based on line properties and the features and capabilities of each modem. The CCITT standards supported by the modem are also part of the negotiation. Let us look at these standards as well.

CCITT STANDARDS

CCITT (French abbreviation for International Telegraph and Telephone Consultive Committee) standards define the maximum operating speed (as well as other features) available in a modem (which is a function of the modulation techniques used). Table E–4 lists the CCITT standards.

Earlier, low-speed standards not shown are the Bell 103 (300 bps using FSK) and Bell 212A (1200 bps using quadrature modulation). V.22 is similar in operation to Bell 212A and is more widely accepted outside the United States.

The V.90 standard, finalized in early 1998, outlines the details of modem communication at 56 Kbps, currently the fastest speed available for regular modems. Fax modems have their own set of standards.

Table E–4
CCITT standards.

Standard	Data Rate (bps)
V.22	1200
V.22 bis	2400
V.32	9600
V.32 bis	14,400
V.32 terbo	19,200
V.34	28,800/33,600
V.90	56K

ISDN MODEMS

ISDN (Integrated Services Digital Network) is a special connection available from the telephone company that provides 64-Kbps digital service. An ISDN modem will typically connect to a *basic rate ISDN* (BRI) line, which contains two full-duplex 64-Kbps B channels (for voice/data) and a 16-Kbps D channel (for control). This allows up to 128-Kbps communication. ISDN modems are more expensive than ordinary modems and require you to have an ISDN line installed before you can use it.

CABLE MODEMS

One of the most inexpensive, high-speed connections available today is the cable modem. A cable modem connects between the television cable supplying your home and a network interface card in your computer. Two unused cable channels are used to provide data rates in the hundreds of thousands of bits per second. For example, downloading a 6MB file over a cable modem takes less than 20 seconds (during several tests of a new cable modem installation). That corresponds to 2,400,000 bps! Of course, the actual data rate available depends on many factors, such as the speed the data is transmitted from the other end and any communication delays. But unlike all other modems, the cable modem has the capability to be staggeringly fast, due to the high bandwidth available on the cable. In addition, a cable modem is typically part of the entire package from the cable company and is returned when you terminate service. The cost is roughly the same as the cost of basic cable service.

FAX/DATA MODEMS

It is difficult to find a modem manufactured today that does not have fax capabilities built into it. Since fax/data modems are relatively inexpensive, it does not make sense to purchase a separate fax machine (unless it is imperative that you be able to scan a document before transmission). Word-processing programs now support the use of a fax/data modem, helping to make the personal computer almost an entire office by itself.

PROTOCOLS

A *protocol* is a prearranged communication procedure that two or more parties agree on. When two modems are communicating over telephone lines (during a file transfer from a computer bulletin board or an America Online session), each modem has to agree on the technique used for transmission and reception of data. Table E–5 shows some of the more common protocols.

Protocol	Operation
Xmodem	Blocks of 128 bytes are transmitted. A checksum byte is used to validate received data. Bad data is retransmitted.
Xmodem CRC	Xmodem using Cyclic Redundancy Check to detect errors.
Xmodem-1K	Essentially Xmodem CRC with 1024-byte blocks.
Ymodem	Similar to Xmodem-1K. Multiple files may be transferred with one command.
Zmodem	Uses 512-byte blocks and CRC for error detection. Can resume an interrupted transmission from where it left off.
Kermit	Transmits data in packets whose sizes are adjusted to fit the needs of the other machine's protocol.

Table E–5
Modem communication protocols.

The modem software that is supplied with a new modem usually allows the user to specify a particular protocol.

 ## COMMON MODEM PROBLEMS

Table E–6 lists some of the most common problems encountered in telephone modems. As you will see, most of the problems are software related.

Other common problems encountered involve very simple hardware considerations. For example, telephone modems usually come with two separate telephone line connectors.

The purpose of the phone input is to connect a telephone, not the output line from the modem, to the telephone wall jack. The phone input is simply a convenience. It allows the telephone to be used without having to disconnect a telephone line from the computer to the wall telephone jack. If you mistakenly connect the line from the wall telephone jack to the phone input, you will be able to dial out from your communications software, but your

Symptom	Possible Cause(s)
Can't connect	Usually this means that your baud rates or numbers of data bits are not matched. This is especially true if you see garbage on the screen, especially the { character.
Can't see input	You are typing in information but it doesn't appear on the screen. However, if the person on the other side can see what you are typing, it means that you need to turn your local echo on. In this way, what you type will be echoed back to you, and you will see it on your screen.
Get double characters	Here you are typing information and getting double characters. This means that if you type HELLO, you get HHEELLLLOO; at the same time, what the other computer is getting appears normal. This means that you need to turn your local echo off. In this way, you will not be echoing back the extra character. With some systems *half duplex* refers to local echo on, whereas *full duplex* refers to local echo off.

Table E–6
Common telephone modem problems.

system will hang up on you. Make sure that the telephone line that goes to the telephone wall jack comes from the *line output* and not the *phone output* jack of your modem.

Another common hardware problem is a problem in your telephone line. This can be quickly checked by simply using your phone to get through to the other party. If you can't do this, then neither can your computer.

A problem that is frequently encountered in an office or school building involves the phone system used within the building. You may have to issue extra commands on your software in order to get your call out of the building. In this case you need to check with your telecommunications manager or the local phone company.

Sometimes your problem is simply a noisy line. This may have to do with your communications provider or it may have to do with how your telephone line is installed. You may have to switch to a long-distance telephone company that can provide service over more reliable communication lines. Or you may have to physically trace where your telephone line goes from the wall telephone jack. If this is an old installation, your telephone line could be running in the wall right next to the AC power lines. If this is the case, you need to reroute the phone line.

Using LanExplorer

Often it is necessary for a network engineer or a technology student to troubleshoot problems that arise on the network using a software tool called a *protocol analyzer*. Using a protocol analyzer, the network interface card in a computer is put into promiscuous mode, allowing it to see all the traffic that is transmitted on the local network segment. This potentially causes a network security risk because it is possible to capture data that is considered to be confidential, such as passwords, social security numbers, and salary information. Therefore, extreme caution and good judgment should be exercised when using a protocol analyzer.

TRAFFIC MONITORING

A typical use for a protocol analyzer is to collect baseline network traffic data. The baseline historical data is then used to compare against network data collected at a different time. The baseline data can be used as an early warning detection system because it is possible to identify several possible harmful situations. These situations include identification of network capacity issues, DHCP errors, duplicate IP assignments, and network utilization trends. In some situations, it is possible to identify a piece of faulty network equipment that has been causing excessive collisions. The process of investigating a network begins with monitoring all the network traffic to develop the baseline data. The baseline may be taken over the course of several hours, days, or weeks using a product such as LanExplorer from Sunrise Telecom (sunrisetelecom.com).

Figure F–1
Initial LanExplorer
window.

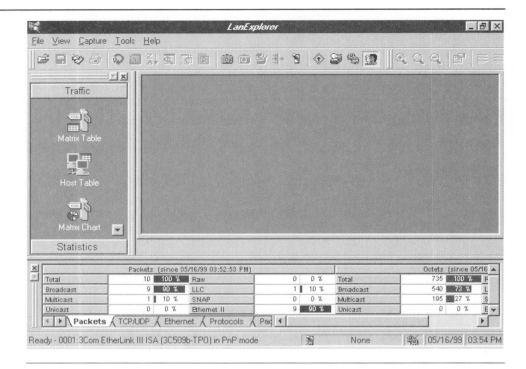

LanExplorer is one of the most popular protocol analyzer packages available. Note that a demonstration copy of LanExplorer is included on the companion CD. The first time LanExplorer is started, it is necessary to select the default network adapter. Since there is usually only *one* network card in a PC, there is only *one* choice available. When more than one network card is present, one of them must be selected. The first screen displayed by LanExplorer after selecting a default adapter is shown in Figure F–1. The LanExplorer screen is divided into three areas. First is the Task Panel, which contains two items, the Traffic option and the Statistics option. The Traffic option allows for quick access to built-in displays. The Statistics option provides access to Distribution and Rate information, which is automatically set. Selections that can be made in the Traffic Task Panel are displays of the Matrix Table, Host Table, Matrix Chart, Host Chart, and Alarm Log. As the items are selected, the corresponding data is displayed in the panel to the right of the Task Panel. At the bottom of the LanExplorer display is the Console Panel, which is used to display a breakdown of the monitored network traffic. Note that as soon as LanExplorer is started, it begins to monitor all the traffic that is present on the network. Let us begin by discussing the various traffic display options.

When the Matrix Table display option is selected by left-clicking on the icon, the panel on the right displays a line of data for each packet that is examined. The information available for examination that is displayed on this screen includes

- Address (host name or host number)
- Octet ratio (bytes of data)
- Total octets
- Total packets
- Duration of the network activity
- Octets in, packets in
- Octets out, packets out
- Broadcast and multicast message counts
- IP packet type
- Time stamp information

Figure F–2 shows a typical Matrix display containing Internet Protocol information. By using the scroll bars, all of the various data elements may be examined.

Moving down the list of Traffic Task Panel options, the Host Table is displayed, as in Figure F–3. As the traffic is monitored, statistics are gathered for

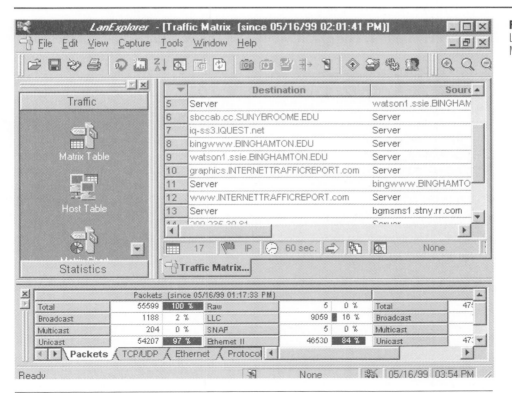

Figure F–2
LanExplorer Traffic Matrix display.

Figure F–3
LanExplorer Host
Table display.

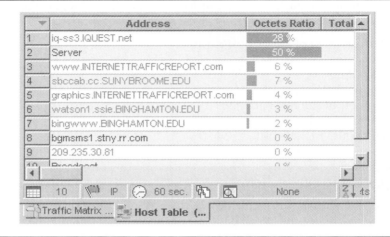

Figure F–3
LanExplorer Host
Table display.

each of the hosts that is transmitting data on the network. The graphical bar chart displayed in Figure F–3 indicates the hosts with the highest ratio of traffic.

The Traffic Matrix Chart shows the same information that was listed in the table format, but now is displayed graphically using a pie chart as illustrated in Figure F–4. The graphical display shows a breakdown of the traffic

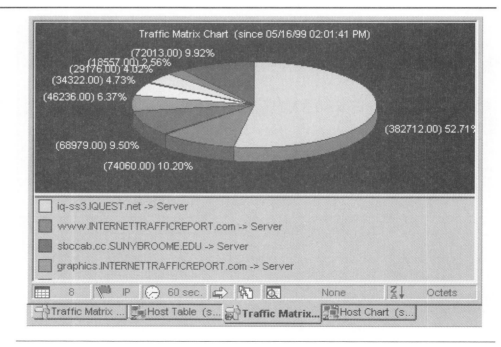

Figure F–4
LanExplorer Traffic
Matrix Chart.

data, by both a count and a percentage. The names of the hosts with the highest traffic are displayed in ascending order as space permits. As the traffic patterns change, the pie chart is automatically updated.

The remaining item in the Traffic Task panel is the Alarm Log. The Alarm Log is used to keep track of all security-related issues such as plain-text password transmissions, DHCP address issues, duplicate IP network assignments, and many other important items. You are encouraged to check the items on the Alarm Log frequently because many potential security issues may be identified.

The LanExplorer Console window located at the bottom of the display contains information about all the traffic being monitored. Figure F–5 shows

Figure F–5
LanExplorer Console window display information.

Packets (since 05/16/99 01:17:33 PM)						Octets (since 05/16		
Total	56768	100 %	Raw	5	0 %	Total	47625478	100 %	F
Broadcast	1250	2 %	LLC	9070	16 %	Broadcast	124077	0 %	L
Multicast	209	0 %	SNAP	5	0 %	Multicast	30188	0 %	S
Unicast	55309	97 %	Ethernet II	47688	84 %	Unicast	47471213	100 %	E

◄ ► \ **Packets** ⟨ TCP/UDP ⟨ Ethernet ⟨ Protocols ⟨ Pac ◄ ►

(a) Packet statistics.

Packets (since 05/16/99 01:17:33 PM)								
FTP	37988	67 %	NNTP	0	0 %	FTP		3
Telnet	0	0 %	NetBIOS	816	1 %	Telnet		
SMTP/POP3/IMAP4	0	0 %	SNMP	0	0 %	SMTP/POP3/IMAP4		
HTTP(S)	6874	12 %	Others	660	1 %	HTTP(S)		

◄ ► \ Packets ⟨ **TCP/UDP** ⟨ Ethernet ⟨ Protocols ⟨ Pac ◄ ►

(b) TCP/UDP statistics.

Transmit (since 05/16/99 01:17:33 PM)				Receive (since 05/16/99 01:17:33 PM)		
OK	4230	Error	1	OK	52244	Error	1
1 Collision	22	Collision	0			No Buffer	1
1+ Collision	28	Late Collision	0			CRC	0
Deferral	611	Underrun	1			Alignment	0

◄ ► \ Packets ⟨ TCP/UDP \ **Ethernet** ⟨ Protocols ⟨ Pac ◄ ►

(c) Ethernet statistics.

Packets (since 05/16/99 01:17:33 PM)						Octets (since 05/16/99 01:17:3		
NetBIOS	8887	15 %	AppleTalk	0	0 %	NetBIOS	7834077	16 %	AppleTalk
IP	51756	85 %	SNA	6	0 %	IP	40110014	84 %	SNA
IPX	237	0 %	Vines	0	0 %	IPX	34478	0 %	Vines
XNS	0	0 %	DEC	0	0 %	XNS	0	0 %	DEC

◄ ► \ Packets ⟨ TCP/UDP ⟨ Ethernet \ **Protocols** ⟨ Pac ◄ ►

(d) Protocol statistics.

(continued on next page)

Figure F–5
(continued)

Packet Size (since 05/16/99 01:17:33 PM)						
64	19567	32 %	256-511		2509	4 %
65-127	6949	11 %	512-1023		1505	2 %
128-255	1102	2 %	1024-1518		29460	45 %

◄ ► TCP/UDP Ethernet Protocols **Packet Size** ◄

(e) Packet size statistics.

the various information displayed in the Console window. The first tab contains information about the Packet Statistics, which is displayed in Figure F–5(a). The total number of packets as well as the packet type is identified. Figure F–5(b) shows a breakdown of the TCP/UDP Internet Protocol packets. Figure F–5(c) shows all of the Ethernet statistics. Figure F–5(d) shows what type of protocols have been monitored on the network, and Figure F–5(e) completes the list of available information by providing a breakdown of the various sizes of the packets that have been transmitted.

Each of the categories presented in the Console window display can be very important when developing a baseline of activity for a network or when performing troubleshooting.

PACKET CAPTURE

Aside from the process of passively monitoring the network traffic, LanExplorer can also capture network traffic. Simply by selecting the Start option from the Capture pull-down menu or using the toolbar icon, LanExplorer will keep a copy of each packet of information transmitted. When the capture process is "in progress," the screen shown in Figure F–6 is displayed. The number of packets captured, number of octets captured, packets seen, octets seen, elapsed time, filter information, and buffer usage is all displayed in real time.

When the buffer is full or the Stop Capture command is executed, the user is presented with a screen similar to Figure F–7. Although it looks very much like the Traffic Matrix display discussed earlier, packets that are captured may be decoded. To decode a packet, the program user simply double-clicks the specific line in the display. This causes the Protocol Decode window to automatically be displayed, as shown in Figure F–8. The Protocol Decode window contains two areas. First, the raw data window is displayed at the top of the screen. Second, the protocol-specific breakdown is displayed at the bottom. The Source Address that has been selected in the Protocol area has a corresponding selection in the raw data display. Notice that the same source

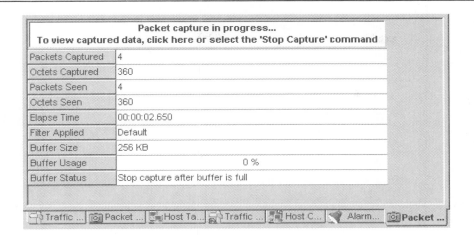

Figure F–6
LanExplorer packet capture status display.

Figure F–7
LanExplorer captured packet display.

address is highlighted in both areas. Choosing the Save option creates a copy of this decoded information in a text file. Figure F–9 shows the data that is written to the text file.

Packet Capture Filters

Many times when monitoring or troubleshooting a network, it is necessary to monitor only a small portion of the data being transmitted. For example, Lan-Explorer can be used to look for network traffic from a specific host computer or look for a specific type of protocol. This is accomplished by setting up a

Figure F–8
LanExplorer Protocol
Decode display
window.

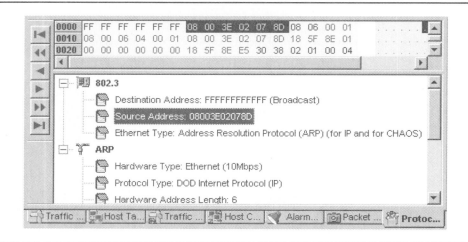

Figure F–9
Decoded LanExplorer
packet saved in text
format.

```
Capture 1:Packet 88

Destination Source       Protocol      Summary  Size    Time Tick
-------------------------------------------------------------------
24.95.142.229   24.95.142.1   ARP    Request   60   05/16/99 15:27:33.767

Addr.   Hex. Data                                      ASCII
0000:   FF FF FF FF FF FF 08 00 3E 02 07 8D 08 06 00 01   ........>.......
0010:   08 00 06 04 00 01 08 00 3E 02 07 8D 18 5F 8E 01   ........>...._..
0020:   00 00 00 00 00 00 18 5F 8E E5 30 38 02 01 00 04   ......._..08....
0030:   18 5F 8E F8 03 03 A9 90 00 00 00 00               ._..........

802.3 [0000:000D]
  0000:0005   Destination Address: FFFFFFFFFFFF (Broadcast)
  0006:000B   Source Address: 08003E02078D
  000C:000D   Ethernet Type: Address Resolution Protocol (ARP) (for IP and
for CHAOS)
ARP [000E:0029]
  000E:000F   Hardware Type: Ethernet (10Mbps)
  0010:0011   Protocol Type: DOD Internet Protocol (IP)
  0012:0012   Hardware Address Length: 6
  0013:0013   Protocol Address Length: 4
  0014:0015   Opcode: Request
  0016:001B   Source HW Address: 08003E02078D
  001C:001F   Source IP Address: 24.95.142.1
  0020:0025   Destination HW Address: 000000000000
  0026:0029   Destination IP Address: 24.95.142.229
```

packet capture *filter.* Packet filter selections are made from either the network layer or address. Figure F–10(a) shows the check box options available when selecting Layer 3+ IP/ARP and TCP/UDP categories. Each item that contains

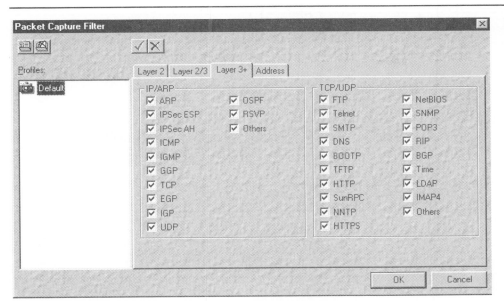

(a) Layer 3+ filter selection options.

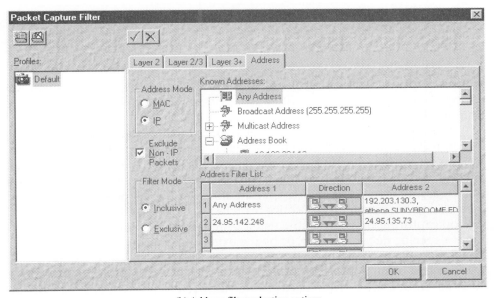

(b) Address filter selection options.

Figure F–10
Packet Capture Filter
configuration
options.

a check mark is identified for capture. Figure F–10(b) shows the Address
packet capture filter. Notice that the address may be a MAC address or an IP
address. Addresses in the Known Addresses box may be dragged down to the

Figure F–11
Packet Capture
Trigger events
window.

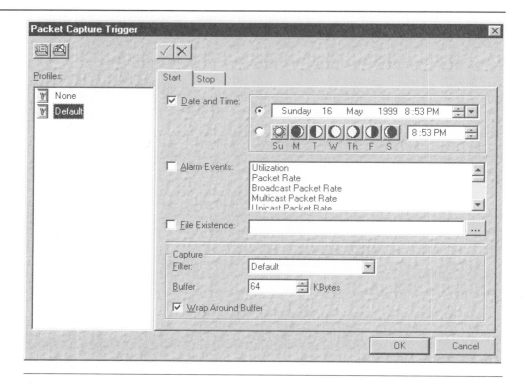

Figure F–11
Packet Capture
Trigger events
window.

Address Filter list as required. The Filter Mode is used to specify whether the addresses listed in the address filter list are inclusive or exclusive, allowing for unlimited filter choices.

By using a filter, much of the networking traffic is eliminated from the buffer, thereby saving only the traffic that is desired. Note that it is also possible to set a trigger event, which will cause LanExplorer to begin the packet capture. This helps guarantee that the network traffic that is captured follows the triggering event. This makes investigating network problems much easier by isolating the information. Notice from Figure F–11 that it is possible to start or stop capturing network traffic using trigger events based on a date and/or time, a specific network event, or by the existence of a specific file.

Rather than pay thousands of dollars for a hardware-based protocol analyzer, spend a fraction of the amount on a software-based protocol analyzer such as LanExplorer. Your networking knowledge and experience will increase rapidly.

G

Network Certification

The rapid and continual growth of communication technology has created an ongoing need for skilled network technicians and administrators. In addition to a technical degree of some kind, employers are now also looking for further proof of an individual's competence in networking. This need has spawned a number of different network certifications such as

- Cisco CCIE
- Microsoft MCSE
- CompTIA Network+

Let us examine the requirements of each certification.

CISCO CCIE

The Cisco CCIE (Cisco Certified Internetworking Expert) allows one to choose from several tracks (such as Routing and Switching, WAN Switching, and Design). The certification involves a written exam and a hands-on lab exam. Visit www.cisco.com for more information.

MICROSOFT MCSE

The Microsoft MCSE (Microsoft Certified Systems Engineer) is one of several certifications offered by Microsoft. The MCSE certification involves taking five core exams and two elective exams. The core exams are strongly based in the Windows 2000 area. Visit www.microsoft.com and search for MCSE for additional information.

COMPTIA NETWORK+

The CompTIA (Computing Technology Industry Association) Network+ is for network technicians who have accumulated 18 to 24 months of experience in their field. One test is used to certify that an individual has the necessary skills for the information technology industry. Visit

www.comptia.org/networkplus/index.htm

for more information.

SAMPLE NETWORK CERTIFICATION TEST QUESTION

Bill and Mary have to assemble a small network of four computers for a demonstration. Three computers run Windows 95 and the fourth runs Windows 98. During the demonstration the computers will need to share files.

Bill connects each machine to a 10baseT hub with UTP cables he pulls out of a box. Mary adjusts the network properties of each computer, setting each one the same way. When they are finished, three of the computers can share files, but the fourth one (a Windows 95 machine) is not even visible under Network Neighborhood.

Bill examines the UTP cable from the fourth machine and discovers it is a crossover cable. He replaces it with a straight-through cable and reboots the fourth computer. What effect does this have on the problem?

a. Solves it completely.
b. Only allows files less than 32K to be shared.
c. Has no effect; the problem still exists.

TESTING SERVICES

Sylvan Prometric is one provider of the Microsoft and CompTIA exams, as well as many others. Visit Sylvan Prometric for additional information at www.sylvanprometric.com.

Telecommunication Technologies

The world of telecommunications is getting both larger and smaller at the same time. From a hardware standpoint, more equipment is being installed every day, connecting more and more people, businesses, and organizations.

At the same time, the pervasiveness of the World Wide Web has made it easy to communicate with someone practically anywhere on the planet. The world does not seem as large as it once did.

In this appendix we will examine the many different telecommunication technologies available and see the part they play in our everyday communication.

TDM

Time-division multiplexing, or TDM, is a technique used by the telephone company to combine multiple digitized voice channels over a single wire. Telephone conversations are digitized into 8-bit PCM (pulse code modulation) samples and sampled 8000 times per second. This gives 64,000 bps for a single conversation. Now, using a multiplexer, if we rapidly switch from one channel to another, it is possible to transmit the 8-bit samples for 24 different conversations over a single wire. All that is required is a fast bit rate on the single wire. Figure H–1 shows a timing diagram for the TDM scheme on a basic carrier called a *T1 carrier*. The T1 provides 1.544 Mbps multiplexed data for twenty-four 64,000 bps channels. The 8 bits for each channel (192 bits total) plus a framing bit (a total of 193 bits) are transmitted 8000 times per second.

Figure H–1
Time-division
multiplexing.

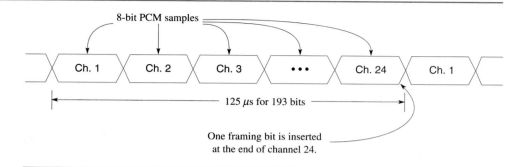

Table H–1
T-carrier services.

Level	Number of voice channels	Data Rate (Mbps)
1	24	1.544
2	96	6.312
3	672	44.736
4	4032	274.176

Table H–1 shows the different levels of T-carrier service available.

CIRCUIT SWITCHING

In the early days of the telephone system, large rotary switches were used to switch communication lines and make the necessary connections to allow end-to-end communication. The switches completed a circuit, hence the name *circuit switching*.

Eventually these slow, mechanical switches were replaced with fast, electronic switches. Also called an *interconnection network,* a switch is used to direct a signal to a specific output (such as the telephone you are calling).

Figure H–2 shows one way to switch a set of eight signals. This type of switch is called a *crossbar switch*. Connections between input and output signals are made by closing switches at specific intersections within the 8-by-8 grid of switches. Only one switch is turned on in any row or column (unless we are broadcasting). Since each intersection contains a switch that may be open or closed, one control bit is required to represent the position of each switch. The pattern for the first row of switches in Figure H–2 is 01000000. The pattern for the second row is 00000100. A total of 64 control bits are required.

A nice feature of the crossbar switch is that any mapping between input and output is possible.

If the cost of 64 switches is too much for your communication budget, a different type of switch can be used to switch eight signals, but with less than half

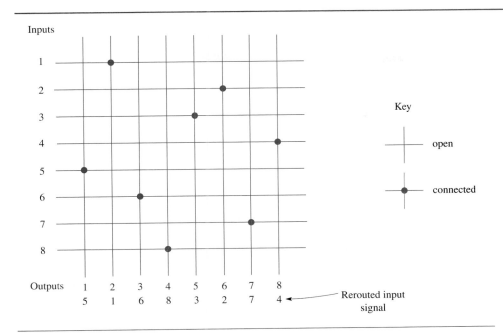

the number of switches. Called a *multistage switch,* it relies on several stages of smaller switches connected in complex ways. Figure H–3 shows a sample three-stage switch capable of switching eight signals. Each smaller switch can be configured as a straight-through or crossover switch, with a single control bit specifying the mode. Now, with only 12 smaller switches, the control information has shrunk from 64 bits in the crossbar switch to only 12 bits. The number of switches is 24 (one switch for straight-through, one switch for crossover, times 12), which is less than half of the 64 required in the crossbar switch.

The price we pay for the simplified hardware in the multistage switch is a smaller number of switching possibilities. For example, in Figure H–3 is it possible to set up the 12 smaller switches so that the output maps to 87654321? The answer is no, indicating that the multistage switch may block some signals from getting to the correct output. This problem is usually temporary, since memory buffers are typically used to store data that cannot be transmitted right away.

PACKET SWITCHING

Figure H–4 shows a simple WAN connecting four networks (A, B, C, and D). Suppose that a machine on network A wants to send a large chunk of data to a machine on network D. Using packet switching, the large chunk of data is broken down into smaller blocks and transmitted as a series of packets.

Figure H–3
Eight-signal multi-stage switch.

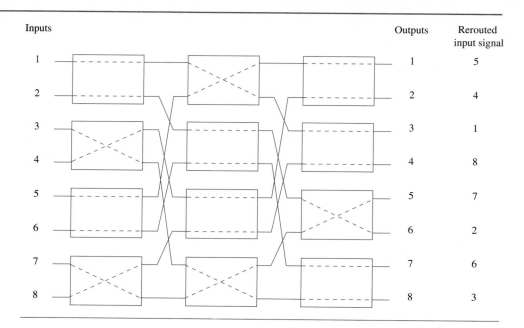

Inputs	Outputs	Rerouted input signal
1	1	5
2	2	4
3	3	1
4	4	8
5	5	7
6	6	2
7	7	6
8	8	3

Figure H–4
Sample WAN.

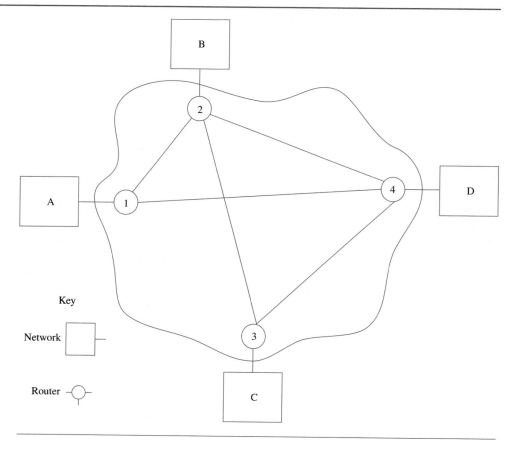

Due to the nature of traffic on shared networks, some packets may go directly from router 1 to router 4 (one hop), whereas others may go from router 1 to router 2, then to router 4 (two hops). A three-hop route is also possible. Thus, it is likely that packets arrive at network D out of order. This is a characteristic of packet switching. Packets can be reassembled in the correct order by including a sequence number within the packet. Even so, this characteristic makes packet switching unsuitable for digitized phone conversations, which, unlike an e-mail message, cannot wait for gaps to be filled in at some unknown later time. These features provide a means for choosing between circuit switching and packet switching.

FRAME RELAY

Packet switching was designed during a time when digital communication channels were not very reliable. To compensate for errors in a channel, a handshaking arrangement of send-and-acknowledge packets was used to guarantee reliable data transfers. This error protocol added time-consuming overhead to the packet switching network, with transmitting stations constantly waiting for acknowledgments before continuing.

Frame relay takes advantage of the improvement in communication technology (fiber links, for example, have a very low error rate compared with copper links) and relies on fewer acknowledgments during a transfer. Only the receiving station need send an acknowledgment.

With fewer acknowledgments and a lower error rate, frame relay provides a significant improvement in communications technology.

ATM

Asynchronous transfer mode (ATM), also called *cell relay,* uses fixed-size cells of data and supports voice, data, or video at either 155.52 Mbps or 622.08 Mbps. Cells are 53 bytes each, with 5 bytes reserved for a header and the remaining 48 for data, as indicated in Figure H–5. The reason for using fixed-size cells is to simplify routing decisions at intermediate nodes in the ATM system.

5-Byte Header	48-Byte Payload

Figure H–5
An ATM cell.

Figure H–6
ATM header fields.

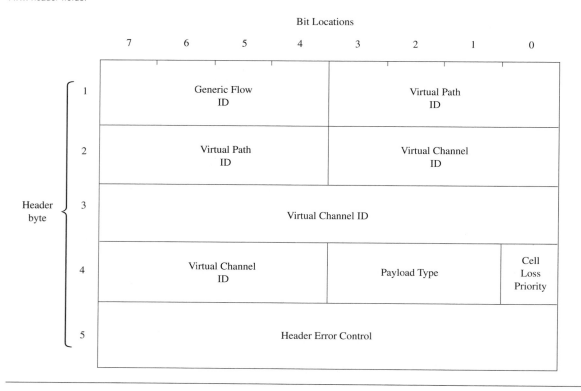

ATM uses communication connections called *virtual channel* connections. A virtual channel is set up between the end-to-end stations on the network and fixed-size cells are sent back and forth. Decisions concerning routing are resolved using information supplied in the ATM header, which is shown in Figure H–6. Notice the entries for virtual path and virtual channel identifiers.

 ISDN

The simplest Integrated Services Data Network (ISDN) connection is called a *basic rate interface,* and consists of two 64-Kbps B channels (for data) and one 16-Kbps D channel (for signaling). The design of ISDN supports circuit-switching, packet-switching, and frame operation. When ISDN is carried over a T1 line (1.544 Mbps), twenty-three 64-Kbps B channels and one 64-Kbps D channel are possible.

 **SONET**

The Synchronous Optical Network (SONET) technology was designed to take advantage of the high speed of a fiber connection between networks. As Table H–2 indicates, the lowest-speed SONET signal level (STS-1) runs at 51.84 Mbps. That is equivalent to more than nine hundred 56-Kbps modems running simultaneously (minus a few for overhead). STS-48 has 48 times the bandwidth of STS-1, so you can imagine how many telephone calls can be carried over a single fiber link.

There are additional benefits to using fiber: It is not susceptible to electrical noise, it can be run farther distances than copper wire before requiring a repeater to extend the signal, and it is easier to repair.

Figure H–7 shows the format of a SONET STS-1 frame. A total of 810 bytes are transmitted in a 125-microsecond time slot. Several bytes from each row of the frame are used for control/status information, such as several 64-Kbps user channels, 192-Kbps and 576-Kbps control, maintenance, and status channels, and several additional signaling items.

SONET level	Data Rate (Mbps)
STS*-1	51.84
STS-3	155.52
STS-9	466.56
STS-12	622.08
STS-18	933.12
STS-24	1244.16
STS-36	1866.24
STS-48	2488.32

Table H–2
SONET signal hierarchy.

*STS (Synchronous Transport Signal)

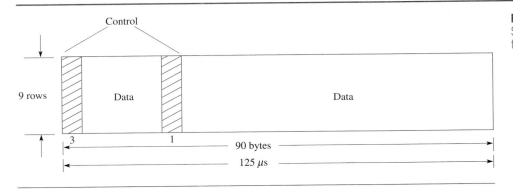

Figure H–7
SONET STS-1 frame format.

🖥️🖥️ FDDI

The Fiber Distributed Data Network (FDDI) was developed to provide 100-Mbps connections between LANs over a wide geographical area. Dual fiber rings are used, with the second ring serving as a backup for the first ring, called the *primary* ring. A token-passing scheme similar to token-ring technology is used to allow access to the ring.

The use of fiber allows longer distances between stations (or LANs). The FDDI physical layer allows for up to 100 fiber repeaters in the ring, with a spacing of 2 kilometers between repeaters. Thus, the size of the FDDI ring covers a perimeter of 200 kilometers (more than 124 miles). This is an attractive technology for long-distance communication.

🖥️🖥️ DENSE WAVE DIVISION MULTIPLEXING (DWDM)

The demands of network users and their applications has pushed even the speed limits of the available fiber-based SONET and FDDI technologies. To provide relief, technology was developed to allow *multiple* channels of light to coexist on the same fiber (by carefully varying the wavelength of the optical carrier, hence the terms *dense* and *division*). Thus, instead of a single OC-48 optical stream (2.4 Gbps), there may be as many as 40 different OC-48 streams, giving a total of 100-Gbps bandwidth. Even more than 40 optical channels will be possible in the future, with 128 channels already being discussed.

Additional benefits of DWDM are

- Easy mixing of different optical carriers
- Longer fiber segments (800 kilometers or more)
- Good for long-haul, point-to-point connections

With fiber optics as the fastest communication medium currently available, DWDM provides one way to keep up with the ever-increasing demand for bandwidth.

🖥️🖥️ MOBILE COMMUNICATION

Almost by definition, mobile communication implies the use of wireless technologies. The traditional cellular technologies are quickly migrating from analog to digital signals that offer additional features and significantly enhanced security benefits. Older geosynchronous satellite communication systems are being replaced by low earth orbit satellite communication systems that can provide wireless coverage for the entire planet.

Wireless technology is based on the concept of having transmitters and receivers. The transmission of wireless signals falls into two categories: omnidirectional and directional. Omnidirectional signals propagate from the transmitter in all directions similar to the transmitter used for an AM or FM radio

Wireless Technology	Application
Digital Cellular	Voice, Data
Wireless LAN	Voice, Data, Video
Personal Communication System	Voice, Data, Video, Fax, Global Positioning

Table H–3
Wireless technologies applications.

station. A directional signal is focused at the receiver. Using a combination of these two types of signals, many different applications of the technology are possible. Some of these applications are shown in Table H–3.

To accompany the new wireless technologies, the IEEE 802.11 specifications provide a software framework on which to build. A new protocol, DFWMAC (Distributed Foundation Wireless MAC), was created to work in the MAC layer of the OSI network model. A modified version of Ethernet called CSMA/CA (Collision Sense Multiple Access/Collision Avoidance) is used to transmit data in the network.

 TELECOMMUNICATION CAREERS

The sophistication of the wide variety of telecommunication equipment requires expertise that is typically beyond that obtained in an ordinary electronics or engineering technology program. Fully developed telecommunication degree programs are now available that train the student in all aspects of the field, using state-of-the-art equipment, such as optical time domain reflectometers, network analyzers, and digital sampling oscilloscopes. Becoming a telecommunication technician or engineer would be a challenging and rewarding pursuit.

Answers to Odd-Numbered Self-Test Questions

Chapter 1
1. True   3. False   5. b   7. b   9. c   11. a   13. c   15. fully connected
17. Data-Link 19. Wireless

Chapter 2
1. False   3. False   5. False   7. a   9. b   11. c   13. b   15. virtual
17. Carrier Sense Multiple Access, Collision Detection   19. virtual private

Chapter 3
1. False   3. False   5. False   7. False   9. a   11. a   13. a   15. c   17. d
19. e   21. combo   23. five   25. mode

Chapter 4
1. False   3. False   5. True   7. b   9. a   11. b   13. seven   15. 16   17. four

Chapter 5
1. False   3. False   5. False   7. c   9. c   11. b   13. active   15. bus
17. concentrators

Chapter 6
1. False   3. False   5. True   7. True   9. b   11. b   13. b   15. least
17. hierarchy   19. environmental   21. straight-through

Chapter 7
1. True   3. False   5. False   7. b   9. b   11. stop   13. Access   15. Server

Chapter 8
1. False   3. True   5. False   7. d   9. c   11. c   13. e   15. b   17. addresses
19. dotted decimal notation

Chapter 9
1. False   3. False   5. True   7. False   9. a   11. a   13. c   15. zone   17. domain
19. host

Chapter 10
1. False   3. True   5. False   7. False   9. c   11. c   13. a   15. Content   17. router
19. 25   21. spanning

Chapter 11
1. False   3. True   5. False   7. c   9. b   11. management information
13. authentication   15. security

Chapter 12
1. False   3. True   5. True   7. False   9. c   11. b   13. a   15. Multimedia Internet
Mail Extensions   17. cc   19. server

Chapter 13
1. False   3. True   5. True   7. False   9. c   11. b   13. c   15. response
17. NOP, 241   19. GET, RETR

Chapter 14
1. True   3. False   5. False   7. b   9. b   11. lossless   13. 8000   15. multicasting
backbone

Chapter 15
1. False   3. True   5. False   7. c   9. a   11. HTML   13. active   15. HTTP

Chapter 16
1. False   3. True   5. True   7. b   9. c   11. b   13. b   15. a   17. logical   19. TCP

Chapter 17
1. False   3. True   5. False   7. a   9. a   11. Extended User Interface
13. Accessories   15. Internet service provider

Chapter 18
1. False   3. True   5. False   7. False   9. c   11. c   13. a   15. d   17. a   19. e
21. workgroup   23. one   25. Dynamic Host Configuration Protocol

Chapter 19
1. False   3. True   5. False   7. False   9. b   11. b   13. a   15. Berkeley   17. footprint
19. linuxconf

Chapter 20
1. True   3. False   5. True   7. b   9. b   11. a   13. NDS   15. IPX/SPX   17. time
19. OS/2 Warp